Lecture Notes in Computer Science 13991

Founding Editors

Gerhard Goos, Germany
Juris Hartmanis, USA

Editorial Board Members

Elisa Bertino, USA
Wen Gao, China

Bernhard Steffen⬤, Germany
Moti Yung⬤, USA

Advanced Research in Computing and Software Science

Subline of Lecture Notes in Computer Science

Subline Series Editors

Giorgio Ausiello, *University of Rome 'La Sapienza', Italy*
Vladimiro Sassone, *University of Southampton, UK*

Subline Advisory Board

Susanne Albers, *TU Munich, Germany*
Benjamin C. Pierce, *University of Pennsylvania, USA*
Bernhard Steffen⬤, *University of Dortmund, Germany*
Deng Xiaotie, *Peking University, Beijing, China*
Jeannette M. Wing, *Microsoft Research, Redmond, WA, USA*

More information about this series at https://link.springer.com/bookseries/558

Leen Lambers · Sebastián Uchitel
Editors

Fundamental Approaches to Software Engineering

26th International Conference, FASE 2023
Held as Part of the European Joint Conferences
on Theory and Practice of Software, ETAPS 2023
Paris, France, April 22–27, 2023
Proceedings

 Springer

Editors
Leen Lambers
Brandenburg University of Technology
Cottbus-Senftenberg
Cottbus, Germany

Sebastián Uchitel
CONICET/University of Buenos Aires
Buenos Aires, Argentina

Imperial College London
London, UK

ISSN 0302-9743   ISSN 1611-3349 (electronic)
Lecture Notes in Computer Science
ISBN 978-3-031-30825-3   ISBN 978-3-031-30826-0 (eBook)
https://doi.org/10.1007/978-3-031-30826-0

ETAPS Foreword

Welcome to the 26th ETAPS! ETAPS 2023 took place in Paris, the beautiful capital of France. ETAPS 2023 was the 26th instance of the European Joint Conferences on Theory and Practice of Software. ETAPS is an annual federated conference established in 1998, and consists of four conferences: ESOP, FASE, FoSSaCS, and TACAS. Each conference has its own Program Committee (PC) and its own Steering Committee (SC). The conferences cover various aspects of software systems, ranging from theoretical computer science to foundations of programming languages, analysis tools, and formal approaches to software engineering. Organising these conferences in a coherent, highly synchronized conference programme enables researchers to participate in an exciting event, having the possibility to meet many colleagues working in different directions in the field, and to easily attend talks of different conferences. On the weekend before the main conference, numerous satellite workshops took place that attracted many researchers from all over the globe.

ETAPS 2023 received 361 submissions in total, 124 of which were accepted, yielding an overall acceptance rate of 34.3%. I thank all the authors for their interest in ETAPS, all the reviewers for their reviewing efforts, the PC members for their contributions, and in particular the PC (co-)chairs for their hard work in running this entire intensive process. Last but not least, my congratulations to all authors of the accepted papers!

ETAPS 2023 featured the unifying invited speakers Véronique Cortier (CNRS, LORIA laboratory, France) and Thomas A. Henzinger (Institute of Science and Technology, Austria) and the conference-specific invited speakers Mooly Sagiv (Tel Aviv University, Israel) for ESOP and Sven Apel (Saarland University, Germany) for FASE. Invited tutorials were provided by Ana-Lucia Varbanescu (University of Twente and University of Amsterdam, The Netherlands) on heterogeneous computing and Joost-Pieter Katoen (RWTH Aachen, Germany and University of Twente, The Netherlands) on probabilistic programming.

As part of the programme we had the second edition of TOOLympics, an event to celebrate the achievements of the various competitions or comparative evaluations in the field of ETAPS.

ETAPS 2023 was organized jointly by Sorbonne Université and Université Sorbonne Paris Nord. Sorbonne Université (SU) is a multidisciplinary, research-intensive and worldclass academic institution. It was created in 2018 as the merge of two first-class research-intensive universities, UPMC (Université Pierre and Marie Curie) and Paris-Sorbonne. SU has three faculties: humanities, medicine, and 55,600 students (4,700 PhD students; 10,200 international students), 6,400 teachers, professor-researchers and 3,600 administrative and technical staff members. Université Sorbonne Paris Nord is one of the thirteen universities that succeeded the University of Paris in 1968. It is a major teaching and research center located in the north of Paris. It has five campuses, spread over the two departments of Seine-Saint-Denis and Val d'Oise: Villetaneuse, Bobigny, Saint-Denis, the Plaine Saint-Denis and Argenteuil. The university has more than 25,000 students in different fields, such as health, medicine, languages, humanities, and science. The local organization team consisted of Fabrice Kordon (general co-chair), Laure Petrucci (general co-chair), Benedikt Bollig (workshops), Stefan Haar (workshops), Étienne André (proceedings and tutorials), Céline Ghibaudo (sponsoring), Denis Poitrenaud (web), Stefan Schwoon (web), Benoît Barbot (publicity), Nathalie Sznajder (publicity), Anne-Marie Reytier (communication), Hélène Pétridis (finance) and Véronique Criart (finance).

ETAPS 2023 is further supported by the following associations and societies: ETAPS e.V., EATCS (European Association for Theoretical Computer Science), EAPLS (European Association for Programming Languages and Systems), EASST (European Association of Software Science and Technology), Lip6 (Laboratoire d'Informatique de Paris 6), LIPN (Laboratoire d'informatique de Paris Nord), Sorbonne Université, Université Sorbonne Paris Nord, CNRS (Centre national de la recherche scientifique), CEA (Commissariat à l'énergie atomique et aux énergies alternatives), LMF (Laboratoire méthodes formelles), and Inria (Institut national de recherche en informatique et en automatique).

The ETAPS Steering Committee consists of an Executive Board, and representatives of the individual ETAPS conferences, as well as representatives of EATCS, EAPLS, and EASST. The Executive Board consists of Holger Hermanns (Saarbrücken), Marieke Huisman (Twente, chair), Jan Kofroň (Prague), Barbara König (Duisburg), Thomas Noll (Aachen), Caterina Urban (Inria), Jan Křetínský (Munich), and Lenore Zuck (Chicago).

Other members of the steering committee are: Dirk Beyer (Munich), Luís Caires (Lisboa), Ana Cavalcanti (York), Bernd Finkbeiner (Saarland), Reiko Heckel (Leicester), Joost-Pieter Katoen (Aachen and Twente), Naoki Kobayashi (Tokyo), Fabrice Kordon (Paris), Laura Kovács (Vienna), Orna Kupferman (Jerusalem), Leen Lambers (Cottbus), Tiziana Margaria (Limerick), Andrzej Murawski (Oxford), Laure Petrucci (Paris), Elizabeth Polgreen (Edinburgh), Peter Ryan (Luxembourg), Sriram Sankaranarayanan (Boulder), Don Sannella (Edinburgh), Natasha Sharygina (Lugano), Pawel Sobocinski (Tallinn), Sebastián Uchitel (London and Buenos Aires), Andrzej Wasowski (Copenhagen), Stephanie Weirich (Pennsylvania), Thomas Wies (New York), Anton Wijs (Eindhoven), and James Worrell (Oxford).

I would like to take this opportunity to thank all authors, keynote speakers, attendees, organizers of the satellite workshops, and Springer-Verlag GmbH for their support. I hope you all enjoyed ETAPS 2023.

Finally, a big thanks to Laure and Fabrice and their local organization team for all their enormous efforts to make ETAPS a fantastic event.

April 2023

Marieke Huisman
ETAPS SC Chair
ETAPS e.V. President

Preface

This book contains the proceedings of FASE 2023, the 26th International Conference on Fundamental Approaches to Software Engineering, held in Paris, France, in April 2023, as part of the annual European Joint Conferences on Theory and Practice of Software (ETAPS 2023).

FASE is concerned with the foundations on which software engineering is built. We solicited four categories of papers, research, empirical, new ideas and emerging results, and tool demonstrations; all of which should make novel contributions to making software engineering a more mature and soundly-based discipline.

The contributions accepted for presentation at the conference were carefully selected by means of a thorough double-blind review process which included no less than 3 reviews per paper. We received 50 submissions, which after a reviewing period of nine weeks and intensive discussion resulted in 16 accepted papers, representing a 32% acceptance rate.

We also ran an artifact track where authors of accepted papers optionally submitted artifacts described in their papers for evaluation. 10 artifacts were submitted for evaluation, 8 of which were successfully evaluated.

In addition, FASE 2023 hosted the 5th International Competition on Software Testing (Test-Comp 2023), which is an annual comparative evaluation of automatic tools for test generation. A total of 13 tools participated this year, from seven countries. The tools were developed in academia and in industry. The submitted tools and the submitted system-description papers were reviewed by a separate program committee: the Test-Comp jury. Each tool and paper was assessed by at least three reviewers. These proceedings contain the competition report and one selected system description of a participating tool. Two sessions in the FASE program were reserved for the presentation of the results: the summary by the Test-Comp chair and of the participating tools by the developer teams in the first session, and the community meeting in the second session.

We thank the ETAPS 2023 general chair, Marieke Huisman, the ETAPS 2023 organizers, Fabrice Kordon and Laure Petrucci, as well as the FASE SC chair, Andrzej Wasowksi, for their support during the whole process. We thank our invited speaker, Sven Apel, for his keynote. We thank all the authors for their hard work and willingness to contribute. We thank all the Program Committee members, external reviewers, who invested time and effort in the selection process to ensure the scientific quality of the program. Last but not least, we thank the Test-Comp chair Dirk Beyer, the artifact evaluation committee chairs, Marie-Christine Jakobs and Carlos Diego Nascimento Damasceno, and their evaluation committees.

April 2023   Leen Lambers
                                                                      Sebastián Uchitel

Organization

FASE—Program Committee Chairs

Leen Lambers   BTU Cottbus-Senftenberg, Germany
Sebastián Uchitel   University of Buenos Aires, Argentina and Imperial
                            College London, UK

FASE—Steering Committee Chair

Andrzej Wasowki   IT University of Copenhagen, Denmark

FASE—Steering Committee

Einar Broch Johnsen   University of Oslo, Norway
Reiner Hähnle   Technische Universität Darmstadt, Germany
Reiko Heckel   University of Leicester, UK
Leen Lambers   BTU Cottbus-Senftenberg, Germany
Tiziana Margaria   University of Limerick, Ireland
Perdita Stevens   University of Edinburgh, UK
Gabriele Taentzer   Philipps-Universität Marburg, Germany
Sebastián Uchitel   University of Buenos Aires, Argentina
                            and Imperial College London, UK
Heike Wehrheim   Carl von Ossietzky Universität Oldenburg, Germany
Manuel Wimmer   JKU Linz, Austria

FASE—Program Committee

Erika Abraham   RWTH Aachen University, Germany
Rui Abreu   University of Porto, Portugal
Domenico Bianculli   University of Luxembourg, Luxembourg
Ana Cavalcanti   University of York, UK
Stijn De Gouw   The Open University, The Netherlands
Antinisca Di Marco   University of L'Aquila, Italy
Sigrid Eldh   Mälardalen University and Ericsson, Sweden
Carlo A. Furia   USI Università della Svizzera Italiana, Switzerland
Alessandra Gorla   IMDEA Software Institute, Spain
Einar Broch Johnsen   University of Oslo, Norway
Axel Legay   UCLouvain, Belgium
Lina Marsso   University of Toronto, Canada
Marjan Mernik   University of Maribor, Slovenia
Fabrizio Pastore   University of Luxembourg, Luxembourg
Leila Ribeiro   Universidade Federal do Rio Grande do Sul, Brazil
Gwen Salaün   University of Grenoble Alpes, France

Paola Spoletini	Kennesaw State University, USA
Daniel Strüber	Chalmers University of Technology and University of Gothenburg, Sweden
Silvia Lizeth Tapia Tarifa	University of Oslo, Norway
Rachel Tzoref-Brill	IBM Research, Israel
Daniel Varro	Linköping University, Sweden and McGill University, Canada
Anna Maria Vollmer	Fraunhofer, Germany
Manuel Wimmer	Johannes Kepler University Linz, Austria

FASE—Artifact Evaluation Committee Chairs

Marie-Christine Jakobs	Technische Universität Darmstadt, Germany
Carlos Diego Nascimento Damasceno	Radboud University, The Netherlands

FASE—Artifact Evaluation Committee

Joshua Dawes	University of Luxembourg, Luxembourg
Elena Gómez-Martínez	Universidad Autónoma de Madrid, Spain
Boyue Caroline Hu	University of Toronto, Canada
Eduard Kamburjan	University of Oslo, Norway
Dylan Marinho	LORIA, Université de Lorraine, France
Kristóf Marussy	Budapest University of Technology and Economics, Hungary
Pedro Ribeiro	University of York, UK
Lucas Sakizloglou	BTU Cottbus-Senftenberg, Germany
Italo Santos	Northern Arizona University, USA
Maya Retno Ayu Setyautami	Universitas Indonesia, Indonesia
Michele Tucci	Charles University, Czechia

Test-Comp—Program Committee and Jury

Dirk Beyer (Chair)	LMU Munich, Germany
Marie-Christine Jakobs (CoVeriTest)	TU Darmstadt, Germany
Rafael Sá Menezes (ESBMC-kind)	University of Manchester, UK
Kaled Alshmrany (FuSeBMC)	University of Manchester, UK
Mohannad Aldughaim (FuSeBMC_IA)	University of Manchester, UK
Gidon Ernst (Legion/SymCC)	LMU Munich, Germany

Thomas Lemberger (PRTest)	QAware GmbH, Germany
Marek Trtík (Symbiotic)	Masaryk University, Brno, Czechia
Joxan Jaffar (TracerX)	National University of Singapore, Singapore
Raveendra Kumar M. (VeriFuzz)	Tata Consultancy Services, India
Filipe Marques (WASP-C)	INESC-ID, Lisbon, Portugal

FASE—Additional Reviewers

Babikian, Aren
Baranov, Eduard
Barnett, Will
Baxter, James
Bubel, Richard
Chen, Boqi
d'Aloisio, Giordano
Damasceno, Carlos Diego Nascimento
David, Istvan
De Boer, Frank
Din, Crystal Chung
Faqrizal, Irman
Feng, Nick
Hu, Caroline
Jongmans, Sung-Shik
Kamburjan, Eduard

Kobialka, Paul
Lang, Frédéric
Lazreg, Sami
Lina Marsso, Nick Feng
Marussy, Kristóf
Marzi, Francesca
Metongnon, Lionel
Pun, Violet Ka I
Raz, Orna
Schivo, Stefano
Schlatte, Rudolf
Soueidi, Chukri
Ye, Kangfeng
Zavattaro, Gianluigi
Ziv, Avi

Brains on Code: Towards a Neuroscientific Foundation of Program Comprehension (Abstract of an Invited Talk)

Sven Apel

Saarland University, Saarland Informatics Campus

Abstract. Research on program comprehension has a fundamental limitation: program comprehension is a cognitive process that cannot be directly observed, which leaves considerable room for misinterpretation, uncertainty, and confounders. In the project Brains On Code, we are developing a neuroscientific foundation of program comprehension. Instead of merely observing whether there is a difference regarding program comprehension (e.g., between two programming methods), we aim at precisely and reliably determining the key factors that cause the difference. This is especially challenging as humans are the subjects of study, and inter-personal variance and other confounding factors obfuscate the results. The key idea of Brains On Code is to leverage established methods from cognitive neuroscience to obtain insights into the underlying processes and influential factors of program comprehension.

Brains On Code pursues a multimodal approach that integrates different neuro-physiological measures as well as a cognitive computational modeling approach to establish the theoretical foundation. This way, Brains On Code lays the foundations of measuring and modeling program comprehension and offers substantial feedback for programming methodology, language design, and education. With Brains On Code, addressing longstanding foundational questions such as "How can we reliably measure program comprehension?", "What makes a program hard to understand?", and "What skills should programmers have?" comes into reach. Brains On Code does not only help answer these questions, but also provides an outline for applying the methodology beyond program code (models, specifications, requirements, etc.).

Keywords: Program comprehension · Neuro-imaging · Computational cognitive modeling

Contents

Regular Contributions

ACoRe: Automated Goal-Conflict Resolution 3
 Luiz Carvalho, Renzo Degiovanni, Matías Brizzio, Maxime Cordy,
 Nazareno Aguirre, Yves Le Traon, and Mike Papadakis

A Modeling Concept for Formal Verification of OS-Based Compositional
Software 26
 Leandro Batista Ribeiro, Florian Lorber, Ulrik Nyman,
 Kim Guldstrand Larsen, and Marcel Baunach

Compositional Automata Learning of Synchronous Systems 47
 Thomas Neele and Matteo Sammartino

Concolic Testing of Front-end JavaScript 67
 Zhe Li and Fei Xie

Democratizing Quality-Based Machine Learning Development through
Extended Feature Models 88
 Giordano d'Aloisio, Antinisca Di Marco, and Giovanni Stilo

Efficient Bounded Exhaustive Input Generation from Program APIs 111
 Mariano Politano, Valeria Bengolea, Facundo Molina,
 Nazareno Aguirre, Marcelo F. Frias, and Pablo Ponzio

Feature-Guided Analysis of Neural Networks 133
 Divya Gopinath, Luca Lungeanu, Ravi Mangal, Corina Păsăreanu,
 Siqi Xie, and Huafeng Yu

JavaBIP meets VerCors: Towards the Safety of Concurrent Software
Systems in Java 143
 Simon Bliudze, Petra van den Bos, Marieke Huisman, Robert Rubbens,
 and Larisa Safina

Model-based Player Experience Testing with Emotion Pattern Verification 151
 Saba Gholizadeh Ansari, I. S. W. B. Prasetya, Davide Prandi,
 Fitsum Meshesha Kifetew, Mehdi Dastani, Frank Dignum,
 and Gabriele Keller

Opportunistic Monitoring of Multithreaded Programs. 173
   Chukri Soueidi, Antoine El-Hokayem, and Yliès Falcone

Parallel Program Analysis via Range Splitting 195
   Jan Haltermann, Marie-Christine Jakobs, Cedric Richter,
   and Heike Wehrheim

Runtime Enforcement Using Knowledge Bases. 220
   Eduard Kamburjan and Crystal Chang Din

Specification and Validation of Normative Rules for Autonomous Agents 241
   Sinem Getir Yaman, Charlie Burholt, Maddie Jones, Radu Calinescu,
   and Ana Cavalcanti

Towards Log Slicing 249
   Joshua Heneage Dawes, Donghwan Shin, and Domenico Bianculli

Vamos: Middleware for Best-Effort Third-Party Monitoring 260
   Marek Chalupa, Fabian Muehlboeck, Stefanie Muroya Lei,
   and Thomas A. Henzinger

Yet Another Model! A Study on Model's Similarities for Defect
and Code Smells. 282
   Geanderson Santos, Amanda Santana, Gustavo Vale,
   and Eduardo Figueiredo

Competition Contributions

Software Testing: 5th Comparative Evaluation: Test-Comp 2023. 309
   Dirk Beyer

FuSeBMC_IA: Interval Analysis and Methods for Test Case Generation
(Competition Contribution). 324
   Mohannad Aldughaim, Kaled M. Alshmrany, Mikhail R. Gadelha,
   Rosiane de Freitas, and Lucas C. Cordeiro

Correction to: Feature-Guided Analysis of Neural Networks C1
   Divya Gopinath, Luca Lungeanu, Ravi Mangal, Corina Păsăreanu,
   Siqi Xie, and Huafeng Yu

Author Index 331

Regular Contributions

ACoRe: Automated Goal-Conflict Resolution

Luiz Carvalho[1], Renzo Degiovanni[1], Matías Brizzio[2,3], Maxime Cordy[1],
Nazareno Aguirre[4], Yves Le Traon[1], Mike Papadakis[1]

[1] SnT, University of Luxembourg, Luxembourg City, Luxembourg
{luiz.carvalho,renzo.degiovanni,maxime.cordy,yves.traon,mike.papadakis}@uni.lu
[2] IMDEA Software Institute, Madrid, Spain
matias.brizzio@imdea.org
[3] Universidad Politécnica de Madrid, Madrid, Spain
[4] Universidad Nacional de Río Cuarto and CONICET, Río Cuarto, Argentina
naguirre@dc.exa.unrc.edu.ar

Abstract. System goals are the statements that, in the context of software requirements specification, capture how the software should behave. Many times, the understanding of stakeholders on what the system should do, as captured in the goals, can lead to different problems, from clearly contradicting goals, to more subtle situations in which the satisfaction of some goals inhibits the satisfaction of others. These latter issues, called *goal divergences*, are the subject of *goal conflict analysis*, which consists of identifying, assessing, and resolving divergences, as part of a more general activity known as goal refinement.

While there exist techniques that, when requirements are expressed formally, can automatically identify and assess goal conflicts, there is currently no automated approach to support engineers in *resolving* identified divergences. In this paper, we present ACoRe, the first approach that automatically proposes potential resolutions to goal conflicts, in requirements specifications formally captured using linear-time temporal logic. ACoRe systematically explores syntactic modifications of the conflicting specifications, aiming at obtaining resolutions that disable previously identified conflicts, while preserving specification consistency. ACoRe integrates modern multi-objective search algorithms (in particular, NSGA-III, WBGA, and AMOSA) to produce resolutions that maintain coherence with the original conflicting specification, by searching for specifications that are either *syntactically* or *semantically* similar to the original specification.

We assess ACoRe on 25 requirements specifications taken from the literature. We show that ACoRe can successfully produce various conflict resolutions for each of the analyzed case studies, including resolutions that resemble specification repairs manually provided as part of conflict analyses.

1 Introduction

Many software defects that come out during software development originate from incorrect understandings of what the software being developed should do [24].

© The Author(s) 2023
L. Lambers and S. Uchitel (Eds.): FASE 2023, LNCS 13991, pp. 3–25, 2023.
https://doi.org/10.1007/978-3-031-30826-0_1

These kinds of defects are known to be among the most costly to fix, and thus it is widely acknowledged that software development methodologies must involve phases that deal with the elicitation, understanding, and precise specification of *software requirements*. Among the various approaches to systematize this requirements phase, the so-called *goal-oriented requirements engineering* (GORE) methodologies [13,55] provide techniques that organize the modeling and analysis of software requirements around the notion of *system goal*. Goals are prescriptive statements that capture how the software to be developed should behave, and in GORE methodologies are subject to various activities, including goal decomposition, refinement, and the assignment of goals [3,13,15,39,55,56].

The characterization of requirements as formally specified system goals enables tasks that can reveal flaws in the requirements. Formally specified goals allow for the analysis and identification of *goal divergences*, situations in which the satisfaction of some goals inhibits the satisfaction of others [9,16]. These divergences arise as a consequence of *goal conflicts*. A *conflict* is a condition whose satisfaction makes the goals inconsistent. Conflicts are dealt with through *goal-conflict analysis* [58], which comprises three main stages: *(i)* the *identification* stage, which involves the identification of conflicts between goals; *(ii)* the *assessment* stage, aiming at evaluating and prioritizing the identified conflicts according to their likelihood and severity; and *(iii)*, the *resolution stage*, where conflicts are resolved by providing appropriate countermeasures and, consequently, transforming the goal model, guided by the criticality level.

Goal conflict analysis has been the subject of different automated techniques to assist engineers, especially in the conflict identification and assessment phases [16,18,43,56]. However, no automated technique has been proposed for dealing with goal conflict *resolution*. In this paper, we present ACoRE, the first automated approach that deals with the goal-conflict resolution stage. ACoRE takes as input a set of goals formally expressed in Linear-Time Temporal Logic (LTL) [45], together with previously identified conflicts, also given as LTL formulas. It then searches for candidate *resolutions*, i.e., syntactic modifications to the goals that remain consistent with each other, while disabling the identified conflicts. More precisely, ACoRE employs modern search-based algorithms to efficiently explore syntactic variants of the goals, guided by a syntactic and semantic similarity with the original goals, as well as with the inhibition of the identified conflicts. This search guidance is implemented as (multi-objective) fitness functions, using Levenshtein edit distance [42] for syntactic similarity, and approximated LTL model counting [8] for semantic similarity. ACoRE exploits this fitness function to search for candidate resolutions, using various alternative search algorithms, namely a Weight-Based Genetic Algorithm (WBGA) [29], a Non-dominated Sorted Genetic Algorithm (NSGA-III) [14], an Archived Multi-Objective Simulated Annealing search (AMOSA) [6], and an unguided search approach, mainly used as a baseline in our experimental evaluations.

Our experimental evaluation considers 25 requirements specifications taken from the literature, for which goal conflicts are automatically computed [16]. The results show that ACoRE is able to successfully produce various conflict resolutions for each of the analysed case studies, including resolutions that resemble specification repairs manually provided as part of conflict analyses. In this assessment, we measured their similarity concerning the ground-truth, i.e., to the manually written repairs, when available. The genetic algorithms are able to resemble 3 out of 8 repairs in the ground truth. Moreover, the results show that ACoRe generates more non-dominated resolutions (their finesses are not subsumed by other repairs in the output set) when adopting genetic algorithms (NSGA-III or WBGA), compared to AMOSA or unguided search, favoring genetic multi-objective search over other approaches.

2 Linear-Time Temporal Logic

2.1 Language Formalism

Linear-Time Temporal Logic (LTL) is a logical formalism widely used to specify reactive systems [45]. In addition, GORE methodologies (e.g. KAOS) have also adopted LTL to formally express requirements [55] and taken advantage of the powerful automatic analysis techniques associated with LTL to improve the quality of their specifications (e.g., to identify inconsistencies [17]).

Definition 1 (LTL Syntax). *Let AP be a set of propositional variables. LTL formulas are inductively defined using the standard logical connectives, and the temporal operators $\bigcirc$ (next) and $\mathcal{U}$ (until), as follows:*

(a) constants true and false are LTL formulas;
(b) every $p \in AP$ is an LTL formula;
(c) if φ and ψ are LTL formulas, then $\neg\varphi$, $\varphi \vee \psi$, $\bigcirc\varphi$ and $\varphi\mathcal{U}\psi$ are also LTL formulas.

LTL formulas are interpreted over infinite traces of the form $\sigma = s_0\, s_1 \ldots$, where each s_i is a propositional valuation on 2^{AP} (i.e., $\sigma \in 2^{AP^\omega}$).

Definition 2 (LTL Semantic). *We say that trace $\sigma = s_0, s_1, \ldots$ satisfies a formula φ, written $\sigma \models \varphi$, if and only if φ holds at the initial state of the trace, i.e. $(\sigma, 0) \models \varphi$. The last notion is inductively defined on the shape of φ as follows:*

(a) $(\sigma, i) \models p \Leftrightarrow p \in s_i$
(b) $(\sigma, i) \models (\phi \vee \psi) \Leftrightarrow (\sigma, i) \models \phi$ or $(\sigma, i) \models \psi$
(c) $(\sigma, i) \models \neg\phi \Leftrightarrow (\sigma, i) \not\models \phi$
(d) $(\sigma, i) \models \bigcirc\phi \Leftrightarrow (\sigma, i+1) \models \phi$
(e) $(\sigma, i) \models (\phi \, \mathcal{U} \, \psi) \Leftrightarrow \exists_{k \geq 0} : (\sigma, k) \models \psi$ and $\forall_{0 \leq j < k} : (\sigma, j) \models \phi$

Intuitively, formulas with no temporal operator are evaluated in the first state of the trace. Formula $\bigcirc\varphi$ is true at position i, iff φ is true in position $i+1$. Formula $\varphi\mathcal{U}\,\psi$ is true in σ iff formula φ holds at every position until ψ holds.

Definition 3 (Satisfiability). *An LTL formula φ is said satisfiable (SAT) iff there exists at least one trace satisfying φ.*

We also consider other typical connectives and operators, such as, $\wedge$, $\Box$ (always), $\Diamond$ (eventually) and $\mathcal{W}$ (weak-until), that are defined in terms of the basic ones. That is, $\phi \wedge \psi \equiv \neg(\neg\phi \vee \neg\psi)$, $\Diamond\phi \equiv true\,\mathcal{U}\phi$, $\Box\phi \equiv \neg\Diamond\neg\phi$, and $\phi\mathcal{W}\psi \equiv (\Box\phi) \vee (\phi\mathcal{U}\psi)$.

2.2   Model Counting

The *model counting* problem consists of calculating the number of models that satisfy a formula. Since the models of LTL formulas are infinite traces, it is often the case that analysis is restricted to a class of canonical *finite* representation of *infinite* traces, such as lasso traces or tree models. Notably, this is the case in bounded model checking for instance [7].

Definition 4 (Lasso Trace). *A lasso trace σ is of the form $\sigma = s_0 \ldots s_i(s_{i+1} \ldots s_k)^\omega$, where the states $s_0 \ldots s_k$ conform the base of the trace, and the loop from state s_k to state s_{i+1} is the part of the trace that is repeated infinitely many times.*

For example, an LTL formula $\Box(p \vee q)$ is satisfiable, and one satisfying lasso trace is $\sigma_1 = \{p\}; \{p, q\}^\omega$, wherein the first state p holds, and from the second state both p and q are valid forever. Notice that the base in the lasso trace σ_1 is the sequence containing both states $\{p\}; \{p, q\}$, while the state $\{p, q\}$ is the sequence in the loop part.

Definition 5 (LTL Model Counting). *Given an LTL formula φ and a bound k, the (bounded) model counting problem consists in computing how many lasso traces of at most k states exist for φ. We denote this as $\#(\varphi, k)$.*

Since existing approaches for computing the exact number of lasso traces are ineffective [25], Brizzio et. al [8] recently developed a novel model counting approach that approximates the number (of prefixes) of lasso traces satisfying an LTL formula. Intuitively, instead of counting the number of lasso traces of length k, the approach of Brizzio et. al [8] aims at approximating the number of bases of length k corresponding to some satisfying lasso trace.

Definition 6 (Approximate LTL Model Counting). *Given an LTL formula φ and a bound k, the approach of Brizzio et. al [8] approximates the number of bases $w = s_0 \ldots s_k$, such that for some i, the lasso trace $\sigma = s_0 \ldots (s_i \ldots s_k)^\omega$ satisfies φ (notice that prefix w is the base of σ). We denote $\#\textsc{Approx}(\varphi, k)$ to the number computed by this approximation.*

ACoRe uses $\#\textsc{Approx}$ model counting to compute the semantic similarity between the original specification and the candidate goal-conflict resolutions.

3 The Goal-Conflict Resolution Problem

Goal-Oriented Requirements Engineering (GORE) [55] drives the requirements process in software development from the definition of high-level goals that state how the system to be developed should behave. Particularly, goals are prescriptive statements that the system should achieve within a given domain. The domain properties are descriptive statements that capture the domain of the problem world. Typically, GORE methodologies use a logical formalism to specify the expected system behavior, e.g., KAOS uses Linear-Time Temporal Logic for specifying requirements [55]. In this context, a *conflict* essentially represents a condition whose occurrence results in the loss of satisfaction of the goals, i.e., that makes the goals *diverge* [56,57]. Formally, it can be defined as follows.

Definition 7 (Goal Conflicts). *Let $G = \{G_1, \ldots, G_n\}$ be a set of goals, and Dom be a set of domain properties, all written in LTL. Goals in G are said to diverge if and only if there exists at least one Boundary Condition (BC), such that the following conditions hold:*

- *logical inconsistency:* $\{Dom, BC, \bigwedge_{1 \leq i \leq n} G_i\} \models false$

  minimality: for each $1 < i < n$, $\{Dom, BC, \bigwedge_{j \neq i} G_j\} \not\models false$

- *non-triviality:* $BC \neq \neg(G_1 \wedge \ldots \wedge G_n)$

Intuitively, a BC captures a particular combination of circumstances in which the goals cannot be satisfied. The first condition establishes that, when BC holds, the conjunction of goals $\{G_1, \ldots, G_n\}$ becomes inconsistent. The second condition states that, if any of the goals are disregarded, then consistency is recovered. The third condition prohibits a boundary condition to be simply the negation of the goals. Also, the minimality condition prohibits that BC be equals to *false* (it has to be consistent with the domain *Dom*).

Goal-conflict analysis [55,56] deals with these issues, through three main stages: (1) The goal-conflicts identification phase consists in generating boundary conditions that characterize divergences in the specification; (2) The assessment stage consists in assessing and prioritizing the identified conflicts according to their likelihood and severity; (3) The resolution stage consists in resolving the identified conflicts by providing appropriate countermeasures. Let us consider the following examples found in our empirical evaluation and commonly presented in related works.

Example 1 (Mine Pump Controller - MPC). Consider the Mine Pump Controller (MPC) widely used in related works that deal with formal requirements and reactive systems [16,35]. The MPC describes a system that is in charge of activating or deactivating a pump (p) to remove the water from the mine, in the presence of possible dangerous scenarios. The MP controller monitors environmental magnitudes related to the presence of methane (m) and the high level of water (h) in the mine. Maintaining a high level of water for a while may produce flooding in the mine, while the methane may cause an explosion when the pump is switched on. Hence, the specification for the MPC is as follows:

$$Dom : \Box((p \wedge \bigcirc(p)) \rightarrow \bigcirc(\bigcirc(\neg h)) \quad G_1 : \Box(m \rightarrow \bigcirc(\neg p)) \quad G_2 : \Box(h \rightarrow \bigcirc(p))$$

Domain property Dom describes the impact into the environment of switching on the pump (p). For instance, when the pump is kept on for 2 unit times, then the water will decrease and the level will not be high $(\neg h)$. Goal G_1 expresses that the pump should be off when methane is detected in the mine. Goal G_2 indicates that the pump should be on when the level of water is high.

Notice that this specification is consistent, for instance, in cases in which the level of water never exceeds the high threshold. However, approaches for goal-conflict identification, such as the one of Degiovanni et al. [16], can detect a conflict between goals in this specification.

The identified goal-conflict describes a divergence situation in cases in which the level of water is high and methane is present at the same time in the environment. Switching off the pump to satisfy G_1 will result in a violation of goal G_2; while switching on the pump to satisfy G_2 will violate G_1. This divergence situation clearly evidence a conflict between goals G_1 and G_2 that is captured by a boundary condition such $BC = \Diamond(h \wedge m)$.

In the work of Letier et al. [40] two resolutions were manually proposed that precisely describe what should be the software behaviour in cases where the divergence situation is reached. The first resolution proposes to refine goal G_2, by weakening it, requiring to switch on the pump only when the level of water is high and no methane is present in the environment.

Example 2 (Resolution 1 - MPC).

$$Dom : \Box((p \wedge \bigcirc(p)) \rightarrow \bigcirc(\bigcirc(\neg h)))$$
$$G_1 : \Box(m \rightarrow \bigcirc(\neg p)) \quad G_2' : \Box(h \wedge \neg m \rightarrow \bigcirc(p))$$

With a similar analysis, the second resolution proposes to weaken G_1, requiring switching off the pump when methane is present and the level of water is not high.

Example 3 (Resolution 2 - MPC).

$$Dom : \Box((p \wedge \bigcirc(p)) \rightarrow \bigcirc(\bigcirc(\neg h)))$$
$$G_1' : \Box(m \wedge \neg h \rightarrow \bigcirc(\neg p)) \quad G_2 : \Box(h \rightarrow \bigcirc(p))$$

The *resolution* stage aims at removing the identified goal-conflicts from the specification, for which it is necessary to modify the current specification formulation. This may require weakening or strengthening the existing goals, or even removing some and adding new ones.

Definition 8 (Goal-Conflict Resolution). *Let* $G = \{G_1, \ldots, G_n\}$, *Dom, and BC be the set of goals, the domain properties, and an identified boundary condition, respectively written in LTL. Let* $M : S_1 \times S_2 \mapsto [0,1]$ *and* $\epsilon \in [0,1]$ *be* *a similarity metric between two specifications and a threshold, respectively. We say that a resolution $R = \{R_1, \ldots, R_m\}$ resolves goal-conflict BC, if and only if, the following conditions hold:*

- *consistency: $\{Dom, R\} \not\models false$*
- *resolution: $\{BC, R\} \not\models false$*
- *similarity: $M(G, R) < \epsilon$*

Intuitively, the first condition states that the refined goals in R remain consistent within the domain properties *Dom*. The second condition states that *BC* does not lead to a divergence situation in the resolution R (i.e., refined goals in R know exactly how to deal with the situations captured by *BC*). Finally, the last condition aims at using a similarity metric M to control for the degree of changes applied to the original formulation of goals in G to produce the refined goals in resolution R.

Notice that the similarity metric M is general enough to capture similarities between G and R of different natures. For instance, $M(G, R)$ may compute the *syntactic similarity* between the text representations of the original specification of goals in G and the candidate resolution R, where the number of tokens edited from G to R is the aim. On the other hand, $M(G, R)$ may compute a semantic similarity between G and R, for instance, to favour resolutions that weaken the goals (i.e. $G \rightarrow R$), or strengthen the goals (i.e. $R \rightarrow G$) or that maintain most of the original behaviours (i.e. $\#G - \#R < \epsilon$).

Precisely, ACoRE will explore syntactic modifications of goals from G, leading to newly refined goals in R, with the aim at producing candidate resolutions that are consistent with the domain properties *Dom* and resolve conflict *BC*. Assuming that the engineer is competent and the current specification is very close to the intended one [19,1], ACoRE will integrate two similarity metrics in a multi-objective search process to produce resolutions that are syntactically and semantically similar to the original specification. Particularly, ACoRE can generate exactly the same resolutions for the MPC previously discussed, manually developed by Letier et al. [40].

4   ACoRe: Automated Goal-Conflict Resolution

ACoRE takes as input a specification $S = (Dom, G)$, composed by the domain properties *Dom*, a set of goals G, and a set $\{BC_1, \ldots, BC_k\}$ of identified boundary conditions for S. ACoRE uses search to iteratively explore variants of G to produce a set $R = \{R_1, \ldots, R_n\}$ of resolutions, where each $R_i = (Dom, G^i)$, that maintain two sorts of similarities with the original specification, namely, syntactic and semantic similarity between S and each R_i. Figure 1 shows an overview of the different steps of the search process implemented by ACoRE.

ACoRE instantiates multi-objective optimization (MOO) algorithms to efficiently and effectively explore the search space. Currently, ACoRE implements four MOO algorithms, namely, the *Non-Dominated Sorting Genetic Algorithm III* (NSGA-III) [14], a *Weight-based genetic algorithm (WBGA)* [29], an *Archived*

Multi-objective Simulated Annealing (AMOSA) [6] approach, and an *unguided search* approach we use as a baseline. Let us first describe some common components shared by the algorithms (namely, the search space, the multi-objectives, and the evolutionary operators) and then get into the particular details of each approach (such as the fitness function and selection criteria).

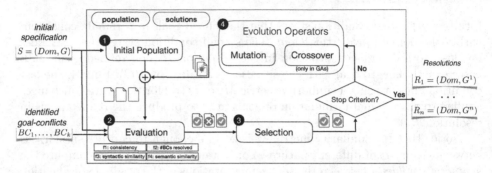

Fig. 1: Overview of ACoRE.

4.1   Search Space and Initial Population

Each individual $cR = (Dom, G')$, representing a candidate resolution, is a LTL specification over a set AP of propositional variables, where Dom captures the domain properties and G' the refined system goals. Notice that domain properties Dom are not changed through the search process since these are descriptive statements. On the other hand, ACoRE performs syntactic alterations to the original set of goals G to obtain the new set of refined goals G' that potentially resolve the conflicts given as input.

The initial population represents a sample of the search space from which the search starts. ACoRE creates one or more individuals (depending on the multi-objective algorithm being used) as the initial population by applying the mutation operator (explained below) to the specification S given as input.

4.2   Multi-Objectives: Consistency, Resolution and Similarities

ACoRE guides the search with *four objectives* that check for the validity of each of the conditions needed to be a valid goal-conflict resolution, namely, consistency, resolution and two similarity metrics (cf. Definition 8).

Given a resolution $cR = (Dom, G')$, the first objective $Consistency(cR)$ evaluates if the refined goals G' are consistent with the domain properties by using SAT solving.

$$Consistency(cR) = \begin{cases} 1 & \text{if } Dom \wedge G' \text{ is satisfiable} \\ 0.5 & \text{if } Dom \wedge G' \text{ is unsatisfiable, but } G' \text{ is satisfiable} \\ 0 & \text{if } G' \text{ is unsatisfiable} \end{cases}$$

The second objective $ResolvedBCs(cR)$ computes the ratio of boundary conditions resolved by the candidate resolution cR, among the total number of boundary conditions given as input. Hence, $ResolvedBCs(cR)$ returns values between 0 and 1, and is defined as follows:

$$ResolvedBCs(cR) = \frac{\sum_{i=1}^{k} isResolved(BC_i, G')}{k}$$

$isResolved(cR, BC_i)$ returns 1, if and only if $BC_i \wedge G'$ is satisfiable; otherwise, returns 0. Intuitively, when $BC_i \wedge G'$ is satisfiable, it means that the refined goals G' satisfies the resolution condition of Definition 8 and thus, BC_i is no longer a conflict for candidate resolution cR. In the case that cR resolves all the (k) boundary conditions, the objective $ResolvedBCs(cR)$ will return 1.

With the objective of prioritising resolutions that are in some sense similar to the original specification among the dissimilar ones, ACoRe integrates two similarity metrics. ACoRe considers one *syntactic* and one *semantic* similarity metric that will help the algorithms to focus the search in the vicinity of the specification given as input.

Precisely, objective $Syntactic(S, cR)$ refers to the distance between the text representations of the original specification S and the candidate resolution cR. To compute the syntactic similarity between LTL specifications, we use Levenshtein distance [42]. Intuitively, the Levenshtein distance between two words is the minimum number of single-character edits (insertions, deletions, or substitutions) required to change one word into the other. Hence, $Syntactic(S, cR)$, is computed as:

$$Syntactic(S, cR) = \frac{maxLength - Levenshtein(S, cR)}{maxLength}$$

where $maxLength = max(length(S), length(cR))$. Intuitively, $Syntactic(S, cR)$ represents the ratio between the number of tokens changed from S to obtain cR among the maximum number of tokens corresponding to the largest specification.

On the other hand, our semantic similarity objective $Semantic(S, cR)$ refers to the system *behaviour* similarities described by the original specification and the candidate resolution. Precisely, $Semantic(S, cR)$ computes the ratio between the number of behaviours present in both, the original specification and candidate resolution, among the total number of behaviours described by the specifications. To efficiently compute the objective $Semantic(S, cR)$, ACoRe uses model counting and the approximation previously described in Definition 6. Hence, given a bound k for the lasso traces, the semantic similarity between S and cR is computed as:

$$Semantic(S, cR) = \frac{\#\text{APPROX}(S \wedge cR, k)}{\#\text{APPROX}(S \vee cR, k)}$$

Notice that, small values for $Semantic(S, cR)$ indicate that the behaviours described by S are divergent from those described by cR. In particular, in cases that S and cR are contradictory (i.e., $S \wedge cR$ is unsatisfiable), $Semantic(S, cR)$ is

0. As this value gets closer to 1, both specifications characterize an increasingly large number of common behaviors.

4.3   Evolutionary Operators

New individuals are generated through the application of the evolution operators. Particularly, our approach ACORE implements two standard operators used for evolving LTL specifications [17,43], namely a mutation and a crossover operators. Below, we provide some examples of the application of these operators, and please refer to the complementary material for a detailed formal definition.

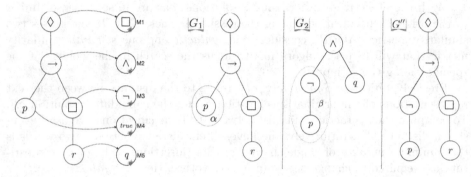

Fig. 2: Mutation operator.   Fig. 3: Crossover operator.

Given a candidate individual $cR' = (Dom, G')$, the *mutation* operator selects a goal $g' \in G'$ to mutate, leading to a new goal g'', and produces a new candidate specification $cR'' = (Dom, G'')$, where $G'' = G'[g' \mapsto g'']$, that is, G'' looks exactly as G' but goal g' is replaced by the mutated goal g''.

For instance, Figure 2 shows 5 possible mutations that we can generate for formula $\Diamond(p \to \Box r)$. Mutation M1 replaces $\Diamond$ by $\Box$, leading to $M1 : \Box(p \to \Box r)$. Mutation $M2 : \Diamond(p \wedge \Box r)$ replaces $\to$ by $\wedge$. Mutation $M3 : \Diamond(p \to \neg r)$ replaces $\Box$ by $\neg$. Mutation $M4 : \Diamond(true \to \Box r)$, reduces to $\Diamond\Box r$, replaces p by $true$. While mutation $M5 : \Diamond(p \to \Box q)$ replaces r by q.

On the contrary, the *crossover* operator takes two individuals $cR^1 = (Dom, G^1)$ and $cR^2 = (Dom, G^2)$, and produces a new candidate resolution $cR'' = (Dom, G'')$ by combining portions of both specifications. In other words, it takes one goal from each individual, i.e. $G_1 \in G^1$ and $G_2 \in G^2$, and generates a new goal G'' that is obtained by replacing a subformula α of G_1 by a subformula β taken from G_2. For instance, Figure 3 provides an illustration of how this operator works. Particularly, subformula $\alpha : p$ is selected from goal $G_1 : \Diamond(p \to \Box r)$, while subformula $\beta : \neg p$ is selected from goal $G_2 : \neg p \wedge q$. Hence, by replacing in G_1 subformula α by subformula β, the crossover operators generate a new goal $G'' : \Diamond(\neg p \to \Box r)$.

It is worth mentioning that the four multi-objective search algorithms implemented by ACoRe use the mutation operator to evolve the population. However, only two of the algorithms that implement two different genetic algorithms (i.e. NSGA-III and WBGA) use the crossover operator to evolve the population.

4.4   Multi-Objective Optimisation Search Algorithms

In a *multi-objective optimisation* (MOO) problem there is a set of solutions, called the *Pareto-optimal* (PO) set, which is considered to be equally important. Given two individuals x_1 and x_2 from the search-space S, and $f_1, \ldots, f_n$ a set of (maximising) fitness functions, where $f_i : S \to \mathbb{R}$, we say that x_1 dominates x_2 if (a) x_1 is not worse than x_2 in all objectives and (b) x_1 is strictly better than x_2 at least in one objective. Typically, MOO algorithms evolve the candidate population with the aim to converge to a set of *non-dominated* solutions as close to the true PO set as possible and maintain as diverse a solution set as possible. There are many variants of MOO algorithms that have been successfully applied in practice [27]. ACoRe implements four multi-objective optimization algorithms to explore the search space to generate goal-conflict resolutions.

AMOSA. The Archived Multi-objective Simulated Annealing (AMOSA) [6] is an adaptation of the simulated annealing algorithm [34] for multi-objectives. AMOSA only analyses one (current) individual per iteration, and a new individual is created by the application of the mutation operator. AMOSA has two particular features that make it promising for our purpose. During the search, it maintains an "archive" with the non-dominated candidates explored so far, that is, candidates whose fitness values are not subsumed by other generated individuals. Moreover, when a new individual is created that does not dominate the current one, it is not immediately discarded and can still be selected among the current individual with some probability that depends on the "temperature" (a function that decreases over time). At the beginning the temperature is high, then new individuals with worse fitness than the current element, are likely to be selected, but this probability decreases over the iterations. This strategy helps in avoiding local maximums and exploring more diverse potential solutions.

WBGA. ACoRe also implements a classic *Weight-based genetic algorithm (WBGA)* [29]. In this case, WBGA maintains a fixed number of individuals in each iteration (a configurable parameter), and applies both the mutation and crossover operators to generate new individuals. WBGA computes the fitness value for each objective and combines them into a single fitness f defined as:

$$f(S, cR) = \alpha * Consistency(cR) + \beta * ResolvedBCs(cR) +$$
$$\gamma * Syntax(S, cR) + \delta * Semantic(S, cR)$$

where weights $\alpha = 0.1$, $\beta = 0.7$, $\gamma = 0.1$, and $\delta = 0.1$ are defined by default (empirically validated), but these can be configured to other values if desired. In each iteration, WBGA sorts all the individuals according to their fitness value (descending order) and selects best ranked individuals to survive to the next iteration (other selectors can be integrated). Finally, WBGA reports all the resolutions found during the search.

NSGA-III. ACoRE also implements the Non-Dominated Sorting Genetic Algorithm III (NSGA-III) [14] approach. It is a variant of a genetic algorithm that also uses mutation and crossover operators to evolve the population. In each iteration, it computes the fitness values for each individual and sorts the population according to the Pareto dominance relation. Then it creates a partition of the population according the level of the individuals in the Pareto dominance relation (i.e., non-dominated individuals are in Level-1, Level-2 contains the individuals dominated only by individuals in Level-1, and so on). Thus, NSGA-III selects only one individual per non-dominated level with the aim of diversifying the exploration and reducing the number of resolutions in the final Pareto-front.

ACoRE also implements an **Unguided Search** algorithm that does not use any of the objectives to guide the search. It randomly selects individuals and applies the mutation operator to evolve the population. After generating a maximum number of individuals (a given parameter of the algorithm), it checks which ones constitute a valid resolution for the goal-conflicts given as input.

5   Experimental Evaluation

We start our analysis by investigating the effectiveness of ACoRE in resolving goal-conflicts. Thus, we ask:

RQ1 *How effective is* ACoRE *at resolving goal-conflicts?*

To answer this question, we study the ability of ACoRE to generate resolutions in a set of 25 specifications for which we have identified goal-conflicts.

Then, we turn our attention to the *"quality"* of the resolution produced by ACoRE and study if ACoRE is able to replicate some of the manually written resolutions gathered from the literature (ground-truth). Thus, we ask:

RQ2 *How able is* ACoRE *to generate resolutions that match with resolutions provided by engineers (i.e. manually developed)?*

To answer RQ2, we check if ACoRE can generate resolutions that are equivalent to the ones manually developed by the engineer.

Finally, we are interested in analyzing and comparing the performance of the four search algorithms integrated by ACoRE. Thus, we ask:

RQ3 *What is the performance of* ACoRE *when adopting different search algorithms?*

To answer RQ3, we basically employ standard quality indicators (e.g. hypervolume (HV) and inverted generational distance (IGD)) to compare the Pareto-front produced by ACoRE when the different search algorithms are employed.

5.1   Experimental Procedure

We consider a total of 25 requirements specifications taken from the literature and different benchmarks. These specifications were previously used by goal-conflicts identification and assessment approaches [4,16,17,18,43,56].

Table 1: LTL Requirements Specifications and Goal-conflicts Identified.

Specification	#Dom + #Goals	#BCs	Specification	#Dom + #Goals	#BCs
minepump	3	14	rrcs	4	14
simple arbiter-v1	4	28	achieve-avoid pattern	3	16
simple arbiter-v2	4	20	retraction pattern-1	2	2
prioritized arbiter	7	11	retraction pattern-2	2	10
arbiter	3	20	RG2	2	9
detector	2	15	lily01	3	5
ltl2dba27	1	11	lily02	3	11
round robin	9	12	lily11	3	5
tcp	2	11	lily15	3	19
atm	3	24	lily16	6	38
telephone	5	4	ltl2dba theta-2	1	3
elevator	2	3	ltl2dba R-2	1	5
			simple arbiter icse2018	11	20

We start by running the approach of Degiovanni et al. [17] on each subject to identify a set of boundary conditions. Table 1 summarises, for each case, the number of domain properties and goals, and the number of boundary conditions (i.e. goal-conflicts) computed with the approach of Degiovanni et al. [17]. Notice that we use the set of "weakest"[1] boundary conditions returned by [17], in the sense that by removing all of these we are guaranteed to remove all the boundary conditions computed.

Then, we run ACoRe to generate resolutions that remove all the identified goal-conflicts. We configure ACoRe to explore a maximum number of 1000 individuals with each algorithm. We repeat this process 10 times to reduce potential threats [5] raised by the random elections of the search algorithms.

To answer RQ1, we run ACoRe and report the number of *non-dominated* resolutions produced by each implemented algorithm (i.e. those resolutions whose fitness values are not subsumed by other individuals).

To answer RQ2, we collected from the literature 8 cases in which authors reported a "buggy" version of the specification and a "fixed" version of the same specification. We take the buggy version and compute a set of boundary conditions for it that are later fed into ACoRe to automatically produce a set of resolutions. We then compare the resolutions produced by our ACoRe and the "fixed" versions we gathered from the literature. We basically analyse, by using sat solving, if any of the resolutions produced by ACoRe is equivalent to the manually developed fixed version.

To answer RQ3, we perform an objective comparison of the performance of the four search algorithms implemented by ACoRe by using two standard

---

[1] A formula A is weaker than B, if $B \land \neg A$ is unsatisfiable, i.e., if B implies A.

quality indicators: hypervolume (HV) [62] and inverted generational distance (IGD) [12]. The recent work of Wu et al. [61] indicates that quality indicators HV and IGD are the prefered ones for assessing genetic algorithms and Pareto evolutionary algorithms such as the ones ACoRE implements (NSGA-III, WBGA, and AMOSA). These quality indicators are useful to measure the *convergence*, *spread*, *uniformity*, and *cardinality* of the solutions computed by the algorithms. More precisely, hypervolume (HV) [42,54] is a *volume-based indicator*, defined by the Nadir Point [38,62], that returns a value between 0 and 1, where a value near to 1 indicates that the Pareto-front converges very well to the reference point [42] (also, high values for HV are good indicator of uniformity and spread of the Pareto-front [54]). The Inverted Generational Distance (IGD) indicator is a *distance-based indicator* that also computes convergence and spread [42,54]. In summary, IGD measures the mean distance from each reference point to the nearest element in the Pareto-optimal set [12,54]. We also perform some statistical analysis, namely, the Kruskal-Wallis H-test [37], the Mann-Whitney U-test [44], and Vargha-Delaney A measure $\hat{A}_{12}$ [59], to compare the performance of the algorithms. Intuitively, the *p-value* will tell us if the performance between the algorithms measured in terms of the HV and IGD is statistical significance, while the A-measure will tell us how frequent one algorithm obtains better indicators than the others.

ACoRE is implemented in Java into the JMetal framework [50]. It integrates the LTL satisfiability checker Polsat [41], a portfolio tool that runs in parallel with four LTL solvers, helping us to efficiently compute the fitness functions. Moreover, ACoRE uses the OwL library [36] to parse and manipulate the LTL specifications. The quality indicators also are implemented by the JMetal framework and the statistical tests by the Apache Common Math. We ran all the experiments on a cluster with nodes with Xeon E5 2.4GHz, with 5 CPUs-nodes and 8GB of RAM available per run.

Regarding the setting of the algorithms, the population size of 100 individuals was defined and the fitness evaluation was limited to a number of 1000 individuals. Moreover, the timeout of the model counting and SAT solvers were configured as 300 seconds. The probability of crossover application was 0.1, while mutation operators were always applied. A tournament selection of four solutions was used for NSGA-III, while WBGA instantiated Bolzman's selection with a decrement exponential function. The WBGA was configured to weight the fitness functions as a proportion of 0.1 in the Status, 0.7 in the ResolvedBC, 0.1 in Syntactic, and 0.1 in Semantic. The AMOSA used an archive of crowding distance, while the cooling scheme relied on a decrement exponential function.

The case studies and results are publicly available at https://sites.google.com/view/acore-goal-conflict-resolution/.

6 Experimental Results

6.1 RQ1: Effectiveness of ACoRe

Table 2 reports the average number of non-dominated resolutions produced by the algorithms in the 10 runs. First, it is worth mentioning that when ACoRe uses any of the genetic algorithms (NSGA-III or WBGA), it successfully generates at least one resolution for all the case studies. However, AMOSA fails in producing a resolution for the `lily16` and `simple arbiter icse2018` in 2 and 1 cases of the 10 runs, respectively. Despite that Unguided search succeeds in the majority of the cases, it was not able to produce any resolution for the `prioritized arbiter`, and failed in producing a resolution in 5 out of the 10 runs for the `simple-arbiter-v2`.

Table 2: Effectiveness of ACoRe in producing resolutions.

Specification	NSGA-III	WBGA	AMOSA	Unguided
minepump	5.0	**6.5**	1.8	5.1
simple arbiter-v1	**4.8**	3.1	2.0	4.1
simple arbiter-v2	6.1	6.1	1.8	1.1
prioritized arbiter	3.1	**3.7**	2.2	0.0
arbiter	**5.8**	2.7	3.0	5.5
detector	4.9	4.8	3.2	**6.1**
ltl2dba27	3.0	**4.2**	3.5	4.0
round robin	**7.0**	4.2	4.7	4.7
tcp	6.4	4.9	2.0	**7.4**
atm	3.9	**6.3**	3.3	4.5
telephone	**4.7**	4.4	2.2	4.5
elevator	**5.9**	**5.9**	3.6	4.8
rrcs	5.5	**5.7**	1.4	3.3
achieve pattern	5.0	**5.9**	2.5	2.8
retraction pattern-1	4.1	4.0	2.7	**4.6**
retraction pattern-2	**6.1**	4.8	2.6	6.0
RG2	3.3	**5.2**	1.5	4.3
lily01	**5.1**	**5.1**	1.5	4.1
lily02	2.4	**3.8**	1.9	1.9
lily11	**7.1**	5.0	2.2	5.8
lily15	**6.1**	4.1	1.2	5.8
lily16	**6.5**	3.2	0.8	3.8
ltl2dba theta-2	1.9	**2.8**	1.9	1.2
ltl2dba R-2	1.0	**2.1**	1.9	**2.1**
simple arbiter icse2018	**3.8**	3.7	0.9	3.5

Table 3: ACoRe effectiveness in producing an exact or more general resolution than the manually written one.

Specification	NSGA-III	WBGA	AMOSA	Unguided
minepump	✓	✓	✓	✓
simple arbiter-v1				
simple arbiter-v2	✓	✓		
prioritized arbiter				
arbiter				
detector	✓	✓		✓
ltl2dba27				
round robin				

Second, the genetic algorithms (NSGA-III and WBGA) generate on average more (non-dominated) resolutions than AMOSA and unguided search. The results point out that WBGA generates more (non-dominated) resolutions than others in 13 out of the 25 cases, and NSGA-III is the one that produces more (non-dominated) resolutions in 11 cases. Considering the genetic algorithms together, we can observe that they outperform the AMOSA and unguided search in 21 out of the 25 cases, and coincide in one case (`ltl2dba R-2`). Finally, the Unguided Search generates more resolutions in 3 cases, namely, `detector`, `TCP`, and `retraction-pattern-1`. Interestingly, the different algorithms of ACoRE produce on average between 1 and 8 non-dominated resolutions, which we consider is a reasonable number of options that the engineer can manually inspect and validate to select the most appropriate one.

> ACoRE generates more non-dominated resolutions when adopting genetic algorithms. On average, ACoRE produces between 1 and 8 non-dominated resolutions that can be presented to the engineer for analysis and validation.

6.2 RQ2: Comparison with the Ground-truth

Table 3 presents the effectiveness of ACoRE in generating a resolution that is equivalent or more general than the ones manually developed by engineers. Overall, ACoRE is able to reproduce same resolutions in 3 out of 8 of the cases, namely, for the `minepump` (our running example), `simple arbiter-v2`, and `detector`. Like for RQ1, the genetic algorithms outperform AMOSA and unguided search in this respect. Particularly, the Unguided Search can replicate the resolution for the `detector` case, in which AMOSA fails.

> Overall, the genetic algorithms can produce same or more general resolutions than the ground-truth in 3 out of the 8 cases, outperforming AMOSA (1 out of the 8) and unguided search (2 out of the 8).

6.3 RQ3: Comparing the Multi-objective Optimization Algorithms

For each set of non-dominated resolutions generated by the different algorithms, we compute the quality indicators HV and IGD for the syntactic and semantic similarity values. The reference point is the best possible value for each objective which is 1. These will allow us to determine which algorithm converges the most to the reference point and produces more diverse and optimal resolutions.

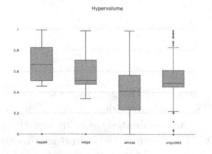
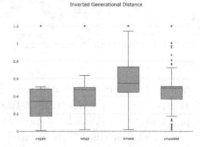

Fig. 4: HV of the Pareto-optimal sets generated by ACoRE.

Fig. 5: IGD of the Pareto-optimal sets generated by ACoRE.

Figures 4 and 5 show the boxplots for each quality indicator. NSGA-III obtains on average much better HV and IGD than the rest of the algorithms. Precisely, it obtains on average 0.66 of HV (while higher the better) and 0.34 of IGD (while lower the better), outperforming the other algorithms.

To confirm this result we compare the quality indicators in terms of non-parametric statistical tests: (i) Kruskal–Wallis test by ranks and (ii) the Mann-Whitney U-test. The α value defined in the Kruskal-Wallis test by ranks is 0.05 and the Mann-Whitney U-test is 0.0125. Moreover, we also complete our assessment by using Vargha and Delaney's $\hat{A}_{12}$, a non-parametric effect size measurement. Table 4 summarises the results when we compare pair-wise each one of the approaches. We can observe that NSGA-III in near 80% of the cases obtains resolutions with better quality indicators than AMOSA and Unguided search (and the differences are statistically significant). We can also observe that NSGA-III obtains higher HV (IGD) than WBGA in 66% (65%) of the cases. From Table 4 we can also observe that WBGA outperforms both AMOSA and unguided search. Moreover, we can observe that AMOSA is the worse performing algorithm according to the considered quality indicators.

Table 4: HV and IGD quality indicators for the generated resolutions.

		WBGA		AMOSA		Unguided	
		HV	IGD	HV	IGD	HV	IGD
NSGAIII	p-value	< 0.00001	< 0.00001	< 0.00001	< 0.00001	< 0.00001	< 0.00001
	$\hat{A}_{12}$	0.66	0.65	0.84	0.83	0.80	0.76
WBGA	p-value	-	-	< 0.00001	< 0.00001	< 0.00001	< 0.00001
	$\hat{A}_{12}$	-	-	0.74	0.74	0.64	0.61
AMOSA	p-value	-	-	-	-	< 0.00001	< 0.00001
	$\hat{A}_{12}$	-	-	-	-	0.36	0.36

Overall, both statistical tests evidence that NSGA-III leads to a set of resolutions with better quality indicators (HV and IGD) than the rest of the algorithms. WBGA is the one in the second place, outperforming the unguided search and AMOSA. While AMOSA shows the lowest performance based on the quality indicators, even worse than the unguided search in several cases.

7 Related Work

Several manual approaches have been proposed to identify inconsistencies between goals and resolve them once the requirements were specified. Among them, Murukannaiah et al. [49] compares a genuine analysis of competing hypotheses against modified procedures that include requirements engineer thought process. The empirical evaluation shows that the modified version presents higher completeness and coverage. Despite the increase in quality, the approach is limited to manual applicability performed by engineers as well previous approaches [56].

Various informal and semi-formal approaches [28,32,33], as well as more formal approaches [21,23,26,30,51,53], have been proposed for detecting logically inconsistent requirements, a strong kind of conflicts, as opposed to this work that focuses on a weak form of conflict, called divergences (cf. Section 3).

Moreover, recent approaches have been introduced to automatically identify goal-conflicts. Degiovanni *et al.* [18] introduced an automated approach where boundary conditions are automatically computed using a tableaux-based LTL satisfiability checking procedure. Since it exhibits serious scalability issues, the work of Degiovanni *et al.* [17] proposes a genetic algorithm that mutates the LTL formulas in order to find boundary conditions for the goal specifications. The output of this approach can be fed into ACoRE to produce potential resolutions for the identified conflicts (as shown in the experimental evaluation).

Regarding specification repair approaches, Wang *et al.* [60] introduced ARepair, an automated tool to repair a faulty model formally specified in Alloy [31]. ARepair takes a faulty Alloy model and a set of failing tests and applies mutations to the model until all failing tests become passing. In the case of ACoRE, the identified goal conflicts are the ones that guide the search, and candidates are aimed to be syntactic and semantically similar to the original specification.

In the context of reactive synthesis [22,46,52], some approaches were proposed to repair imperfections in the LTL specifications that make the unrealisable (i.e., no implementation that satisfies the specification can be synthesized). The majority of the approaches focus on learning missing assumptions about the environment that make them unrealisable [4,10,11,48]. A more recent approach [8], published in a technical report, proposes to mutate both the assumptions and guarantees (goals) until the specification becomes realisable. Precisely, we use the novel model counting approximation algorithm from Brizzio et. al [8] to compute the semantic similarity between the original buggy specification and the resolutions. However, the notion of repair for Brizzio et. al [8] requires a realizable specification, which is very general and does not necessarily lead to quality synthesized controllers [20,47]. In this work, the definition of resolution is fine-grained and focused on removing the identified conflicts, which potentially leads to interesting repairs as we showed in our empirical evaluation.

Alrajeh *et al.* [2] introduced an automated approach to refine a goal model when the environmental context changes. That is, if the domain properties are changed, then this approach will propose changes in the goals to make them consistent with the new domain. The adapted goal model is generated using a new counterexample-guided learning procedure that ensures the correctness of the updated goal model, preferring more local adaptations and more similar goal models. In our work, the domain properties are not changed and the adaptions are made to resolve the identified inconsistencies, and instead of counterexamples, our search is guided by syntactic and semantic similarity metrics.

8   Conclusion

In this paper, we presented ACoRE, the first automated approach for goal-conflict resolution. Overall, ACoRE takes a goal specification and a set of conflicts previously identified, expressed in LTL, and computes a set of resolutions that removes such conflicts. To assess and implement ACoRe that is a search-based approach, we adopted three multi-objective algorithms (NSGA-III, AMOSA, and WBGA) that simultaneously optimize and deal with the trade-off among the objectives. We evaluated ACoRe in 25 specifications that were written in LTL and extracted from the related literature. The evaluation showed that the genetic algorithms (NSGA-III and WBGA) typically generate more (non-dominated) resolutions than AMOSA and an Unguided Search we implemented as a baseline in our evaluation. Moreover, the algorithms generate on average between 1 and 8 resolutions per specification, which may allow the engineer to manually inspect and select the most appropriate resolutions. We also observed that the genetic algorithms (NSGA-III and WBGA) outperform AMOSA and Unguided Search in terms of several quality indicators: number of (non-dominated) resolutions and standard quality indicators (HV and IGD) for multi-objective algorithms.

Acknowledgements. This work is supported by the Luxembourg National Research Funds (FNR) through the CORE project grant C19/IS/13646587/RASoRS.

References

1. Allen Troy Acree, Timothy Alan Budd, Richard A. DeMillo, Richard J. Lipton, and Frederick Gerald Sayward. Mutation analysis. techreport GIT-ICS-79/08, Georgia Institute of Technology, Atlanta, Georgia, 1979.
2. Dalal Alrajeh, Antoine Cailliau, and Axel van Lamsweerde. Adapting requirements models to varying environments. In *Proceedings of the 42nd International Conference on Software Engineering, ICSE 2020, Seoul, South Korea, May 23-29, 2020*, 2020.
3. Dalal Alrajeh, Jeff Kramer, Alessandra Russo, and Sebastin Uchitel. Learning operational requirements from goal models. In *Proceedings of the 31st International Conference on Software Engineering*, ICSE '09, pages 265–275, Washington, DC, USA, 2009. IEEE Computer Society.
4. Rajeev Alur, Salar Moarref, and Ufuk Topcu. Counter-strategy guided refinement of GR(1) temporal logic specifications. In *Formal Methods in Computer Aided Design, FMCAD 2013, Portland, OR, USA, October 20-23, 2013*, pages 26–33, 2013.
5. Andrea Arcuri and Lionel Briand. A practical guide for using statistical tests to assess randomized algorithms in software engineering. In *Proceedings of the 33rd International Conference on Software Engineering*, ICSE '11, page 1–10, New York, NY, USA, 2011. Association for Computing Machinery.
6. Sanghamitra Bandyopadhyay, Sriparna Saha, Ujjwal Maulik, and Kalyanmoy Deb. A simulated annealing-based multiobjective optimization algorithm: AMOSA. *IEEE Trans. Evol. Comput.*, 12(3):269–283, 2008.
7. Armin Biere, Alessandro Cimatti, Edmund M. Clarke, and Yunshan Zhu. Symbolic model checking without bdds. In *Proceedings of the 5th International Conference on Tools and Algorithms for Construction and Analysis of Systems*, TACAS '99, pages 193–207, London, UK, UK, 1999. Springer-Verlag.

8. Matías Brizzio, Renzo Degiovanni, Maxime Cordy, Mike Papadakis, and Nazareno Aguirre. Automated repair of unrealisable LTL specifications guided by model counting. *CoRR*, abs/2105.12595, 2021.

9. Antoine Cailliau and Axel van Lamsweerde. Handling knowledge uncertainty in risk-based requirements engineering. In *23rd IEEE International Requirements Engineering Conference, RE 2015, Ottawa, ON, Canada, August 24-28, 2015*, pages 106–115, 2015.

10. Davide G. Cavezza and Dalal Alrajeh. Interpolation-based GR(1) assumptions refinement. *CoRR*, abs/1611.07803, 2016.

11. Krishnendu Chatterjee, Thomas A. Henzinger, and Barbara Jobstmann. Environment assumptions for synthesis. In Franck van Breugel and Marsha Chechik, editors, *CONCUR 2008 - Concurrency Theory*, pages 147–161, Berlin, Heidelberg, 2008. Springer Berlin Heidelberg.

12. Carlos A. Coello Coello and Margarita Reyes Sierra. A study of the parallelization of a coevolutionary multi-objective evolutionary algorithm. In Raúl Monroy, Gustavo Arroyo-Figueroa, Luis Enrique Sucar, and Humberto Sossa, editors, *MICAI 2004: Advances in Artificial Intelligence*, pages 688–697, Berlin, Heidelberg, 2004. Springer Berlin Heidelberg.

13. Anne Dardenne, Axel van Lamsweerde, and Stephen Fickas. Goal-directed requirements acquisition. In *SCIENCE OF COMPUTER PROGRAMMING*, pages 3–50, 1993.

14. Kalyanmoy Deb and Himanshu Jain. An evolutionary many-objective optimization algorithm using reference-point-based nondominated sorting approach, part i: Solving problems with box constraints. *IEEE Transactions on Evolutionary Computation*, 18(4):577–601, 2014.

15. Renzo Degiovanni, Dalal Alrajeh, Nazareno Aguirre, and Sebastián Uchitel. Automated goal operationalisation based on interpolation and sat solving. In *ICSE*, pages 129–139, 2014.

16. Renzo Degiovanni, Pablo F. Castro, Marcelo Arroyo, Marcelo Ruiz, Nazareno Aguirre, and Marcelo F. Frias. Goal-conflict likelihood assessment based on model counting. In *Proceedings of the 40th International Conference on Software Engineering, ICSE 2018, Gothenburg, Sweden, May 27 - June 03, 2018*, pages 1125–1135, 2018.

17. Renzo Degiovanni, Facundo Molina, Germán Regis, and Nazareno Aguirre. A genetic algorithm for goal-conflict identification. In *Proceedings of the 33rd ACM/IEEE International Conference on Automated Software Engineering, ASE 2018, Montpellier, France, September 3-7, 2018*, pages 520–531, 2018.

18. Renzo Degiovanni, Nicolás Ricci, Dalal Alrajeh, Pablo F. Castro, and Nazareno Aguirre. Goal-conflict detection based on temporal satisfiability checking. In *Proceedings of the 31st IEEE/ACM International Conference on Automated Software Engineering, ASE 2016, Singapore, September 3-7, 2016*, pages 507–518, 2016.

19. Richard A. DeMillo, Richard J. Lipton, and Frederick G. Sayward. Hints on test data selection: Help for the practicing programmer. *IEEE Computer*, 11(4):34–41, 1978.

20. Nicolás D'Ippolito, Víctor A. Braberman, Nir Piterman, and Sebastián Uchitel. Synthesizing nonanomalous event-based controllers for liveness goals. *ACM Trans. Softw. Eng. Methodol.*, 22(1):9, 2013.

21. Christian Ellen, Sven Sieverding, and Hardi Hungar. Detecting consistencies and inconsistencies of pattern-based functional requirements. In *Proc. of the 19th Intl. Conf. on Formal Methods for Industrial Critical Systems*, pages 155–169, 2014.

22. E. Allen Emerson and Edmund M. Clarke. Using branching time temporal logic to synthesize synchronization skeletons. *Sci. Comput. Program.*, 2(3):241–266, 1982.
23. Neil A. Ernst, Alexander Borgida, John Mylopoulos, and Ivan J. Jureta. Agile requirements evolution via paraconsistent reasoning. In *Proc. of the 24th Intl. Conf. on Advanced Information Systems Engineering*, pages 382–397, 2012.
24. Daniel Méndez Fernández, Stefan Wagner, Marcos Kalinowski, Michael Felderer, Priscilla Mafra, Antonio Vetro, Tayana Conte, M.-T. Christiansson, Des Greer, Casper Lassenius, Tomi Männistö, M. Nayabi, Markku Oivo, Birgit Penzenstadler, Dietmar Pfahl, Rafael Prikladnicki, Günther Ruhe, André Schekelmann, Sagar Sen, Rodrigo O. Spínola, Ahmet Tuzcu, Jose Luis de la Vara, and Roel Wieringa. Naming the pain in requirements engineering - contemporary problems, causes, and effects in practice. *Empirical Software Engineering*, 22(5):2298–2338, 2017.
25. Bernd Finkbeiner and Hazem Torfah. Counting models of linear-time temporal logic. In Adrian Horia Dediu, Carlos Martín-Vide, José Luis Sierra-Rodríguez, and Bianca Truthe, editors, *Language and Automata Theory and Applications - 8th International Conference, LATA 2014, Madrid, Spain, March 10-14, 2014. Proceedings*, volume 8370 of *Lecture Notes in Computer Science*, pages 360–371. Springer, 2014.
26. David Harel, Hillel Kugler, and Amir Pnueli. Synthesis revisited: Generating statechart models from scenario-based requirements. In *Formal Methods in Software and Systems Modeling: Essays Dedicated to Hartmut Ehrig on the Occasion of His 60th Birthday*, pages 309–324, 2005.
27. Mark Harman, S. Afshin Mansouri, and Yuanyuan Zhang. Search-based software engineering: Trends, techniques and applications. *ACM Comput. Surv.*, 45(1):11:1–11:61, December 2012.
28. J.H. Hausmann, R. Heckel, and G. Taentzer. Detection of conflicting functional requirements in a use case-driven approach. In *ICSE*, pages 105–115, 2002.
29. John H. Holland. *Adaptation in Natural and Artificial Systems: An Introductory Analysis with Applications to Biology, Control, and Artificial Intelligence*. MIT Press, 1992.
30. Anthony Hunter and Bashar Nuseibeh. Managing inconsistent specifications: Reasoning, analysis, and action. *ACM TOSEM*, 7(4):335–367, 1998.
31. Daniel Jackson. *Software Abstractions - Logic, Language, and Analysis*. MIT Press, 2006.
32. M. Kamalrudin. Automated software tool support for checking the inconsistency of requirements. In *ASE*, pages 693–697, 2009.
33. Massila Kamalrudin, John Hosking, and John Grundy. Improving requirements quality using essential use case interaction patterns. In *ICSE*, pages 531–540, 2011.
34. S. Kirkpatrick, C. D. Gelatt, and M. P. Vecchi. Optimization by simulated annealing. *SCIENCE*, 220(4598):671–680, 1983.
35. J. Kramer, J. Magee, M. Sloman, and A. Lister. CONIC: an integrated approach to distributed computer control systems. *Computers and Digital Techniques, IEE Proceedings E*, 130(1):1+, 1983.
36. Jan Kretínský, Tobias Meggendorfer, and Salomon Sickert. Owl: A library for ω-words, automata, and LTL. In Shuvendu K. Lahiri and Chao Wang, editors, *Automated Technology for Verification and Analysis - 16th International Symposium, ATVA 2018, Los Angeles, CA, USA, October 7-10, 2018, Proceedings*, volume 11138 of *Lecture Notes in Computer Science*, pages 543–550. Springer, 2018.
37. William H Kruskal and W Allen Wallis. Use of ranks in one-criterion variance analysis. *Journal of the American statistical Association*, 47(260):583–621, 1952.

38. Maciej Laszczyk and Paweł B. Myszkowski. Survey of quality measures for multi-objective optimization: Construction of complementary set of multi-objective quality measures. *Swarm and Evolutionary Computation*, 48:109–133, 2019.

39. Emanuel Letier. Goal-oriented elaboration of requirements for a safety injection control system. Technical report, Université catholique de Louvain, 2002.

40. Emmanuel Letier. *Reasoning about Agents in Goal-Oriented Requirements Engineering*. PhD thesis, Université catholique de Louvain, 2001.

41. Jianwen Li, Geguang Pu, Lijun Zhang, Yinbo Yao, Moshe Y. Vardi, and Jifeng He. Polsat: A portfolio LTL satisfiability solver. *CoRR*, abs/1311.1602, 2013.

42. Miqing Li and Xin Yao. Quality evaluation of solution sets in multiobjective optimisation: A survey. *ACM Comput. Surv.*, 52(2), mar 2019.

43. Weilin Luo, Hai Wan, Xiaotong Song, Binhao Yang, Hongzhen Zhong, and Yin Chen. How to identify boundary conditions with contrasty metric? In *43rd IEEE/ACM International Conference on Software Engineering, ICSE 2021, Madrid, Spain, 22-30 May 2021*, pages 1473–1484. IEEE, 2021.

44. H. B. Mann and D. R. Whitney. On a Test of Whether one of Two Random Variables is Stochastically Larger than the Other. *The Annals of Mathematical Statistics*, 18(1):50 – 60, 1947.

45. Zohar Manna and Amir Pnueli. *The Temporal Logic of Reactive and Concurrent Systems*. Springer-Verlag New York, Inc., New York, NY, USA, 1992.

46. Zohar Manna and Pierre Wolper. Synthesis of communicating processes from temporal logic specifications. *ACM Trans. Program. Lang. Syst.*, 6(1):68–93, 1984.

47. Shahar Maoz and Jan Oliver Ringert. On well-separation of GR(1) specifications. In *Proceedings of the 24th ACM SIGSOFT International Symposium on Foundations of Software Engineering, FSE 2016, Seattle, WA, USA, November 13-18, 2016*, pages 362–372, 2016.

48. Shahar Maoz, Jan Oliver Ringert, and Rafi Shalom. Symbolic repairs for GR(1) specifications. In *Proceedings of the 41st International Conference on Software Engineering, ICSE 2019, Montreal, QC, Canada, May 25-31, 2019*, pages 1016–1026, 2019.

49. P.K. Murukannaiah, A.K. Kalia, P.R. Telangy, and M.P. Singh. Resolving goal conflicts via argumentation-based analysis of competing hypotheses. In *Proc. 23rd IEEE Int. Requirements Engineering Conf.*, pages 156–165, 2015.

50. Antonio J. Nebro, Juan J. Durillo, and Matthieu Vergne. Redesigning the jmetal multi-objective optimization framework. In *Proceedings of the Companion Publication of the 2015 Annual Conference on Genetic and Evolutionary Computation*, GECCO Companion '15, page 1093–1100, New York, NY, USA, 2015. Association for Computing Machinery.

51. Tuong Huan Nguyen, Bao Quoc Vo, Markus Lumpe, and John Grundy. KBRE: a framework for knowledge-based requirements engineering. *Software Quality Journal*, 22(1):87–119, 2013.

52. A. Pnueli and R. Rosner. On the synthesis of a reactive module. In *Proceedings of the 16th ACM SIGPLAN-SIGACT Symposium on Principles of Programming Languages*, POPL '89, pages 179–190, New York, NY, USA, 1989. ACM.

53. George Spanoudakis and Anthony Finkelstein. Reconciling requirements: a method for managing interference, inconsistency and conflict. *Annals of Software Engineering*, 3(1):433–457, 1997.

54. Ryoji Tanabe and Hisao Ishibuchi. An analysis of quality indicators using approximated optimal distributions in a 3-d objective space. *IEEE Trans. Evol. Comput.*, 24(5):853–867, 2020.

55. Axel van Lamsweerde. *Requirements Engineering - From System Goals to UML Models to Software Specifications.* Wiley, 2009.
56. Axel van Lamsweerde, Robert Darimont, and Emmanuel Letier. Managing conflicts in goal-driven requirements engineering. *IEEE Trans. Software Eng.*, 24(11):908–926, 1998.
57. Axel van Lamsweerde and Emmanuel Letier. Integrating obstacles in goal-driven requirements engineering. In *Proceedings of the 20th International Conference on Software Engineering*, ICSE '98, pages 53–62, Washington, DC, USA, 1998. IEEE Computer Society.
58. Axel van Lamsweerde and Emmanuel Letier. Handling obstacles in goal-oriented requirements engineering. *IEEE Trans. Softw. Eng.*, 26(10):978–1005, October 2000.
59. András Vargha and Harold D. Delaney. A critique and improvement of the "cl" common language effect size statistics of mcgraw and wong. *Journal of Educational and Behavioral Statistics*, 25(2):101–132, 2000.
60. Kaiyuan Wang, Allison Sullivan, and Sarfraz Khurshid. Arepair: A repair framework for alloy. In *2019 IEEE/ACM 41st International Conference on Software Engineering: Companion Proceedings (ICSE-Companion)*, pages 103–106, 2019.
61. Jiahui Wu, Paolo Arcaini, Tao Yue, Shaukat Ali, and Huihui Zhang. On the preferences of quality indicators for multi-objective search algorithms in search-based software engineering. *Empirical Softw. Engg.*, 27(6), nov 2022.
62. Eckart Zitzler, Lothar Thiele, Marco Laumanns, Carlos M. Fonseca, and Viviane Grunert da Fonseca. Performance assessment of multiobjective optimizers. An analysis and review. *IEEE Transactions on Evolutionary Computation*, 7:117–132, 2003.

A Modeling Concept for Formal Verification of OS-Based Compositional Software

Leandro Batista Ribeiro[1]([⊠]), Florian Lorber[2], Ulrik Nyman[2],
Kim Guldstrand Larsen[2], and Marcel Baunach[1]

[1] Graz University of Technology, Graz, Austria
{lbatistaribeiro,baunach}@tugraz.at
[2] Aalborg University, Aalborg, Denmark
{florber,ulrik,kgl}@cs.aau.dk

Abstract. The use of formal methods to prove the correctness of compositional embedded systems is increasingly important. However, the required models and algorithms can induce an enormous complexity. Our approach divides the formal system model into layers and these in turn into modules with defined interfaces, so that reduced formal models can be created for the verification of concrete functional and non-functional requirements. In this work, we use UPPAAL to (1) model an RTOS kernel in a modular way and formally specify its internal requirements, (2) model abstract tasks that trigger all kernel functionalities in all combinations or scenarios, and (3) verify the resulting system with regard to task synchronization, resource management, and timing. The result is a fully verified model of the operating system layer that can henceforth serve as a dependable foundation for verifying compositional applications w.r.t. various aspects, such as timing or liveness.

Keywords: Embedded Systems · Real-Time Operating Systems · Formal Methods · Uppaal · Software Composition.

Availability of Artifacts

All UPPAAL models and queries are available at https://doi.org/10.6084/m9.figshare.21809403. Throughout the paper, model details are omitted for the sake of readability or due to space constraints. In such cases, the symbol ⟨ᗺ⟩ indicates that details can be found in the provided artifacts.

1 Introduction

Embedded systems are everywhere, from simple consumer electronics (wearables, home automation, etc.) to complex safety-critical devices. e.g., in the automotive, aerospace, medical, and nuclear domains. While bugs on non-critical devices are at most inconvenient, errors on safety-critical systems can lead to catastrophic

L. Lambers and S. Uchitel (Eds.): FASE 2023, LNCS 13991, pp. 26–46, 2023.
https://doi.org/10.1007/978-3-031-30826-0_2

consequences, with severe financial or even human losses [19,21]. Therefore, it is of utmost importance to guarantee dependable operation for safety-critical systems at all times. Common practice in industry to validate safety-critical systems is still extensive testing [4]. However, this approach only proves the absence of errors in known cases, but it cannot prove general system correctness.

While general correctness can be proven with formal methods, they still face resistance from practitioners [24], as they are considered resource-intensive and difficult to integrate into existing development processes [14]. However, potential cost reduction or strict regulations might contribute to their adoption. For example, the use of formal methods can facilitate the acceptance of medical devices by regulatory agencies [13], and is already prescribed as part of future development processes in some domains [30,31].

The software running in embedded devices is commonly composed of applications running on top of an Operating System (OS). Throughout the device life cycle, there are usually many more updates on the application than on the OS. Moreover, the application software is tailored for specific needs, while the OS is a foundation that diverse applications can use. Therefore, it is highly desirable to have a formally verified OS, which does not need to be re-verified when applications are modified. The complete formal verification of software involves the creation of models and their verification. Furthermore, all transition steps from models to machine code must be verified.

In this paper, we focus on the modeling stage by using the model-checking tool UPPAAL [23] to model typical features and functionality of modern real-time operating systems and to formally specify requirements to verify the model. Once the OS model is proven correct, it can be used by OS-based software models and reduce the verification effort, since OS requirements do not need to be re-verified.

Our contributions in this paper are (1) an approach that allows the modularization of formal models with defined interfaces, so that these can be assembled as models of the overall system; (2) based on this, guidelines to create a self-contained OS model that facilitates the creation of application models, which can be combined to verify various aspects of the overall software; (3) a concept for creating abstract task models to verify the OS model against the specified requirements.

As a proof of concept and to evaluate our approach in terms of performance and scalability, we formally model typical syscalls that represent the kernel interface towards the higher software levels. We then verify the modeled kernel features under all conceivable situations. For this, we create models that abstract the full software stack, and then verify timing, task synchronization, and resource management with feasible resource expense. The result is a formally verified OS model that can henceforth be used as a foundation for the modeling and verification of complex OS-based applications.

In this paper, **we do not address** the correctness of concrete OS implementations or the completeness of specified requirements, i.e., this paper does not aim to prove the correctness of the code-to-model translation, or that all require-

Table 1. Common task states on RTOSes.

State	Description
Running	Task is currently being executed.
Waiting	Task is waiting for an event, a resource , or a timeout.
Ready	Task could be executed, but higher priority tasks or the OS are running.
Suspended	Task is terminated or not yet started.

ments are specified. Still, the provided models and requirements are sufficient to demonstrate the proposed concept.

The remainder of this paper is organized as follows: in Section 2 we present relevant concepts for our proposed approach. In Section 3 we describe our approach to model the software layers modularly. In Section 4 we introduce abstract tasks and discuss the verification of OS requirements. In Section 5, we analyze and evaluate the proposed concept. In Section 6 we present related work. Finally, Section 7 summarizes this paper and shows potential future work.

2   Background

2.1   Real-Time Operating System (RTOS)

Complex OSes quickly lead to state explosion when model-checking. Therefore, we focus on a small common set of features of modern RTOSes that enables real-time behavior, namely preemptive multitasking, priority-driven scheduling, task synchronization, resource management, and time management. Priority inheritance protocols are not addressed in this paper, because they are not necessary to demonstrate our proposed concept. However, they can be integrated by modifying the related syscalls.

Tasks are the basic execution unit of RTOS-based software. They run in user mode and have fewer privileges than the kernel, which runs in kernel mode. Tasks have individual priorities and execute concurrently, and interact with the OS via *syscalls*. Tasks can be in one of the four states shown in Table 1. Specific implementations might not contain all states. For example, in this paper we model tasks as infinite loops, which never terminate. Thus, they have no suspended state. RTOSes commonly contain an idle task, which runs when no other task is in the ready state.

The Kernel is responsible for providing services to tasks and for interacting with the hardware. It initializes the system on startup and switches between tasks at runtime. Kernel execution can be triggered by tasks or interrupts through a fixed interface only.

Syscalls and Interrupt Service Routines (ISRs) are special functions that are exclusively provided by the kernel and define its interface. While user mode software can only interact with the OS through syscalls, ISRs can only be triggered by the hardware. The modeled syscalls and ISR are covered in Section 3.

Time Management is an important feature of RTOSes. The kernel (1) maintains an internal timeline to which all tasks can relate, and (2) allows tasks to specify timing requirements.

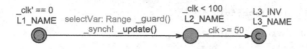

Fig. 1. A general UPPAAL timed automaton template.

Events can be used for inter-task communication and to react on interrupts. They provide a unified synchronization mechanism across hardware and software, in which tasks can signal each other, and interrupts can trigger tasks.

Resources coordinate the access of tasks to exclusively shared components, like hardware (e.g., I/O peripherals) or virtual entities (e.g., data structures). They can be requested from the OS and are assigned depending on availability and the priority of waiting tasks.

The Scheduler is responsible for coordinating the interleaving of tasks according to one or more predefined policies, such as fixed-priority, Rate-Monotonic Scheduling (RMS), and Earliest Deadline First (EDF).

2.2 UPPAAL

For modeling and verification, we choose the model-checking tool UPPAAL [23], in which systems are formalized as a network of timed automata with additional functions and data structures that are executed and changed on edges. Since we model preemptive tasks, we use UPPAAL 4.1, which supports stopwatch automata[10] and enables the elegant modeling of preemption. While a formal definition of timed automata is provided in [7], we still describe the features relevant for this work. Examples in this section refer to Fig. 1.

Timed automata are composed of (labeled) *locations* and *edges*. In UPPAAL, timed automata are specified with the concept of *templates*, which are similar to classes in object-oriented programming. For the verification, the templates are instantiated into *processes* (analogous to objects). All instantiated processes execute concurrently in a UPPAAL model. However, they can still be modeled in a fashion that executes them sequentially, which we adopted in our models.

Locations. *Standard locations* are represented by a circle (L2_NAME). The *initial location* (L1_NAME) is represented by a double circle. *Committed locations* (L3_NAME) have a letter "C" within the circle, and they are used to connect multi-step atomic operations. Different from standard locations, time does not pass while any automata are in a committed location. Locations can have names and invariants. Location names can be used in requirement specifications, and ease the readability of automata. A location invariant (e.g., _clk<100) is an expression that must hold while the automaton is in that corresponding location.

Edges connect locations in a directional manner. Edge transitions are instantaneous, i.e., they introduce zero time overhead. Edges can have a select statement(selectVar : Range), a guard (_guard()), a synchronization (_synch!), and an update operation (_update()). A select statement non-deterministically chooses a value from a range of options and assigns it to a variable. A guard controls whether or not its edge is enabled. An update operation is a sequence of

```
1 typedef int [5 , 10] from5to10_t;
2
3 const from5to10_t VALID = 10;
4 from5to10_t invalid = 4; // verification failure
5
6 typedef struct {from5to10_t var1;} newStruct_t;
```

Listing 1.1. Bounded types and data structures in UPPAAL.

expressions to be executed. Finally, processes can synchronize and communicate via channels.

Communication channels (_synch) allow processes to send output (_synch!) or listen for input (_synch?). UPPAAL supports handshake and broadcast communication. When a synchronizing transition is triggered, both the sender and the listener(s) move to the next location simultaneously, assuming their guards allow for the transition to be taken. The update operation happens first at the sender side, allowing the sender to communicate numeric values via shared variables. In our approach, this is used to pass function/syscall parameters and return values between model modules.

Time is modeled with clock variables (_clk). The timing behavior is controlled with clock constraint expressions in invariants and guards. For example, the invariant _clk < 100 and the guard _clk >= 50 indicate that the transition from L2_NAME to L3_NAME happens when _clk is in the interval [50, 100). In general, all clock variables progress continuously and synchronously. However, the stopwatch feature of UPPAAL 4.1 provides a way to stop one or more clocks in any location, namely by setting the clock derivative to zero (_clk' == 0). When the derivative is not written in the location invariant, its default value (1) is used and the clock progresses normally. For our system models, stopwatches are used to measure and verify the execution time of preemptive tasks. A task's clock progresses only if the task is in the running state, otherwise it is stopped.

Functions, data structures and bounded data types are defined in UPPAAL in a C-like language. Bounded types are very convenient for detecting unwanted values during the verification, which is immediately aborted in case a variable is assigned a value outside its type range. The syntax is exemplified in Listing 1.1.

Formal verification. UPPAAL performs symbolic model-checking to exhaustively verify the specified system requirements. The UPPAAL specification language allows expressing liveness, safety, and reachability properties.

An important operator offered by UPPAAL is "-- >" (leads to): p -- > q means that whenever p holds, q shall also eventually hold. This notation is particularly useful to detect task starvation: if a task in the ready state does not lead to its running state, it is starved. A deadlock in the UPPAAL verification query language is used to detect system states that are not able to progress, i.e., states of the model in which no edges are enabled. Throughout this paper, such situations are referred to as UPPAAL *deadlock*. It must not be confused with *deadlock*, which refers only to task deadlocks due to cyclic waiting on resources.

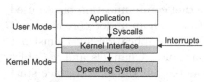

Fig. 2. Model layers as abstraction of the software stack.

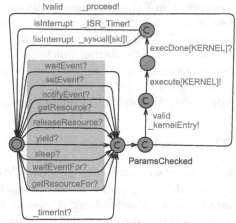

Fig. 4. Kernel interface template. Syscalls highlighted 🔗.

Fig. 3. Modeling of kernel execution time.

3 Model Design

In this section, we propose a general modular approach to model OSes and (abstractions of) application tasks. Our overall goal is to formally prove that a system meets all (non-)functional requirements, which we divide into OS-internal and overall software composition requirements. The characteristics of each category are described in Section 4.

We logically divide the UPPAAL model into three layers, as shown in Fig. 2. The application[3] contains tasks that run in user mode and can use OS services through syscalls. The kernel interface is responsible for switching between user and kernel mode, and to invoke the appropriate OS services or functionality upon syscalls or interrupts.

In this paper, we primarily focus on the operating system layer and how to model it with the goal to simplify the later modeling of the application layer. The result is a strict layering of the overall software model, where modules above the OS layer can be added, removed or updated without re-verifying the OS itself.

To demonstrate the applicability of our approach, we create an OS model 🔗 (composed of sub-models) based on common features of modern RTOSes: preemptive multitasking, priority-driven scheduling, and syscalls for task synchronization, resource management, and time management. The modeling techniques are generic, and any concrete OS can be similarly modeled.

3.1 Naming Convention

For readability, there is a naming convention for communication channels and variables throughout the entire model: Channels starting with an underscore

---

[3] For this paper, user libraries and middleware services are abstracted into the application layer and are not discussed separately.

(e.g., _proceed! in Fig. 4) represent internal kernel communication or are used for interrupt handling. Similarly, variables starting with an underscore represent internal kernel data structures. As for real code, the application layer must not directly access such OS-internal functions or variables. Channels and variables that can be accessed by the application layer as part of the OS interface start with a letter (e.g., sleep? in Fig. 4). Unfortunately, UPPAAL does not support such scope separation and the naming convention is used only as visual aid.

3.2   The Kernel Interface

The kernel interface must offer all possibilities to switch from user to kernel mode, modeled with communication channels. Triggering such channels from automata in the application layer represents a syscall in the real code.

Fig. 4 depicts our modeled kernel interface. A context switch (_kernelEntry!) occurs either upon syscalls, if the parameters are valid (valid 🗗), or upon a timer interrupt (_timerInt). Supporting more interrupts (or syscalls) can be achieved by adding their corresponding automata, and respective edges into the kernel interface.

Kernel Execution and Kernel Overhead. Our modeling approach can precisely reflect the runtime overhead introduced in a preemptive system by the OS kernel itself. This allows a more accurate verification of the behavior of embedded systems compared to approaches that abstract away the OS layer. While different types of OS overhead can be modeled, we initially focus on timing.

Therefore, the kernel interface in Fig. 4 triggers a separate automaton for the kernel timing (execute[KERNEL]!), as shown in Fig. 3. The execution time interval [bcet, wcet] contains the time required to enter the kernel, process the invoked syscall or ISR, execute further kernel functions (e.g., the scheduler), and exit the kernel. This concentrated timing computation is possible because the kernel executes atomically (in contrast to the preemptive tasks).

Next, after taking kernel timing into consideration (execDone[KERNEL]?), we trigger the automata for the functional part of the actual syscall or ISR. The variable sid in _syscall[sid]! is updated along the syscall edges 🗗 and identifies the ID of the invoked syscall. The same approach can be used for modeling multiple interrupts.

3.3   The Operating System

The OS model must contain the internal data structures as well as the UPPAAL templates for the scheduler and for all syscalls. For this paper, we created the OS model based on the *SmartOS* [28] implementation.

Data Structures and Tight Bounds. We must declare all OS variables and arrays with data types of the tightest possible boundaries, according to the system parameters. Listing 1.2 shows a few examples from our OS model.

A beneficial consequence is a strict verification that does not tolerate any value out of range. In such cases, the verification immediately fails and aborts.

```
1  // 1 - System Parameters
2  const int NTASKS, NEVENTS, NRESOURCES, MMGR;
3  // 2 - Type Definitions
4  typedef struct {
5      int[0,NTASKS] qCtr;            // the number of tasks in ready queue
6      ExtTaskId_t readyQ[NTASKS];    // the ready queue containing all tasks
7                                     // in ready state sorted by priority
8  } SCB_t; // Scheduler Control Block
9  typedef int [0 , NTASKS - 1] TaskId_t;
10 // 3 - Declaration of Control Blocks
11 TCB_t _TCB[NTASKS];        // Task CBs
12 RCB_t _Res[NRESOURCES];    // Resource CBs
13 SCB_t _sched;              // Scheduler CB
```

Listing 1.2. Tight bounds on type and array definitions 📖

In other words, if the verification finishes, there is a guarantee that no boundary violation has occurred.

The Scheduler must be the only part of the OS model allowed to manipulate the ready queue (see Listing 1.2) and dispatch Ready tasks for execution.

Before the first task is dispatched, the system must be fully initialized. To ensure this, we must use a single initial committed location, from which an initializing edge transition occurs. Fig. 5 shows this behavior on the scheduler. The function startOS() initializes all the internal data structures of the OS. Next, because the following location is also committed, the scheduler immediately dispatches the highest priority Ready task, and switches to user mode (uppermost edge). The scheduler then must wait for instructions (proceed?, _schedule?, etc.), which are issued by syscalls or ISRs, and must adapt the ready queue accordingly 📖.

Syscalls. Each syscall must have a dedicated UPPAAL template, which models its semantics, i.e., the manipulation of related OS data structures, and interactions with the scheduler. Syscalls can be triggered (1) from the kernel interface (_syscall[sid]!) or (2) from other syscalls. Their general structure is an initial non-committed location, followed by a sequence of transitions through committed locations, making the syscall execution atomic, as shown in Fig. 6.

Task slices. While syscall automata model the behavior of the OS, task slices model different aspects of task execution, as shown in Fig. 7. They can directly communicate with task models (e.g., in Fig. 7(c), start/end a real-time block), or progress upon kernel operations (e.g., in Fig. 7(d), state change upon scheduler actions). The latter is completely transparent to task models. The use of task slices facilitates the modeling of tasks (Section 3.4) and the formal specification and verification of requirements (Section 4).

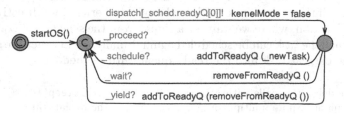

Fig. 5. The priority-driven scheduler 📖.

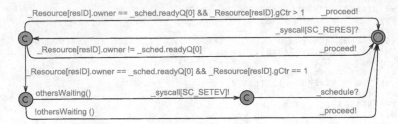

Fig. 6. The `releaseResource` syscall model .

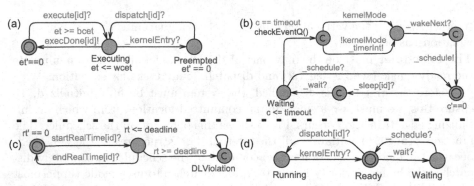

Fig. 7. Modeled task slices: (a) Task Execution, (b) Task Timeout, (c) Task Real-Time, (d) Task States.

Task Execution Time. This task slice represents the user-space execution time of (code blocks within) a task. It abstracts away the code functionality, but allows the modeling of a [bcet, wcet] range. While the specification of the range itself is shown in Section 3.4, the helper template is shown in Fig. 7(a). Its structure is similar to the kernel execution time template in Fig. 3. However, we cannot assure that the execution of code in user mode is atomic, and must therefore consider preemption: If a _kernelEntry! occurs while a task is in the Executing location, it goes to Preempted, where the task execution is paused, i.e., the execution time clock et is paused (et'==0).

Task Timeout. This task slice is responsible for handling timeouts of syscalls (e.g., sleep), and thus it must trigger timer interrupts. Our version is depicted in Fig. 7(b)[4]. The clock c is used to keep track of elapsed time. The location Waiting can be left in two different ways: either the timeout expires (edge with c==timeout), or the task receives the requested resource/event (edge with _schedule?) before the timeout. If c==timeout, a timer interrupt is generated (_timerInt!) if the system is not in kernel mode. Otherwise, we directly proceed to the next location, where we wait for a signal from the scheduler (_wakeNext?) indicating that the task can be scheduled again. Finally, we instruct the scheduler to insert the current task into the ready queue with _schedule!.

---

[4] In our model, all syscalls with a timeout internally use _sleep[id] . Other approaches might require multiple outgoing edges from the initial state.

Task Real-Time. This task slice is used to verify real-time behavior, as it can detect deadline violations. This task slice acts as an observer of the response times during verification, and has no influence on OS data structures or locations.

As shown in Fig. 7(c), there is a local clock rt, which is used to compute the response time of a code sequence. It remains paused unless startRealTime[id]? is triggered by the corresponding task. This happens in the task model (as shown in Section 3.4) and indicates that the task is about to start the execution of a code sequence with timing constraints. rt then progresses until the task triggers endRealTime[id]?. If this happens before the deadline is reached, the process returns to its initial state and is ready for another real-time block. Otherwise, the system goes to the DLViolation error state. The self-loop in the error state is used to avoid a UPPAAL deadlock[5].

Task States. This task slice allows the detection of task starvation. A task starves if it never runs (again). A special case of starvation is task deadlock, which can be detected by additionally analyzing the OS internal data structures and identifying cyclic waiting on resources. Fig. 7(d) shows the modeled task states (as locations) and the actions that trigger state transitions.

The use of task slices is an extensible modeling concept: Extra task slices can be added to enable the verification of other (non-)functional requirements, e.g., energy/memory consumption.

3.4   Simple Application Modeling

The OS model, kernel interface, and task slices are designed with a common goal: Simplify the modeling of application tasks and make the overall system verification more efficient. With our concept, task models just need to use the provided interfaces (channels) and pass the desired parameters.

In summary, a task can be modeled with three simple patterns, as exemplified in Fig. 8:

❶ syscalls: invocation by triggering the corresponding channel, then waiting for dispatch[id]? (from the scheduler),

❷ execution of regular user code between execute[id]! and execDone[id]? (from Task Execution Time task slice),

❸ specification of real-time blocks between startRealTime! and endRealTime!.

As an example, Fig. 8 models the task source code from Listing 1.3 as a UPPAAL task. The variables p1 and p2 are used to pass data between different processes, e.g., for syscall parameters.

For ❶ and ❷, the use of the guard amIRunning(id) is crucial for the correct behavior of the task. It allows a task to proceed only if it is Running. The absence of this guard would allow any task to execute, regardless of priorities or task states.

For ❸, this guard is not necessary when starting or ending real-time blocks, though. If a task reaches the beginning of a real-time block, the response time

---

[5] In our approach, an UPPAAL deadlock indicates a modeling mistake.

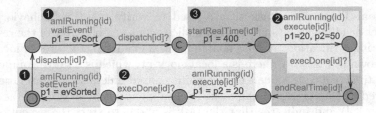

Fig. 8. UPPAAL model of the code from Listing 1.3.

```
 1  OS_TASKENTRY (taskSort){
 2      while (1){
 3  ❶     waitEvent (evSort);
 4  ❸     // START: Real-Time Task block. Deadline=400
 5  ❸❷ quickSort (buffer, BUFSIZE);  // Execution Block: BCET=20, WCET=50
 6  ❸     // END: Real-Time Task block
 7  ❷     for (...) printf ("\n\%u", buffer[i]); // Execution Block: BCET=WCET=20
 8  ❶     setEvent (evSorted);
 9      }
10  }
```

Listing 1.3. Source code of a task.

computation must be immediately started, even if the task is preempted. Similarly, after the execution of a real-time block, the response time computation must be stopped immediately.

4 Requirements and Verification

4.1 Composition Requirements

These requirements refer to task properties that are influenced by other tasks running in the system, such as freedom from starvation and from deadline violations 🔗.

If a composition requirement is violated, the underlying cause is usually a badly composed or implemented task set, which makes it impossible for all tasks to coexist. However, it is also possible that an error in the OS leads to a violation of the composition requirements. In order to exclude this second possibility when verifying the complete system model, we must formally verify the OS model first.

4.2 OS Requirements

The OS requirements refer to OS properties that must always hold (invariants), regardless of the number of tasks in the system or of how these tasks interact with the OS (or with each other through the OS). As described in Section 3.3, the OS model is composed of data structures and multiple UPPAAL templates, which must be consistent at all time (general requirement). For example, if a task is in the Waiting location in the task timeout task slice, it must also be in the Waiting location in the task states task slice. In UPPAAL, we can verify this requirement with the query:

```
A[] forall (Tasks) TaskTimeout.Waiting imply TaskStates.Waiting 🔗
```

This example shows an important point when extending our concept: Whenever new task slices are added to verify other (non-)functional requirements of the application, additional OS requirements must be specified to verify the consistency of the new task slice with pre-existing parts of the OS model.

4.3   Verifying the Requirements

For a given software (i.e., OS and application), we can prove correctness w.r.t. the OS and composition requirements by verifying all associated queries. However, we cannot yet claim that the OS model is correct in general (i.e., independent from the task composition), because we do not know if all possible OS operations were considered in all possible scenarios during the verification. Therefore, a complete re-verification of both layers is required in case the application changes.

To avoid the repeated and resource-expensive re-verification of the OS requirements for each task set, we must prove that the OS model is correct in general. We can then limit the re-verification to the application layer. To achieve this goal, we need to make sure that all possible OS operations are verified in all possible scenarios and execution orders. One possible strategy is to create different task sets to reach different scenarios, similar to test case generation. However, this strategy requires the prior identification of relevant scenarios, and the creation of the corresponding task sets. Additionally, it is hard to guarantee that all scenarios were indeed identified. Therefore, we introduce a new concept that inherently covers all scenarios: abstract tasks. They unite all possible behaviors of concrete tasks, i.e., they can trigger any action at any time. A task set with N abstract tasks thus represents the behavior of all possible task sets with N (concrete) tasks. Thus, by definition, all possible scenarios will be reached (UPPAAL exhaustive approach).

Abstract Tasks. Real tasks, as exemplified in Listing 1.3, are strictly sequential. Thus, a (concrete) task model is a predefined sequence of steps, as discussed in Section 3.4, and shown in Fig. 8. Their key characteristic is that only one outgoing edge is enabled in any location at any point in time.

The abstract task is depicted in Fig. 9. Unlike a concrete task, it has multiple outgoing edges enabled, which open all possible options to progress: ❶ syscalls with valid parameters and ❷ user code execution (execute[id]!). Thus, the behavior of any concrete task can also be achieved with the abstract task.

While different actions are performed by taking different edges, the parameters are non-deterministicaly chosen in the select statements for each syscall. The UPPAAL state space exploration mechanisms guarantee that all values of the select statements are considered for each edge.

Select statements are not necessary for the timing parameters EX_TIME and SL_TIME. Fixed values have less impact on the state space, and are enough to fire all edges from the task execution and task timeout (Fig. 7(a) and Fig. 7(b), respectively). We define the timing parameters ⑥ in a way that all edges are eventually fired and the state space remains small enough for a feasible verification.

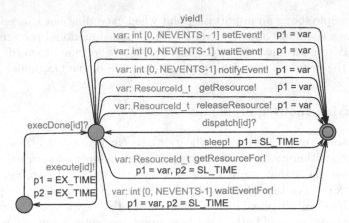

Fig. 9. The abstract task model.

Non-Goals of Verification with Abstract Tasks. With abstract tasks, it is meaningless to verify if **composition requirements** are satisfied at task level. Abstract tasks – by definition – lead to states where composition requirements are violated[6]. The goal of abstract tasks is to ensure that the OS itself works correctly even if the task composition is flawed, e.g., if it leads to starvation or livelocks. This is achieved by verifying the OS requirements in all conceivable scenarios (in the end of Section 4.4, we show how to verify that flawed composition scenarios are also reached). Additionally, we do not explore **invalid values** of variables./parameters. Out-of-bound values lead to verification failure, and when invalid syscall parameters are detected in the kernel interface, no functionality is triggered in the OS. Thus, checking for invalid values would increase the state space without adding new behaviors.

4.4   OS Model Verification

A single set of abstract tasks provides a reliable way of verifying scenarios that could otherwise only be reached with numerous concrete task sets. To fully verify the OS model, we must compose the abstract task set so that it triggers all OS operations in all possible scenarios (covering all corner cases).

Within our model, we can control four system parameters that affect the OS verification: NTASKS, NEVENTS, NRESOURCES, and MMGR[7], cf. Listing 1.2. We use a **short notation** to represent the system configuration. For example, 5-3-4-2 represents a configuration with NTASKS = 5 (idle task + 4 others), NEVENTS = 3, NRESOURCES = 4, and MMGR = 2. The goal is to find the minimal configuration that reaches all possible scenarios, and thus allows the complete verification of the OS model with minimal verification effort.

---

[6] Unless the OS offers guarantees by design, e.g., if it implements the Highest Locker Protocol (HLP), task deadlock scenarios must not be reachable.

[7] Maximum multiple getResource, i.e., the upper limit of the resource counter.

Model Coverage. In order to cover the whole model, the verification must traverse all edges, and entirely cover the C-like code of update operations.

Edge Coverage. If there is at least one edge in the model that is not traversed during verification, the model is surely not fully verified; unreachable edges could also indicate design flaws in the model. Therefore, the first step of the verification addresses the edge coverage. We add boolean markers in strategic edges, which are set to true when the corresponding edge is taken. We then verify if all markers are ever true:

`E<> forall (i : int [0, NEDGES-1]) edge[i]==true`

Edge Scenarios. A single edge can be traversed in multiple scenarios, due to composite guards (with the pattern **(A or B or C ...)**) or update operations (parameter passing or functions). For the composite guards, we must verify that each of its components is reachable with queries with the following pattern [图]:

`E<> Location and A`

For the update operations, we ensure that an edge is traversed with all possible parameter values via select statements, which cover all valid parameter values. The functions demand a more careful analysis. It is necessary to identify all corner cases, and verify their reachability. For example, to verify the corner cases of a list insertion, we can use the following queries:

`E<> InsertLocation and firstPosInsertion`
`E<> InsertLocation and lastPosInsertion`
`E<> InsertLocation and intermediatePosInsertion`

After an iterative process of increasing the configuration and verifying the aforementioned properties, we found the smallest configuration that entirely covers our OS model: 4-1-1-2.

OS and Composition Requirements. The goal of the verification of the OS model is to guarantee that all OS requirements are met. In conjunction with the full model coverage verification, we prove that they are met regardless of the operations performed by individual tasks on top of the OS.

However, to ensure that the OS model is correct, we still must prove that the OS requirements are also met in states where composition requirements are violated. For that, we must identify all situations that violate composition requirements, and verify their reachability. For example, the reachability of a deadlock scenario can be verified with the query [图]:

`E<> Res1.owner == Task1 and Res2.owner == Task2 and`
`Task1.waits == Res2 and Task2.waits == Res1`

The deadlock scenario reveals that 4-1-1-2 is not sufficient to reach all composition scenarios, since at least two resources are required to cause it. For the modeled OS features, all composition scenarios are reachable with 4-1-2-2.

Algorithm 1 Finding the minimal configuration.

1: **procedure** FINDMINIMALCONFIG (FEATURES)
2:     $minConf \leftarrow$ 0-0-...-0
3:     foreach (f: Features)
4:         $conf \leftarrow$ getMinimalFeatureConfig(f)
5:         $minConf \leftarrow$ getMaxParams($minConf, conf$)
6:     return $minConf$

---

5   Analysis and Evaluation

So far, we verified 4-1-2-2^8, and confirmed that it satisfies all specified OS requirements and the necessary aspects discussed in Section 4: (1) traverse all model edges at least once; (2) invoke syscalls with all possible parameters; (3) reach all corner cases of edge update operations; (4) satisfy all of the components of composite guards; (5) reach valid and invalid composition scenarios; In this section, we analyze how the minimal configuration is obtained in the general case, and the scalability of the approach. We then reason why bigger configurations are not necessary for the verification.

5.1   Compositional Approach to Deriving the Minimal Configuration

The verification of the OS model is essentially the verification of its set of supported features. Thus, the composition of all minimal configurations needed to verify individual features is used to verify properties of the entire OS.

We assume that feature developers/experts provide the minimal configuration based on the corner cases and composition scenarios of their feature. We then build the minimal configuration by using the highest value of each parameter of each analyzed feature, as described in Algorithm 1. For example, the dominating features^9 in our OS model are resource management (3-0-2-2) and event passing (4-1-0-0), which lead to the resulting configuration 4-1-2-2.

5.2   Scalability: Resource Consumption for Verification

First, we show a concrete analysis of our approach, namely the number of explored states, CPU Time, and memory consumption during verification. Additionally, we show how each system parameter influences these values.

The verification was performed with UPPAAL 4.1.26 x64, running on a machine with Ubuntu 18.04.5 LTS, a 16 core Intel(R) Xeon(R) CPU E5-2690 v3 @ 2.60GHz, 64GB DDR4 memory @ 1600MHz, and 8GB swap.

State Space. In order to explore all states with a low processing overhead, we verify the query "A[] **true**". Fig. 10 and Table 2 show the number of explored states with different system configurations. The leftmost point (Delta = 0) in

---

^{8} see Section 4.4 for configuration notation.
^{9} No other feature has higher parameter values.

Table 2. Verification time (minutes) and memory consumption (MB).

		A[]true		OS Requirements	
Configuration	State space	Time	Memory	Time	Memory
C-(51-50-2-2)	574,266	1.5	640	76.0	738
4-1-2-2	5,369,534	0.6	470	30.7	470
4-1-2-4	14,963,367	2.5	1,787	124.3	1,788
5-1-2-2	85,077,164	13.2	6,655	644.2	6,656
4-3-2-2	116,606,955	14.7	10,189	689.0	10,189
4-1-4-2	570,284,574	75.8	47,800	3,774.6	47,800

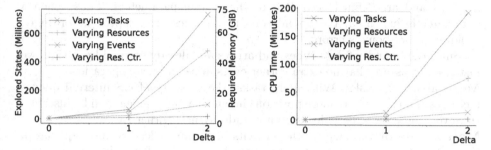

Fig. 10. Verification overhead for different configurations.

Fig. 10 represents our proposed minimal system configuration 4-1-2-2. We then vary one of the parameters, while all others are constant. For example, the "Varying Events" line on Delta = 1 shows the number of states for 4-2-2-2; and the "Varying Res. Ctr." line on Delta = 2 the number of states for 4-1-2-4.

The curves from Fig. 10 show that NTASKS has the biggest impact in the state space, and that MMGR has the lowest. While MMGR affects only the upper bound of the resource counters, NTASKS affects all kernel data structures, since each task can call any of the syscalls, which drive the modifications on the kernel data structures. In fact, the verification of 6-1-2-2 did not finish. It required more than 72GB of RAM, and the process was killed by Linux. Until short before, we could already count 950 million explored states.

It is important to highlight that the scalability is much better when simple concrete tasks are modeled. To demonstrate it, we modeled a concrete task set with sequential execution (without preemption) and used the configuration C-(51-50-2-2) ⬚, where C- indicates it is a configuration for a concrete task set. Table 2 shows that verifying "A[]**true**" explored only 574,266 states. Additionally, ongoing research on reducing the state-space, like for instance with partial-order reduction [22], will enable the verification of ever larger systems.

Memory consumption and CPU time. For the tested configurations, memory and CPU time follow a pattern similar to the number of explored states (Fig. 10). However, the number of states is not the only factor influencing resource consumption. The verification of C-(51-50-2-2) took longer and used more memory than the verification of 4-1-4-2, even though the state space is almost 10 times smaller (see Table 2). The size of individual states also plays an important role, because they are stored/read into/from memory during the verification. In our OS model, NTASKS, NEVENTS, and NRESOURCES contribute to the state size, since bigger values increase the size/amount of data structures.

5.3 Sufficiency of 4-1-2-2 Configuration for our OS Model

We cannot run the verification of the OS model with arbitrarily big system configurations, due to the state space explosion problem. Therefore, we reason that, despite creating a larger state space, bigger configurations do not create any new scenarios in the OS layer.

As discussed in Section 3.3, the bounds of all data types are as tight as possible, and are defined according to the system parameters. Thus, when a parameter is increased, the bounds of the variables are adapted accordingly, avoiding out-of-bounds errors.

Since the bounds of data types and arrays are already covered by design, we just need to assure that no extra corner cases arise on queue operations.

More abstract tasks. With more tasks, the capacity of OS internal queues increases. Thus, there are more positions in which a new element can be inserted. However, these new possibilities do not add any new corner cases.

More events or resources. More events or resources lead to more queues in the system, but do not change the capacity of the queues. Thus, these parameters do not affect queue operations w.r.t. verification.

Higher limit for counting resources. When a task T (that already owns a resource R) requests R once again, R's internal counter is incremented. Still, a higher limit does not create new corner cases w.r.t. verification.

Composition Scenarios. Bigger system configurations do not create new scenarios, but only new settings for the existing ones, e.g., starvation of different tasks, or deadlocks involving different sets of tasks and resources.

6 Related Work

Similar to our approach, with the goal to verify compositional requirements, Ironclad [18] covers the full software stack. It uses Dafny [25] and Boogie [6] to verify assembly code, but it addresses only security requirements. Borda *et al.* [8] propose a language to model self-adaptive cyber-physical systems modularly and a technique to support compositional verification. However, timing requirements are not addressed. Giese *et al.*[12] address compositional verification of real-time systems modeled in UML. Components are verified in isolation, and the correctness of the system is derived by ensuring that the composition is syntactically correct. However, this is only possible if the components do not share resources. UPPAAL has been used for schedulability analysis of compositional avionic software [17], and for conformance testing with requirements specified as pre- and post-condition functions [29].

Regarding modeling and verification of OSes, on a more abstract level, Alkhammash *et al.*[5] propose guidelines for modeling FreeRTOS[1] using Event-B[3]. Cheng *et al.* formally specify the behavior of FreeRTOS tasks [11] and verify it using the Z/Eves theorem prover[26], but, unlike our approach, they do not address timing, resource sharing, or interrupts.

On a less abstract level, closer to the real implementation, seL4 [20] proves the functional correctness of the C code of the kernel. Furthermore, it guarantees that the binary code correctly reflects the semantics of the C code. Hyperkernel [27] formally verifies the functional correctness of syscalls, exceptions and interrupts. The verification is performed at the LLVM intermediate representation level [32] using the Z3 SMT solver[9]. CertikOS[16] is the first work that formally verifies a concurrent OS kernel. They use the Coq proof assistant[2], a C-like programming language, and a verified compiler [15]. These approaches focus exclusively on the functional correctness of the OS kernel.

We have not found a work that can verify timing, resource sharing, task synchronization, and interrupts in a compositional context. That is what our work enables, after proving the correctness of the OS model.

7 Conclusions and Future Work

In this paper, we presented a UPPAAL modeling approach for verifying compositional software, exemplified with an OS model containing a common set of features present in modern RTOSes. Since the proposed techniques and patterns are general, they can be used to model any concrete OS. We showed how to model the OS aiming to simplify the modeling of application tasks (Section 3). We also introduced separate *OS requirements* and *composition requirements*, and showed how they can be formally specified (Section 4) to decouple the verification of the OS and the application layer. We then proposed the concept of *abstract tasks* (Section 4.3) and reasoned that the OS model can be fully verified with a minimal set of such tasks, which interact through OS primitives (e.g., events and shared resources) and thus trigger all OS functions in all possible scenarios (Section 4.4). Finally, we evaluated the resource consumption of the verification process, reasoned about the sufficiency of the used minimal configuration, and analyzed the benefits of the proposed concept (Section 5).

With the OS model proven correct, there is no need to re-verify it when the upper layers are modified, which saves time and resources on the verification of concrete task sets. We consider this as particularly beneficial for developing and maintaining highly dependable systems, where, e.g., the task composition and functionality may change during updates. Another benefit of our approach is the potential use on test case generation for the application software.

This work opens a variety of directions for future work. We currently work on task slices to verify further (non-)functional requirements. Besides, we continuously improve the model design for a better trade-off between abstraction level and verification overhead, including the avoidance of potential state space explosions. Tools to convert between source code and UPPAAL templates shall reduce the modeling gap, i.e., the discrepancy between the formal model and the actual implementation. While our *models* allow the verification of applications on top of an OS, a limitation is that model correctness does not yet mean implementation correctness. For that, the full path from models to machine code must be verified.

References

1. FreeRTOS. https://freertos.org/. [Online; accessed 20-January-2023].
2. The Coq proof assistant. https://coq.inria.fr/. [Online; accessed 20-January-2023].
3. Jean-Raymond Abrial. *Modeling in Event-B: system and software engineering.* Cambridge University Press, 2010.
4. Benny Akesson, Mitra Nasri, Geoffrey Nelissen, Sebastian Altmeyer, and Robert I Davis. A comprehensive survey of industry practice in real-time systems. *Real-Time Systems*, 2021.
5. Eman H Alkhammash et al. Modeling guidelines of FreeRTOS in Event-B. In *Shaping the Future of ICT*. CRC Press, 2017.
6. Mike Barnett, Bor-Yuh Evan Chang, Robert DeLine, Bart Jacobs, and K. Rustan M. Leino. Boogie: A Modular Reusable Verifier for Object-Oriented Programs. In *Formal Methods for Components and Objects*, Berlin, Heidelberg, 2006. Springer Berlin Heidelberg.
7. Gerd Behrmann, Alexandre David, and Kim G Larsen. A tutorial on Uppaal. *Formal methods for the design of real-time systems*, 2004.
8. Aimee Borda, Liliana Pasquale, Vasileios Koutavas, and Bashar Nuseibeh. Compositional Verification of Self-Adaptive Cyber-Physical Systems. In *2018 IEEE/ACM 13th Int'l Symposium on Software Engineering for Adaptive and Self-Managing Systems (SEAMS)*, 2018.
9. Robert Brummayer and Armin Biere. Boolector: An Efficient SMT Solver for Bit-Vectors and Arrays. In *Tools and Algorithms for the Construction and Analysis of Systems*, Berlin, Heidelberg, 2009.
10. Franck Cassez and Kim Larsen. The impressive power of stopwatches. In *International Conference on Concurrency Theory*. Springer, 2000.
11. Shu Cheng, Jim Woodcock, and Deepak D'Souza. Using formal reasoning on a model of tasks for FreeRTOS. *Formal Aspects of Computing*, 27(1), 2015.
12. Holger Giese et al. Towards the Compositional Verification of Real-Time UML Designs. In *9th European Software Engineering Conference Held Jointly with 11th ACM SIGSOFT Int'l Symposium on Foundations of Software Engineering*, New York, NY, USA, 2003.
13. Mario Gleirscher, Simon Foster, and Jim Woodcock. New Opportunities for Integrated Formal Methods. *ACM Comput. Surv.*, 52(6), oct 2019.
14. Tomás Grimm, Djones Lettnin, and Michael Hübner. A Survey on Formal Verification Techniques for Safety-Critical Systems-on-Chip. *Electronics*, 7(6), 2018.
15. Ronghui Gu et al. Deep Specifications and Certified Abstraction Layers. *ACM SIGPLAN Notices*, 50(1), jan 2015.
16. Ronghui Gu et al. CertiKOS: An Extensible Architecture for Building Certified Concurrent OS Kernels. In *12th USENIX Symposium on Operating Systems Design and Implementation (OSDI 16)*, Savannah, GA, November 2016. USENIX Association.
17. Pujie Han, Zhengjun Zhai, Brian Nielsen, and Ulrik Nyman. A Compositional Approach for Schedulability Analysis of Distributed Avionics Systems. In *1st Int'l Workshop on Methods and Tools for Rigorous System Design (MeTRiD@ETAPS)*, Greece, EPTCS, 2018.
18. Chris Hawblitzel et al. Ironclad Apps: End-to-End Security via Automated Full-System Verification. In *11th USENIX Symposium on Operating Systems Design and Implementation (OSDI 14)*, Broomfield, CO, October 2014. USENIX Association.

19. Joseph Herkert, Jason Borenstein, and Keith Miller. The Boeing 737 MAX: Lessons for engineering ethics. *Science and engineering ethics*, 26(6), 2020.
20. Gerwin Klein et al. SeL4: Formal Verification of an OS Kernel. In *ACM SIGOPS 22nd Symposium on Operating Systems Principles*, SOSP '09, New York, NY, USA, 2009.
21. John C. Knight. Safety Critical Systems: Challenges and Directions. In *24th Int'l Conference on Software Engineering*, ICSE '02, New York, NY, USA, 2002.
22. Kim G. Larsen, Marius Mikučionis, Marco Muñiz, and Jiří Srba. Urgent partial order reduction for extended timed automata. In Dang Van Hung and Oleg Sokolsky, editors, *Automated Technology for Verification and Analysis*, pages 179–195, Cham, 2020. Springer International Publishing.
23. Kim G Larsen, Paul Pettersson, and Wang Yi. UPPAAL in a nutshell. *Int'l journal on software tools for technology transfer*, 1997.
24. Thierry Lecomte et al. Applying a Formal Method in Industry: A 25-Year Trajectory. In *Formal Methods: Foundations and Applications*, Cham, 2017. Springer International Publishing.
25. K. Rustan M. Leino. Dafny: An Automatic Program Verifier for Functional Correctness. In *Logic for Programming, Artificial Intelligence, and Reasoning*, Berlin, Heidelberg, 2010. Springer Berlin Heidelberg.
26. Irwin Meisels and Mark Saaltink. The Z/EVES reference manual (for version 1.5). *Reference manual, ORA Canada*, 1997.
27. Luke Nelson et al. Hyperkernel: Push-Button Verification of an OS Kernel. In *26th Symposium on Operating Systems Principles*, SOSP '17, New York, NY, USA, 2017. Association for Computing Machinery.
28. Tobias Scheipel, Leandro Batista Ribeiro, Tim Sagaster, and Marcel Baunach. SmartOS: An OS Architecture for Sustainable Embedded Systems. In *Tagungsband des FG-BS Frühjahrstreffens 2022*, Bonn, 2022. Gesellschaft für Informatik e.V.
29. Abhishek Singh, Meenakshi D'Souza, and Arshad Ebrahim. *Conformance Testing of ARINC 653 Compliance for a Safety Critical RTOS Using UPPAAL Model Checker*. New York, NY, USA, 2021.
30. UNECE. UN Regulation No. 156 – Uniform provisions concerning the approval of vehicles with regards to software update and software updates management system. [online] https://unece.org/sites/default/files/2021-03/R156e.pdf.
31. Virginie WIELS et al. Formal Verification of Critical Aerospace Software. *Aerospace Lab*, May 2012.
32. Jianzhou Zhao et al. Formalizing the LLVM Intermediate Representation for Verified Program Transformations. In *39th Annual ACM SIGPLAN-SIGACT Symposium on Principles of Programming Languages*, POPL '12, New York, NY, USA, 2012. Association for Computing Machinery.

Compositional Automata Learning of Synchronous Systems

Thomas Neele[1]($\boxtimes$) and Matteo Sammartino[2,3]

[1] Eindhoven University of Technology, Eindhoven, The Netherlands
t.s.neele@tue.nl
[2] Royal Holloway University of London, Egham, UK
University College London, London, UK
matteo.sammartino@rhul.ac.uk

Abstract. Automata learning is a technique to infer an automaton model of a black-box system via queries to the system. In recent years it has found widespread use both in industry and academia, as it enables formal verification when no model is available or it is too complex to create one manually. In this paper we consider the problem of learning the individual components of a black-box synchronous system, assuming we can only query the whole system. We introduce a *compositional* learning approach in which several learners cooperate, each aiming to learn one of the components. Our experiments show that, in many cases, our approach requires significantly fewer queries than a widely-used non-compositional algorithm such as L*.

1 Introduction

Automata learning is a technique for inferring an automaton from a black-box system by interacting with it and observing its responses. It can be seen as a game in which a *learner* poses queries to a *teacher* – an abstraction of the target system – with the intent of inferring a model of the system. The learner can ask two types of queries: a *membership* query, asking if a given sequence of actions is allowed in the system; and an *equivalence* query, asking if a given model is correct. The teacher must provide a counter-example in case the model is incorrect. In practice, membership queries are implemented as tests on the system, and equivalence queries as conformance test suites.

The original algorithm L* proposed by Dana Angluin in 1987 [3] allowed learning DFAs; since then it has been extended to a variety of richer automata models, including symbolic [5] and register [7,26] automata, automata for ω-regular languages [4], and automata with fork-join parallelism [18], to mention recent work. Automata learning enables formal verification when no formal model is available and also reverse engineering of various systems. Automata learning has found wide application in both academia and industry. Examples are: the verification of neural networks [31], finding bugs in specific implementations of security [29,12] and network protocols [11], or refactoring legacy software [30].

L. Lambers and S. Uchitel (Eds.): FASE 2023, LNCS 13991, pp. 47–66, 2023.
https://doi.org/10.1007/978-3-031-30826-0_3

In this paper we consider the case when the system to be learned consists of several concurrent components that interact in a synchronous way; the components themselves are not accessible, but their number and respective input alphabets are known. It is well-known that the composite state-space can grow exponentially with the number of components. If we use L* to learn such a system as a whole, it will take a number of queries that is proportional to the whole state-space – many more than if we were able to apply L* to the individual components. Since in practice queries are implemented as tests performed on the system (in the case of equivalence queries, exponentially many tests are required), learning the whole system may be impractical if tests take a non-negligible amount of time, e.g., if each test needs to be repeated to ensure accuracy of results or when each test requires physical interaction with a system.

In this work we introduce a *compositional* approach that is capable of learning models for the individual components, by interacting with an ordinary teacher for the *whole* system. This is achieved by translating queries on a single component to queries on the whole system and interpreting their results on the level of a single component. The fundamental challenge is that components are *not* independent: they interact synchronously, meaning that sequences of actions in the composite system are realised by the individual components performing their actions in a certain relative order. The implications are that: (i) the answer to some membership queries for a specific component may be *unknown* if the correct sequence of interactions with other components has not yet been discovered; and (ii) counter-examples for the global system cannot univocally be decomposed into counter-examples for individual components, therefore some of them may result in *spurious* counter-examples that need to be corrected later.

To tackle these issues, we make the following contributions:

- A *compositional learning framework*, orchestrating several instances of (an extension of) L* with the purpose to learn models for the individual components from an ordinary monolithic teacher. An adapter transforms queries on single components into queries to the monolithic teacher.
- An extension of L* that can deal with unknown membership query results and spurious counter-examples; when plugged into the aforementioned framework, we obtain a learning algorithm for our setting.
- An implementation of our approach as a tool COAL based on the state-of-the-art automata learning library LearnLib [22], accompanied by a comprehensive set of experiments: for some of the larger systems, our approach requires up to six orders of magnitude fewer membership queries and up to ten times fewer equivalence queries than L* (applied to the monolithic system).

The rest of this paper is structured as follows. We introduce preliminary concepts and notation in Section 2. Our learning framework is presented in Section 3. Section 4 discusses the details of our implementation and the results of our experiments. Related work is highlighted in Section 5 and Section 6 concludes.

2 Preliminaries

Notation and terminology. We use Σ to denote a *finite alphabet* of action symbols, and Σ^* to denote the set of finite sequences of symbols in Σ, which we call *traces*; we use ϵ to denote the empty trace. Given two traces $s_1, s_2 \in \Sigma^*$, we denote their concatenation by $s_1 \cdot s_2$; for two sets $S_1, S_2 \subseteq \Sigma^*$, $S_1 \cdot S_2$ denotes element-wise concatenation. Given $s \in \Sigma^*$, we denote by $Pref(s)$ the set of prefixes of s, and by $Suff(s)$ the set of its suffixes; the notation lifts to sets $S \subseteq \Sigma^*$ as expected. We say that $S \subseteq \Sigma^*$ is *prefix-closed* (resp. *suffix-closed*) whenever $S = Pref(S)$ (resp. $S = Suff(S)$). The *projection* $\sigma_{\restriction \Sigma'}$ of σ on an alphabet $\Sigma' \subseteq \Sigma$ is the sequence of symbols in σ that are also contained in Σ'. Finally, given a set S, we write $|S|$ for its cardinality.

In this work we represent the state-based behaviour of a system as a *labelled transition system*.

Definition 1 (Labelled Transition System). *A* labelled transition system *(LTS) is a four-tuple $L = (S, \to, \hat{s}, \Sigma)$, where*

- *S is a set of states, which we refer to as the* state space;
- *$\to \subseteq S \times \Sigma \times S$ is a transition relation, which we write in infix notation as $s \xrightarrow{a} t$, for $(s, a, t) \in \to$.*
- *$\hat{s} \in S$ is an initial state; and*
- *Σ is a finite set of actions, called the* alphabet.

We say that L is deterministic *whenever for each $s \in S$, $a \in \Sigma$ there is at most one transition from s labelled by a.*

Some actions in Σ may not be allowed from a given state. We say that an action a is *enabled* in s, written $s \xrightarrow{a}$, if there is t such that $s \xrightarrow{a} t$. This notation is also extended to traces $\sigma \in \Sigma^*$, yielding $s \xrightarrow{\sigma} t$ and $s \xrightarrow{\sigma}$. The language of L is the set of traces enabled from the starting state, formally:

$$\mathcal{L}(L) = \{\sigma \in \Sigma^* \mid \hat{s} \xrightarrow{\sigma}\} \ .$$

From here on, we only consider deterministic LTSs. Note that this does not reduce the expressivity, in terms of the languages that can be encoded.

Remark 1. Languages of LTSs are always prefix-closed, because every prefix of an enabled trace is necessarily enabled. Prefix-closed languages are accepted by a special class of deterministic finite automata (DFA), where all states are final except for a sink state, from which all transitions are self-loops. Our implementation (see Section 4) uses these models as underlying representation of LTSs.

We now introduce a notion of parallel composition of LTSs, which must synchronise on shared actions.

Definition 2. *Given n LTSs where $L_i = (S_i, \to_i, \hat{s}_i, \Sigma_i)$ for $1 \leq i \leq n$, their parallel composition, notation $\|_{i=1}^{n} L_i$, is an LTS over the alphabet $\bigcup_{i=1}^{n} \Sigma_i$, defined as follows:*

- *the state space is $S_1 \times S_2 \times \cdots \times S_n$;*
- *the transition relation is given by the following rule*

$$\frac{s_i \xrightarrow{a}_i t_i \quad \text{for all } i \text{ such that } a \in \Sigma_i \qquad s_j = t_j \quad \text{for all } j \text{ such that } a \notin \Sigma_j}{(s_1, \ldots, s_n) \xrightarrow{a} (t_1, \ldots, t_n)}$$

- *the initial state is $(\hat{s}_1, \ldots, \hat{s}_n)$.*

Intuitively, a certain action a can be performed from $(s_1, \ldots, s_n)$ only if it can be performed by all component LTSs that have a in their alphabet; all other LTSs must stay idle. We say that an action a is *local* if there is exactly one i such that $a \in \Sigma_i$, otherwise it is called *synchronising*. The parallel composition of LTSs thus forces individual LTSs to cooperate on synchronising actions; local actions can be performed independently. We typically refer to the LTSs that make up a composite LTS as *components*. Synchronisation of components corresponds to communication between components in real-world settings.

Example 1. Consider the left two LTSs below with the respective alphabets $\{a, c\}$ and $\{b, c\}$. Their parallel composition is depicted on the right.

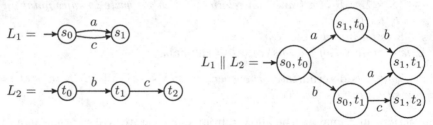

Here a and b are local actions, whereas c is synchronising. Note that, despite L_1 being able to perform c from its initial state s_0, there is no c transition from (s_0, t_0), because c is not initially enabled in L_2. First L_2 will have to perform b to reach t_1, where c is enabled, which will allow $L_1 \parallel L_2$ to perform c. $\qquad \square$

We sometimes also apply parallel composition to sets of traces: $\parallel_i S_i$ is equivalent to $\parallel T_i$, where each T_i is a tree-shaped LTS that accepts exactly S_i, *i.e.*, $\mathcal{L}(T_i) = S_i$. In such cases, we will explicitly mention the alphabet each T_i is assigned. This notation furthermore applies to single traces: $\parallel_i \sigma_i = \parallel_i \{\sigma_i\}$.

2.1 L* algorithm

We now recall the basic L* algorithm. Although the algorithm targets DFAs, we will present it in terms of deterministic LTSs, which we use in this paper (these are a sub-class of DFAs, see Remark 1). The algorithm can be seen as a game in which a *learner* poses queries to a *teacher* about a target language $\mathcal{L}$ that only the teacher knows. The goal of the learner is to learn a *minimal* deterministic LTS with language $\mathcal{L}$. In practical scenarios, the teacher is an abstraction of the target system we wish to learn a model of. The learner can ask two types of queries:

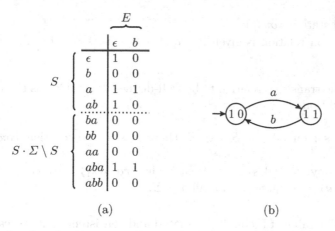

		ϵ	b
	ϵ	1	0
S	b	0	0
	a	1	1
	ab	1	0
	ba	0	0
	bb	0	0
$S \cdot \Sigma \setminus S$	aa	0	0
	aba	1	1
	abb	0	0

(a)   (b)

Fig. 1: A closed and consistent observation table and the LTS that can be constructed from it.

- **Membership query:** is a trace s in the target language $\mathcal{L}$? The teacher will return a Yes/No answer.
- **Equivalence query:** does a given *hypothesis* LTS H accept $\mathcal{L}$? The teacher will return Yes/No; a No answer comes with a *counter-example*, i.e., a trace in $\mathcal{L}(H) \,\Delta\, \mathcal{L}$, where Δ denotes the symmetric difference.

The learner organises the information received in response to queries in an *observation table*, which is a triple (S, E, T), consisting of a finite, prefix-closed set $S \subseteq \Sigma^*$, a finite, suffix-closed set $E \subseteq \Sigma^*$, and a function $T : (S \cup S \cdot \Sigma) \cdot E \to \{0, 1\}$. The function T can be seen as a table in which rows are labelled by traces in $S \cup S \cdot \Sigma$, columns by traces in E, and cells $T(s \cdot e)$ contain 1 if $s \cdot e \in \mathcal{L}$ and 0 otherwise.

Example 2. Consider the prefix-closed language $\mathcal{L}$ over the alphabet $\Sigma = \{a, b\}$ consisting of traces where a and b alternate, starting with a; for instance $aba \in \mathcal{L}$ but $abb \notin \mathcal{L}$. An observation table generated by a run of L* targeting this language is shown in Figure 1a. ⊔⊓

Let $row_T : S \cup S \cdot \Sigma \to (E \to \{0, 1\})$ denote the function $row_T(s)(e) = T(s \cdot e)$ mapping each row of T to its content (we omit the subscript T when clear from the context). The crucial observation is that T approximates the Nerode congruence [28] for $\mathcal{L}$ as follows: s_1 and s_2 are in the same congruence class only if $row(s_1) = row(s_2)$, for $s_1, s_2 \in S$. Based on this fact, the learner can construct a hypothesis LTS from the table, in the same way the minimal DFA accepting a given language is built via its Nerode congruence:[3]

- the set of states is $\{row(s) \mid s \in S, row(s)(\epsilon) = 1\}$;

---

[3] For the minimal DFA, the set of states is $\{row(s) \mid s \in S\}$; here we only take accepting states as we are building an LTS.

- the initial state is $row(\epsilon)$;
- the transition relation is given by $row(s) \xrightarrow{a} row(s \cdot a)$, for all $s \in S$ and $a \in \Sigma$.

In order for the transition relation to be well-defined, the table has to satisfy the following conditions:

- **Closedness:** for all $s \in S, a \in \Sigma$, there is $s' \in S$ such that $row_T(s') = row_T(s \cdot a)$.
- **Consistency:** for all $s_1, s_2 \in S$ such that $row_t(s_1) = row_t(s_2)$, we have $row_T(s_1 \cdot a) = row_T(s_2 \cdot a)$, for all $a \in \Sigma$.

Example 3. The table of Example 2 is closed and consistent. The corresponding hypothesis LTS, which is also the minimal LTS accepting $\mathcal{L}$, is shown in Figure 1b. □

The algorithm works in an iterative fashion: starting from the empty table, where S and E only contain ϵ, the learner extends the table via membership queries until it is closed and consistent, at which point it builds a hypothesis and submits it to the teacher in an equivalence query. If a counter-example is received, it is incorporated in the observation table by adding its prefixes to S, and the updated table is again checked for closedness and consistency. The algorithm is guaranteed to eventually produce a hypothesis H such that $\mathcal{L}(H) = \mathcal{L}$, for which an equivalence query will be answered positively, causing the algorithm to terminate.

3 Learning Synchronous Components Compositionally

In this section, we show how to compositionally learn an unknown system $M = M_1 \parallel \cdots \parallel M_n$ consisting of n parallel LTSs. To achieve this, we assume that we are given: (i) a teacher for M; and (ii) the respective alphabets $\Sigma_1, \ldots, \Sigma_n$ of $M_1, \ldots, M_n$. To achieve this, we propose the architecture in Figure 2. We have n leaners, which are instances of (an extension of) the L* algorithm, one for each component M_i. The instance L_i^* can pose queries for M_i to an *adapter*, which converts them to queries on M. The resulting yes/no answer (and possibly counter-example) is translated back to information about M_i, which is returned to leaner L_i^*. To achieve this, the adapter moreover choreographs the learners to some extent: before an equivalence query $H \overset{?}{=} M$ can be sent to the teacher, the adapter must first receive equivalence queries $H_i \overset{?}{=} M_i$ from each learner.

We first discuss the implementation of the adapter and show its limitations. To deal with these limitations, we next propose a couple of extensions to L* (Section 3.2). Completeness claims are stated in Section 3.3. Several optimisations are discussed in Section 3.4.

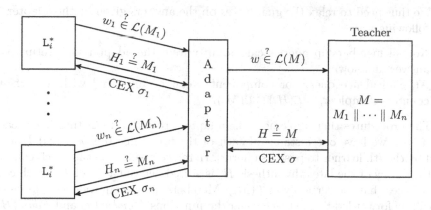

Fig. 2: Architecture for learning LTS M consisting of components $M_1 \parallel \cdots \parallel M_n$.

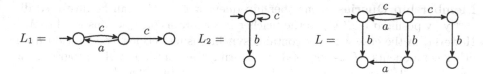

Fig. 3. Running example consisting of two LTSs L_1 and L_2 and their parallel composition L. The respective alphabets are $\{a,c\}$, $\{b,c\}$ and $\{a,b,c\}$.

3.1   Query Adapter

As sketched above, our adapter answers queries on each of the LTSs M_i, based on information obtained from queries on M. However, the application of the parallel operator causes loss of information, as the following example illustrates. We will use the LTSs below as a running example throughout this section.

Example 4. Consider the LTSs L_1, L_2 and $L = L_1 \parallel L_2$ depicted in Figure 3. Their alphabets are $\{a,c\}$, $\{b,c\}$ and $\{a,b,c\}$, respectively.

Suppose we sent a membership query bc to the teacher and we receive as answer that $bc \notin \mathcal{L}(L)$. At this point, we do not have sufficient information to deduce about the respective projections whether $bc_{\restriction\{a,c\}} = c \notin \mathcal{L}(L_1)$ or $bc_{\restriction\{b,c\}} = bc \notin \mathcal{L}(L_2)$ (or both). In this case, only the latter holds. Similarly, if a composite hypothesis $H = H_1 \parallel H_2$ is rejected with a negative counter-example $ccc \notin \mathcal{L}(L)$, we cannot deduce whether this is because $ccc \notin \mathcal{L}(L_1)$ or $ccc \notin \mathcal{L}(L_2)$ (or both). Here, however, the former is true but the latter is not, *i.e.*, ccc is not a counter-example for H_2 at all.   □

Generally, given negative information on the composite level ($\sigma \notin \mathcal{L}(M)$), it is hard to infer information for a single component M_i, whereas positive information ($\sigma \in \mathcal{L}(M)$) easily translates back to the level of individual components.

We thus need to relax the guarantees on the answers given by the adapter in the following way:

1. Not all membership queries can be answered, the adapter may return the answer 'unknown'.
2. An equivalence query for component i can be answered with a *spurious* counter-example $\sigma_i \in \mathcal{L}(H_i) \cap \mathcal{L}(M_i)$.

The procedures that implement the adapter are stated in Listing 1. For each $1 \leq i \leq n$, we have one instance of each of the functions $Member_i$ and $Equiv_i$, used by the ith learner to pose its queries. Here, we assume that for each component i, a copy of the latest hypothesis H_i is stored, as well as a set P_i which contains traces that are certainly in $\mathcal{L}(M_i)$. Membership and equivalence queries on M will be forwarded to the teacher via the functions $Member(\sigma)$ and $Equiv(H)$, respectively.

Membership Queries A membership query $\sigma \in \mathcal{L}(M_i)$ can be answered directly by posing $\sigma \in \mathcal{L}(M)$ to the teacher if σ contains only actions local to M_i. However, in the case where σ contains synchronising actions, cooperation from other components M_j is required. So, during the runtime of the program, for each i we collect traces in a set P_i, for which it is certain that $P_i \subseteq \mathcal{L}(M_i)$. That is, P_i contains traces which were returned as positive counter-examples (line 16) or membership queries (line 5). Recall from Section 2 that we can construct tree-LTSs to compute $\|_{j \neq i} P_j$, where each P_i has alphabet Σ_i. By construction, we have $\mathcal{L}(\|_{j \neq i} P_j) \subseteq \mathcal{L}(\|_{j \neq i} M_j)$, and so we have an under-approximation of the behaviour of other components, possibly including some synchronising actions they can perform. If we find in $\mathcal{L}(\|_{j \neq i} P_j)$ a trace σ' such that σ and σ' contain the same sequence of synchronising actions (line 2, stored in set Π), we construct an arbitrary interleaving (respecting synchronising actions) of σ and σ' and forward it to the teacher (line 4). Such an interleaving is a trace $\sigma_{int} \in \mathcal{L}(\sigma \| \sigma')$ of maximal length. Note that a $\sigma' \in \Pi$ trivially exists if σ does not contain synchronising actions. If, on the other hand, no such σ' exists, we do not have sufficient information on how other LTSs M_j can cooperate, and we return 'unknown' (line 7).

Example 5. Refer to the running example in Figure 3. Suppose that the current knowledge about L_2 is $H_2 = \{\epsilon, b\}$. When $Member_1(c)$ is called, $\Pi = \emptyset$, because there is no trace $\sigma' \in P_2$ that is equal to c when restricted to $\{a, c\}$, therefore *unknown* is returned. Intuitively, since the second learner has not yet discovered that c or bc (or some other trace containing a c) is in its language, the adapter is unable to turn the query c on L_1 into a query for the composite system.   □

Example 6. Suppose now that $cac \in P_1$, *i.e.*, we already learned that $cac \in \mathcal{L}(L_1)$. When posing the membership query $cbc \in \mathcal{L}(L_2)$, the adapter finds that cac and cbc contain the same synchronising actions (*viz.* cc) and constructs an interleaving, for example $cabc$. The teacher answers negatively to the query $cabc \in \mathcal{L}(L)$, and thus we learn that $cbc \notin \mathcal{L}(L_2)$.   □

Listing 1: Membership and equivalence query procedures for component i.

Input: Alphabets $\Sigma_1, \ldots, \Sigma_n$ of the components
Data: for each i, the latest hypothesis H_i and a set P_i of traces, initially $\{\epsilon\}$.

```
1  Function Member_i(σ)
2  │  Π := {σ' ∈ L(||_{j≠i} P_j) | σ'_{↾Σ_i} = σ_{↾Σ_other}} where Σ_other = ⋃_{j≠i} Σ_j;
3  │  if Π ≠ ∅ then
4  │  │   answer := Member(σ_int) for some σ' ∈ Π and some maximal
   │  │     σ_int ∈ L(σ || σ') ;                    /* construct interleaving */
5  │  │   if answer = yes then P_i := P_i ∪ {σ};
6  │  │   return answer
7  │  else return unknown;
8  Function Equiv_i(H')
9  │  H_i := H';
10 │  while true do
11 │  │   barrier(n) ;   /* wait until this point is reached for every i */
12 │  │   construct H = ||_i H_i;
13 │  │   switch Equiv(H) do
14 │  │   │   case yes do return yes;
15 │  │   │   case (no, σ) do
16 │  │   │   │   if σ ∉ L(H) then P_i := P_i ∪ {σ_{↾Σ_i}};
17 │  │   │   │   if a ∈ Σ_i, where σ = σ'a, and σ ∈ L(H) ↔ σ_{↾Σ_i} ∈ L(H_i) then
18 │  │   │   │   │   return (no, σ_{↾Σ_i})
```

Equivalence Queries For equivalence queries, the adapter offers functions $Equiv_i$. To construct a corresponding query on the composite level, we first need to gather a hypothesis H_i for each i. Thus, we synchronise all learners in a barrier (line 11), after which a composite hypothesis can be constructed and forwarded to the teacher (lines 12, 13). An affirmative answer can be returned directly, while in the negative case we investigate the returned counter-example σ. If σ is a positive counter-example, we add its projection to P_i (line 16). By the assumption that σ is shortest[4], H and M agree on all $\sigma' \in Pref(\sigma) \setminus \{\sigma\}$. Thus, σ only concerns H_i if the last action in σ is contained in Σ_i. Furthermore, we need to check whether H and H_i agree on σ: it can happen that $\sigma_{\upharpoonright \Sigma_i} \in \mathcal{L}(H_i)$ but $\sigma \notin \mathcal{L}(H)$ due to other hypotheses not providing the necessary communication opportunities. If both conditions are satisfied (line 17), we return the projection of σ on Σ_i (line 18). Otherwise, we cannot conclude anything about H_i at this moment and we iterate (line 10). In that case, we effectively wait for other hypotheses H_j, with $j \neq i$, to be updated before trying again. A termination argument is provided later in this section.

---

[4] This assumption can be satisfied in practice by using a lexicographical ordering on the conformance test suite the teacher generates to decide equivalence.

Example 7. Again considering our running example (Figure 3), suppose the two learners call in parallel the functions $Equiv_1(H_1)$ and $Equiv_2(H_2)$. The provided hypotheses and their parallel composition are as follows:

$$H_1 = \quad \rightarrow\!\bigcirc\!\underset{a}{\overset{c}{\rightleftarrows}}\!\bigcirc \qquad H_2 = \quad \rightarrow\!\bigcirc\!\circlearrowright\, b\ c \qquad H_1 \parallel H_2 = \quad \rightarrow\!\bigcirc\!\underset{a}{\overset{c}{\rightleftarrows}}\!\bigcirc\!\begin{smallmatrix}b\\ \end{smallmatrix}$$

The adapter forwards $H = H_1 \parallel H_2$ to the teacher, which returns the counter-example cc. The last symbol, c, occurs in both alphabets, but $cc \in \mathcal{L}(H)$ does not hold and $cc_{\restriction \Sigma_2} \in \mathcal{L}(H_2)$ does, so only $Equiv_1(H_1)$ returns (no, cc). The call to $Equiv_2(H_2)$ hangs in the while loop of line 10 until $Equiv_1$ is invoked with a different hypothesis.   □

Example 8. Suppose now that the hypotheses and their composition are:

$$H_1 = \quad \rightarrow\!\bigcirc\!\underset{a\ c}{\overset{c}{\rightleftarrows}}\!\bigcirc \qquad H_2 = \quad \rightarrow\!\bigcirc\!\overset{c}{\underset{}{\circlearrowright}}\!\overset{b}{\rightarrow}\!\bigcirc \qquad H_1 \parallel H_2 = \quad$$

When we submit $Equiv(H_1 \parallel H_2)$, we may receive the negative counter-example ccc, which is a shortest counter-example. This counter-example does not contain any information to suggest that it only applies to H_1. It is a spurious counter-example for H_2, since that *should* contain the trace ccc.   □

3.2   L* extensions

As explained in the previous section, the capabilities of our adapter are limited compared to an ordinary teacher. We thus extend L* to deal with the answer 'unknown' to membership queries and to deal with spurious counter-examples.

Answer 'unknown'. The setting of receiving incomplete information through membership queries first occurred in [15], and is also discussed in [24]. Here we briefly recall the ideas of [15]. To deal with partial information from membership queries, the concept of an observation table is generalised such that the function $T : (S \cup S \cdot \Sigma) \cdot E \to \{0, 1\}$ is a partial function, that is, for some cells we have no information. Based on T, we now define the function $row : S \cup S \cdot \Sigma \to E \to \{0, 1, ?\}$ to fill the cells of the table: $row_T(s)(e) = T(se)$ if $T(se)$ is defined and ? otherwise. We refer to '?' as a *wildcard*; its actual value is currently unknown and might be learned at a later time or never at all. To deal with the uncertain nature of wildcards, we introduce a relation $\approx$ on rows, where $row(s_1) \approx row(s_2)$ iff for every $e \in E$, $row(s_1)(e) \neq row(s_2)(e)$ implies that $row(s_1)(e) = ?$ or $row(s_2)(e) = ?$. Note that $\approx$ is not an equivalence relation since it is not transitive. Closedness and consistency are defined as before, but now use the new relation $\approx$. We say an LTS M is *consistent* with T iff for all $s \in \Sigma^*$ such that $T(s)$ is defined, we have $T(s) = 1$ iff $s \in \mathcal{L}(M)$.

As discussed earlier, Angluin's original L* algorithm relies on the fact that, for a closed and consistent table, there is a unique minimal DFA (or, in our case, LTS) that is consistent with T. However, the occurrence of wildcards in the observation table may allow multiple minimal LTSs that are consistent with T. Such a minimal consistent LTS can be obtained with a SAT solver, as described in [19].

Similar to Angluin's original algorithm, this extension comes with some correctness theorems. First of all, it terminates outputting the minimal LTS for the target language. Furthermore, each hypothesis is consistent with all membership queries and counter-examples that were provided so far. Lastly, each subsequent hypothesis has at least as many states as the previous one, but never more than the minimal LTS for the target language.

Spurious Counter-Examples. We now extend this algorithm with the ability to deal with spurious counter-examples. Any *negative* counter-example $\sigma \in \mathcal{L}(H_i)$ might be spurious, *i.e.*, it is actually the case that $\sigma \in \mathcal{L}(M_i)$. Since L* excludes σ from the language of all subsequent hypotheses, we might later get the same trace σ, but now as a *positive* counter-example. In that case, the initial negative judgment from the equivalence teacher was spurious.

One possible way of dealing with spurious counter-examples, is adding to L* the ability to *overwrite* entries in the observation table in case a spurious counter-example is corrected. However, this may cause the learner to diverge if infinitely many spurious counter-examples are returned. Therefore, we instead choose to add a backtracking mechanism to ensure our search will converge. The pseudo code is listed in Listing 2; we refer to this as $L^*_{?,b}$ (L* with wildcards and backtracking).

We have a mapping BT that stores backtracking points; BT is initialised to the empty mapping (line 1). Lines 5-11 ensure the observation table is closed and consistent in the same way as L*, but use the relation $\approx$ on rows instead. Next, we construct a minimal hypothesis that is consistent with the observations in T (line 12). This hypothesis is posed as an equivalence query. If the teacher replies with a counter-example σ for which $T(\sigma) = 0$, then σ was a spurious counter-example, so we backtrack and restore the observation table from just before $T(\sigma)$ was introduced (line 15). Otherwise, we store a backtracking point for when σ later turns out to be spurious (line 17); this is only necessary if σ is a negative counter-example. Note that not all information is lost when backtracking: the set P_i stored in the adapter is unaffected, so some positive traces are carried over after backtracking. Finally, we incorporate σ into the observation table (line 18). When the teacher accepts our hypothesis, we terminate.

We finish this section with an example that shows how spurious counter-examples may be resolved.

Listing 2: Learning with wildcards and backtracking.

```
1 Set BT to ∅;
2 Initialise S and E to {ε};
3 Extend T to S ∪ S · Σᵢ by calling Memberᵢ;
4 repeat
5    while (S, E, T) is not closed and consistent do
6       if (S, E, T) is not consistent then
7          Find s₁, s₂ ∈ S, a ∈ Σᵢ, e ∈ E such that rowₜ(s₁) ≈ rowₜ(s₂) and
             T(s₁ · a · e) ≉ T(s₂ · a · e);
8          Add a · e to S and extend T by calling Memberᵢ;

9       if (S, E, T) is not closed then
10         Find s₁ ∈ S, a ∈ Σᵢ such that rowₜ(s₁ · a) ≉ rowₜ(s) for all s ∈ S;
11         Add s₁ · a to S and extend T by calling Memberᵢ;

12   Call Equivᵢ(H) for some minimal LTS H consistent with T;
13   if Teacher replies with counter-example σ then
14      if T(σ) = 0 then            /* σ corrects an earlier spurious CEX */
15         (S, E, T) := BT(σ);

16      else if σ ∈ L(H) then                      /* σ might be spurious */
17         BT(σ) := (S, E, T);

18      Add σ and all its prefixes to S and extend T by calling Memberᵢ;

19 until Teacher replies yes to conjecture H;
20 return H;
```

Example 9. Refer again to the LTSs of our running example in Figure 3. Consider the situation after proposing the hypotheses of Example 8 and receiving the counter-example *ccc*, which is spurious for the second learner.

In the next iteration, $Member_2$ can answer some membership queries, such as *cbc*, necessary to expand the table of the second learner. This is enabled by the fact that P_1 contains *cc* from the positive counter-example of Example 7 (line 2 of Listing 1). The resulting updated hypotheses are as follows.

Now the counter-example to composite hypothesis $H_1' \parallel H_2'$ is *cacc*. The projection on Σ_2 is *ccc*, which directly contradicts the counter-example received in the previous iteration. This spurious counter-example is thus repaired by backtracking in the second learner. The invocation of $Equiv_1(H_1')$ by the first learner does not return this counter-example, since $H_1' \parallel H_2'$ and H_1' do not agree on *cacc*, so the check on line 17 of Listing 1 fails.

Finally, in the next iteration, the respective hypotheses coincide with L_1 and L_2 and both learners terminate.   □

3.3   Correctness

As a first result, we show that our adapter provides correct information on each of the components when asking membership queries. This is required to ensure that information obtained by membership queries does not conflict with counter-examples. Proofs are omitted for space reasons.

Theorem 1. *Answers from $Member_i$ are consistent with $\mathcal{L}(M_i)$.*

Before presenting the main theorem on correctness of our learning framework, we first introduce several auxiliary lemmas. In the following, we assume n instances of $L_{?,b}^*$ run concurrently and each queries the corresponding functions $Member_i$ and $Equiv_i$, as per our architecture (Figure 2). First, a counter-example cannot be spurious for all learners; thus at least one learner obtains valid information to progress its learning.

Lemma 1. *Every counter-example obtained from $Equiv(H)$ is valid for at least one learner.*

The next lemma shows that even if a spurious counter-example occurs, this does not induce divergence, since it is always repaired by a corresponding positive counter-example in finite time.

Lemma 2. *If $Equiv(H)$ always returns a shortest counter-example, then each spurious counter-example is repaired by another counter-example within a finite number of invocations of $Equiv(H)$, the monolithic teacher.*

Our main theorem states that a composite system is learned by n copies of $L_{?,b}^*$ that each call our adapter (see Figure 2).

Theorem 2. *Running n instances of $L_{?,b}^*$ terminates, and on termination we have $H_1 \parallel \cdots \parallel H_n = M_1 \parallel \cdots \parallel M_n$.*

Remark 2. We cannot claim the stronger result that $H_i = M_i$ for all i, since different component LTSs can result in the same parallel composition. For example, consider the below LTSs, both with alphabet $\{a\}$:

$$H_1 = \; \rightarrow\!\bigcirc \qquad H_2 = \; \rightarrow\!\bigcirc\!\circlearrowright a$$

Here we have $H_1 \parallel H_2 = H_1 \parallel H_1$. The equivalence oracle thus may also return *yes* even when the component LTSs differ slightly.

3.4   Optimisations

There are a number of optimisations that can dramatically improve the practical performance of our learning framework. We briefly discuss them here.

First, finding whether there is a trace $\sigma' \in \Pi$ (line 2 of Listing 1) can quickly become expensive once the sets P_i grow larger. We thus try to limit the size of each P_i without impacting the amount of information it provides on the synchronisation opportunities offered by component M_i. Therefore, when we derive that $\sigma \in \mathcal{L}(M_i)$, we only store the shortest prefix ρ of σ such that ρ and σ contain the same synchronising actions. That is, $\sigma = \rho \cdot \rho'$ and ρ' contains only actions local to M_i. Furthermore, we construct $\|_{j \neq i} P_j$ only once after each call to $Equiv_i$ and we cache accesses to $\|_{j \neq i} P_j$, such that it is only traversed once when performing multiple queries σ^1, σ^2 for which it holds that $\sigma^1_{\restriction \Sigma_{other}} = \sigma^2_{\restriction \Sigma_{other}}$. A possibility that we have not explored is applying *partial-order reduction* to eliminate redundant interleavings in $\|_{j \neq i} P_j$.

Since the language of an LTS is prefix-closed, we can – in some cases – extend the function T that is part of the observation table without performing membership queries. Concretely, if $T(\sigma) = 0$ then we can set $T(\sigma \cdot \sigma') = 0$ for any trace σ'. Dually, if $T(\sigma \cdot \sigma') = 1$ then we set $T(\sigma) = 1$.

4   Experiments

We created an experimental implementation of our algorithms in a tool called COAL (COmpositional Automata Learner) [27], implemented in Java. It relies on LearnLib [22], a library for automata learning, which allows us to re-use standard data structures, such as observation tables, and compare our framework to a state-of-the-art implementation of L*. To extract a minimal LTS from an observation table, we first attempt the inexact blue-fringe variant of RPNI [20] (as implemented in LearnLib). If this does not result in an LTS that is minimal, we resort to an exact procedure based on a SAT translation; we use the Z3 solver [10].

Our experiments are run on a machine with an Intel Core i3 3.6GHz, with 16GB of RAM, running Ubuntu 20.04. For each experiment, we use a time-out of 30 minutes.

4.1   Random Systems

We first experiment with a large number of composite systems where each of the component LTSs is randomly generated. This yields an accurate reflection of actual behavioural transition systems [16]. Each component LTS has a random number of states between 5 and 9 (inclusive, uniformly distributed) and a maximum number of outgoing edges per state between 2 and 4 (inclusive, uniformly distributed).

We assign alphabets to the components LTSs in five different ways that reflect real-world communication structures, see Figure 4. Here, each edge represents a communication channel that consists of two synchronising actions; each component LTS furthermore has two local actions. The hyperedge in *multiparty* indicates multiparty communication: the two synchronising actions in such a system are shared by all component LTSs. The graph that represents the *bipartite* communication structure is always complete, and the components are evenly distributed between both sides. *Random* is slightly different: it contains $2(n-1)$

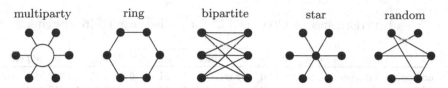

Fig. 4: Communication structure of the randomly generated systems. Dots represent components LTSs; edges represent shared synchronising actions.

edges, where n is the number of components, each consisting of one action; we furthermore ensure the random graph is connected.

For our five communication structures, we create ten instances for each number of components between 4 and 9; this leads to a total benchmark set of 300 LTSs. Out of these, 47 have more than 10,000 states, including 12 LTSs of more than 100,000 states. The largest LTS contains 379,034 states. *Bipartite* often leads to relatively small LTSs, due to its high number of synchronising actions.

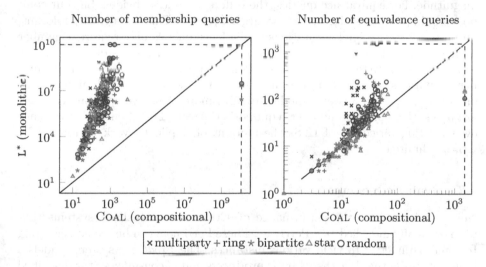

Fig. 5: Performance of L* and compositional learning on random models.

On each LTS, we run the classic L* algorithm and COAL, and record the number of queries posed to the teacher.[5] The result is plotted in Figure 5; note the log scale. Here, marks that lie on the dashed line indicate a time-out or out-of-memory for one of the two algorithms.

COAL outperforms the monolithic L* algorithm in the number of membership queries for all cases (unless it fails). In more than half of the cases, the

---

[5] The number of queries is the standard performance measure for query learning algorithms; runtime is less reliable, as it depends on the specific teacher implementation.

Table 1: Performance of COAL and L* for realistic composite systems.

				COAL				L*		
model	scaling	comp	states	time(s)	memQ	eqQ	spCE	time(s)	memQ	eqQ
CloudOps $W=1, C=1, N=3$		5	690	1.06	957	24	0	1.85	2,740,128	88
CloudOps $W=1, C=1, N=4$		6	1,932	1.13	1,004	26	0	16.99	22,252,120	216
CloudOps $W=2, C=1, N=3$		5	3,858	47.13	8,897	41	3	8.94	12,574,560	99
CloudOps $W=2, C=1, N=4$		6	10,824	48.20	8,811	36	3	84.02	91,178,900	227
ProdCons $K=5, P=1, C=1$		3	246	0.51	285	13	3	0.34	160,126	30
ProdCons $K=5, P=2, C=1$		4	962	0.54	401	13	0	2.35	2,523,625	91
ProdCons $K=5, P=3, C=2$		6	13,001	1.65	1,239	16	0	65.42	60,186,235	187
ProdCons $K=5, P=3, C=3$		7	45,302	3.21	2,276	16	0	241.37	222,567,729	193
ProdCons $K=3, P=2, C=2$		5	2,273	0.61	456	13	0	1.66	2,141,165	43
ProdCons $K=5, P=2, C=2$		5	3,329	1.29	596	15	1	6.36	6,984,705	93
ProdCons $K=7, P=2, C=2$		5	4,385	0.97	799	15	0	17.56	15,792,997	135

difference is at least three orders of magnitude; it can even reach six orders of magnitude. For equivalence queries, the difference is less obvious, but our compositional approach scales better for larger systems. This is especially relevant, because in practice implementations equivalence queries may require a number of membership queries that is exponential in the size of the system. Multiparty communication systems benefit most from compositional learning. The number of spurious counter-examples that occurs for these models is limited: about one on average. Only twelve models require more than five spurious counter-examples; the maximum number required is thirteen. This is encouraging, since even for this varied set of LTSs the amount of duplicate work performed by COAL is limited.

4.2   Realistic Systems

Next, we investigate the performance of COAL on two realistic systems that were originally modelled as a Petri net. These Petri nets can be scaled according to some parameters to yield various instances. The *ProdCons* system models a buffer of size K that is accessed by P producers and C consumers; it is described in [32, Fig. 8]. The *CloudOpsManagement* net is obtained from the 2019 Model Checking Contest [2], and describes the operation of C containers and operating systems and W application runtimes in a cloud environment. Furthermore, we scale the number N of application runtime components. We generate the LTS that represents the marking graph of these nets and run L* and COAL; the results are listed in Table 1. For each system, we list the values of scaling parameters, the number of components and the number of states of the LTS. For COAL and L*, we list the runtime and the number of membership and equivalence queries; for COAL we also list the number of spurious counter-examples (column spCE).

The results are comparable to our random experiments: COAL outperforms L* in number of queries, especially for larger systems. For the two larger CloudOps-

Management instances, the increasing runtime of COAL is due to the fact that two of the components grow as the parameter W increases. The larger number of states causes a higher runtime of the SAT procedure for constructing a minimal LTS.

We remark that in our experiments, the teacher has direct access to the LTS we aim to learn, leading to cheap membership and equivalence queries. Thus, in this idealised setting, L* incurs barely any runtime penalty for the large number of queries it requires. Using a realistic teacher implementation would quickly cause time-outs for L*, making the results of our experiments less insightful.

5   Related Work

Finding ways of projecting a known concurrent system down into its components is the subject of several works, e.g., [8,17]. In principle, it would be possible to learn the system monolithically and use the aforementioned results. However, as shown in Section 4, this may result in a substantial query blow-up.

Learning approach targeting various concurrent systems exist in the literature. As an example of the monolithic approach above, the approach of [6] learns asynchronously-communicating finite state machines via queries in the form of message sequence charts. The result is a monolithic DFA that is later broken down into components via an additional synthesis procedure. This approach thus does not avoid the exponential blow-up in queries. Another difference with our work is that we consider synchronous communication.

Another monolithic approach is [18], which provides an extension of L* to *pomset automata*. These automata are acceptors of partially-ordered multisets, which model concurrent computations. Accordingly, this relies on an oracle capable of processing pomset-shaped queries; adapting the approach to an ordinary sequential oracle – as in our setting – may cause a query blow-up.

A severely restricted variant of our setting is considered in [13], which introduces an approach to learn *Systems of Procedural Automata*. Here, DFAs representing procedures are learned independently. The constrained interaction of such DFAs allows for deterministically translating between component-level and system-level queries, and for univocally determining the target of a counterexample. Our setting is more general – arbitrary (not just pair-wise) synchronisations are allowed at any time – hence these abilities are lost.

Two works that do not allow synchronisation at all are [23,25]. In [23] individual components are learned without any knowledge of the component number and their individual alphabets, however components cannot synchronise (alphabets are assumed to be disjoint). This is a crucial difference with our approach, which instead has to deal with unknown query results and spurious counterexamples precisely due to the presence of synchronising actions. An algorithm for learning Moore machines with decomposable outputs is propose in [25]. This algorithm spawns several copies of L*, one per component. This approach is not applicable to our setting, as we do not assume decomposable output and allow dependencies between components.

Other approaches consider teachers that are unable to reply to membership queries [1,14,15,24]; they all use SAT-based techniques to construct automata. The closest works to ours are: [24], considering the problem of compositionally learning a property of a concurrent system with full knowledge of the components; and [1], learning an unknown component of the *serial* composition of two automata. In none of these works spurious counter-examples arise.

6   Conclusion

We have shown how to learn component systems with synchronous communication in a compositional way. Our framework uses an adapter and a number of concurrent learners. Several extensions to L* were necessary to circumvent the fundamental limitations of the adapter. Experiments with our tool COAL show that our compositional approach offers much better scalability than a standard monolithic approach.

In future work, we aim to build on our framework in a couple of ways. First, we want to apply these ideas to all kinds of extensions of L* such as TTT [21] (for reducing the number of queries) and algorithms for learning extended finite state machines [7]. Our expectation is that the underlying learning algorithm can be replaced with little effort. Next, we want to eliminate the assumption that the alphabets of individual components are known a priori. We envisage this can be achieved by combining our work and [23].

We also would like to explore the integration of learning and model-checking. A promising direction is *learning-based assume-guarantee reasoning*, originally introduced by Cobleigh et. al. in [9]. This approach assumes that models for the individual components are available. Using our approach, we may be able to drop this assumption, and enable a fully black-box compositional verification approach.

Acknowledgements. We thank the anonymous reviewers for their useful comments, and Tobias Kappé for suggesting several improvements. This research was partially supported by the EPSRC Standard Grant *CLeVer* (EP/S028641/1).

References

1. Abel, A., Reineke, J.: Gray-Box Learning of Serial Compositions of Mealy Machines. In: NFM. pp. 272–287 (2016). https://doi.org/10.1007/978-3-319-40648-0_21
2. Amparore, E., et al.: Presentation of the 9th Edition of the Model Checking Contest. In: TACAS2019. LNCS, vol. 11429, pp. 50–68 (2019). https://doi.org/10.1007/978-3-030-17502-3_4
3. Angluin, D.: Learning regular sets from queries and counterexamples. Information and Computation **75**(2), 87–106 (1987). https://doi.org/10.1016/0890-5401(87)90052-6
4. Angluin, D., Fisman, D.: Learning regular omega languages. Theor. Comput. Sci. **650**, 57–72 (2016). https://doi.org/10.1016/j.tcs.2016.07.031

5. Argyros, G., D'Antoni, L.: The Learnability of Symbolic Automata. In: CAV. pp. 427–445 (2018). https://doi.org/10.1007/978-3-319-96145-3_23
6. Bollig, B., Katoen, J., Kern, C., Leucker, M.: Learning Communicating Automata from MSCs. IEEE Trans. Software Eng. **36**(3), 390–408 (2010). https://doi.org/10.1109/TSE.2009.89
7. Cassel, S., Howar, F., Jonsson, B., Steffen, B.: Active learning for extended finite state machines. Formal Aspects Comput. **28**(2), 233–263 (2016). https://doi.org/10.1007/s00165-016-0355-5
8. Castellani, I., Mukund, M., Thiagarajan, P.S.: Synthesizing Distributed Transition Systems from Global Specifications. In: FSTTCS. LNCS, vol. 1738, pp. 219–231 (1999). https://doi.org/10.1007/3-540-46691-6_17
9. Cobleigh, J.M., Giannakopoulou, D., Pasareanu, C.S.: Learning Assumptions for Compositional Verification. In: TACAS. Lecture Notes in Computer Science, vol. 2619, pp. 331–346. Springer (2003). https://doi.org/10.1007/3-540-36577-X_24
10. De Moura, L., Bjørner, N.: Z3: An efficient SMT Solver. In: TACAS 2008. LNCS, vol. 4963, pp. 337–340 (2008). https://doi.org/10.1007/978-3-540-78800-3_24
11. Fiterau-Brostean, P., Janssen, R., Vaandrager, F.W.: Combining Model Learning and Model Checking to Analyze TCP Implementations. In: CAV2016. LNCS, vol. 9780, pp. 454–471 (2016). https://doi.org/10.1007/978-3-319-41540-6_25
12. Fiterau-Brostean, P., Jonsson, B., Merget, R., de Ruiter, J., Sagonas, K., Somorovsky, J.: Analysis of DTLS Implementations Using Protocol State Fuzzing. In: USENIX (2020), https://www.usenix.org/conference/usenixsecurity20/presentation/fiterau-brostean
13. Frohme, M., Steffen, B.: Compositional learning of mutually recursive procedural systems (2021). https://doi.org/10.1007/s10009-021-00634-y
14. Grinchtein, O., Leucker, M.: Learning Finite-State Machines from Inexperienced Teachers. In: ICGI. pp. 344–345 (2006). https://doi.org/10.1007/11872436_30
15. Grinchtein, O., Leucker, M., Piterman, N.: Inferring Network Invariants Automatically. In: IJCAR. pp. 483–497 (2006). https://doi.org/10.1007/11814771_40
16. Groote, J.F., van der Hofstad, R., Raffelsieper, M.: On the random structure of behavioural transition systems. Science of Computer Programming **128**, 51–67 (2016). https://doi.org/10.1016/j.scico.2016.02.006
17. Groote, J.F., Moller, F.: Verification of parallel systems via decomposition. In: CONCUR 1992. LNCS, vol. 630, pp. 62–76 (1992). https://doi.org/10.1007/BFb0084783
18. van Heerdt, G., Kappé, T., Rot, J., Silva, A.: Learning Pomset Automata. In: FoSSaCS2021. LNCS, vol. 12650, pp. 510–530 (2021). https://doi.org/10.1007/978-3-030-71995-1_26
19. Heule, M.J.H., Verwer, S.: Exact DFA Identification Using SAT Solvers. In: ICGI 2010. LNCS, vol. 6339, pp. 66–79 (2010). https://doi.org/10.1007/978-3-642-15488-1_7
20. de la Higuera, C.: Grammatical Inference: Learning Automata and Grammars. Cambridge University Press, USA (2010)
21. Isberner, M., Howar, F., Steffen, B.: The TTT Algorithm: A Redundancy-Free Approach to Active Automata Learning. In: RV2014. LNCS, vol. 8734, pp. 307–322 (2014). https://doi.org/10.1007/978-3-319-11164-3_26
22. Isberner, M., Howar, F., Steffen, B.: The Open-Source LearnLib: A Framework for Active Automata Learning. In: CAV2015. LNCS, vol. 9206, pp. 487–495 (2015). https://doi.org/10.1007/978-3-319-21690-4_32

23. Labbaf, F., Groote, J.F., Hojjat, H., Mousavi, M.R.: Compositional Learning for Interleaving Parallel Automata. In: FoSSaCS 2023. LNCS, Springer (2023)
24. Leucker, M., Neider, D.: Learning Minimal Deterministic Automata from Inexperienced Teachers. In: ISoLA. pp. 524–538 (2012). https://doi.org/10.1007/978-3-642-34026-0_39
25. Moerman, J.: Learning Product Automata. In: ICGI. vol. 93, pp. 54–66. PMLR (2018), http://proceedings.mlr.press/v93/moerman19a.html
26. Moerman, J., Sammartino, M., Silva, A., Klin, B., Szynwelski, M.: Learning nominal automata. In: POPL. pp. 613–625 (2017). https://doi.org/10.1145/3009837.3009879
27. Neele, T., Sammartino, M.: Replication package for the paper "Compositional Automata Learning of Synchronous Systems" (2023). https://doi.org/10.5281/zenodo.7503396
28. Nerode, A.: Linear automaton transformations 9(4), 541–544. (1958)
29. de Ruiter, J., Poll, E.: Protocol State Fuzzing of TLS Implementations. In: USENIX. pp. 193–206 (2015), https://www.usenix.org/conference/usenixsecurity15/technical-sessions/presentation/de-ruiter
30. Schuts, M., Hooman, J., Vaandrager, F.W.: Refactoring of Legacy Software Using Model Learning and Equivalence Checking: An Industrial Experience Report. In: IFM. LNCS, vol. 9681, pp. 311–325 (2016). https://doi.org/10.1007/978-3-319-33693-0_20
31. Shih, A., Darwiche, A., Choi, A.: Verifying Binarized Neural Networks by Angluin-Style Learning. In: SAT. vol. 11628, pp. 354–370 (2019). https://doi.org/10.1007/978-3-030-24258-9_25
32. Zuberek, W.: Petri net models of process synchronization mechanisms. In: SMC1999. vol. 1, pp. 841–847. IEEE (1999). https://doi.org/10.1109/ICSMC.1999.814201

Concolic Testing of Front-end JavaScript

Zhe Li[✉] and Fei Xie

Portland State University, Portland, OR 97201, USA
{zl3,xie}@pdx.edu

Abstract. JavaScript has become the most popular programming language for web front-end development. With such popularity, there is a great demand for thorough testing of client-side JavaScript web applications. In this paper, we present a novel approach to concolic testing of front-end JavaScript web applications. This approach leverages widely used JavaScript testing frameworks such as *Jest* and *Puppeteer* and conducts concolic execution on JavaScript functions in web applications for unit testing. The seamless integration of concolic testing with these testing frameworks allows injection of symbolic variables within the native execution context of a JavaScript web function and precise capture of concrete execution traces of the function under test. Such concise execution traces greatly improve the effectiveness and efficiency of the subsequent symbolic analysis for test generation. We have implemented our approach on *Jest* and *Puppeteer*. The application of our *Jest* implementation on *Metamask*, one of the most popular Crypto wallets, has uncovered 3 bugs and 1 test suite improvement, whose bug reports have all been accepted by *Metamask* developers on Github. We also applied our *Puppeteer* implementation to 21 Github projects and detected 4 bugs.

Keywords: Concolic Testing · JavaScript · Front-end Web Application.

1 Introduction

JavaScript (JS), as the most popular web frond-end programming language, is used by 95.1% of websites [23]. Many of such websites handle sensitive information such as financial transactions and private conversions. Errors in these websites not only affect user experiences, but also endanger safety, security, and privacy of users. Therefore, these websites, particularly their dynamic functions that are often implemented in JS, must be thoroughly tested to detect software bugs. There have been many testing frameworks for JS applications, such as *Jest* and *Puppeteer*. These frameworks provide a systematic way to test JS applications and reduce the tedious testing setup, particularly for unit testing. However, although these testing frameworks simplify the execution of testing, they do not provide test data for web applications. Such test data still needs to be provided manually by application developers, which is often very time-consuming and laborious. And achieving high code and functional coverage on web applications with high-quality test data still remains a challenge [34].

L. Lambers and S. Uchitel (Eds.): FASE 2023, LNCS 13991, pp. 67–87, 2023.
https://doi.org/10.1007/978-3-031-30826-0_4

Symbolic execution has shown great promises in software testing, particularly in test data generation [29]. It exercises software with symbolic inputs, explores its execution paths systematically, and generates test data for the paths explored symbolically. However, symbolic execution may suffer from path explosions when the software has too many paths to explore [26]. Concolic testing addresses path explosion by combining concrete execution with symbolic execution. The software is first exercised with a concrete input and the resulting concrete execution trace is then analyzed symbolically to explore paths that are adjacent to the concrete trace. Concolic testing has achieved many successes in software testing [25]. It is strongly desirable to apply concolic testing to front-end JS web application to generate high-quality test data automatically, so manually efforts can be reduced and test coverage can be improved. However, front-end JS applications pose major challenges to concolic testing. These applications typically execute in the contexts of web browsers, which tends to be complex, and they are usually event-driven, user-interactive, and string-intensive [35].

In this paper, we present a novel approach to concolic testing of front-end JS web application. This approach leverages widely used JS testing frameworks such as *Jest* and *Puppeteer* and conducts concolic execution on JS web functions for unit testing [39]. These testing frameworks isolate the web function under test from the context of its embedding web page by mocking the environment and provide the test data that drives the function. This isolation of web function provides an ideal target for application of concolic testing. We integrate concolic testing APIs into these testing frameworks. The seamless integration of concolic testing allows injection of symbolic variables within the native execution context of a JS web function and precise capture of concrete execution traces of this function. As the testing framework executes the function under test with test data, parts or all of the test data can be made symbolic and the resulting execution traces of the function are captured for later symbolic analysis. Concise execution traces greatly improve the effectiveness and efficiency of the subsequent symbolic analysis for test generation. The new test data generated by the symbolic analysis is again fed back to the testing frameworks to drive further concolic testing.

We have implemented our approach on *Jest* and *Puppeteer*. The application of our *Jest* implementation to *Metamask*, one of the most popular Crypto wallets, has uncovered 3 bugs and 1 test suite improvement, whose bug reports have been accepted by *Metamask* developers on Github. We have also applied our *Puppeteer* implementation to 21 Github projects and detected 4 bugs.

2   Background

2.1   Front-end JavaScript Testing Frameworks

In a general software testing framework, a test case is designed to exercise a single, logical unit of behavior in an application and ensure the targeted unit operates as expected [21]. Typically, it is structured as a tuple $\{P, C, Q\}$:

- P are the preconditions that must be met so that the function under test can be executed.
- C is the function under test, containing the logic to be tested.
- Q are the post assertions of the test case that are expected to be true.

As shown in Figure 1, a front-end JS testing framework inspects the web application in the browser for JS functions to test. It utilizes testing libraries to

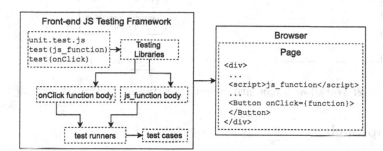

Fig. 1: Front-end JS testing framework workflow

obtain the web pages, parses them and stores page functions and their context information individually so that test runners can run the functions browser-less [4] The test runner sets up the three parts of a test case for each JS function under test and then executes the test case. The front-end JS testing framework helps isolate the JS function under test and provides the execution context for testing the function, which is an ideal entry for our application of the concolic testing to front-end JS.

2.2   In-situ Concolic Testing of Backend JavaScript

In [9], a new approach has been introduced to applying concolic testing to backend JS in-situ, i.e., scripts are executed in their native environments (e.g., Node.js) as part of concolic execution and test cases generated are directly replayed in these environments [13]. As illustrated in Figure 2, the concrete execution step of concolic testing as indicated by the dashed box on top is conducted in the native execution environment for JS, where the trace of this concrete execution is captured. The trace is then analyzed in the symbolic execution step of concolic testing to generate test cases that are then fed back into the native concrete execution to drive further test case generation. This approach has been implemented on the Node.js execution environment and its V8 JS engine [24]. As a script is executed with Node.js, its binary-level execution trace is captured and later analyzed through symbolic execution for test case generation. It also offers the flexibility of customizing trace as needed. We leverage this functionality in our approach.

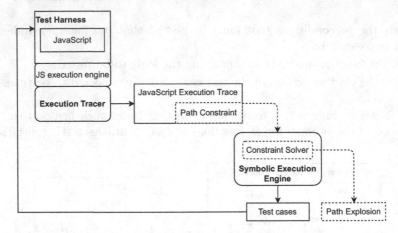

Fig. 2: Workflow for in-situ concolic testing of backend JavaScript

3 Approach

3.1 Overview

Our approach strives to apply concolic testing on front-end JS web applications to generate effective test data for unit-testing of these applications. Below are the specific design goals for our approach:

- **Front-end JS Extraction.** JS web functions need to be extracted from web pages to execute independently to reduce complexity for concolic testing.
- **Execution Context Construction.** JS web functions under test need to have the same execution environments as they are executed in the web pages.
- **Non-intrusive and Effective Concolic Testing.** Concolic execution on JS web applications needs to require minimal changes on both the applications and the symbolic engine and generate useful test cases effectively.

With the above goals in mind, we design an approach to concolic testing of front-end JS web application, which leverages the JS testing frameworks such as Jest and Puppeteer and conducts concolic execution on JS web functions for unit testing. The seamless integration of concolic testing with these testing frameworks is achieved through extending in-situ concolic testing of backend JS applications. Figure 3 illustrates how the integration is realized:

1. Workflow 1 in Figure 3a illustrates the original capability of in-situ concolic testing of backend JS applications. It tests pure JS functions from NPM JS libraries. The execution tracer captures the traces of the pure JS functions and feeds them to the symbolic execution engine to generate new test data.
2. Workflow 2 in Figure 3b illustrates a naïve application of in-situ concolic testing to a JS web application. However, in-situ concolic testing cannot handle web elements, e.g., <HTML> tags, without the capability of a browser.

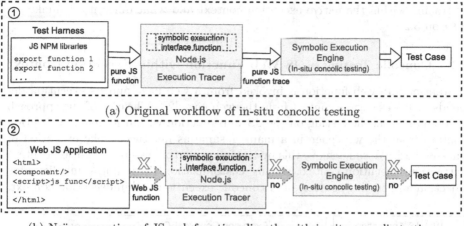

(a) Original workflow of in-situ concolic testing

(b) Naïve execution of JS web function directly with in-situ concolic testing

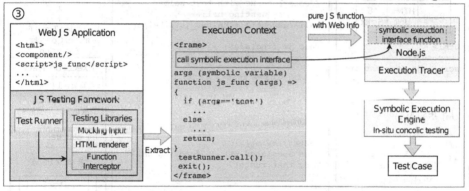

(c) Workflow for enabling effective in-situ concolic testing on front-end JS

Fig. 3: Overview for concolic testing of front-end JS

3. Workflow 3 in Figure 3c illustrates how we leverage a JS testing framework to extract the front-end JS web function and its execution context from the web page. In the extraction, we encapsulate them as a pure JS function augmented with the web page information, inject symbolic values and capture execution traces for later symbolic analysis by calling the symbolic execution interface functions within the extracted execution context. We then utilize the test runner of the JS testing framework to initiate and drive concolic testing within the execution context to generate new test data.

This workflow allows faithful simulation of the execution context of a JS web function without the presence of a web browser. It enables injection of symbolic variables and captures of concrete execution traces within the execution context of the JS web function under test. A concise and accurate concrete execution trace can greatly improve the effectiveness and efficiency of the following symbolic analysis for test generation. We explain how to decide the starting point of tracing within the native execution context and what difference it makes in Section 3.2.

3.2   Concolic Testing of JS Web Function within Execution Context

A front-end JS web function is invoked from a web page and its execution depends on the execution context from the web page [28]. The core of our approach is to enable concolic testing on the JS web function within its native execution context from the web page in a manner same as in-situ concolic execution of back-end JS. We can achieve this by the following three steps: execution context extraction, execution context tracing customization (including symbolic value injection and tracing control), and concolic execution within execution context.

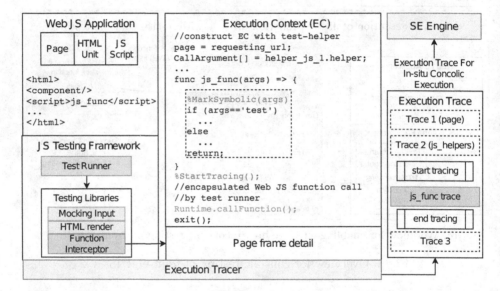

Fig. 4: Concolic testing of JS Web function within execution context

Execution Context Extraction To transform a JS web function to a pure JS function without losing its context of a web page, we introduce a `function interceptor` to the JS testing framework to serve this purpose. As shown in Figure 4, the `function interceptor` completes the following tasks to finish this transformation in order to suit later in-situ concolic testing in the back-end:

- First, the `function interceptor` requests the page frame detail of the web page where the targeted JS web function resides, utilizing the existing mocking data and the `HTML render` function. The mocking data and the `HTML render` function are usually created manually and included in the unit test suite.
- Second, from the page frame detail, the `function interceptor` identifies the function body in a pure JS form given the function name. To preserve the

JS function's native web environment, it extracts the associated execution context of the web page. This is realized by calling helper functions provided by the testing libraries of the JS testing framework. The execution context contains everything that is needed for the pure JS function to be executed in the web page, which includes the arguments of the function, its concrete dependency objects set by mocking data and the function scope.

– Third, the `function interceptor` delivers a complete function in the pure JS form encapsulated with its associated web execution context by assembling them, and then makes it accessible for the test runner of the JS testing framework so that the test runner can initiate the concolic execution in the execution context when running the test suite.

Execution Context Tracing Customization In-situ concolic testing offers the capability of tracing inside the V8 JS engine to capture the execution trace that closely matches the JS bytecode interpretation [9,22]. The conciseness of an execution trace determines the efficiency and the effectiveness of later symbolic analysis and test case generation. Therefore, to make the most of this capability, we pinpoint the locations of where to introduce symbolic values and start tracing during the extraction of the execution context, before we commence concolic testing on the encapsulated JS web function with its execution context. In situ concolic testing provides interface functions for introducing the symbolic values (`MarkSymbolic()`) and tracing control (`StartTracing()`). We use these interface functions to customize execution context tracing as needed.

Symbolic Value Injection and Tracing Control A JS testing frameworks uses a test runner to execute its test suites. As shown in Figure 5, the test runner prepares the dependencies for setting up the testing environment and loads the JS libraries the test suites need before starting run the individual function under test. In order to avoid tracing the unnecessary startup overhead of the test runner

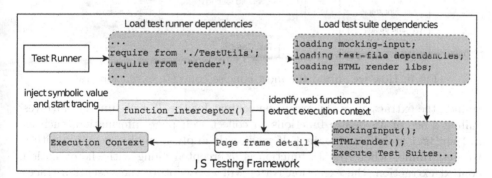

Fig. 5: How to avoid unnecessary tracing of the test runner setup by delaying injection of symbolic values and start of tracing

(indicated by the red box in Figure 5), we choose to inject symbolic values inside the execution context and start tracing when the test runner actually executes the encapsulated function, by calling the interface functions the in-situ concolic testing provides. This way the execution tracer only captures the execution trace of the encapsulated JS web function. The locations for injecting symbolic values and starting tracing are indicated in the "Execution Context (EC)" box in Figure 4 and the captured execution trace is indicated by the "Execution Trace" box in the right corner of Figure 4.

Most Concise Execution Trace Figure 6 shows why our approach can obtain the most concise execution trace for the JS web function driven by the test runner of the JS testing framework. Apart from the overhead caused by the test

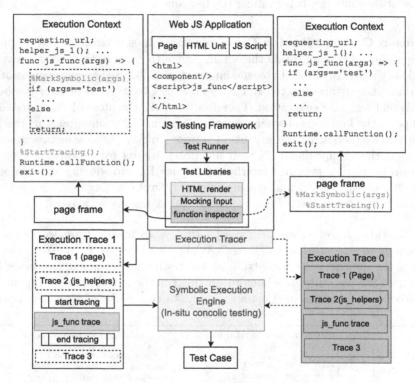

Fig. 6: How we obtain the most concise concrete execution trace

runner, the extraction of the execution context for the JS web function involves calling a set of JS helper functions to collect web page information, such as helper_js_1 and JSHandle_js_1. If we directly apply symbolic execution within the test runner where the JS function is intercepted along with the execution context extraction, the execution tracer will also capture the execution traces of the test runner and the testing helper functions from the testing libraries shown as "Execution Trace 0" in the right-hand side of Figure 6. We modified the test runner to mark symbolic variables and enable tracing control within the execution context. Instead of starting tracing when the test runner starts, we defer the tracing of the execution to when and where the test runner actually executes the encapsulated function under test in the extracted execution context, indicated by the "Execution Trace 1" in the left-hand side of Figure 6. This way we minimize the extend of execution tracing needed.

Concolic Testing within Execution Context We leverage the test runner of the JS testing framework to initiate and start the in-situ concolic testing of the JS web function under test. Typically the test runner starts running the JS web function with an existing unit test. In our approach, the execution of the unit test triggers the `function interceptor`, which starts the process of extracting the execution context and encapsulating the target JS web function. During this process, symbolic values are injected and tracing is started in the right place as described in previous sections. The resulting pure JS application is then executed by in-situ concolic testing. Newly generated test data is fed back to the JS testing framework to drive further concolic testing.

4   Implementations

In this section, we demonstrate the feasibility of our approach to concolic testing of front-end JS functions by implementing it on two popular JS testing frameworks, namely Puppeteer and Jest assisted by the *React* testing library [18,14].

4.1   Implementation on Puppeteer

Puppeteer is a testing framework developed by the Chrome team and implemented as a Node.js library [14]. It provides a high-level API to interact with headless (or full) Chrome. It can simulate browser functions using testing libraries. Puppeteer can execute JS functions residing in a web page without a browser. Puppeteer allows us to easily navigate pages and fetch information about those pages. In the implementation of our approach on Puppeteer, we augment it with the implementation of the `function interceptor` to identify the targeted web JS functions and extract their execution contexts from the web pages and encapsulate them for in-situ concolic testing.

Encapsulating JS Web Function with Execution Context As shown in Figure 7, Puppeteer communicates with the browser [15]. One browser instance can own multiple browser contexts. A `Browser Context` instance defines a browsing session and can have more than one pages. The `Browser Context` provides a way to operate an independent browser session [3]. A `Page` has at least one frame. Each frame has a default execution context. The default execution context is where the frame's JavaScript is executed. This context is returned by `frame.executionContext()` method, which gives the detail about a page frame. We implement the `function interceptor` in the *Execution Context* class under the browser context to collect necessary information for encapsulating a JS function with its associated web execution context. The *Execution Context* class

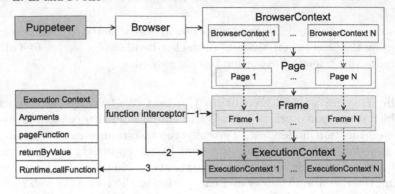

Fig. 7: How Puppeteer executes a JS function in a web page

represents a context for JS execution in the web page. We modified it to identify the page function, its arguments and return value [5]. The `pageFunction` is the function in the HTML page to be evaluated in the execution context, which is in a pure JS form. For example, Listing 1.1 shows a front-end application example written with the *Express* web development framework [6]. This example contains a web page (from line 7 to line 17) with a JS web function marked by `<script>` tag in line 15. The `${path}` points to the JS file that contains the implementation of the JS web function, as shown in Listing 1.2. Our approach is able to encapsulate the pure JS form of the web JS function (its implementation) with its associated web execution context.

Listing 1.1: An example of a front-end web application using Express framework

```
1   const app = express()
2     .use(middleware(compiler, { serverSideRender: true }))
3     .use((req, res) => {
4       const webpackJson =
              res.locals.webpack.devMiddleware.stats.toJson()
5       const paths = getAllJsPaths(webpackJson)
6       res.send(
7         '<!DOCTYPE html>
8         <html>
9           <head>
10            <title>Test</title>
11          </head>
12          <body>
13            <div id="root"></div>
14            ${paths.map((path) =>
15            '<script src="${path}"></script>').join('')}
16          </body>
17        </html>'
18      )
19    })
```

Listing 1.2: An example of a front-end JS script under Express framework

```
1  function foo(args) {
2      if(args === 'foo'){
3          return 'match';
4      }
5      return 'not match';
6  }
7  module.exports = foo;
```

Execution Context Tracing Customization We utilize the *page.evaluate* function of the *Puppeteer* testing framework to drive the JS function under test and extend it with the `function interceptor`. As described in Figure 8, to enable customized execution context tracing, the `function interceptor` introduces symbolic variables and set the starting point for tracing within the web execution context of the JS function wrapped by the `<script>` tag in the web page. This way, we make it possible for the test runner to initiate concolic testing when it starts running the test suites so that JS function can be tested concolically and automatically without tracing additional overheads. Since the `Execution Context` is triggered by the `evaluate` function in unit tests. We target applications from GitHub that uses *Puppeteer* to test front-end features and utilizes `evaluate` in unit testing. We will discuss the results later in Section 5.

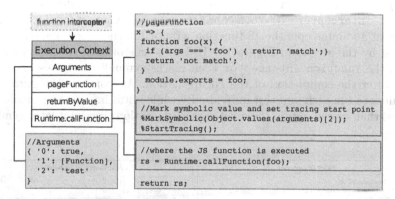

Fig. 8: How we set symbolic variables in the execution context and enable customized execution context tracing in *Puppeteer*

4.2 Implementation on Jest with React Testing Library

Another implementation of our approach is on the *Jest* testing framework assisted by the *React* testing library for unit testing. The *React* testing library is a lightweight library for testing *React* components that wrap the JS functions with the HTML elements [18]. As shown in Figure 9, there are three components in the application as indicated by the numbers. Components allow the splitting of a UI into independent, reusable pieces, and designing each piece in isolation. *React* is flexible; however, it has a strict rule: all *React* components must act as pure functions with respect to their inputs [16]. We refer to them as "functional components". They accept arbitrary inputs (called "props") and return React elements describing what should appear on the web page [17]. An individual component can be reused in different combinations. Therefore, the correctness of an individual component is important with the respect to the correctness of their compositions. In our implementation, we only consider components that have at least one input.

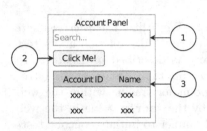

Fig. 9: Example React Components

Jest has a test runner, which allows us to run tests from the command line. Jest also provides additional utilities such as mocks, stubs, etc., besides the utilities of test cases, assertions, and test suites. We use Jest's mock data to set up the testing environment for the front-end components defined with *React*. Figure 10 shows how we leverage and extend *Jest* assisted by *React* testing library to apply the in-situ concolic testing to React component. To encapsulate the JS function in the component with its execution context, we aug-

mented the **render** function, whose functionality is to render the *React* component function and props as an individual unit for *Jest* to execute from the web page, with the **function interceptor**. Through the **render** function, the **function interceptor** extracts a complete execution context for the functional component and intercepts the JS function wrapped in the functional component indicated by the arrows in Figure 10. To enable customized execution context tracing, the **function interceptor** then marks symbolic variables and starts tracing after the completion of the encapsulation. At last, we configure *Jest*'s test runner to run each unit test individually while initiating in-situ concolic execution so that we can obtain the most concise execution traces for later symbolic analysis.

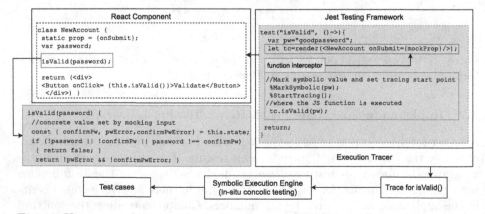

Fig. 10: How to apply in-situ concolic testing on React components using *Jest*

5 Evaluations

For evaluations, we apply our approach to in-situ concolic testing on front-end JS web application projects that come with unit test suites. They are utilizing Jest with *React* testing library and Puppeteer. In these evaluations, we target the String and Number types as symbolic variables for the functions under test.

5.1 Evaluation of *Puppeteer* Implementation on Github Projects

We have selected 21 GitHub projects utilizing *Puppeteer*. We test them using the *Puppeteer* framework extended with our concolic testing capability. As a result, we discovered 4 bugs triggered from their web pages and 2 of them originated from their dependency libraries.

Evaluation Setup We selected GitHub projects with the following properties as as our targets:

(1) They use *Puppeteer* for unit testing of their JS web features;
(2) They have JS functions in web pages and such functions have at least one argument whose type is string or number;
(3) They utilize evaluate in their unit tests.

We have developed a script based on such properties and used the searching API provided by GitHub to collect applicable projects [20]. 21 projects were collected. Table 1 summarizes the demographics of the 21 GitHub projects collected by our script. We calculated the statistics using *ls-files* [7] combined with *cloc* provided by GitHub [8]. The LoC/JS is the LoC (lines of code) of all JS files, which includes the JS files of the libraries the project depends on. The LoC/HTML is the LoC of HTML files, which indicates the volume of its front-end web contents. The LoC of unit tests (LoC/unit test) includes the unit test files ending with .test.js. The test ratio is the ratio between the LoC/unit test over the LoC/JS, indicating the availability of unit tests for the projects. Before evaluation, we configure these projects to use the extended Puppeteer framework instead of the original one.

Result Analysis We ran each project with our approach for 30 minutes. On average, our implementation generates 200 to 400 test cases for each function. Table 2 summarizes the bugs detected. For polymer, our method generates two types of test cases that trigger two different bugs in user password validation functionalities of the project: 1) a generated test case induces execution to skip an *if* branch, which causes the password to be undefined, leading to the condition !password || this.password === password to return true, which should have returned false. We have fixed this bug by changing the operator || to &&. 2) test cases containing *unicode* characters fail password pattern matching using regular expression without g flag, i.e., /[!@#$%&*(),.?":|<>]/.test(value). For InsugarTrading, a test case of a string not containing comma is generated for

Table 1: Selected Projects that utilize *Puppeteer* for unit testing

name	LoC/JS	LoC/HTML	LoC/unit test	test ratio
keepfast	15835	514	58	8.61
DragAndScale*	982	16	370	77.49
affiliate	306	13	197	64.37
ecowetrics	3363	339	0	0
phantomas	5973	655	1440	24.10
polymer*	5399	157	2045	37.87
Insugar*	1967	32	410	20.84
wolkenkit*	1618	15	0	0
vidi	192048	2430	3505	1.82
vue*	849	125	0	0
weatherzen	333	45	0	0
querystringme	835	12	191	22.87
avocode*	5330	9	0	0
Odoo	1303	528	92	7.06
easy	54620	25141	4081	7.47
drag-and-scale	1100	24	548	88.09
My-first*	22729	808	0	0
boxtree	2033	48	1434	70.53
foundation	967	0	18	1.86
treezjs	109975	1475	8519	7.74
TicTacToe	543	442	243	44.75

`str.split(',')` function. The return value of an empty array causes errors in the dependency library `cookie-connoisseur`. A number out-of-bound error is discovered in the `changeCell()` function of TicTacToe. For phantomas, function `phantomas` has a check for `url` to be the string type but does not have pattern matching for it. A generated test case with an invalid `url` causes an exception in function `addScriptToEvaluateOnNewDocument` of *chromeDevTools*.

Table 2: Bugs detected in web applications using Puppeteer from Github

GitHub Projects	Bugs	Error Sources
polymer	Passwords fail validate and match	validator-match.js
InsugarTrading	Empty array caused by invalid string	cookie-connoisseur
TicTacToe	changeCell() out of bound	game.js
phantomas	Invalid string for url due to lack of pattern matching	chromeDevTools

We identified two traits of the projects for which we did not detect bugs in. (1) A project does not fit the design of our Puppeteer implementation, i.e., `evaluate` is not used in the test suite. (2) The applicable JS part is small and well tested.

5.2   Evaluation of Jest Implementation on *Metamask*

In evaluation of the implementation of our concolic testing approach on Jest, we focus on Metamask's browser extension for Chrome. MetaMask is a software crypto-currency wallet used to interact with the Ethereum blockchain. It allows users to access their Ethereum wallet through a browser extension or mobile app, which can then be used to interact with decentralized applications [12]. *Metamask* extension utilizes the `render` functionality for testing JS functions in *React* components. We focus on front-end JS web functions, *React* component functions in particular. They reside in the `ui` folder of the *metamask-extension* project.

Testing Coverage Statistics of *Metamask* We select the `ui` folder as our evaluation target for two reasons: (1) *React* components of *metamask-extension* are mostly defined and implemented under this folder; (2) the functions in this folder is under tested. Figure 11 shows the current testing coverage statistics of the `ui` folder of *metamask-extension* [1]. We can see that only one sub-folder of `ui` (which also happens to be named as `ui`) has a relatively high coverage of 82.03%. Most other folders have coverage under 70% or even lower coverage.

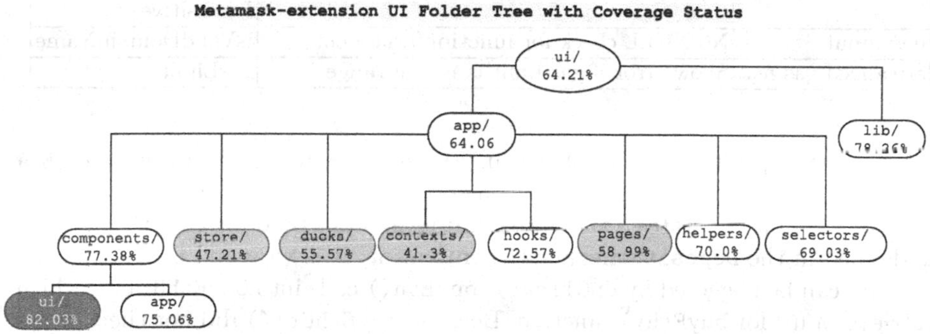

Fig. 11: Coverage statistics of `ui` folder of Metamask-extension

Evaluation Setup In the unit testing workflow of *metamask-extension*, there is a global configuration for all unit test suites of UI components. This is because one component's functionality may depend on other components. Therefore, *metamask-extension* needs to be executed as an instance to support unit testing. To evaluate the implementation of in-situ concolic testing for *React* components, we need an independent environment for each component function wrapped with a single test file. This test file only contains one function under test. Therefore, each test file is an independent in-situ concolic testing runner for a function in a component. We implement an evaluation setup script to complete this task. This script automatically prepares the evaluation environment for in-situ concolic testing of a *React* component. Specifically, it does the following work under the folder where the target component resides:

- *Jest* Configuration. Configure *Jest* for the individual component test file with an independent `jest.config.js`
- Babel Configuration. Configure `Babel` for the component test file to take JS native syntax, which is required by in-situ concolic testing. This is because *metamask-extension* JS source files are transformed using `Babel`.

– Dependency Installation. Collect and install dependencies for the target component. Such dependencies can be components or libraries.

Result Analysis After we set up the evaluation environment, we can conduct our evaluation in a sandbox on the test network of *Metamask*. We have uncovered 3 bugs and 1 test suite improvement as shown in Table 3. We have filed them as bug reports through GitHub. They have been accepted by *Metamask* developers. Along the way, we also found some similar test cases that *Metamask*'s bot reported.

Table 3: Bugs Detected in Metamask under UI folder

Features	Bugs	Functions
buy-eth	Missing checks for if the returned url is null causes page to return 500 in test network	buyEth
token-search	Syntax error without boundary checking	isEqualCase-Insensitive
ens-input	No NULL check for function argument	isValidDomainName
advanced-gas-fee	Show error if gas limit is not in range	gasLimit

For the buy-eth feature as shown in Figure 12, a test network error with a respond code of 500 was triggered when testing the Ether deposit functionality. Concolic testing generates a test case of an invalid `chainId` for `buyEth()`, which is defined in the `DepositEtherModal` component. It is wrapped by a `<Button>` tag and can be triggered by `onClick()`. `buyEth()` calls into `buyEthUrl()`, which retrieves a url for `buyEth()` function. Because `buyEthUrl()` did not check if the url is valid or null before it calls `openTab(url)` with the returned url. And there is also no validation for input in the component implementation. Additionally, this process was not wrapped in a `try/catch` block. We caught this error in our evaluation. We tested 16 component folders and discovered that *metamask-extension* most likely will ignore input checking if inputs are not directly from users. `chainId` is retrieved from mock data in this case, which is generated by our concolic engine.

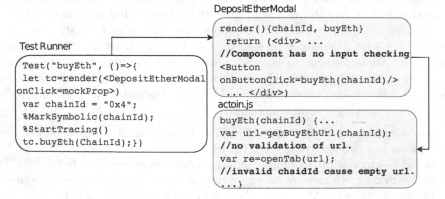

Fig. 12: Error trace of the bug discovered in buy-eth

For the token-search feature, we uncovered a bug triggered by an empty string. In the TokenSearch component, function handleSearch() is wrapped by <TextField> with onChange method. It calls isEqualCaseInsensitive() with an empty string as its second argument without boundary checking. Function isEqualCaseInsensitive is defined in utils.js, which provides shared functions. We found that the unit testing for utils.js do not have test suites for that function, while the same bug is not found in the experiment conducted on the send.js file. In send.js, function validateRecipientUserInput also calls the incorrect function isEqualCaseInsensitive. However, since send.js checks for both empty string and null inputs before calling the faulty function, it avoids the potential error in utils.js.

For the ens-input feature, in the onChange method of component EnsInput's <input/>, the function isValidDomain is called. Our approach generated test cases with unacceptable ASCII characters in the domain name, e.g., %ff.bar. We replay this test case, function isValidDomain returns true when it should return false. In Listing 1.3, function isValidDomain returns the value of the condition match !== undefined. This test case made through regex matching and returned null but null is not equal to undefined in JS.

Listing 1.3: A code segment of utils.js with function isValidDomain showing incorrect behavior in line 8

```
1  function isValidDomainName(\%ff bar) {
2    var match = punycode
3      .toASCII(address)
4      .match(
5        /^(?:[a-z0-9](?:[-a-z0-9]*[a-z0-9])?\.)+[a-z0-9][-a
           -z0-9]*[a-z0-9]$/u,
6      );
7    //After match function, returning string match=null;
         therefore, match !== undefined return true.
8    return match !== undefined;
9  }
```

For the advanced-gas-fee feature, we found the updateGasLimit(gasLimit) function (expecting a numeric input) in the <FormField> component has wrong behavior when given a string input containing only digits such as "908832". The function simply sets the gas limit to 0 without emitting error. We do not consider this as a bug since component <FormField> restricted the input to be numeric in the HTML element. After we filed it, this has been marked with the area-testSuite tag on GitHub by developers as a test suite improvement.

6   Related Work

Our approach is closely related to work on symbolic execution for JS. Most of them aim at back-end/standalone JS programs, primarily target specific bug patterns and depend on whole-program analysis. Jalangi works on pure JS programs and instruments the source JS code to collect path constraints and data for replaying [38]. COSETTE is another symbolic execution engine for JS using an intermediate representation, namely JSIL, translated from JS [36]. ExpoSE applies symbolic execution on standalone JS and uses JALANGI as its symbolic execution engine. ExpoSE's contribution is in addressing the limitation that JALANGI has, which is to support regular expressions for JS [33]. There are few symbolic analysis frameworks for JS web applications. Oblique injects symbolic JS library into the page's HTML. When a user loads the page, it conducts a symbolic page load to explore the possible behaviors of a web browser and a web server during the page load process. It generates a list of pre-fetch `url` for client-side to speed up page load [30]. It is an extension of the ExpoSE concolic engine. SymJS is a framework for testing client-side JS script and mainly focus on automatically discovering and exploring web events [31]. It modifies Rhino JS engine for symbolic execution [27,19]. Kudzu targets AJAX applications and focuses on discovering code injection vulnerabilities by implementing a dynamic symbolic interpreter that takes a simplified intermediate language for JS [37]. To the best of our knowledge, there has been no publicly available symbolic execution engines targeting JS functions embedded in front-end web pages [32].

Another related approach to JS testing is fuzzing, which typically uses code coverage as feedback to test generation. There are a few fuzzers for JS, e.g., *jsfuzz* [11] and *js-fuzz* [10], which are largely based on the fuzzing logic of AFL (American fuzzy lop) [2] and re-implemented it for JS. We view fuzzing and symbolic/concolic testing as complementing techniques: fuzzing for broader exploration of JS while symbolic/concolic testing for deeper exploration.

7   Conclusions

We have presented a novel approach to apply concolic execution to front-end JS. The approach makes use of an in-situ concolic executor for JS and leverages the functionality of JS testing frameworks as test runners and web content extractors. Our approach works in three steps: (1) extracting JS functions from web pages using with JS testing framework; (2) integrating the in-situ concolic testing interface in the execution context for the JS Web functions; (3) utilizing the testing framework's test runner and its mock data as the driver for concolic execution to generate additional test data for the JS web function under test.

We have conducted evaluation on open-source projects from Github and on *Metamask*'s UI features, which are proper targets for our implementations on Puppeteer and Jest respectively. We have found bugs in each evaluation, whose bug reports have been accepted on GitHub. This contributes to both bug finding and test suite improvement for the applications tested. The results show that our approach to concolic testing frontend JS is both practically and effective.

Acknowledgements. This research received financial support in part from National Science Foundation (Grant #: 1908571).

References

1. Metamask-extension coveralls. https://coveralls.io/github/MetaMask/metamask-extension (Mar 2021)
2. Afl: American fuzzy lop. http://lcamtuf.coredump.cx/afl/ (Jan 2022)
3. Browser context. https://pptr.dev/api/puppeteer.browser (Oct 2022)
4. Building a javascript testing framework. https://cpojer.net/posts/building-a-javascript-testing-framework#building-a-testing-framework (Oct 2022)
5. Executioncontext class. https://pub.dev/documentation/puppeteer/latest/puppeteer/ExecutionContext-class.html (Oct 2022)
6. Express. https://expressjs.com/ (Oct 2022)
7. git-ls-files. https://git-scm.com/docs/git-ls-files (Oct 2022)
8. git-ls-files. https://github.com/AlDanial/cloc (Oct 2022)
9. Zhe, L., Fei, X.: In-situ concolic testing of javascript. In: Proceedings of the 30th IEEE International Conference on Software Analysis, Evolution and Reengineering (2023)
10. js-fuzz. https://github.com/connor4312/js-fuzz (Jan 2022)
11. Jsfuzz: coverage-guided fuzz testing for javascript. https://github.com/fuzzitdev/jsfuzz (Jan 2022)
12. Metamask. https://metamask.io/ (Oct 2022)
13. Node.js. https://nodejs.org/en/ (Oct 2022)
14. Puppeteer. https://pptr.dev/ (Oct 2022)
15. Puppeteer architecture. https://devdocs.io/puppeteer (Oct 2022)
16. React component. https://reactjs.org/docs/react-component.html (Oct 2022)
17. React component. https://reactjs.org/docs/components-and-props.html (Oct 2022)
18. React testing library. https://testing-library.com/docs/react-testing-library/intro/ (Oct 2022)
19. Rhino: Javascript in java. http://mozilla.github.io/rhino (Oct 2022)
20. Search: The search api lets you to search for specific items on github. https://docs.github.com/en/rest/search (Oct 2022)
21. Six essential frameworks for creating automated tests. https://dzone.com/refcardz/javascript-test-automation-frameworks (Oct 2022)
22. Understanding v8's bytecode. https://medium.com/dailyjs/understanding-v8s-bytecode-317d46c94775 (Oct 2022)
23. Usage statistics of javascript as client-side programming language on websites. https://w3techs.com/technologies/details/cp-javascript (Oct 2022)
24. v8. https://v8.dev/ (Oct 2022)
25. Araki, L.Y., Peres, L.M.: A systematic review of concolic testing with aplication of test criteria. In: ICEIS (2018)
26. Baldoni, R., Coppa, E., D'elia, D.C., Demetrescu, C., Finocchi, I.: A survey of symbolic execution techniques. ACM Comput. Surv. **51**(3) (May 2018). https://doi.org/10.1145/3182657, https://doi.org/10.1145/3182657
27. JIN, X.o., ZHONG, B.y., LI, X.: Research and implementation of interpreting javascript dynamic web page based on rhino engine [j]. Computer Technology and Development **2**(002) (2008)

28. Jueckstock, J., Kapravelos, A.: Visiblev8: In-browser monitoring of javascript in the wild. In: Proceedings of the Internet Measurement Conference. p. 393–405. IMC '19, Association for Computing Machinery, New York, NY, USA (2019). https://doi.org/10.1145/3355369.3355599, `https://doi.org/10.1145/3355369.3355599`

29. King, J.C.: Symbolic execution and program testing. Commun. ACM **19**(7), 385–394 (jul 1976). https://doi.org/10.1145/360248.360252, `https://doi.org/10.1145/360248.360252`

30. Ko, R., Mickens, J., Loring, B., Netravali, R.: Oblique: Accelerating page loads using symbolic execution. In: 18th USENIX Symposium on Networked Systems Design and Implementation (NSDI 21). pp. 289–302. USENIX Association (Apr 2021), `https://www.usenix.org/conference/nsdi21/presentation/ko`

31. Li, G., Andreasen, E., Ghosh, I.: Symjs: automatic symbolic testing of javascript web applications. In: Proceedings of the 22nd ACM SIGSOFT International Symposium on Foundations of Software Engineering. pp. 449–459 (2014)

32. Li, Y.F., Das, P.K., Dowe, D.L.: Two decades of web application testing—a survey of recent advances. Information Systems **43**, 20–54 (2014)

33. Loring, B., Mitchell, D., Kinder, J.: Expose: practical symbolic execution of standalone javascript. In: Proceedings of the 24th ACM SIGSOFT International SPIN Symposium on Model Checking of Software. pp. 196–199 (2017)

34. Mirshokraie, S., Mesbah, A., Pattabiraman, K.: Jseft: Automated javascript unit test generation. In: 2015 IEEE 8th International Conference on Software Testing, Verification and Validation (ICST). pp. 1–10. IEEE (2015)

35. Powers, B., Vilk, J., Berger, E.D.: Browsix: Bridging the gap between unix and the browser. In: Proceedings of the Twenty-Second International Conference on Architectural Support for Programming Languages and Operating Systems. p. 253–266. ASPLOS '17, Association for Computing Machinery, New York, NY, USA (2017). https://doi.org/10.1145/3037697.3037727, `https://doi.org/10.1145/3037697.3037727`

36. Santos, J.F., Maksimović, P., Grohens, T., Dolby, J., Gardner, P.: Symbolic execution for javascript. In: Proceedings of the 20th International Symposium on Principles and Practice of Declarative Programming. pp. 1–14 (2018)

37. Saxena, P., Akhawe, D., Hanna, S., Mao, F., McCamant, S., Song, D.: A symbolic execution framework for javascript. In: 2010 IEEE Symposium on Security and Privacy. pp. 513–528 (2010). https://doi.org/10.1109/SP.2010.38

38. Sen, K., Kalasapur, S., Brutch, T., Gibbs, S.: Jalangi: A selective record-replay and dynamic analysis framework for javascript. In: Proceedings of the 2013 9th Joint Meeting on Foundations of Software Engineering. pp. 488–498 (2013)

39. Thakkar, M.: Unit Testing Using Jest, pp. 153–174. Apress, Berkeley, CA (2020). https://doi.org/10.1007/978-1-4842-5869-9_5, `https://doi.org/10.1007/978-1-4842-5869-9_5`

Democratizing Quality-Based Machine Learning Development through Extended Feature Models*

Giordano d'Aloisio^(✉) , Antinisca Di Marco , and Giovanni Stilo

University of L'Aquila, L'Aquila, Italy
giordano.daloisio@graduate.univaq.it
{antinisca.dimarco,giovanni.stilo}@univaq.it

Abstract. ML systems have become an essential tool for experts of many domains, data scientists and researchers, allowing them to find answers to many complex business questions starting from raw datasets. Nevertheless, the development of ML systems able to satisfy the stakeholders' needs requires an appropriate amount of knowledge about the ML domain. Over the years, several solutions have been proposed to automate the development of ML systems. However, an approach taking into account the new quality concerns needed by ML systems (like fairness, interpretability, privacy, and others) is still missing.

In this paper, we propose a new engineering approach for the quality-based development of ML systems by realizing a workflow formalized as a Software Product Line through Extended Feature Models to generate an ML System satisfying the required quality constraints. The proposed approach leverages an experimental environment that applies all the settings to enhance a given Quality Attribute, and selects the best one. The experimental environment is general and can be used for future quality methods' evaluations. Finally, we demonstrate the usefulness of our approach in the context of multi-class classification problem and fairness quality attribute.

Keywords: Machine Learning System · Software Quality · Feature Models · Software Product Line · Low-code development

1 Introduction

Machine Learning (ML) systems are increasingly becoming used instruments, applied to all application domains and affecting our real life. The development

---

* This work has been partially supported by EMELIOT national research project, which has been funded by the MUR under the PRIN 2020 program (Contract 2020W3A5FY) and by European Union – Horizon 2020 Program under the scheme "INFRAIA-01-2018-2019 – Integrating Activities for Advanced Communities", Grant Agreement n.871042, "SoBigData++: European Integrated Infrastructure for Social Mining and Big Data Analytics" (http://www.sobigdata.eu)

L. Lambers and S. Uchitel (Eds.): FASE 2023, LNCS 13991, pp. 88–110, 2023.
https://doi.org/10.1007/978-3-031-30826-0_5

of ML systems usually requires a good knowledge of the underlying ML approaches to choose the best techniques and models to solve the targeted problem. Many methods have been developed in the last years to automate some ML systems development phases and help non-technical users [61,31,34]. However, these techniques do not consider the *quality properties* essential for ML systems, such as dataset's Privacy, model's Interpretability, Explainability, and Fairness [50,46,12]. Indeed, if we consider the impact that ML applications have in our lives, it is clear how assuring that these quality properties are satisfied is of paramount importance (look for instance at some of the 17 sustainable development goals proposed by the United Nations [51]).

In this paper, we present MANILA (Model bAsed developmeNt of machIne Learning systems with quAlity), a novel approach which will democratize the quality-based development of ML systems by means of a low-code platform [62]. The goal of our approach is to provide an environment for the automatic configuration of experiments that automatically selects the ML System (i.e., ML Algorithm and quality enhancing method) better satisfying a given quality requirement. The requirement is satisfied by finding the best trade-off among the involved quality attributes. This will simplify the work of the data scientist and will make the quality-based development of ML systems also accessible to non-technical users (in other words, *democratize*).

Hence, the main contributions of this paper are the following:

– The identification of key quality attributes in ML systems by selecting the more adopted ones in the literature;
– The specification and realization of a general workflow for the quality-based development of ML systems. This workflow is derived from our experience in the quality-based development of ML systems. It leverages an experimental environment that evaluates all the methods to enhance a given quality attribute, and selects the one performing better. Such workflow can be modelled as a Software Product Line (SPL);
– The specification of an Extended Feature Models (ExtFM) [38,9] that implements the SPL, where the variation points are identified by all the components needed to generate a quality experiment. The ExtFM guides the data scientist through a low-code workflow configuration;
– The generation, from the workflow configuration, of an actual Python implementation of the experiment to find the ML System that better satisfies a given quality constraint. The generated experimental environment is general and can be used in the future to evaluate other methods to enhance a given quality property.

This paper is organized as follows: in section 2 we discuss related works related to quality engineering of ML systems. In section 3, we present the selected quality attributes and discuss how they affect ML systems. Section 4 is devoted to presenting a general workflow to choose the ML system achieving the best-given quality attributes. This general workflow has been the motivating scenario for MANILA. In section 5, we present MANILA by describing in detail the implemented ExtFM and explaining each step of the quality-based development of ML systems. Section 6 is dedicated to a proof of concept of the developed modelling framework by reproducing a case study. Section 7 describes some threats to validity, and finally, section 8 presents some discussions, describes future work, and wraps up the paper.

2   Related Work

The problem of quality assurance in machine learning systems has gained much relevance in the last years. Many articles highlight the needing of defining and formalizing new standard quality attributes for machine learning systems [30,65,70] [50,12,46]. Most of the works in the literature focus either on the identification of the most relevant quality attributes for ML systems or on the formalization of them in the context of ML systems development.

Concerning the identification of quality attributes in ML systems, the authors of [40,72] identify three main components in which quality attributes can be found: **Training Data**, **ML Models** and **ML Platforms**. The quality of **Training Data** is usually evaluated with properties such as *privacy, bias, number of missing values, expressiveness*. For **ML Model**, the authors mean the trained model used by the system. The quality of this component is usually evaluated by *fairness, explainability, interpretability, security*. Finally, the **ML Platform** is the implementation of the system, which is affected mostly by *security* and *performance reliability and availability*. Muccini et al. identify in [50] a set of quality properties as stakeholders' constraints and highlight the needing of considering them during the *Architecture Definition* phase. The quality attributes are: *data quality, ethics, privacy, fairness, ML models' performance*, etc. Martinez-Fernàndez et al. also highlight in [46] the needing of formalizing quality properties in ML systems and to update the software quality requirements defined by ISO 25000 [36]. The most relevant properties highlighted by the authors concern: *ML safety, ML ethics*, and *ML explainability*. In our work, we focus on quality properties that arises during the development of ML systems such as, *fairness, explainability, interpretability*, and dataset's *privacy*, while we leave other quality properties (e.g., *performance*) that arises during other phases (e.g., deployment) for future works.

Many solutions have been proposed to formalize and model standard quality assurance process in ML systems. Amershi et al., have been the first authors to identify a set of common steps that identify each ML system development [5]. In particular, each ML system is identified by nine stages that go from data collection and cleaning, to model training and evaluation, and finally to the deployment and monitoring of the ML model. Their work has been the foundation of many subsequent papers on quality modelling of ML systems. *CRISP_ML* (*Cross-Industry Standard Process model for Machine Learning*) is a process model proposed by Studer et al. [66], extending the more known *CRISP_DL* [45] process model to ML systems. They identify a set of common phases for the building of ML systems namely: *Business and Data understanding, Data preparation, Modeling, Evaluation, Deployment, Monitoring and Maintenance.*

For each phase, the authors identify a set of functional quality properties to guarantee the quality of such systems. Similarly, the *Quality for Artificial Intelligence* (*Q4AI*) consortium proposed a set of guidelines [32] for the quality assurance of ML systems for specific domains: *generative systems, operational data in process systems, voice user interface system, autonomous driving* and *AI OCR*. For each domain, the authors identify a set of properties and metrics to ensure quality. Concerning the modelling of quality requirements, Azimi et al. proposed a layered model for the quality assurance of machine learning systems in the context of Internet of Things (IoT) [7]. The model is made of two layers: *Source Data* and *ML Function/Model*. For the *Source Data*, a set of quality attributes are defined: *completeness, consistency, conformity, accuracy, integrity, timeliness*. Machine learning models are instead classified into *predictors, estimators* and *adapters* and a set of quality attributes are defined for each of them: *accuracy, correctness, completeness, effectiveness, optimality*. Each system is then influenced by a subset of quality characteristics based on the type of ML model and the required data. Ishikawa proposed, instead, a framework for the quality evaluation of an ML system [35]. The framework defines these components for ML applications: *dataset, algorithm, ML component* and *system*, and, for each of them, proposed an argumentation approach to assess quality. Finally, Siebert et al. [64] proposed a formal modelling definition for quality requirements in ML systems. They start from the process definition in [45] and build a meta-model for the description of quality requirements. The meta-model is made of the following classes: *Entity* (which can be defined at various levels of abstraction, such as the whole system or a specific component of the system), *Property* (also expressed at different levels of abstraction), *Evaluation* and *Measure* related to the property. Starting from this meta-model, the authors build a tree model to evaluate the quality of the different components of the system. From this analysis, we can conclude that there is a robust research motivation in formalizing and defining new quality attributes for ML systems. Many attempts have been proposed to solve these issues, and several quality properties, metrics and definitions of ML systems can now be extracted from the literature. However a framework that actually guides the data scientist through the development of a ML systems satisfying quality properties is still missing.In this paper, we aim to solve these concerns by proposing MANILA, a novel approach which will democratize the quality-based development of ML systems by means of a low-code platform. In particular, we model a general workflow for the quality-based development of ML systems as a SPL through the ExtFM formalism. Next, we demonstrate how it is possible to generate an actual implementation of such workflow from a low-code experiment configuration and how this workflow is actually able to find the best methods to satisfy a given quality requirement. Recalling the ML development process of [5], MANILA focuses on the *model training* and *model evaluation* development steps by guiding the data scientist in selecting the ML system (i.e., ML algorithm and quality-enhancing method) better satisfying a given quality attribute.

Concerning the adoption of Feature Models to model ML systems, a similar approach has been used by Di Sipio et al. in [24]. In their work, the authors use Feature Models to model ML pipelines for Recommender Systems. The variation points are identified by all the components needed to implement a recommender system (e.g., the ML algorithm to use or the python libraries for the implementation). However, they do not consider quality attributes in their approach.

Finally, concerning assessing quality attributes in ML systems, there is an intense research activity primarily related to the fairness-testing domain [20]. In general, the problem of fairness assurance can be defined as a search-based problem among different ML algorithms and fairness methods [20]. Many tools have been proposed for the automatic fairness test, such as [18,63,69] to cite a few. However, these tools tend to require programming skills and thus are unfriendly to nontechnical stakeholders [20]. In our work, we aim to fill this gap by proposing a low-code framework that, generating and executing suitable experiments, supports (also not expert) users in the quality-based development of ML systems, by returning the trained ML model with best quality.

3   Considered Quality Attributes

In software engineering, a quality requirement specifies criteria that can be used to quantify or qualify the operation of a system rather than to specify its behaviours [19]. To analyse an ML system from a qualitative perspective, we must determine the Quality Attributes (QA) that we can use to judge the system's operation, influencing the ML designers' decisions. We refer to the literature for ML systems to identify the QA to consider [46,50,30,40,70]. In this work, we consider a sub-set of the identified QA, i.e., *Effectiveness*, *Fairness*, *Interpretability*, *Explainability*, and *Privacy*.

Effectiveness. This QA is used to define how good the model must be in predicting outcomes [13]. There are different metrics in the literature to address the Effectiveness of an ML model. Among the most common metrics, we cite *Precision*: fraction of true positives (TP) to the total positive predictions [14]; *Recall*: fraction of TP to the total positive items in the dataset [14]; *F1 Score*: harmonic mean of *Precision* and *Recall* [67]; *Accuracy*: fraction of True Positives (TP) and True Negatives (TN) above the total of predictions [60]. This attribute can be considered crucial in developing an ML system and must always be accounted in the quality evaluation of ML systems [72,13].

Fairness. A ML model can be defined *fair* if it has no prejudice or favouritism towards an individual or a group based on their inherent or acquired characteristics identified by the so-called *sensitive variables* [47]. Sensitive variables are variables of the dataset that can cause prejudice or favouritism towards individuals having a particular value of that variable (e.g., *sex* is a very common sensitive variable, and *women* can be identified as the unprivileged group [47,16,42]). Several metrics can assess the discrimination of an ML system towards sensitive groups (*group fairness metrics*) or single individuals (*individual-fairness metrics*) [47,16].

Interpretability. *Interpretability* can be defined as the ability of a system to enable user-driven explanations of how a model reaches the produced conclusion [15]. Interpretability is one QA that can be estimated without executing an actual ML system. Indeed, ML methods are classified as *whitebox*, i.e., interpretable (e.g., Decision Trees or linear models), and *black-box*, i.e., not interpretable (e.g., Neural Networks) [49]. Interpretability is a very strong property that can hold only for white-box approaches (such as decision trees). Instead, black-box methods (such as neural networks) require the addition of *explainability*-enhancing methods to have their results interpretable [43].

Explainability. *Explainability* can be defined as the ability to make black-box methods' results (which are not interpretable) interpretable [43]. Enhancing the Interpretability of black-box methods has become crucial to guarantee the trustworthiness of ML systems, and several methods have been implemented for this purpose [43]. The quality of explanations can be measured with several metrics that can be categorised as *application-grounded* metrics, which involve an evaluation of the explanations with end-users, *human-grounded* metrics, which include evaluations of explanations with non-domain-experts, and *functionally-grounded* metrics, which use proxies based on a formal definition of interpretability [73].

Privacy. *Privacy* can be defined as the susceptibility of data or datasets to revealing private information [21]. Several metrics can assess the ability to link personal data to an individual, the level of detail or correctness of sensitive information, background information needed to determine private information, etc [71].

4   Motivating Scenario

Today, a data scientist, required to realize an ML system satisfying a given quality constraint, has no automatic support in the development process. Indeed, she follows and manually executes a general experiment workflow aiming at evaluating a set of ML systems obtained by assembling quality assessment and improvement algorithms with the ones solving the specific ML tasks. By running the defined experiment, she aims to find the optimal solution satisfying a given QA constraint.

Algorithm 1 reports the pseudo-code of a generic experiment to assess a generic QA during the development of an ML system. This code has been derived from our previous experience in the quality-based development of ML Systems and by asking researchers studying ML development and quality assessment how they evaluate such properties during ML systems development.

The first step in the experiment workflow is selecting the dataset to use (in this work, we assume that the dataset has already been preprocessed and is ready to train the ML model). Next, the data scientist selects the ML algorithms, the methods enhancing a QA, and the appropriate quality metrics for the evaluation. Then, for each of the chosen ML algorithms, she applies the selected quality methods accordingly to their type, there can be the following options:

Algorithm 1: Quality-evaluation experiment pseudo-code

---

1 select dataset d;
2 select set of ML Algorithms;
3 select set of QA Methods and Metrics;
4 **for** $m \in$ *ML Algorithms* **do**
5   **for** $q \in$ *QA Methods* **do**
6   **if** *q works on d* **then**
7             $\lfloor$ apply q on d;
8   **if** *q works on m before training* **then**
9             $\lfloor$ apply q on m;
10         $f =$ train m;
11   **if** *q works on f* **then**
12            $\lfloor$ apply q on f;
13   compute selected metrics on f;
14 choose report technique;
15 evaluate the results;
16 $Q =$ best QA Method;
17 $M =$ best ML Algorithm;
18 $F =$ train M with full dataset applying Q;
19 **return** F

- if the quality method works on the training set, it has to be applied to the dataset before training the ML algorithm;
- if the quality method works on the ML algorithm before training, then it has to be applied to the ML algorithm before the training phase;
- if the method works on the trained ML algorithm (i.e., f in the code), then it has to be applied after the training of the ML algorithm.

Finally, the data scientist computes the selected metrics for the specific pair of ML and QA methods. After repeating the process for all the selected methods, she chooses a report technique (e.g., table or chart), evaluates the obtained results collected in the report and trains with the entire dataset the ML algorithm performing better by applying the quality method that better achieves the QA. If the data scientist has a threshold to achieve, then she can verify if at least one of the ML and quality methods combinations satisfies the constraint. If so, one of the suitable pair is selected. Otherwise, she has to relax the threshold and repeat the process again.

The workflow described in Algorithm 1 can be generalized as a process of common steps describing any experiment in the considered domain. Figure 1 sketches such a generalization. First, the data scientist selects all the features of the experiment, i.e., the dataset, the ML Methods, the methods assuring a specific QA and the related metrics. we call such a step *Features Selection*. Next, she runs the quality methods using the general approach described in algorithm 1 and evaluates the results (namely, *Experiment Execution*). If the results are

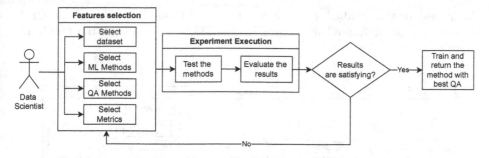

Fig. 1: Manual execution of the quality experiment workflow

satisfying (i.e., they satisfy the quality constraints), then the method with the best QA is returned. Otherwise, the data scientist have to repeat the process.

The described workflow is the foundation of MANILA that aims to formalise and democratise it by providing a SPL and ExtFM-based low-code framework that supports her in development of quality ML systems.

5   MANILA Approach

In this section, we describe MANILA, a framework to formalise and democratise the quality-based development of ML systems. This work is based on the quality properties and the experiment workflow described in sections 3 and 4, respectively.

Our approach aims to automate and ease the quality-based development of ML systems. We achieve this goal by proposing a framework to automatically generate a configuration of an experiment to find the ML system (i.e., ML algorithm and quality enhancing method) better satisfying a given QA. This framework will accelerate the quality-based development of ML systems making it accessible also to not experts.

Recalling the experimental workflow described in section 4, the set of ML models, quality methods and metrics can be considered *variation points* of each experiment, differentiating them from one another. For this reason, we can think of this family of experiments as a Software Product Line (SPL) specified by a Feature Model [6]. Indeed, Feature Models allow us to define a template for families of software products with standard features (i.e., components of the final system) and a set of variability points that differentiate the final systems [38,29]. Features in the model follow a tree-like parent-child relationship and could be *mandatory* or *optional* [29]. Sibling features can belong to an *Or-relationship* or an *Alternative-relationship* [29]. Finally, there could be *Cross-tree* relationships among features not in the same branch. These relationships are expressed using logical propositions [29]. However, traditional Feature Models do not allow associating attributes to features, which are necessary in our case to represent a proper experiment workflow (for instance, to specify the label of the dataset or the number of rounds in a cross-validation [58]). Hence, we relied on the concept of Extended Feature Models [38,9] to represent the family of experiments workflows.

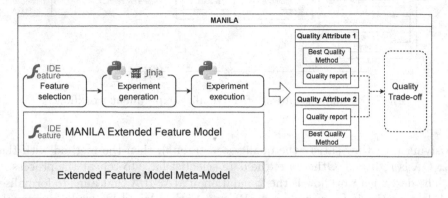

Fig. 2: MANILA approach

Figure 2 details a high-level picture of MANILA, where each rounded box represents a step in the quality-driven development process, while square boxes represent artefacts. Dotted blocks represent steps which have not been implemented yet and will be considered in future works.

The basis of MANILA is the Extended Feature Model (ExtFM), based on the existing ExtFM Meta-Model. The ExtFM is the template of all possible experiments a data scientist can perform and guides her through the quality-based development of an ML system. The first step in the development process is the features selection, in which the data scientist selects all the components of the quality-testing experiment. Next, a Python script implementing the experiment is automatically generated from the selected features. Finally, the experiment is executed, and for each QA selected, it returns:

1. a quality report reporting for each quality method and ML algorithm the related metrics;
2. the ML algorithm with the applied quality enhancing method that better performs with the given QA, trained and ready for production.

In the future, MANILA will analyse the quality reports of each selected QA in order to find the best trade-off among them (for instance, by means of Pareto-front functions). The architecture of MANILA makes it easy to extend. In fact, adding a new method or metric to MANILA just translates to adding a new feature to the ExtFM and adding the proper code implementing it.

Near each step, we report the tools involved in its implementation. The source code of the implemented artefacts is available on Zenodo [23], and GitHub [22]. In the following, we detail the ExtFM and each process step.

5.1 Extended Feature Model

As already mentioned, the ExtFM is the basis of MANILA approach since it defines the template of all possible experiments a data scientist can generate. It has been implemented using *FeatureIDE*, an open-source graphical editor which allows the definition of ExtFMs [68]. Figure 3 shows a short version of the im-

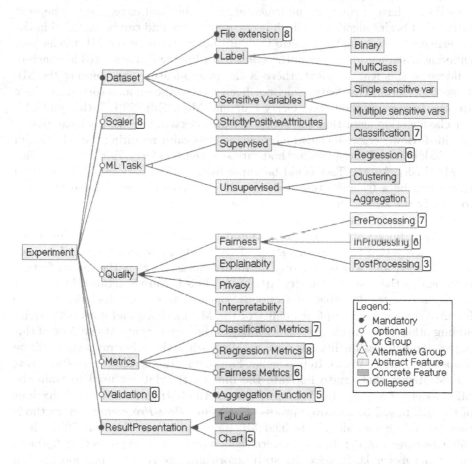

Fig. 3: Short version of the implemented Extended Feature Model

plemented ExtFM[1]. In particular, each experiment is defined by seven macro features, which are then detailed by children's features.

The first mandatory feature is the Dataset. The Dataset has a file extension (e.g., CSV, EXCEL, JSON, and others), and a Label which can be Binary or Multi-Class. The Label feature has two attributes specifying his name and

---

[1] The whole picture can be downloaded here https://anonymous.4open.science/r/
manila-101D/imgs/feature-model.png

the positive value (used to compute fairness metrics). The Dataset could also have one or more sensitive variables that identify sensitive groups subject to unfairness [47]. The sensitive variables have a set of attributes to specify their name and the privileged and unprivileged groups [47]. Finally, there is a feature to specify if the Dataset has only positive attributes. This feature has been included to define a cross-tree constraint with a scaler technique that requires only positive attributes (see table 1). All these features are modelled as abstract since they do not have a concrete implementation in the final experiment. The next feature is a Scaler algorithm, which is not mandatory and can be included in the experiment to scale and normalize the data before training the ML model [54]. Different scaler algorithms from the *scikit-learn* library [55] are listed as concrete children of this feature. Next, there is the macro-feature representing the ML Task to perform. This feature has not been modelled as mandatory since there are two fairness methods (i.e. Gerry Fair and Meta Fair [39,17]) that embed a fair classification algorithm and so, if they are selected, the ML Task can not be specified. However, we included a cross-tree constraint requiring the selection of ML Task if any of these two methods are selected ($\neg$ Gerry Fair $\wedge$ $\neg$ Meta Fair $\Rightarrow$ ML Task). An ML Task could be Supervised or Unsupervised. A Supervised task could be a Classification task or a Regression task and has an attribute to specify the size of the training set. These two abstract features are then detailed by a set of concrete implementations of ML methods selected from the *scikit-learn* library [55]. The Unsupervised learning task could be a Clustering or an Aggregation task. At this stage of the work, these two features have not been detailed and will be explored in future works. Next is the macro feature representing the system's Quality Attributes. This feature is detailed by the four quality attributes described in section 3. Effectiveness is not included in these features since it is an implicit quality of the ML methods and does not require adding other components (i.e. algorithms) in the experiment. At the time of this paper, the Fairness quality has been detailed, while the other properties will be deepened in future works. In particular, Fairness methods can be *Pre-Processing* (i.e. strategies that try to mitigate the bias on the dataset used to train the ML model [47,37,27]), *In-Processing* (i.e. methods that modify the behaviour of the ML model to improve fairness [47,3]), and *Post-Processing* (i.e. methods that re-calibrate an already trained ML model to remove bias [47,56]). These three features are detailed by several concrete features representing fairness-enhancing methods. In selecting such algorithms, we selected methods with a solid implementation, i.e., algorithms integrated into libraries such as *AIF360* [8] or *Fairlearn* [11] or algorithms with a stable source code such as *DEMV* [26] or *Blackbox* [56]. All these quality features have been implemented with an *Or-group* relationship. Forward, the macro feature represents the Metrics to use in the experiment. Metrics are divided among Classification Metrics, Regression Metrics and Fairness Metrics. Each metric category has a set of concrete metrics selected from the *scikit-learn* library [55] and the *AIF360* library [8]. Based on the ML Task and the Quality Attributes selected, the data scientist must select the proper metrics to assess Correctness and the other Quality Attributes. This constraint is formalized by cross-tree relationships among features (see table 1). In addition, a set of Aggregation Functions must be selected if more than one metric is selected. The aggregation function combines the value of the other metrics to give an overall view of the method's behaviour. Forward, there is the optional macro feature identifying the Validation function. Validation functions are different strategies to evaluate the Quality Attributes of an ML model [57]. Several Validation functions are available as children features, and there is an attribute to specify the number of groups in case of cross-validation [57]. The last macro-feature is related to the presentation of the results. Recalling the experiment workflow described in section 4, the results are the metrics' values derived from the execution of the experiment. The results can be presented in a tabular way or using proper charts. Different chart types are available as concrete children features. Finally, table 1 lists the cross-tree constraints defined

Table 1: Extended Feature Model cross-tree constraints

Cross-tree constraints
Single Sensitive Var $\Rightarrow \neg$ Sampling $\wedge \neg$ Blackbox $\wedge \neg$ DIR
Fairness $\Rightarrow$ Sensitive Variables
MultiClass $\Rightarrow \neg$ Reweighing $\wedge \neg$ DIR $\wedge \neg$ Optimized Preprocessing $\wedge \neg$ LFR $\wedge \neg$ Adversarial Debiasing $\wedge \neg$ Gerry Fair $\wedge \neg$ Meta Fair $\wedge \neg$ Prejudice Remover $\wedge \neg$ Calibrated EO $\wedge \neg$ Reject Option
Regression $\Rightarrow \neg$ PostProcessing $\wedge \neg$ Reweighing $\wedge \neg$ DIR $\wedge \neg$ DEMV $\wedge \neg$ Optimized Preprocessing $\wedge \neg$ LFR $\wedge \neg$ Adversarial Debiasing $\wedge \neg$ Gerry Fair $\wedge \neg$ Meta Fair $\wedge \neg$ Prejudice Remover
Exponentiated Gradient $\vee$ Grid Search $\Rightarrow \neg$ MLP Classifier $\wedge \neg$ MLP Regressor
$\neg$ GerryFair $\wedge \neg$ MetaFair $\Rightarrow$ ML Task
Classification $\Longleftrightarrow$ Classification Metrics $\wedge \neg$ Regression Metrics
Classification Metrics $\Longleftrightarrow \neg$ Regression Metrics
Regression $\Longleftrightarrow$ Regression Metrics $\wedge \neg$ Classification Metrics
Fairness $\Rightarrow$ Fairness Metrics
Box Cox Method $\Rightarrow$ Strictly Positive Attributes

in our model. These constraints are useful to guide the data scientist through selecting proper fairness-enhancing methods or metrics based on the Dataset's characteristics (i.e., label type or the number of sensitive variables) or the ML Task.

5.2   Features Selection

From the depicted ExtFM, the data scientist can define her experiment by specifying the needed features inside a *configuration file*. A *configuration file* is an XML file describing the set of selected features and the possible attribute values. The constraints among features defined in the ExtFM will guide the data scientist in the selection by not allowing the selection of features that are in contrast with already selected ones. The editor used to implement the ExtFM [68] provides a GUI for the specification of configuration files, making this process accessible to non-technical users.

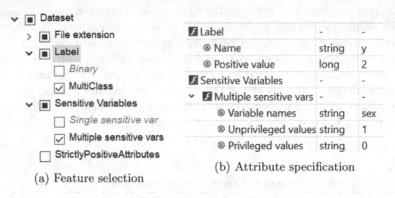

(a) Feature selection

(b) Attribute specification

Fig. 4: Feature selection and attribute specification process

Figure 4 depicts how the features selection and attribute specification processes are done in MANILA. In particular, figure 4a details how the features of the Dataset are selected inside the configuration. Note how features in contrast with already selected ones are automatically disabled by the system (e.g., the *Binary* feature is disabled since the *MultiClass* feature is selected). This automatic cut of the ExtFM guides the data scientist in defining configurations that always lead to valid (i.e., executable) experiments. Figure 4b details how attributes can be specified during the definition of the configuration. In particular, the rightmost column in figure 4b displays the attribute value specified by the data scientist (e.g., the name of the label is y, and the positive value is 2). During the *experiment generation* step, a process will automatically check if all the required attributes (e.g., label name) have been defined. Otherwise, it will ask the data scientist to fill them.

5.3   Experiment generation

From the XML file describing an experiment configuration, it is possible to generate a Python script implementing the defined experiment.

```
<feature automatic="selected" manual="undefined" name="Dataset"/
    >
<feature automatic="selected" manual="undefined" name="Label">
    <attribute name="Positive value" value="2"/>
    <attribute name="Name" value="contr_use"/>
</feature>
<feature automatic="unselected" manual="undefined" name="Binary"
    />
```

```
<feature automatic="undefined" manual="selected" name="
    MultiClass"/>
```

Listing 1.1: Portion of configuration file

Listing 1.1 shows a portion of the configuration file derived from the feature selection process. In particular, it can be seen how the Dataset and the Label features have been automatically selected by the system (features with name="Dataset" and name="Label" and automatic="selected"), the Multi-Class feature has been manually selected by the data scientist (feature with name="MultiClass" and manual="selected"), and the Binary feature was not selected (feature with name="Binary" and both automatic and manual unselected). In addition, the name and the value of two Label attributes (i.e., Positive value equal to 2 and Name equal to contr_use) are reported.

The structure of the configuration file makes it easy to be parsed by a proper script. In MANILA, we implemented a Python parser that reads the configuration file given as input and generates a set of scripts implementing the defined experiment. The parser can be invoked using the Python interpreter with the following command shown in listing 1.2.

```
$ python generator.py -n <CONFIGURATION FILE PATH>
```

Listing 1.2: Python parser invocation

In particular, the parser first checks if all the required attributes (e.g., the label's name) are set. If some of them are not set, it asks the data scientist to fill them in before continuing the parsing. Otherwise, it selects all the features with automatic="selected" or manual="select" and uses them to fill a Jinja2 template [53]. The generated quality-evaluation experiment follows the same structure of algorithm 1. It is embedded inside a Python function that takes as input the dataset to use (listing 1.3). An example of a generated file can be accessed on the GitHub [22] or Zenodo [23] repository.

```
def experiment(data):
    # quality evaluation experiment
```

Listing 1.3: Quality-testing experiment signature

In addition to the main file, MANILA generates also a set of Python files needed to execute the experiment and an environment.yml file containing the specification of the *conda* [1] environment needed to perform the experiment. All the files are generated inside a folder named gen.

5.4 Experiment Execution

The generated experiment can be invoked directly through the Python interpreter using the command given in listing 1.4. Otherwise, it can be called through a REST API or any other interface such as a desktop application, or a Scientific Workflow Management System like *KNIME* [44,10]. This generality of our experimental workflow, makes it very flexible and suitable to many use-cases.

```
$ python main.py -d <DATASET PATH>
```
Listing 1.4: Experiment invocation

The experiment applies each ML algorithm with each quality method and returns a report using the adequate selected metrics along with the method achieving the best QA. It is worth noting how each quality method is evaluated individually on the selected ML algorithm, and for each QA, a corresponding report is returned by the system. Figure 5 reports an example of how the quality

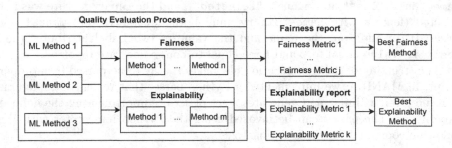

Fig. 5: Quality evaluation process example

evaluation process is done in MANILA. In this example, the data scientist has selected three ML algorithms and wants to assure Fairness and Explainability. She has selected n methods to assure Fairness and m methods to assure Explainability. In addition, she has selected j metrics for Fairness and k metrics for Explainability. Then, the testing process performs two parallel set of experiments. In the first, it applies the n fairness methods to each ML algorithm accordingly and computes the j fairness metrics. In the second, it applies the m Explainability methods to the ML algorithms and computes the k Explainability metrics. Finally, the process returns two reports synthesising the obtained results for Fairness and Explainability along with the ML algorithms with the best Fairness and Explainability, respectively. If the data scientist chooses to see the results in tabular form (i.e., selects the **Tabular** feature in the ExtFM), then the results are saved in a CSV file. Otherwise, the charts displaying the results are saved as PNG files. The ML algorithm returned by the experiment is instead saved as a *pickle* file [2]. We have chosen this format since it is a standard format to store serialized objects in Python and can be easily imported in other scripts.

Finally, it is worth noting how the generated experiment workflow is written in Python and can be customised to address particular stakeholders' needs or evaluate other quality methods.

6   Proof of Concept

To prove the ability of MANILA in supporting the quality-based development of ML systems, we implemented with MANILA a fair classification system to predict the frequency of contraceptive use by women, using a famous dataset in the Fairness literature [42]. This use case is reasonable since fairness has acquired much importance in recent years, partly because of the sustainable goals of the UN [51]. The first step in the quality development process is feature

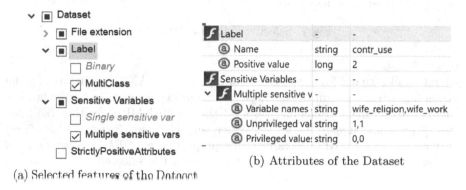

(a) Selected features of the Dataset

(b) Attributes of the Dataset

Fig. 6: Dataset specification

selection. The ML task to solve is a multi-class classification problem [4], hence in the ExtFM we selected the feature *MultiClass* for the *Label* and we specified its name and the positive value to consider for the fairness evaluation (*long-term use*). We will use a CSV dataset file, so we specified this feature in the configuration. Finally, accordingly to the literature [42], we specified that the dataset has multiple sensitive variables to consider for fairness, and we specified their names and privileged and unprivileged values. Figure 6 reports the selected features of the Dataset and the attributes specified.

Next, we specified that we want to use a *Standard Scaler* algorithm to normalize the data and we selected the following ML algorithms for classification: *Logistic Regression*[48], *Support Vector Classifier*[52], and *Gradient Boosting Classifier*[28]. Figure 7 reports the Fairness methods we want to test. Note how many methods have been automatically disabled by the system based on the features already selected[2]. Further, we specified the metrics we want to use to evaluate Fairness and Effectiveness: *Accuracy* [60], *Zero One Loss* [25], *Disparate Impact* [27], *Statistical Parity* [41], and *Equalized Odds* [33], and the *Harmonic Mean* as aggregation function (we have chosen this aggregation function since it is widely used in the literature). Finally, we specified that we want to perform a *10-fold* cross validation [59] and that we want the results in tabular form without the

---

[2] In particular, these methods have been disabled because they do not support multi-class classification or multiple sensitive variables

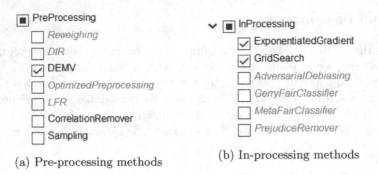

(a) Pre-processing methods

(b) In-processing methods

Fig. 7: Selected Fairness methods

generation of a chart. From the given configuration, MANILA generates all the python files needed to run the quality-assessment experiment. In particular, the generated experiment trains and tests all the selected ML algorithm (i.e., *Logistic Regression, Support Vector Classifier,* and *Gradient Boosting Classifier*) applying all the selected fairness methods properly (i.e., *DEMV, Exponentiated Gradient,* and *Grid Search*). Finally, it computes the selected metrics on the trained ML algorithms and returns a report of the metrics along with the fully trained ML algorithm with the best fairness. All the generated files are available on Zenodo [23] and Github [22]. The generated experiment was executed di-

Table 2: Generated results

Fairness Method	ML Model	Stat Par	Eq Odds	ZO Loss	Disp Imp	Accuracy	HMean
demv	svm	0.004	0.216	0.273	0.708	0.546	0.705
demv	gradient	-0.006	0.197	0.276	0.689	0.561	0.702
demv	logreg	0.003	0.193	0.225	0.676	0.511	0.7
grid	gradient	-0.057	0.21	0.167	0.749	0.443	0.694
eg	gradient	-0.09	0.183	0.309	0.658	0.546	0.685
grid	logreg	-0.012	0.241	0.26	0.815	0.445	0.679
eg	svm	-0.109	0.16	0.337	0.549	0.546	0.652
eg	logreg	-0.107	0.218	0.35	0.543	0.509	0.617
grid	svc	-0.197	0.273	0.295	0.197	0.435	0.301

rectly from the python interpreter, and the obtained results are available in table 2. In the table are reported the Fairness enhancing methods, the ML algorithms and all the metrics computed. The table has been automatically ordered based on the given aggregation function (i.e., the rightmost column *HMean*). From the results, we can see that the Support Vector Classifier (i.e., *svc* in the table) and the *DEMV* fairness method can achieve the best Fairness and Effectiveness trade-off, since they have the highest *HMean* value (highlighted in green in table 2). Hence, the ML algorithm returned by the experiment is the Support Vector Classifier, trained with the full dataset after the application of the DEMV algorithm.

7   Threats to Validity

Although the QA considered in MANILA are the most relevant and the most cited in the literature, there could be other QA highly affecting the environment/end users of the ML system that are not focused prominently by existing papers. In addition, the proposed experimental workflow is based on the considered QA; there could be other QA not considered at the time of this paper that should be evaluated differently.

8   Conclusion and Future Work

In this paper, we have presented MANILA, a novel approach to democratize the quality-based development of ML systems. First, we have identified the most influential quality properties in ML systems by selecting the quality attributes that are most cited in the literature. Next, we have presented a general workflow for the quality-based development of ML systems. Finally, we described MANILA in detail by first explaining how the general workflow can be formalized through an ExtFM. Next, we detailed all the steps required to develop a quality ML system using MANILA. We started from the low-code configuration of the experiment to perform; we described how a Python implementation could be generated from such a configuration. Finally, we showed how the execution of the experiment could identify the method better satisfying a given quality requirement. We have demonstrated the ability of MANILA in guiding the data scientists through the quality-based development of ML systems by implementing a *fair* multi-class classification system to predict the use of contraceptive methods by women.

In future, we plan to improve MANILA by extending the ExtFM with additional methods enhancing other quality attributes and by implementing in the framework the trade-off analysis that combines the different quality attribute evaluations when required by means of Pareto-front functions. MANILA appears to be easy to use and very general, able to embed different quality attributes that are quantitatively measured. To demonstrate our intuition, we will conduct a user evaluation of MANILA, to evaluate its usability by involving experts and not experts of the quality ML system development. Some groups we aim to involve are: master students in computer science and applied data science (i.e., non-expert users), data scientists working in industries, and researchers studying ML development and quality assessment (i.e., expert users). In addition, since MANILA supports the configuration of an experiment by running all possible combinations of the selected features, a limit of the proposed approach can be its complexity and the time needed to obtain the results. Such limitation is mitigated by the feature selection step, which demands the user to choose which features to include in the experiment. As future work, to enlarge the MANILA usage, we will better study such aspects and provide guidelines to the users on how to mitigate such potential limitations.

References

1. Conda website, https://docs.conda.io/
2. Pickle documentation, https://docs.python.org/3/library/pickle.html
3. Agarwal, A., Beygelzimer, A., Dudik, M., Langford, J., Wallach, H.: A Reductions Approach to Fair Classification. In: Proceedings of the 35th International Conference on Machine Learning. pp. 60–69. PMLR (Jul 2018), https://proceedings.mlr.press/v80/agarwal18a.html, iSSN: 2640-3498
4. Aly, M.: Survey on multiclass classification methods. Neural Netw 19(1-9), 2 (2005)
5. Amershi, S., Begel, A., Bird, C., DeLine, R., Gall, H., Kamar, E., Nagappan, N., Nushi, B., Zimmermann, T.: Software Engineering for Machine Learning: A Case Study. In: 2019 IEEE/ACM 41st International Conference on Software Engineering: Software Engineering in Practice (ICSE-SEIP). pp. 291–300. IEEE, Montreal, QC, Canada (May 2019). https://doi.org/10.1109/ICSE-SEIP.2019.00042, https://ieeexplore.ieee.org/document/8804457/
6. Apel, S., Batory, D., Kästner, C., Saake, G.: Feature-oriented software product lines. Springer (2016)
7. Azimi, S., Pahl, C.: A layered quality framework for machine learning-driven data and information models. In: ICEIS (1). pp. 579–587 (2020)
8. Bellamy, R.K., Dey, K., Hind, M., Hoffman, S.C., Houde, S., Kannan, K., Lohia, P., Martino, J., Mehta, S., Mojsilović, A., et al.: Ai fairness 360: An extensible toolkit for detecting and mitigating algorithmic bias. IBM Journal of Research and Development 63(4/5), 4–1 (2019)
9. Benavides, D., Segura, S., Ruiz-Cortés, A.: Automated analysis of feature models 20 years later: A literature review. Information Systems 35(6), 615–636 (Sep 2010). https://doi.org/10.1016/j.is.2010.01.001, https://www.sciencedirect.com/science/article/pii/S0306437910000025
10. Berthold, M.R., Cebron, N., Dill, F., Gabriel, T.R., Kötter, T., Meinl, T., Ohl, P., Thiel, K., Wiswedel, B.: Knime - the konstanz information miner: Version 2.0 and beyond. SIGKDD Explor. Newsl. 11(1), 26–31 (Nov 2009). https://doi.org/10.1145/1656274.1656280, https://doi-org.univaq.clas.cineca.it/10.1145/1656274.1656280
11. Bird, S., Dudík, M., Edgar, R., Horn, B., Lutz, R., Milan, V., Sameki, M., Wallach, H., Walker, K.: Fairlearn: A toolkit for assessing and improving fairness in AI. Tech. Rep. MSR-TR-2020-32, Microsoft (May 2020), https://www.microsoft.com/en-us/research/publication/fairlearn-a-toolkit-for-assessing-and-improving-fairness-in-ai/
12. Bosch, J., Olsson, H.H., Crnkovic, I.: Engineering AI Systems: A Research Agenda (2021). https://doi.org/10.4018/978-1-7998-5101-1.ch001, https://www.igi-global.com/chapter/engineering-ai-systems/www.igi-global.com/chapter/engineering-ai-systems/266130, iSBN: 9781799851011 Pages: 1-19 Publisher: IGI Global
13. Braiek, H.B., Khomh, F.: On testing machine learning programs. Journal of Systems and Software 164, 110542 (2020). https://doi.org/https://doi.org/10.1016/j.jss.2020.110542, https://www.sciencedirect.com/science/article/pii/S0164121220300248
14. Buckland, M., Gey, F.: The relationship between recall and precision. Journal of the American society for information science 45(1), 12–19 (1994), publisher: Wiley Online Library

15. Carvalho, D.V., Pereira, E.M., Cardoso, J.S.: Machine learning interpretability: A survey on methods and metrics. Electronics 8(8), 832 (2019)
16. Caton, S., Haas, C.: Fairness in machine learning: A survey (2020)
17. Celis, L.E., Huang, L., Keswani, V., Vishnoi, N.K.: Classification with fairness constraints: A meta-algorithm with provable guarantees. In: Proceedings of the conference on fairness, accountability, and transparency. pp. 319–328 (2019)
18. Chakraborty, J., Majumder, S., Yu, Z., Menzies, T.: Fairway: A way to build fair ml software. In: Proceedings of the 28th ACM Joint Meeting on European Software Engineering Conference and Symposium on the Foundations of Software Engineering. pp. 654–665 (2020)
19. Chen, L., Ali Babar, M., Nuseibeh, B.: Characterizing architec- turally significant requirements. IEEE Software 30(2), 38–45 (2013). https://doi.org/10.1109/MS.2012.174
20. Chen, Z., Zhang, J.M., Hort, M., Sarro, F., Harman, M.: Fairness Testing: A Com- prehensive Survey and Analysis of Trends (Aug 2022), http://arxiv.org/abs/ 2207.10223, arXiv:2207.10223 [cs]
21. Clifton, C.: Privacy Metrics. In: LIU, L., ÖZSU, M.T. (eds.) Encyclope- dia of Database Systems, pp. 2137–2139. Springer US, Boston, MA (2009). https://doi.org/10.1007/978-0-387-39940-9_272, https://doi.org/10.1007/ 978-0-387-39940-9_272
22. d'Aloisio, G., Marco, A.D., Stilo, G.: Manila github repository (Jan 2023), https: //github.com/giordanoDaloisio/manila
23. d'Aloisio, G., Marco, A.D., Stilo, G.: Manila zenodo repository (Jan 2023). https://doi.org/10.5281/zenodo.7525759, https://doi.org/10.5281/zenodo. 7525759
24. Di Sipio, C., Di Rocco, J., Di Ruscio, D., Nguyen, D.P.T.: A Low-Code Tool Supporting the Development of Recommender Systems. In: Fifteenth ACM Con- ference on Recommender Systems. pp. 741–744. ACM, Amsterdam Netherlands (Sep 2021). https://doi.org/10.1145/3460231.3478885, https://dl.acm.org/doi/ 10.1145/3460231.3478885
25. Domingos, P., Pazzani, M.: On the Optimality of the Simple Bayesian Classifier under Zero-One Loss. Machine Learning 29(2), 103–130 (Nov 1997). https://doi.org/10.1023/A:1007413511361, https://doi.org/10.1023/A: 1007413511361
26. d'Aloisio, G., D'Angelo, A., Di Marco, A., Stilo, G.: Debiaser for Multiple Variables to enhance fairness in classification tasks. Information Processing & Management 60(2), 103226 (Mar 2023) http://doi.org/10.1016/j.ipm.2022.103226, https:// www.sciencedirect.com/science/article/pii/S0306457322003272
27. Feldman, M., Friedler, S.A., Moeller, J., Scheidegger, C., Venkatasubrama- nian, S.: Certifying and Removing Disparate Impact. In: Proceedings of the 21th ACM SIGKDD International Conference on Knowledge Discov- ery and Data Mining. pp. 259–268. ACM, Sydney NSW Australia (Aug 2015). https://doi.org/10.1145/2783258.2783311, https://dl.acm.org/doi/10. 1145/2783258.2783311
28. Friedman, J.H.: Stochastic gradient boosting. Computational statistics & data analysis 38(4), 367–378 (2002), publisher: Elsevier
29. Galindo, J.A., Benavides, D., Trinidad, P., Gutiérrez-Fernández, A.M., Ruiz- Cortés, A.: Automated analysis of feature models: Quo vadis? Computing 101(5), 387–433 (May 2019). https://doi.org/10.1007/s00607-018-0646-1, http://link. springer.com/10.1007/s00607-018-0646-1

30. Giray, G.: A software engineering perspective on engineering machine learning systems: State of the art and challenges. Journal of Systems and Software p. 111031 (2021)
31. Goncalves Jr., P.M., Barros, R.S.M.: Automating data preprocessing with dmpml and kddml. In: 2011 10th IEEE/ACIS International Conference on Computer and Information Science. pp. 97–103 (2011). https://doi.org/10.1109/ICIS.2011.23
32. Hamada, K., Ishikawa, F., Masuda, S., Myojin, T., Nishi, Y., Ogawa, H., Toku, T., Tokumoto, S., Tsuchiya, K., Ujita, Y., et al.: Guidelines for quality assurance of machine learning-based artificial intelligence. In: SEKE. pp. 335–341 (2020)
33. Hardt, M., Price, E., Price, E., Srebro, N.: Equality of Opportunity in Supervised Learning. In: Advances in Neural Information Processing Systems. vol. 29. Curran Associates, Inc. (2016), `https://proceedings.neurips.cc/paper/2016/hash/9d2682367c3935defcb1f9e247a97c0d-Abstract.html`
34. He, X., Zhao, K., Chu, X.: Automl: A survey of the state-of-the-art. Knowledge-Based Systems **212**, 106622 (2021). https://doi.org/https://doi.org/10.1016/j.knosys.2020.106622, `https://www.sciencedirect.com/science/article/pii/S0950705120307516`
35. Ishikawa, F.: Concepts in quality assessment for machine learning-from test data to arguments. In: International Conference on Conceptual Modeling. pp. 536–544. Springer (2018)
36. ISO: ISO/IEC 25010:2011. Tech. rep. (2011), `https://www.iso.org/cms/render/live/en/sites/isoorg/contents/data/standard/03/57/35733.html`
37. Kamiran, F., Calders, T.: Data preprocessing techniques for classification without discrimination. Knowledge and Information Systems **33**(1), 1–33 (Oct 2012). https://doi.org/10.1007/s10115-011-0463-8, `http://link.springer.com/10.1007/s10115-011-0463-8`
38. Kang, K.C., Cohen, S.G., Hess, J.A., Novak, W.E., Peterson, A.S.: Feature-oriented domain analysis (foda) feasibility study. Tech. rep., Carnegie-Mellon Univ Pittsburgh Pa Software Engineering Inst (1990)
39. Kearns, M., Neel, S., Roth, A., Wu, Z.S.: An empirical study of rich subgroup fairness for machine learning. In: Proceedings of the conference on fairness, accountability, and transparency. pp. 100–109 (2019)
40. Kumeno, F.: Sofware engneering challenges for machine learning applications: A literature review. Intelligent Decision Technologies **13**(4), 463–476 (2019)
41. Kusner, M.J., Loftus, J., Russell, C., Silva, R.: Counterfactual fairness. In: Advances in Neural Information Processing Systems. vol. 30. Curran Associates, Inc. (2017), `https://proceedings.neurips.cc/paper/2017/hash/a486cd07e4ac3d270571622f4f316ec5-Abstract.html`
42. Lim, T.S., Loh, W.Y., Shih, Y.S.: A comparison of prediction accuracy, complexity, and training time of thirty-three old and new classification algorithms. Machine learning **40**(3), 203–228 (2000), publisher: Springer
43. Linardatos, P., Papastefanopoulos, V., Kotsiantis, S.: Explainable ai: A review of machine learning interpretability methods. Entropy **23**(1), 18 (2021)
44. Liu, J., Pacitti, E., Valduriez, P., Mattoso, M.: A survey of data-intensive scientific workflow management. Journal of Grid Computing **13**(4), 457–493 (2015)
45. Martínez-Plumed, F., Contreras-Ochando, L., Ferri, C., Orallo, J.H., Kull, M., Lachiche, N., Quintana, M.J.R., Flach, P.A.: Crisp-dm twenty years later: From data mining processes to data science trajectories. IEEE Transactions on Knowledge and Data Engineering (2019)

46. Martínez-Fernández, S., Bogner, J., Franch, X., Oriol, M., Siebert, J., Trendow-
    icz, A., Vollmer, A.M., Wagner, S.: Software Engineering for AI-Based Systems:
    A Survey. ACM Transactions on Software Engineering and Methodology **31**(2),
    37e:1–37e:59 (Apr 2022). https://doi.org/10.1145/3487043, https://doi.org/10.
    1145/3487043
47. Mehrabi, N., Morstatter, F., Saxena, N., Lerman, K., Galstyan, A.: A Survey on
    Bias and Fairness in Machine Learning. ACM Computing Surveys **54**(6), 1–35
    (Jul 2021). https://doi.org/10.1145/3457607, https://dl.acm.org/doi/10.1145/
    3457607
48. Menard, S.: Applied logistic regression analysis, vol. 106. Sage (2002)
49. Molnar, C.: Interpretable machine learning. Lulu. com (2020)
50. Muccini, H., Vaidhyanathan, K.: Software Architecture for ML-based Systems:
    What Exists and What Lies Ahead. In: 2021 IEEE/ACM 1st Workshop on AI
    Engineering - Software Engineering for AI (WAIN). pp. 121–128 (May 2021).
    https://doi.org/10.1109/WAIN52551.2021.00026
51. Nations, U.: THE 17 GOALS | Sustainable Development, https://sdgs.un.org/
    goals
52. Noble, W.S.: What is a support vector machine? Nature biotechnology **24**(12),
    1565–1567 (2006), publisher: Nature Publishing Group
53. PalletsProject: Jinja website, https://jinja.palletsprojects.com/
54. Patro, S., Sahu, K.K.: Normalization: A preprocessing stage. arXiv preprint
    arXiv:1503.06462 (2015)
55. Pedregosa, F., Varoquaux, G., Gramfort, A., Michel, V., Thirion, B., Grisel, O.,
    Blondel, M., Prettenhofer, P., Weiss, R., Dubourg, V., Vanderplas, J., Passos, A.,
    Cournapeau, D., Brucher, M., Perrot, M., Duchesnay, E.: Scikit-learn: Machine
    learning in Python. Journal of Machine Learning Research **12**, 2825–2830 (2011)
56. Putzel, P., Lee, S.: Blackbox Post-Processing for Multiclass Fairness.
    arXiv:2201.04461 [cs] (Jan 2022), http://arxiv.org/abs/2201.04461, arXiv:
    2201.04461
57. Refaeilzadeh, P., Tang, L., Liu, H.: Cross-validation. Encyclopedia of database
    systems **5**, 532–538 (2009)
58. Refaeilzadeh, P., Tang, L., Liu, H.: Cross-Validation, pp. 1–7. Springer New York,
    New York, NY (2016). https://doi.org/10.1007/978-1-4899-7993-3_565-2
59. Refaeilzadeh, P., Tang, L., Liu, H.: Cross-Validation. In: Encyclopedia of
    Database Systems, pp. 1–7. Springer New York, New York, NY (2016).
    https://doi.org/10.1007/978-1-4899-7993-3_565-2
60. Rosenfield, G., Fitzpatrick-Lins, K.: A coefficient of agreement as a measure of the-
    matic classification accuracy. Photogrammetric Engineering and Remote Sensing
    52(2), 223–227 (1986), http://pubs.er.usgs.gov/publication/70014667
61. Rönkkö, M., Heikkinen, J., Kotovirta, V., Chandrasekar, V.: Automated prepro-
    cessing of environmental data. Future Generation Computer Systems **45**, 13–
    24 (2015). https://doi.org/https://doi.org/10.1016/j.future.2014.10.011, https://
    www.sciencedirect.com/science/article/pii/S0167739X14002040
62. Sahay, A., Indamutsa, A., Di Ruscio, D., Pierantonio, A.: Supporting the under-
    standing and comparison of low-code development platforms. In: 2020 46th Eu-
    romicro Conference on Software Engineering and Advanced Applications (SEAA).
    pp. 171–178. IEEE (2020)
63. Saleiro, P., Kuester, B., Hinkson, L., London, J., Stevens, A., Anisfeld, A., Rodolfa,
    K.T., Ghani, R.: Aequitas: A bias and fairness audit toolkit. arXiv preprint
    arXiv:1811.05577 (2018)

64. Siebert, J., Joeckel, L., Heidrich, J., Trendowicz, A., Nakamichi, K., Ohashi, K., Namba, I., Yamamoto, R., Aoyama, M.: Construction of a quality model for machine learning systems. Software Quality Journal pp. 1–29 (2021)
65. de Souza Nascimento, E., Ahmed, I., Oliveira, E., Palheta, M.P., Steinmacher, I., Conte, T.: Understanding development process of machine learning systems: Challenges and solutions. In: 2019 ACM/IEEE International Symposium on Empirical Software Engineering and Measurement (ESEM). pp. 1–6. IEEE (2019)
66. Studer, S., Bui, T.B., Drescher, C., Hanuschkin, A., Winkler, L., Peters, S., Müller, K.R.: Towards crisp-ml (q): a machine learning process model with quality assurance methodology. Machine Learning and Knowledge Extraction 3(2), 392–413 (2021)
67. Taha, A.A., Hanbury, A.: Metrics for evaluating 3D medical image segmentation: analysis, selection, and tool. BMC Medical Imaging 15(1), 29 (Aug 2015). https://doi.org/10.1186/s12880-015-0068-x, https://doi.org/10.1186/s12880-015-0068-x
68. Thüm, T., Kästner, C., Benduhn, F., Meinicke, J., Saake, G., Leich, T.: Featureide: An extensible framework for feature-oriented software development. Science of Computer Programming 79, 70–85 (2014)
69. Tramer, F., Atlidakis, V., Geambasu, R., Hsu, D., Hubaux, J.P., Humbert, M., Juels, A., Lin, H.: Fairtest: Discovering unwarranted associations in data-driven applications. In: 2017 IEEE European Symposium on Security and Privacy (EuroS&P). pp. 401–416. IEEE (2017)
70. Villamizar, H., Escovedo, T., Kalinowski, M.: Requirements engineering for machine learning: A systematic mapping study. In: SEAA. pp. 29–36 (2021)
71. Xu, R., Baracaldo, N., Joshi, J.: Privacy-Preserving Machine Learning: Methods, Challenges and Directions. arXiv:2108.04417 [cs] (Sep 2021), http://arxiv.org/abs/2108.04417, arXiv: 2108.04417
72. Zhang, J.M., Harman, M., Ma, L., Liu, Y.: Machine learning testing: Survey, landscapes and horizons. IEEE Transactions on Software Engineering (2020)
73. Zhou, J., Gandomi, A.H., Chen, F., Holzinger, A.: Evaluating the Quality of Machine Learning Explanations: A Survey on Methods and Metrics. Electronics 10(5), 593 (Jan 2021). https://doi.org/10.3390/electronics10050593, https://www.mdpi.com/2079-9292/10/5/593, number: 5 Publisher: Multidisciplinary Digital Publishing Institute

Efficient Bounded Exhaustive Input Generation from Program APIs

Mariano Politano[1,4](✉), Valeria Bengolea[1], Facundo Molina[3], Nazareno Aguirre[1,4], Marcelo F. Frias[2,4], and Pablo Ponzio[1,4]

[1] Universidad Nacional de Río Cuarto, Río Cuarto, Argentina
mpolitano@dc.exa.unrc.edu.ar
[2] Instituto Tecnológico de Buenos Aires, Buenos Aires, Argentina
[3] IMDEA Software Institute, Madrid, Spain
[4] CONICET, Buenos Aires, Argentina

Abstract. Bounded exhaustive input generation (BEG) is an effective approach to reveal software faults. However, existing BEG approaches require a precise specification of the *valid* inputs, i.e., a repOK, that must be provided by the user. Writing repOKs for BEG is challenging and time consuming, and they are seldom available in software.

In this paper, we introduce BEAPI, an efficient approach that employs routines from the API of the software under test to perform BEG. Like API-based test generation approaches, BEAPI creates sequences of calls to methods from the API, and executes them to generate inputs. As opposed to existing BEG approaches, BEAPI does not require a repOK to be provided by the user. To make BEG from the API feasible, BEAPI implements three key pruning techniques: *(i)* discarding test sequences whose execution produces exceptions violating API usage rules, *(ii)* state matching to discard test sequences that produce inputs already created by previously explored test sequences, and *(iii)* the automated identification and use of a subset of methods from the API, called *builders*, that is sufficient to perform BEG.

Our experimental assessment shows that BEAPI's efficiency and scalability is competitive with existing BEG approaches, without the need for repOKs. We also show that BEAPI can assist the user in finding flaws in repOKs, by (automatically) comparing inputs generated by BEAPI with those generated from a repOK. Using this approach, we revealed several errors in repOKs taken from the assessment of related tools, demonstrating the difficulties of writing precise repOKs for BEG.

1 Introduction

Automated test generation approaches aim at assisting developers in crucial software testing tasks [2,22], like automatically generating test cases or suites [6,18,10], and automatically finding and reporting failures [23,19,12,20,4,13]. Many of these approaches involve random components, that avoid making a systematic exploration of the space of behaviors, but improve test generation efficiency [23,19,10]. While these approaches have been useful in finding a large

L. Lambers and S. Uchitel (Eds.): FASE 2023, LNCS 13991, pp. 111–132, 2023.
https://doi.org/10.1007/978-3-031-30826-0_6

number of bugs in software, they might miss exploring certain faulty software behaviors due to their random nature. Alternative approaches aim at systematically exploring a very large number of executions of the software under test (SUT), with the goal of providing stronger guarantees about the absence of bugs [20,4,12,14,6,18]. Some of these approaches are based on bounded exhaustive generation (BEG) [20,4], which consists of generating all feasible inputs that can be constructed using bounded data domains. Common targets to BEG approaches have been implementations of complex, dynamic data structures with rich structural constraints (e.g., linked lists, trees, etc). The most widely-used and efficient BEG approaches for testing software [20,4] require the user to provide a formal specification of the constraints that the inputs must satisfy –often a representation invariant of the input (repOK)–, and bounds on data domains [20,4] –often called scopes. Thus, specification-based BEG approaches yield all inputs within the provided scopes that satisfy repOK.

Writing appropriate formal specifications for BEG is a challenging and time consuming task. The specifications must precisely capture the intended constraints of the inputs. Overconstrained specifications lead to missing the generation of valid inputs, which might make the subsequent testing stage miss the exploration of faulty behaviors of the SUT. Underconstrained specifications may lead to the generation of invalid inputs, which might produce false alarms while testing the SUT. Furthermore, sometimes the user needs to take into account the way the generation approach operates, and write the specifications in a very specific way for the approach to achieve good performance [4] (see Section 4). Finally, such precise formal specifications are seldom available in software, hindering the usability of specification-based BEG approaches.

Several studies show that BEG approaches are effective in revealing software failures [20,16,4,33]. Furthermore, the *small scope hypothesis* [3], which states that most software faults can be revealed by executing the SUT on "small inputs", suggests that BEG approaches should discover most (if not all) faults in the SUT, if large enough scopes are used. The challenge that BEG approaches face is how to efficiently explore a huge search space, that often grows exponentially with respect to the scope. The search space often includes a very large number of invalid (not satisfying repOK) and isomorphic inputs [15,28]. Thus, pruning parts of the search space involving invalid and redundant inputs is key to make BEG approaches scale up in practice [4].

In this paper, we propose a new approach for BEG, called BEAPI, that works by making calls to API methods of the SUT. Similarly to API-based test generation approaches [23,19,10], BEAPI generates sequences of calls to methods from the API (i.e., test sequences). The execution of each test sequence yielded by BEAPI generates an input in the resulting BEG set of objects. As usual in BEG, BEAPI requires the user to provide scopes for generation, which for BEAPI includes a maximum test sequence length. Brute force BEG from a user-provided scope would attempt to generate all feasible test sequences of methods form the API with up to a maximum sequence length. This is an intrinsically combinatorial process, that exhausts computational resources before completion even for very small scopes (see Section 4). We propose several pruning techniques that are crucial for the efficiency of BEAPI, and allow it to scale up to significantly larger scopes. First, BEAPI executes test sequences and discards those that correspond to violations of API usage rules (e.g., throwing exceptions that indicate incorrect API usage, such as `IllegalArgumentException` in Java [17,23]). Thus, as opposed to specification-based BEG approaches, BEAPI does not require a `repOK` that precisely describes valid inputs. In contrast, BEAPI requires minimum specification effort in most cases (including most of our case studies in Section 4), which consists of making API methods throw exceptions on invalid inputs (in the "defensive programming" style popularized by Liskov [17]). Second, BEAPI implements state matching [15,28,36] to discard test sequences that produce inputs already created by previously explored sequences. Third, BEAPI employs only a subset of the API methods to create test sequences: a set of methods automatically identified as builders [27]. Before test generation, BEAPI executes an automated builders identification approach [27] to find a smaller subset of the API that is sufficient to yield the resulting BEG set of inputs. Another advantage of BEAPI with respect to specification-based approaches is that it produces test sequences to create the corresponding inputs using methods from the API, making it easier to create tests from BEAPI's output [5].

We experimentally assess BEAPI, and show that its efficiency and scalability are comparable to those of the fastest BEG approach (Korat), without the need for repOKs. We also show that BEAPI can be of help in finding flaws in repOKs, by comparing the sets of inputs generated by BEAPI using the API against the sets of inputs generated by Korat from a `repOK`. Using this procedure, we found several flaws in `repOK`s employed in the experimental assessment of related tools, thus providing evidence on the difficulty of writing `repOK`s for BEG.

2   A Motivating Example

To illustrate the difficulties of writing formal specifications for BEG, consider Apache's `NodeCachingLinkedList`'s (NCL) representation invariant shown in Figure 1 (taken from the ROOPS benchmark[5]). NCLs are composed of a main circular, doubly-linked list, used for data storage, and a cache of previously used nodes implemented as a singly linked list. Nodes removed from the main list are moved to the cache, where they are saved for future usage. When a node is required for an insertion operation, a cache node (if one exists) is reused (instead of allocating a new node). As usual, `repOK` returns true iff the input structure satisfies the intended NCL properties [17]. Lines 1 to 20 check that the main list is a circular doubly-linked list with a dummy head; lines 21 to 33 check that the cache is a null terminated singly linked list (and the consistency of size fields is verified in the process). This `repOK` is written in the way recommended by the authors of Korat [4]. It returns false as soon as it finds a violation of an intended property in the current input. Otherwise, it returns true at the end. This allows Korat to prune large portions of the search space, and improves its

---

[5] https://code.google.com/p/roops/

```
1   public boolean repOK() {
2     if (this.header == null) return false;
3     // Missing constraint: the value of the sentinel node must be null
4     // if (this.header.value != null) return false;
5     if (this.header.next == null) return false;
6     if (this.header.previous == null) return false;
7     if (this.cacheSize > this.maximumCacheSize) return false;
8     if (this.size < 0) return false;
9     int cyclicSize = 0;
10    LinkedListNode n = this.header;
11    do {
12        cyclicSize++;
13        if (n.previous == null) return false;
14        if (n.previous.next != n) return false;
15        if (n.next == null) return false;
16        if (n.next.previous != n) return false;
17        if (n != null) n = n.next;
18    } while (n != this.header && n != null);
19    if (n == null) return false;
20    if (this.size != cyclicSize - 1) return false;
21    int acyclicSize = 0;
22    LinkedListNode m = this.firstCachedNode;
23    Set visited = new HashSet();
24    visited.add(this.firstCachedNode);
25    while (m != null) {
26        acyclicSize++;
27        if (m.previous != null) return false;
28        // Missing constraint: the value of cache nodes must be null
29        // if (m.value != null) return false;
30        m = m.next;
31        if (!visited.add(m)) return false;
32    }
33    if (this.cacheSize != acyclicSize) return false;
34    return true;
35  }
```

Fig. 1. NodeCachingLinkedList's repOK from ROOPS

performance [4]. repOK suffers from underspecification: it does not state that the sentinel node and all cache nodes must have null values (lines 3-4 and 28-29, respectively). Mistakes like these are very common when writing specifications (see Section 4.3), and difficult to discover by manual inspection of repOK. These errors can have serious consequences for BEG. Executing Korat with repOK and a scope of up to 8 nodes produces 54.5 million NCL structures, while the actual number of valid NCL instances is 2.8 million. Clearly, this is a problem for Korat's performance, and for the subsequent testing of the SUT. In addition, the invalid instances generated might trigger false alarms in the SUT in many cases. We discovered these errors in repOK with the help of BEAPI: we automatically contrasted the structures generated using BEAPI and the NCL's API, with those generated using Korat with repOK, for the same scope.

This example shows that writing sound and precise repOKs for BEG is difficult and time consuming. Fine-tuning repOKs to improve the performance of BEG (e.g., for Korat) is even harder. The main advantage of BEAPI is that it requires minimal specification effort to perform BEG. If API methods used for generation are correct, all generated structures are valid by construction. The programmer only needs to make sure that API methods throw exceptions when API usage

```
1  max.objects=3
2  int.range=0:2
3  # strings=str1,str2,str3
4  # omit.fields=NodeCachingLinkedList.DEFAULT_MAXIMUM_CACHE_SIZE
```

Fig. 2. BEAPI's scope definition for NCL (max. nodes 3)

rules are violated, in a defensive programming style [17]. In most cases, this requires checking very simple conditions on the inputs. In our example, the method to add an element to a NCL throws an `IllegalArgumentException` when is called with the `null` element (the implementation of the method takes care that the remaining NCL properties hold).

3 Bounded Exhaustive Generation from Program APIs

We now describe BEAPI's approach. We start with the definition of scope, then present BEAPI's optimizations, and we finally describe BEAPI's algorithm.

3.1 Scope Definition

The definition of scope in Korat involves providing bounded data domains for classes and fields of the SUT, since Korat explores the state space of feasible input candidates, and yields the set of inputs satisfying repOK as a result. Instead, BEAPI explores the search space of (bounded) test sequences that can be formed by making calls to the SUT's API. Thus, we have to provide data domains for the primitive types employed to make such calls, and a bound on the maximum size of the structures we want to keep, from those generated by such API calls. An example configuration file defining BEAPI's scope for the NCL case study is shown in Figure 2. The `max.objects` parameter specifies the maximum number of different objects (reachable from the root) that a structure is allowed to have. Test sequences that create a structure with a larger number of different objects (of any class) than `max.objects` will be discarded (and the structure too). In our example, this implies that BEAPI will not create NCLs with more than 3 nodes. Next, one has to specify the values that will be employed by BEAPI to invoke API routines that take primitive type parameters (e.g., elements to insert into the list). The `int.range` parameter allows one to specify a range of integers, which goes from 0 to 2 in Figure 2. One may also specify domains for other primitive types like floats, doubles and strings, by describing their values by extension. For example, line 3 shows how to define `str1`, `str2` and `str3` as the feasible values for String-typed parameters. Also, we can instruct BEAPI which fields to take into account for structure canonicalization, or which fields to omit (`omit.fields`). This allows the user to control the state matching process (see Section 3.2). For example, uncommenting line 4 would make BEAPI omit the `DEFAULT_MAXIMUM_CACHE_SIZE` in state matching, which in our example is a constant initialized to 20 in the class constructor. In this case, omitting the field does not change anything in terms of the different structures generated by

BEAPI, but in other cases omitting fields may have an impact. The configuration in Figure 2 is enough for BEAPI to generate NCLs with a maximum of 3 nodes, containing integers from 0 to 2 as values, which allowed us to mimic the structures generated by Korat for the same scope.

3.2 State Matching

In test generation with BEAPI, multiple test sequences often produce the same structure, e.g., inserting an element into a list and removing the element afterwards. BEAPI assumes that method executions are deterministic: any execution of a method with the same inputs yields the same results. For the generation of a bounded exhaustive set of structures, for each distinct structure s in the set, BEAPI only needs to save the first test sequence that generates s. All test sequences generated subsequently that also create s can be discarded. As BEAPI works by extending previously generated test sequences (Section 3.4), if we save many test sequences for the same structure, all these sequences would have to be extended with new routines in subsequent iterations of BEAPI, resulting in unnecessary computations. Hence, we implement state matching on BEAPI as follows. We store all the structures produced so far by BEAPI in a canonical form (see below). After executing the last routine $r(p_1, \ldots, p_k)$ of a newly generated test sequence T, we check whether any of r's parameters hold a structure not seen before (not stored). If T does not create any new structure, it is discarded. Otherwise, T and the new structures it generates are stored by BEAPI.

We represent heap-allocated structures as labeled graphs. After the execution of a method, a (non-primitive typed) parameter p holds a reference to the root object r of a rooted heap (i.e. $p = r$), defined below.

Definition 1. *Let O be a set of objects, and P a set of primitive values (including null). Let F be the fields of all objects in O.*

- *A heap is a labeled graph $H = \langle O, E \rangle$ with $E = \{(o, f, v) | o \in O, f \in F, v \in O \cup P\}$.*
- *A rooted heap is a pair $RH = \langle r, H \rangle$ where $r \in O$, $H = \langle O, E \rangle$ is a heap, and for each $v' \in O \cup P$, v' is reachable from r through fields in F.*

The special case $p = null$ can be represented by a rooted heap with a dummy node and a dummy field pointing to *null*. In languages without explicit memory management (like Java), each object is identified by the memory address where is allocated. But changing the memory addresses of objects (while keeping the same graph structure) has no effect in the execution of a program. Heaps obtained by permutations of the memory addresses of their component objects are called *isomorphic heaps*. We avoid the generation of isomorphic heaps by employing a canonical representation for heaps [15,4]. Rooted heaps can be efficiently canonicalized by an approach called *linearization* [15,36], which transforms a rooted heap into a unique sequence of values.

Figure 3 shows the linearization algorithm used by BEAPI, a customized version that reports when objects exceed the scopes and supports ignoring object

```
1   int[] linearize(O root, Heap<O, E> heap, int scope, Regex omitFields) {
2     Map ids = new Map(); // maps nodes into their unique ids
3     return lin(root, heap, scope, ids, omitFields);
4   }
5   int[] lin(O root, Heap<O, E> heap, int scope, Map ids, Regex omitFields) {
6     if (ids.containsKey(root))
7       return singletonSequence(ids.get(root));
8     if (ids.size() == scope)
9       throw new ScopeExceededException();
10    int id = ids.size() + 1;
11    ids.put(root, id);
12    int[] seq = singletonSequence(id);
13    Edge[] fields = sortByField({ <root, f, o> in E }, omitFields);
14    foreach (<root, f, o> in fields) {
15      if (isPrimitive(o))
16        seq.add(uniqueRepresentation(o));
17      else
18        seq.append(lin(o, heap, scope, ids, omitFields));
19    }
20    return seq;
21  }
```

Fig. 3. Linearization algorithm

fields (for the original version see [36]). linearize starts a depth-first traversal of the heap from the root, by invoking lin in line 3. To canonicalize the heap, lin assigns different identifiers to the different objects it visits. Map ids stores the mapping between objects and unique object identifiers. When an object is visited for the first time, it is assigned a new unique identifier (lines 10-11), and a singleton sequence with the identifier is created to represent the object (line 12). Then, the object's fields, sorted in a predefined order (e.g., by name), are traversed and the linearization of each field value is constructed, and the result is appended to the sequence representing the current object (lines 13-19). A field storing a primitive value is represented by a singleton sequence with the primitive value (line 15-16). If a field references an object, a recursive call to lin converts the object into a sequence, which will be appended to the result (line 18). At the end of the loop, seq contains the canonical representation of the whole rooted heap starting at root, and is returned by lin (line 20). When an already visited object is traversed by a recursive call, the object must have an identifier already assigned in ids (line 6), and lin returns the singleton sequence with the object's unique identifier (lines 7). When more than scope objects are reachable from the rooted heap, lin returns an exception to report that the scope has been exceeded (lines 9-10). The exception will be employed later on by BEAPI to discard test sequences that create objects larger than allowed by the scope. linearize also takes as a parameter a regular expression omitFields, that matches the names of the fields that must be omitted during canonicalization (see Section 3.1). To omit such fields, we implemented sortByField (line 13) in such a way that it does not return the edges corresponding to fields whose names match omitFields. This in turn avoids saving the values of omitted fields in the sequence yielded by linearize. Finally, notice that linearization allows for efficient comparison of objects (rooted heaps): two objects are equal if and only if their corresponding sequences yielded by linearize are equal.

3.3   Builders Identification Approach

As the feasible combinations of methods grow exponentially with the number of methods, it is crucial to reduce the number of methods that BEAPI uses to produce test sequences. We employ an automated builders identification approach [27] to find a subset of API methods that are sufficient for the generation of the bounded exhaustive structure sets. We call such routines *builders*. The previous approach to identify a subset of sufficient builders from an API is based on a genetic algorithm, but is computationally expensive [27]. Here, we consider a simpler hill climbing approach (HC), that achieves better performance. HC may of course be less precise, as it may include some methods in the resulting set of builders that might not be needed to produce a bounded exhaustive set of structures. However, HC worked very well and consistently computed minimal sets of builders in our experiments (we checked that the set of builders computed by HC matched the set of builders we manually identified for each case study). Our goal here is to assess the impact of using builders for BEG from an API. Comparing the HC approach against existing techniques is left for future work.

Let API=$m_1, m_2, \ldots, m_n$ be the set of API methods. HC explores the search space of all subsets of methods from API. HC requires the user to provide a scope s (in the same way as in BEAPI). The fitness f(sm) of a given set sm of methods is the number of distinct structures (after canonicalization) that BEAPI generates using the set, for the given scope s. We also give priority in the fitness to sets of methods with less and simpler parameter types (see [27] for further details). The successors succs(sm) for a candidate sm are the sets sm$\cup\{m_i\}$, for each $m_i \in$ API. HC starts by computing the fitness of all singletons $\{c\}$ of constructor methods. The best of the singletons is set as the current candidate curr, and HC starts a typical iterative hill climbing process. At each iteration HC computes f(succ) for each succ $\in$ succs(curr). Let best be the successor with the highest fitness value. Notice that best has exactly one more method than the best candidate of the previous iteration, curr. If f(best) > f(curr), methods in best can be used to create a larger set of structures than those in curr. Thus, HC assigns best to curr, and continues with the next iteration. Otherwise, f(best) <= f(curr), and curr already generates the largest possible set of structures (no method could be added that increases the number of generated structures from curr). At this point, curr is returned as the set of identified builders.

Notice that HC performs many invocations to BEAPI for builders identification. The key insight that makes builders identification feasible is that often builders identified for a relatively small scope are the same set of methods that are needed to create structures of any size. In other words, once the scope for builders computation is large enough, increasing the scope will yield the same set of builders as a result. This result resembles the small scope hypothesis for bug detection [3] (and transcoping [31]). A scope of 5 was enough for builders computation in all our case studies (we manually checked that the computed builders were the right ones in all cases). After builders are identified efficiently using a small scope, we can run BEAPI with the identified builders using a larger scope, for example, to generate bigger objects to exercise the SUT. In most of our case

```
1    BEAPI(List methods, int scope, Map<Type, List<Seq>> primitives, Regex omitFields) {
2      Map<Type, List<Seq>> currSeqs = new Map();
3      currSeqs.addAll({ T->L | T->L in primitives });
4      Set canonicalStrs = new Set();
5      for (int it=0; true; it++) {
6        Map<Type, List<Seq>> newSeqs = new Map();
7        boolean newStrs = false;
8        for (m(T_1,...,T_n):T_r: methods) {
9          Map<Type, List<Seq>> seqsT_1 = currSeqs.getSequencesForType(T_1);
10         ...
11         Map<Type, List<Seq>> seqsT_n = currSeqs.getSequencesForType(T_n);
12         for ((s_1,...,s_n): seqsT_1 × ... ×seqsT_n) {
13           Seq newSeq = createNewSeq(s_1,...,s_n,m);
14           o_1,...,o_n,o_r,failure,exception = execute(newSeq);
15           if (failure) throw new ExecutionFailedException(newSeq);
16           if (exception) continue;
17           c_1,...,c_n,c_r,outOfScope = makeCanonical(o_1,...,o_n,o_r,scope,omitFields);
18           if (outOfScope) continue;
19           if (isReferenceType(T_1) and !canonicalStrs.contains(c_1)) {
20             canonicalStrs.add(c_1);
21             newSeqs.addSeqForType(T_1, newSeq);
22             newStrs = true;
23           }
24           ...
25           if (isReferenceType(T_r) and !canonicalStrs.contains(c_r)) {
26             canonicalStrs.add(c_r);
27             newSeqs.addSeqForType(T_r, newSeq);
28             newStrs = true;
29           }
30         }
31       }
32       if (!newStrs) break;
33       currSeqs.addAll(newSeqs);
34     }
35     return currSeqs.getAllSeqsAsList();
36   }
```

Fig. 4. BEAPI algorithm

studies, builders comprise a constructor and a single method to add elements to the structure. However, our automated builder identification approach showed that, for Red-Black Trees, a remove method was also required (for scopes greater than 3), since there are trees with a particular balance configuration (red and black coloring for the nodes) that cannot be constructed by just adding elements to the tree. In contrast, AVL trees, which are also balanced, do not require the remove method as a builder, and the class constructor and an add routine suffice. This shows that builders identification is non-trivial to perform manually, as it requires a very careful exploration of a very large number of structures and method combinations. Other structures that require more than two builders are binomial and Fibonacci heaps.

3.4   The BEAPI Approach

A pseudocode of BEAPI is shown in Figure 4. BEAPI takes as inputs a list of methods from an API, methods (the whole API, or previously identified builders); the scope for generation, scope; a list of test sequences to create values for each primitive type provided in the scope description, primitives (automat-

ically created from configuration options `int.range`, `strings`, etc., see Fig. 2);
and a regular expression matching fields to be omitted in the canonicalization
of structures, `omitFields`. Notice that methods from more than one class could
be passed in `methods` if one wants to generate objects for several classes in the
same execution of BEAPI, e.g., when methods from one class take objects from
another class as parameters. BEAPI's map `currSeqs` stores, for each type, the
list of test sequences that are known to generate structures of the type. `currSeqs`
starts with all the primitive typed sequences in `primitives` (lines 2-3). At each
iteration of the main loop (lines 5-34), BEAPI creates new sequences for each
available method `m` (line 8), by exhaustively exploring all the possibilities for
creating test sequences using `m` and inputs generated in previous iterations and
stored in `currSeqs` (lines 9-30). The newly created test sequences that generate
new structures in the current iteration are saved in map `newSeqs` (initialized
empty in line 6); all the generated sequences are then added to `currSeqs` at the
end of the iteration (line 33). If no new structures are produced at the current
iteration (`newStrs` is false in line 32), BEAPI's main loop terminates and the list
of all sequences in `currSeqs` is returned (line 35).

Let us now discuss the details of the for loop in lines 9-30. First, all sequences
that can be used to construct inputs for `m` are retrieved in $seqsT_1,...,seqsT_n$.
BEAPI explores each tuple $(s_1,...,s_n)$ of feasible inputs for `m`. Then, it executes
`createNewSeq` (line 13), which constructs a new test sequence `newSeq` by performing the sequential composition of test sequences $s_1,...,s_n$ and routine `m`, and
replacing `m`'s formal parameters by the variables that create the required objects
in $s_1,...,s_n$. `newSeq` is then executed (line 14) and it either produces a failure
(`failure` is set to true), raises an exception that represents an invalid usage of
the API (`exception` is set to true), or its execution is successful and it creates
new objects $o_1,...,o_n,o_r$. In case of a failure, an exception is thrown and `newSeq`
is presented to the user as a witness of the failure (line 15). If a different kind of
exception is thrown, BEAPI assumes it corresponds to an API misuse (see below),
discards the test sequence (line 16) and continues with the next candidate sequence. Otherwise, the execution of `newSeq` builds new objects $o_1,...,o_n,o_r$ (or
values of primitive types) that are canonicalized by `makeCanonical` (line 17) –by
executing `linearize` from Figure 3 on each structure. If any of the structures
produced by `newSeq` exceeds the scope, `makeCanonical` sets `outOfScope` to true,
BEAPI discards `newSeq` and continues with the next one (line 18). If none of the
above happens, `makeCanonical` returns canonical versions of $o_1,...,o_n,o_r$ in
variables $c_1,...,c_n,c_r$, respectively. Afterwards, BEAPI performs state matching by checking that the canonical structure c_1 is of reference type and that
it has not been created by any previous test sequence (line 19). Notice that
`canonicalStrs` stores all of the already visited structures. If c_1 is a new structure, it is added to `canonicalStrs` (line 27), and the sequence that creates c_1,
`newSeq`, is added to the set of test sequences producing structures of type T_1
(`newSeqs` in line 27). Also, `newStrs` is set to true to indicate that at least a
new object has been created in the current iteration (line 22). This process is
repeated for canonical objects $c_2,...,c_n,c_r$ (lines 24-29).

BEAPI distinguishes failures from bad API usage based on the type of the exception (similarly to previous API based test generation techniques [23]). For example, IllegalArgumentException and IllegalStateException correspond to API misuses, and the remaining exceptions are considered failures by default. BEAPI's implementation allows the user to select the exceptions that correspond to failures and those that do not, by setting the corresponding configuration parameters. As mentioned in Section 2, BEAPI assumes that API methods throw exceptions when they fail to execute on invalid inputs. We argue that this is a common practice, called defensive programming [17], that should be followed by all programmers, as it results in more robust code and improves software testing in general [2] (besides helping automated test generation tools). We also argued in Section 2 that the specification effort required for defensive programming is much less than writing precise (and efficient) repOKs for BEG, and that this was true after manually inspecting the source code of our case studies. On the other hand, note that BEAPI can employ formal specifications to reveal bugs in the API, e.g., by executing repOK and check that it returns true on every generated object of the corresponding type (as in Randoop [23]). However, the specifications used for bug finding do not need to be very precise (e.g., the underspecified NCL repOK from Section 2 is fine for bug finding), or written in a particular way (as required by Korat). Other kinds of specifications that are weaker and simpler to write can also be used by BEAPI to reveal bugs, like violations of language specific contracts (e.g., equals is an equivalence relation in Java), metamorphic properties [7], user-provided assertions (assert), etc.

Another advantage of BEAPI is that, for each generated object, it yields a test sequence that can be executed to create the object. This is in contrast with specification based approaches (that generate a set of objects from repOK). Finding a sequence of invocations to API methods that create a specific structure is a difficult problem on its own, that can be rather costly computationally [5], or require significant effort to perform manually. Thus, often objects generated by specification based approaches are "hardwired" when used for testing a SUT (e.g., by using Java reflection), making tests very hard to understand and maintain, as they depend on the low-level implementation details of the structures [5].

4   Evaluation

In this section, we experimentally assess BEAPI against related approaches. The evaluation is organized around the following research questions:

RQ1 *Can BEG be performed efficiently using API routines?*

RQ2 *How much do the proposed optimizations impact the performance of BEG from the API?*

RQ3 *Can BEAPI help in finding discrepancies between* repOK *specifications and the API's object generation ability?*

As case studies, we employ data structures implementations from four benchmarks: three employed in the assessment of existing testing tools (Korat [4],

Kiasan [9], FAJITA [1]), and ROOPS. These benchmarks cover diverse implementations of complex data structures, which are a good target for BEG. We choose these as case studies because the implementations come equipped with repOKs, written by the authors of the benchmarks. The experiments were run on a workstation with an Intel Core i7-8700 CPU (3.2 Ghz) and 16Gb of RAM. We set a timeout of 60 minutes for each individual run. To replicate the experiments, we refer the reader to the paper's artifact [25].

4.1   RQ1: Efficiency of Bounded Exhaustive Generation from APIs

For RQ1 we assess whether or not BEAPI is fast enough to be a useful BEG approach, by comparing it to the fastest BEG approach, Korat [32]. The results of the comparison are summarized in Table 1. For each technique, we report generation times (in seconds), number of generated and explored structures, for increasingly large scopes. Due to space reasons, we show a representative sample of the results (we try to maintain the same proportion of good and bad cases for each technique in the data we report). We include the largest successful scope for each technique; the execution times for the largest scopes are in boldface in the table. In this way, should scalability issues arise, they can be easily identified. For the complete report of the results visit the paper's website [26]. To obtain proper performance results for BEAPI, we extensively tested the API methods of the classes to ensure they were correct for this experiment. We did not try to change the repOKs in any way because that would change the performance of Korat, and one of our goals here is evaluating the performance of Korat using repOKs written by different programmers. Differences in explored structures are expected, since the corresponding search spaces for Korat and BEAPI are different. However, for the same case study and scope, one would expect both approaches to generate the same number of valid structures. This is indeed the case in most experiments, with notable exceptions of two different kinds. Firstly, there are cases where repOK has errors; these cases are grayed out in the tables. Secondly, the slightly different notion of *scope* in each technique can cause discrepancies. This only happens for Red-Black Trees (RBT) and Fibonacci heaps (FibHeap), which are shown in boldface. In these cases certain structures of size n can only be generated from larger structures, with insertions followed by removals and then insertions again to trigger specific balance rearrangements. BEAPI discards generated sequences as soon as they exceed the maximum structure size, hence it cannot generate these structures.

In terms of performance, we have mixed results. In the Korat benchmark, Korat shows better performance in 4 out of 6 cases. In the FAJITA benchmark, BEAPI is better in 3 out of 4 cases. In the ROOPS benchmark, BEAPI is better in 5 out of 7 cases. In the Kiasan benchmark, Korat is faster in 6 of the 7 cases. We observe that BEAPI shows a better performance in structures with more restrictive constraints such as RBT and Binary Search Trees (BST); often these cases have a smaller number of valid structures. Cases where the number of valid structures grows faster with respect to the scope, such as doubly-linked lists (DLList), are better suited for Korat. More structures means BEAPI has

Table 1. Efficiency assessment of BEAPI against Korat

	Class	S	Time Korat	Time BEAPI	Generated Korat	Generated BEAPI	Explored Korat	Explored BEAPI
KORAT	DLList	6	0.24	7.11	55987	55987	521904	335930
		7	2.31	108.08	960800	960800	9875550	6725609
		9	1333.88	TO	435848050		5325611829	
	FibHeap	6	1.26	5.95	573223	54159	1641562	379125
		7	32.87	115.44	17858246	898394	54268866	7187167
		8	1415.77	TO	654214491		2105008180	
	BinHeap	7	0.26	25.32	107416	107416	261788	859337
		8	0.85	163.39	603744	603744	1323194	5433706
		11	2558.32	TO	2835325296		2985116257	
	BST	10	131.18	49.10	223191	223191	216680909	2231922
		11	1137.17	199.46	974427	974427	1679669258	10718710
		12	TO	1341.86		4302645		51631754
FAJITA	SLList	7	5.76	17.87	137257	137257	2055596	960807
		8	8.16	256.49	2396745	2396745	40701876	19173969
		9	190.45	TO	48427561		919451065	
	RBT	11	40.54	33.42	51242	39942	53141999	878743
		12	220.77	79.45	146073	112237	276868584	2693710
		13	1277.67	689.06	428381	314852	1454153331	8186175
	BinTree	10	73.73	51.34	223191	223191	218675679	2231922
		11	634.114	265.57	974427	974427	1689480455	10718710
		12	TO	1578.72		4302645		51631754
	AVL	10	163.50	1.92	7393	7393	349178307	73942
		11	1271.23	5.80	20267	20267	2504382415	222950
		13	TO	45.45		145206		1887693
	RBT	11	58.74	19.72	51242	39942	75814869	878743
		12	318.57	63.16	146073	112237	385422689	2693710
		13	1779.83	206.66	428381	314852	1957228527	8186175
ROOPS	BinHeap	7	.77	44.452	107416	107416	1447594	859337
		8	5.96	97.08	603744	603744	13329584	5433706
		10	1174.91	TO	117157172		2061630115	
	AVL	5	3.54	0.05	1107	62	12277946	317
		6	213.63	0.09	2060	15T	101802289	950
		13	TO	46.71		145206		1887693
	NCL	6	0.65	2.27	800667	11196	805921	134364
		7	8.797	33.89	2739128	160132	16443824	2241862
		8	205.596	769.63	381367044	2739136	381381493	43826192
	BinTree	3	0.173	0.02	65376	15	65596	50
		4	37.546	0.05	121853251	51	121855507	210
		12	TO	966.41		4302645		51631754
	LList	7	0.51	12.62	137257	137257	1410799	960807
		8	7.64	295.94	2396745	2396745	26952027	19173969
		9	176.69	TO	48427561		591734656	
	RBT	11	69.87	31.02	51242	39942	75814869	878743
		12	361.88	81.03	146073	112237	385422689	2693710
		13	2007.29	697.06	428381	314852	1957228527	8186175
	FibHeap	4	1.851	0.13	131444	335	5681553	1683
		5	346.275	0.70	21629930	4381	1295961583	26297
		7	TO	129.01		898394		7187167
KIASAN	BinHeap	6	1.04	1.31	7602	7602	3202245	53222
		7	17.47	13.06	107416	107416	64592184	859337
		8	448.48	96.94	603744	603744	1483194820	5433706
	BST	11	12.184	204.83	974427	974427	69000009	10718710
		12	65.305	1235.67	4302645	4302645	308229505	51631754
		14	1751.4	TO	86211885		7438853941	
	DLL	7	0.614	18.09	137257	137257	2326622	960807
		8	9.824	257.42	2396745	2396745	45449534	19173969
		9	245.787	TO	48427561		1015587001	
	RBT	7	10.76	0.78	911	561	44832139	7866
		8	283.33	1.57	2489	1657	1044561963	26526
		12	TO	84.51		112237		2693710
	DisjSetFast	6	0.198	0.89	52165	544	117456	22890
		7	1.209	8.26	1545157	4397	3398383	246288
		9	1402.376	TO	2201735557		4715569321	
	StackList	6	0.128	4.35	55987	55987	56008	335930
		7	0.517	83.06	960800	960800	960828	6725609
		9	212.919	TO	435848050		435848095	
	BHeap	7	0.654	53.78	3206861	458123	3221407	3665089
		8	8.98	1221.59	64014472	8001809	64124432	72016409
		9	202.804	TO	1447959627		1449279657	
	TreeMap	5	.55	24.95	40526	34276	162375	1028287
		6	2.85	866.71	1207261	1098397	3381725	46132686
		8	1980.70	TO	1626500673		2671020961	

to create more test sequences in each successive iteration, which makes its performance suffer more in such cases. As expected, the way repOKs are written has a significant impact in Korat's performance. For example, for binomial heaps (BinHeap) Korat reaches scope 8 with Roops' repOK, scope 10 with FAJITA's repOK, and scope 11 with Korat's repOK (all equivalent in terms of generated structures). In most cases, repOKs from the Korat benchmark result in better performance, as these are fine-tuned for usage with Korat. Case studies with errors in repOKs are grayed out in the table, and discussed further in Section 4.3. Notice that errors in repOKs can severely affect Korat's performance.

4.2   RQ2: Impact of BEAPI's Optimizations

Table 2. Execution times (sec) of BEAPI under different configurations.

ROOPS					
Class	S	SM/BLD	SM	BLD	NoOPT
AVL	3	.02	.04	.34	-
	4	.03	.07	102.16	-
	5	.05	.11	-	-
	13	46.71	657.17	-	-
NCL	3	.04	1.31	1.37	7.96
	4	.10	9.59	52.17	-
	5	.34	40.54	-	-
	8	769.63	-	-	-
BinTree	3	.02	.04	.23	33.84
	4	.05	.08	85.32	-
	5	.11	.16	-	-
	12	966.41	2281.42	-	-
LList	3	.03	.09	.26	-
	4	.07	.48	115.27	-
	5	.18	118.75	-	-
	8	295.94	-	-	-
RBT	3	.04	.04	39.11	-
	4	.11	.09	-	-
	5	.22	.14	-	-
	12	81.03	2379.44	-	-
FibHeap	3	.04	.09	.94	-
	4	.13	.20	-	-
	5	.70	1.13	-	-
	7	129.01	243.36	-	-
BinHeap	3	.05	.11	2.03	18.38
	4	.09	.34	-	-
	5	.26	.96	-	-
	8	96.94	220.18	-	-

Real World					
Class	S	SM/BLD	SM	BLD	NoOPT
NCL	3	.10	.47	-	-
	4	.41	3.48	-	-
	5	3.33	-	-	-
	6	73.78	-	-	-
TSet	3	.03	.07	56.82	-
	11	21.52	86.06	-	-
	12	69.98	276.85	-	-
	13	226.66	887.83	-	-
TMap	3	.11	.25	-	-
	4	.75	2.36	-	-
	5	15.97	57.64	-	-
	6	839.87	2901.37	-	-
LList	3	.02	.13	.64	-
	6	.96	258.85	-	-
	7	12.98	-	-	-
	8	286.21	-	-	-
HMap	3	.10	11.49	-	-
	4	.55	-	-	-
	5	5.33	-	-	-
	6	119.87	-	-	-

In RQ2 we assess the impact each of BEAPI's proposed optimizations has in BEG. For this, we assess the performance of four different BEAPI configurations: SM/BLD is BEAPI with state matching (SM) and builder identification (BLD) enabled; SM is BEAPI with only state matching (SM) enabled; BLD is BEAPI with only builders (BLD) identification enabled; NoOPT has both optimizations disabled. The left part of Table 2 summarizes the results of this experiment for the ROOPS benchmark; the right part reports preliminary results on five "real world" implementations of data structures: LinkedList (21 API methods), TreeSet (22 API methods), TreeMap (32 methods) and HashMap (29 methods) from `java.util`, and NCL from Apache Collections (20 methods). As most real world implementations, these data structures do not come equipped with repOKs, hence we only employed them in this RQ.

The brute force approach (NoOPT) performs poorly even for the easiest case studies and very small scopes. These scopes are too small and often not enough if one wants to generate high quality test suites. State matching is the most impactful optimization, greatly improving by itself the performance and scalability all around (compare NoOPT and SM results). As expected, builders identification is much more relevant in cases where the number of methods in the API is large (more than 10), and remarkably in the real world data structures (with 20 or more API methods). SM/BLD is more than an order of magnitude faster than SM in `AVL` and `RBT`, and it reaches one more scope in NCL and `LList`. The remaining classes of ROOPS have just a few methods, and the impact of using builders is relatively small. The conclusions drawn from ROOPS apply to the other three benchmarks (we omit their results here for space reasons, visit the paper's website for a complete report [26]). In the real world data structures, using precomputed builders allowed SM/BLD to scale to significantly larger scopes in all cases but `TreeMap` and `TreeSet`, where it significantly improves running times. Overall, the proposed optimizations have a crucial impact in BEAPI's performance and scalability, and both should be enabled to obtain good results

On the cost of builders identification. Due to space reasons we report builders identification times in the paper's website [26]. For the conclusions of this section, it is sufficient to say that scope 5 was employed for builders identification in all cases, and that the maximum runtime of the approach was 65 seconds in the four benchmarks (ROOPS' SLL, 11 methods), and 132 seconds in the real world data structures (`TreeMap`, 32 methods). We manually checked that the identified methods included a set of sufficient builders in all cases. Notice that BEG is often performed for increasingly larger scopes, and the identified builders can be reused across executions. Thus, builder identification times are amortized across different executions, which makes it difficult to calculate how much builder identification times add to BEAPI running times in each case. So we did not include builder identification times in BEAPI running times in any of the experiments. Notice that, for the larger scopes, which arguably are the most important, builders identification time is negligible in relation to generation times.

4.3   RQ3: Analysis of Specifications using BEAPI

RQ3 addresses whether BEAPI can be useful in assisting the user in finding flaws in repOKs, by comparing the set of objects that can be generated using the API and the set of objects generated from the repOK. We devised the following automated procedure. First, we run BEAPI to generate a set SA of structures from the API, and Korat to generate a set SR from repOK, using the same scope for both tools. Second, we canonicalize the structures in both SA and SR using linearization (Section 3.2). Third, we compare sets SA and SR for equality. Differences in this comparison point out a mismatch between repOK and the API. There are three possible outputs for this automated procedure. If SA ⊂ SR, it is possible

Table 3. Summary of flaws found in `repOKs` using BEAPI

Bench.	Class	Error Description	Type
Korat	RBTree	Color of root should not be red	under
Roops	NCL	Key values in the cache should be set to null	under
		Key value of the dummy node in the main list should be null	under
	BinTree	Parent of root node should be null	under
	RBT	Color of root should not be red	under
	AVL	Height computation is wrong (leaves are assigned the wrong value)	error
		Repeated key values should not be allowed	under
	FibHeap	Left and right fields of nodes should not be null	under
		Min node should always contain the minimum value in the heap	under
		If a node has no child its degree should be zero	under
		Child nodes should have smaller keys than their parents	under
		Parent fields of all nodes are forced to be null	over
		Heap with min node set to null is rejected	over
Kiasan	DisjSetFast	The rank of the root can be invalid	under
	BinaryHeap	The first position of an array (dummy) may contain an element	under
Fajita	AVL	Height computation is wrong (leaves are assigned the wrong value)	error

that the API generates a subset of the valid structures, that `repOK` suffers from underspecification (missing constraints), or both. In this case, the structures in SR that do not belong to SA are witnesses of the problem, and the user has to manually analyze them to find out where the error is. Here, we report the (manually confirmed) underspecification errors in `repOKs` that are witnessed by the aforementioned structures. In contrast, when SR ⊂ SA, it can be the case that the API generates a superset of the valid structures, that `repOK` suffers from overspecification (`repOK` is too strong), or both. The structures in SA that do not belong to SR might point out to the root of the error, and again they have to be manually analyzed by the user. We report the (manually confirmed) overspecification errors in `repOKs` that are witnessed by these structures. Finally, it can be the case that there are structures in SR that do not belong to SA, and there are structures (distinct than the former ones) in SA that do not belong to SR. These might be due to faults in the API, flaws in the `repOK`, or both. We report the manually confirmed flaws in `repOKs` witnessed by such structures simply as errors (`repOK` describes a different set of structures than the one it should). Notice that differences in the scope definitions for the approaches might make sets SA and SR differ. This was only the case in the RBT and FibHeap structures, where BEAPI generated a smaller set of structures for the same scope than Korat due to balance constraints (as explained in Section 4.1). However, these "false positives" can be easily revealed, since all the structures generated by Korat were always included in the structures generated by BEAPI if a larger scope was used for the latter approach. Using this insight we manually discarded the "false positives" due to scope differences in RBT and FibHeap.

The results of this experiment are summarized in Table 3. We found out flaws in 9 out of 26 `repOKs` using the approach described above. The high number of flaws discovered evidences that problems in repOKs are hard to find manually, and that BEAPI can be of great help for this task.

5   Related Work

BEG approaches have been shown effective in achieving high code coverage and finding faults, as reported in various research papers [20,16,4,33]. Our goal here is not to assess yet again the effectiveness of BEG suites, but to introduce an approach that is straightforward to use in today's software because it does not require the manual work of writing formal specifications of the properties of the inputs (e.g., repOKs). Different languages have been proposed to formally describe structural constraints for BEG, including Alloy's relational logic (in the so-called declarative style), employed by the TestEra tool [20]; and source code in an imperative programming language (in the so-called operational style), as used by Korat [4]. The declarative style has the advantage of being more concise and simpler for people familiar with it, however this knowledge is not common among developers. The operational style can be more verbose, but as specifications and source code are written in the same language this style is most of the time preferred by developers. UDITA [11] and HyTeK [29] propose to employ a mix of the operational and the declarative styles to write the specifications, as parts of the constraints are often easier to write in one style or the other. With precise specifications both approaches can be used for BEG. Still, to use these approaches developers have to be familiar with both specification styles, and take the time and effort required to write the specifications. Model checkers like Java Pathfinder [34] (JPF) can also perform BEG, but the user has to manually provide a "driver" for the generation: a program that the model checker can use to generate the structures that will be fed to the SUT afterwards. Writing a BEG driver often involves invoking API routines in combination with JPF's nondeterministic operators, hence the developer must familiarize with such operators and put in some manual effort to use this approach. Furthermore, JPF runs over a customized virtual machine in place of Java's standard JVM, so there is a significant overhead in running JPF compared to the use of the standard JVM (employed by BEAPI). The results of a previous study [32] show that JPF is significantly slower than Korat for BEG. Therein, Korat has been shown to be the fastest and most scalable BEG approach at the time of publication [32]. This in part can be explained by its smart pruning of the search space of invalid structures and the elimination of isomorphic structures. In contrast, BEAPI does not require a repOK and works by making calls to the API.

An alternative kind of BEG consists of generating all inputs to cover all feasible (bounded) program paths, instead of generating all feasible bounded inputs. This is the approach of systematic dynamic test generation, a variant of symbolic execution [14]. This approach is implemented by many tools [13,12,24,8], and has been successfully used to produce test suites with high code coverage, reveal real program faults, and for proving memory safety of programs. Kiasan [9] and FA-

JITA [1] are also white-box test case generation approaches that require formal specifications and aim for coverage of the SUT.

Linearization has been employed to eliminate isomorphic structures in traditional model checkers [15,28], and also in software model checkers [35]. A previous study experimented with state matching in JPF and proposed several approaches for pruning the search space for program inputs using linearization, for both concrete and symbolic execution [35]. As stated before, concrete execution in JPF requires the user to provide a driver. The symbolic approach attempts to find inputs to cover paths of the SUT; we perform BEG instead. Linearization has also been employed for test suite minimization [36].

6 Conclusions

Software quality assurance can be greatly improved thanks to modern software analysis techniques, among which automated test generation techniques play an outstanding role [6,18,10,23,19,12,20,4,13]. Random and search-based approaches have shown great success in automatically generating test suites with very good coverage and mutation metrics, but their random nature does now allow these techniques to precisely characterize the families of software behaviors that the generated tests cover. Systematic techniques such as those based on model checking, symbolic execution or bounded exhaustive generation, cover a precise set of behaviors, and thus can provide specific correctness guarantees.

In this paper, we presented BEAPI, a technique that aims at facilitating the application of a systematic technique, bounded exhaustive input generation, by producing structures solely from a component's API, without the need for a formal specification of the properties of the structures. BEAPI can generate bounded exhaustive suites from components with implicit invariants, and reduces the burden of providing formal specifications, and tailoring the specifications for improved generation. Thanks to a number of optimizations, including an automated identification of builder routines and a canonicalization/state matching mechanism, BEAPI can generate bounded exhaustive suites with a performance comparable to that of the fastest specification-based technique Korat [4]. We have also identified the characteristics of a component that may make it more suitable for a specification-based generation, or an API-based generation.

Finally, we have shown how specification based approaches and BEAPI can complement each other, depicting how BEAPI can be used to assess repOK implementations. Using this approach, we found a number of subtle errors in repOK specifications taken from the literature. Thus, techniques that require repOK specifications (e.g, [30]), as well as techniques that require bounded-exhaustive suites (e.g., [21]) can benefit from our presented generation technique.

Acknowledgements This work was partially supported by ANPCyT PICTs 2017-2622, 2019-2050, 2020-2896, an Amazon Research Award, and by EU's Marie Sklodowska-Curie grant No. 101008233 (MISSION). Facundo Molina's work is also supported by Microsoft Research, through a LA PhD Award.

References

1. Abad, P., Aguirre, N., Bengolea, V.S., Ciolek, D.A., Frias, M.F., Galeotti, J.P., Maibaum, T., Moscato, M.M., Rosner, N., Vissani, I.: Improving test generation under rich contracts by tight bounds and incremental SAT solving. In: Sixth IEEE International Conference on Software Testing, Verification and Validation, ICST 2013, Luxembourg, Luxembourg, March 18-22, 2013. pp. 21–30. IEEE Computer Society (2013)
2. Ammann, P., Offutt, J.: Introduction to Software Testing. Cambridge University Press, Cambridge (2016)
3. Andoni, A., Daniliuc, D., Khurshid, S., Marinov, D.: Evaluating the "small scope hypothesis". Tech. rep., MIT CSAIL (10 2002)
4. Boyapati, C., Khurshid, S., Marinov, D.: Korat: automated testing based on java predicates. In: Frankl, P.G. (ed.) Proceedings of the International Symposium on Software Testing and Analysis, ISSTA 2002, Roma, Italy, July 22-24, 2002. pp. 123–133. ACM (2002)
5. Braione, P., Denaro, G., Mattavelli, A., Pezzè, M.: Combining symbolic execution and search-based testing for programs with complex heap inputs. In: Bultan, T., Sen, K. (eds.) Proceedings of the 26th ACM SIGSOFT International Symposium on Software Testing and Analysis, Santa Barbara, CA, USA, July 10 - 14, 2017. pp. 90–101. ACM (2017)
6. Cadar, C., Dunbar, D., Engler, D.R.: KLEE: unassisted and automatic generation of high coverage tests for complex systems programs. In: Draves, R., van Renesse, R. (eds.) 8th USENIX Symposium on Operating Systems Design and Implementation, OSDI 2008, December 8-10, 2008, San Diego, California, USA, Proceedings. pp. 209–224. USENIX Association (2008)
7. Chen, T.Y., Kuo, F.C., Liu, H., Poon, P.L., Towey, D., Tse, T.H., Zhou, Z.Q.: Metamorphic testing: A review of challenges and opportunities. ACM Comput. Surv. **51**(1) (jan 2018)
8. Christakis, M., Godefroid, P.: Proving memory safety of the ANI windows image parser using compositional exhaustive testing. In: D'Souza, D., Lal, A., Larsen, K.G. (eds.) Verification, Model Checking, and Abstract Interpretation - 16th International Conference, VMCAI 2015, Mumbai, India, January 12-14, 2015. Proceedings. Lecture Notes in Computer Science, vol. 8931, pp. 373–392. Springer (2015)
9. Deng, X., Robby, Hatcliff, J.: Kiasan: A verification and test-case generation framework for java based on symbolic execution. In: Leveraging Applications of Formal Methods, Second International Symposium, ISoLA 2006, Paphos, Cyprus, 15-19 November 2006. p. 137. IEEE Computer Society (2006)
10. Fraser, G., Arcuri, A.: Evosuite: automatic test suite generation for object-oriented software. In: Gyimóthy, T., Zeller, A. (eds.) SIGSOFT/FSE'11 19th ACM SIG-SOFT Symposium on the Foundations of Software Engineering (FSE-19) and ESEC'11: 13th European Software Engineering Conference (ESEC-13), Szeged, Hungary, September 5-9, 2011. pp. 416–419. ACM (2011)
11. Gligoric, M., Gvero, T., Jagannath, V., Khurshid, S., Kuncak, V., Marinov, D.: Test generation through programming in UDITA. In: Kramer, J., Bishop, J., Devanbu, P.T., Uchitel, S. (eds.) Proceedings of the 32nd ACM/IEEE International Conference on Software Engineering - Volume 1, ICSE 2010, Cape Town, South Africa, 1-8 May 2010. pp. 225–234. ACM (2010)

12. Godefroid, P., Klarlund, N., Sen, K.: DART: directed automated random testing. In: Sarkar, V., Hall, M.W. (eds.) Proceedings of the ACM SIGPLAN 2005 Conference on Programming Language Design and Implementation, Chicago, IL, USA, June 12-15, 2005. pp. 213–223. ACM (2005)

13. Godefroid, P., Levin, M.Y., Molnar, D.A.: SAGE: whitebox fuzzing for security testing. Commun. ACM **55**(3), 40–44 (2012)

14. Godefroid, P., Sen, K.: Combining model checking and testing. In: Clarke, E.M., Henzinger, T.A., Veith, H., Bloem, R. (eds.) Handbook of Model Checking, pp. 613–649. Springer (2018)

15. Iosif, R.: Symmetry reduction criteria for software model checking. In: Bosnacki, D., Leue, S. (eds.) Model Checking of Software, 9th International SPIN Workshop, Grenoble, France, April 11-13, 2002, Proceedings. Lecture Notes in Computer Science, vol. 2318, pp. 22–41. Springer (2002)

16. Khurshid, S., Marinov, D.: Checking java implementation of a naming architecture using testera. Electron. Notes Theor. Comput. Sci. **55**(3), 322–342 (2001)

17. Liskov, B., Guttag, J.: Program Development in Java: Abstraction, Specification, and Object-Oriented Design. Addison-Wesley Longman Publishing Co., Inc., USA, 1st edn. (2000)

18. Luckow, K.S., Pasareanu, C.S.: Symbolic pathfinder v7. ACM SIGSOFT Softw. Eng. Notes **39**(1), 1–5 (2014)

19. Ma, L., Artho, C., Zhang, C., Sato, H., Gmeiner, J., Ramler, R.: GRT: an automated test generator using orchestrated program analysis. In: Cohen, M.B., Grunske, L., Whalen, M. (eds.) 30th IEEE/ACM International Conference on Automated Software Engineering, ASE 2015, Lincoln, NE, USA, November 9-13, 2015. pp. 842–847. IEEE Computer Society (2015)

20. Marinov, D., Khurshid, S.: Testera: A novel framework for automated testing of java programs. In: 16th IEEE International Conference on Automated Software Engineering (ASE 2001), 26-29 November 2001, Coronado Island, San Diego, CA, USA. p. 22. IEEE Computer Society (2001)

21. Molina, F., Ponzio, P., Aguirre, N., Frias, M.: EvoSpex: An evolutionary algorithm for learning postconditions. In: Proceedings of the 43rd ACM/IEEE International Conference on Software Engineering ICSE 2021, Virtual (originally Madrid, Spain), 23-29 May 2021 (2021)

22. Myers, G.J., Sandler, C., Badgett, T.: The Art of Software Testing. Wiley Publishing, 3rd edn. (2011)

23. Pacheco, C., Lahiri, S.K., Ernst, M.D., Ball, T.: Feedback-directed random test generation. In: 29th International Conference on Software Engineering (ICSE 2007), Minneapolis, MN, USA, May 20-26, 2007. pp. 75–84. IEEE Computer Society (2007)

24. Pham, L.H., Le, Q.L., Phan, Q., Sun, J.: Concolic testing heap-manipulating programs. In: ter Beek, M.H., McIver, A., Oliveira, J.N. (eds.) Formal Methods - The Next 30 Years - Third World Congress, FM 2019, Porto, Portugal, October 7-11, 2019, Proceedings. Lecture Notes in Computer Science, vol. 11800, pp. 442–461. Springer (2019)

25. Politano, M., Bengolea, V., Molina, F., Aguirre, N., Frias, M.F., Ponzio, P.: *Efficient Bounded Exhaustive Input Generation from Program APIs* paper's artifact. https://doi.org/10.5281/zenodo.7574758

26. Politano, M., Bengolea, V., Molina, F., Aguirre, N., Frias, M.F., Ponzio, P.: *Efficient Bounded Exhaustive Input Generation from Program APIs* paper's website. https://sites.google.com/view/bounded-exhaustive-api

27. Ponzio, P., Bengolea, V.S., Politano, M., Aguirre, N., Frias, M.F.: Automatically identifying sufficient object builders from module apis. In: Hähnle, R., van der Aalst, W.M.P. (eds.) Fundamental Approaches to Software Engineering - 22nd International Conference, FASE 2019, Held as Part of the European Joint Conferences on Theory and Practice of Software, ETAPS 2019, Prague, Czech Republic, April 6-11, 2019, Proceedings. Lecture Notes in Computer Science, vol. 11424, pp. 427–444. Springer (2019)

28. Robby, Dwyer, M.B., Hatcliff, J., Iosif, R.: Space-reduction strategies for model checking dynamic software. Electron. Notes Theor. Comput. Sci. **89**(3), 499–517 (2003)

29. Rosner, N., Bengolea, V., Ponzio, P., Khalek, S.A., Aguirre, N., Frias, M.F., Khurshid, S.: Bounded exhaustive test input generation from hybrid invariants. SIGPLAN Not. **49**(10), 655–674 (oct 2014)

30. Rosner, N., Geldenhuys, J., Aguirre, N., Visser, W., Frias, M.F.: BLISS: improved symbolic execution by bounded lazy initialization with SAT support. IEEE Trans. Software Eng. **41**(7), 639–660 (2015)

31. Rosner, N., Pombo, C.G.L., Aguirre, N., Jaoua, A., Mili, A., Frias, M.F.: Parallel bounded verification of alloy models by transcoping. In: Cohen, E., Rybalchenko, A. (eds.) Verified Software: Theories, Tools, Experiments - 5th International Conference, VSTTE 2013, Menlo Park, CA, USA, May 17-19, 2013, Revised Selected Papers. Lecture Notes in Computer Science, vol. 8164, pp. 88–107. Springer (2013)

32. Siddiqui, J.H., Khurshid, S.: An empirical study of structural constraint solving techniques. In: Breitman, K.K., Cavalcanti, A. (eds.) Formal Methods and Software Engineering, 11th International Conference on Formal Engineering Methods, ICFEM 2009, Rio de Janeiro, Brazil, December 9-12, 2009. Proceedings. Lecture Notes in Computer Science, vol. 5885, pp. 88–106. Springer (2009)

33. Sullivan, K.J., Yang, J., Coppit, D., Khurshid, S., Jackson, D.: Software assurance by bounded exhaustive testing. In: Avrunin, G.S., Rothermel, G. (eds.) Proceedings of the ACM/SIGSOFT International Symposium on Software Testing and Analysis, ISSTA 2004, Boston, Massachusetts, USA, July 11-14, 2004. pp. 133–142. ACM (2004)

34. Visser, W., Mehlitz, P.C.: Model checking programs with java pathfinder. In: Godefroid, P. (ed.) Model Checking Software, 12th International SPIN Workshop, San Francisco, CA, USA, August 22-24, 2005, Proceedings. Lecture Notes in Computer Science, vol. 3639, p. 27. Springer (2005)

35. Visser, W., Pasareanu, C.S., Pelánek, R.: Test input generation for java containers using state matching. In: Pollock, L.L., Pezzè, M. (eds.) Proceedings of the ACM/SIGSOFT International Symposium on Software Testing and Analysis, ISSTA 2006, Portland, Maine, USA, July 17-20, 2006. pp. 37–48. ACM (2006)

36. Xie, T., Marinov, D., Notkin, D.: Rostra: A framework for detecting redundant object-oriented unit tests. In: 19th IEEE International Conference on Automated Software Engineering (ASE 2004), 20-25 September 2004, Linz, Austria. pp. 196–205. IEEE Computer Society (2004)

Feature-Guided Analysis of Neural Networks

Divya Gopinath[1]([✉]), Luca Lungeanu[2], Ravi Mangal[3], Corina Păsăreanu[1,3],
Siqi Xie[3], and Huafeng Yu[4]

[1] KBR, NASA Ames, Moffett Field CA 94035, USA
divya.gopinath@nasa.gov
[2] Lynbrook High School, San Jose CA, 95129, USA
[3] Carnegie Mellon University, Pittsburgh PA 15213, USA
[4] Boeing Research & Technology, Santa Clara CA, USA

Abstract. Applying standard software engineering practices to neural
networks is challenging due to the lack of high-level abstractions describing a neural network's behavior. To address this challenge, we propose
to extract high-level task-specific *features* from the neural network internal representation, based on monitoring the neural network activations.
The extracted feature representations can serve as a link to high-level
requirements and can be leveraged to enable fundamental software engineering activities, such as automated testing, debugging, requirements
analysis, and formal verification, leading to better engineering of neural
networks. Using two case studies, we present initial empirical evidence
demonstrating the feasibility of our ideas.

Keywords: Features · Neural Networks · Software Engineering

1 Introduction

The remarkable computational capabilities unlocked by neural networks have
led to the emergence of a rapidly growing class of neural-network based software
applications. Unlike traditional software applications whose logic is driven from
input-output specifications, neural networks are inherently *opaque*, as their logic
is learned from examples of input-output pairs. The lack of high-level abstractions
makes it challenging to interpret the logical reasoning employed by a neural
network and hinders the use of standard software engineering practices such as
automated testing, debugging, requirements analysis, and formal verification that
have been established for producing high-quality software.

In this work, we aim to address this challenge by proposing a *feature-guided*
approach to neural network engineering. Our proposed approach is illustrated
in Figure 1. We draw from the insight that, in a neural network, early layers
typically extract the important features of the inputs and the dense layers close
to the output contain logic in terms of these features to make decisions [12].
The approach therefore first extracts high-level, human-understandable feature
representations from the trained neural network which allows us to formally link
domain-specific, human-understandable features to the internal logic of a trained
model. This in turn enables us to reason about the model through the lens of
the features and to drive the above mentioned software engineering activities.

The original version of this chapter was revised: The affiliations of some of the authors
have been corrected as well as the name of the author Huafeng Yu. The correction to
this chapter is available at https://doi.org/10.1007/978-3-031-30826-0_19

L. Lambers and S. Uchitel (Eds.): FASE 2023, LNCS 13991, pp. 133–142, 2023.
https://doi.org/10.1007/978-3-031-30826-0_7

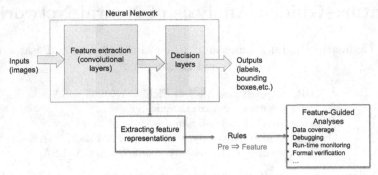

Fig. 1: Proposed Approach

For feature representations, we seek to extract associations between the activation values at the intermediate layers and higher-level abstractions that have clear semantic meaning (e.g., objects in a scene or weather conditions). We present an algorithm to extract these high-level feature representations in the form of *rules* (**pre** $\implies$ **post**) where the precondition (**pre**) is a box over the latent space at an internal layer and the postcondition (**post**) denotes the presence (or absence) of the feature.

The formal, checkable rules enable us to evaluate the quality of the datasets, retrieve and label new data, understand scenarios where models make correct and incorrect predictions, detect incorrect (or out-of-distribution) samples at run-time, and verify models against human-understandable requirements.

We evaluate our algorithm for extracting feature representations and the downstream analyses using two networks trained for computer vision tasks, namely TaxiNet [4,9], a regression model for center-line tracking on airport runways, and YOLOv4-Tiny [14], an object detection model trained on the nuImages [6] dataset for autonomous driving.

2   Extracting Feature Representations

Algorithm 2.1 describes the method for extracting the representation of a particular feature from a trained neural network. A feed-forward neural network $f : \mathbb{R}^n \to \mathbb{R}^m$ is organized in multiple *layers*, each consisting of computational units called *neurons*. Each neuron takes a weighted sum of the outputs from the previous layer and applies a non-linear *activation function* on it. The algorithm requires a *small* dataset D where each raw input is labeled with 0 or 1 indicating whether the feature under consideration is absent or present. The algorithm takes as inputs a neural network f, the dataset D, the index l of the layer used for extracting the feature representations. The first step of the algorithm (line 2) is to construct a new dataset A where each raw input x is replaced by the corresponding activation value a output by layer l ($f^l(x)$ denotes the output of f at layer l for input x). Next, the algorithm invokes a learning procedure to learn a classifier r that separates activation values that map to feature being present from activation values that map to feature absence (line 3).

Algorithm 2.1: Extracting Feature Representations

Inputs: A neural classifier $f \in \mathbb{R}^n \to \mathbb{R}^m$, dataset $D \subseteq \mathbb{R}^n \times \{0,1\}$, $|D| = N$,
   and layer $l \in \{1, \ldots, k-1\}$, where k is the number of layers in f
Output: Representation r for the feature

1 FeatRep(f, D, l):
2      $A := \{(a,y) \mid (x,y) \in D \wedge a = f^l(x)\}$ //f^l is the output of f at layer l
3      $r := $ Learn(A)
4   return r

We use decision tree learning on line 3 to extract feature representations as a set of rules of the form $\texttt{pre} \Rightarrow \{0,1\}$; $\texttt{pre}$ in each rule is a condition on neuron values at layer l, and 0 or 1 indicates whether the rule corresponds to the feature being absent or present. $\texttt{pre}$ is a box in the activation space of layer l, i.e., $\bigwedge_{N_j \in \mathcal{N}_l}(N_j(x) \in [v_j^L, v_j^U])$. Here $\mathcal{N}_l$ is the set of neurons at layer l, and v_j^L and v_j^U are lower and upper bounds for the output of neuron N_j. The rules mined by decision-tree learning partition the activation space at a given inner layer. Some partitions may be impure containing inputs both with and without the feature. We only select pure rules, having 100% precision on d. We return these rules as r. Note that there can be activation values for which no rule in r is satisfied and we are unable to say whether the feature is absent or present.

3 Feature-Guided Analyses

The extracted feature representations as formal, checkable rules enable multiple analyses, as listed below.

- **Data analysis and testing.** We can assess the quality of the training and testing data in terms of coverage of different features. We can leverage the extracted feature representations to automatically retrieve new data that has the necessary features, by checking that the (unlabeled) data satisfies the corresponding rules. We can also use the extracted rules to label new data with their corresponding features, enabling further data-coverage analysis.
- **Debugging and explanations of network behavior.** We can leverage the feature rules to uncover the high-level, human-understandable reasons for a neural network model making correct and incorrect predictions. In the latter case we can repair the model, which involves automatically selecting and training based on inputs with features that caused incorrect predictions.
- **Formulation and analysis of requirements.** Extracted feature representations are the key to enabling verification of models with respect to high-level safety requirements ($\texttt{pre} \Longrightarrow \texttt{post}$). Specifically, the constraint $\texttt{pre}$ in the requirement expressed over features can be translated into a constraint $\texttt{pre}'$ expressed over activation values, by substituting the features with their corresponding representations. The modified requirement $\texttt{pre}' \Longrightarrow \texttt{post}$ can be checked automatically using off-the-shelf verification tools [10].

- **Run-time monitoring.** We can also enforce safety properties at run-time. For instance, we can use `pre'` as above to check (at run-time) whether inputs satisfy a desired precondition, and reject the ones that don't.
- **Conformance with the operational design domain (ODD).** This is a particular instance of the case above, where we use the rules to formally capture the model's expected domain of operation and use a run-time guard to ensure that the model is not used in scenarios outside its ODD. A related problem is out-of-distribution detection, where we can similarly formulate the conditions under which the model is not supposed to operate and use run-time monitoring to enforce it.

One can also check overlap between feature rules, using off-the-shelf decision procedures, to uncover spurious correlations between the different features that are learned by the network. We envision many other applications for these rules, whose exploration we leave for the future.

4   Case Studies

We use two case studies to present initial empirical evidence in support of our ideas. In particular, we show that Algorithm 2.1 with decision tree learning is successful in extracting feature representations. We also demonstrate how these representations can be used for analyzing the behavior of neural networks.

4.1   Center-line Tracking with TaxiNet

We first analyzed TaxiNet, a perception model for center-line tracking on airport runways [4,9]. It takes runway images as input and produces two outputs, cross-track (CTE) and heading angle (HE) errors which indicate the lateral and angular distance respectively of the nose of the plane from the center-line of the runway. We analyzed a CNN model provided by our industry partner, with 24 layers including three dense layers (100/50/10 neurons) before the output layer. It is critical that the TaxiNet model functions correctly and keeps the plane safe without running off the taxiway. The domain experts provided a specification for correct output behavior: $|y_0 - y_{0ideal}| \leq 1.0m \wedge |y_1 - y_{1ideal}| \leq 5$ *degrees*. One can evaluate the model correctness using Mean Absolute Error (MAE) on a test set (CTE:0.366, HE:1.645).

Feature Elicitation We first need to identify the high-level features that are relevant for the task. These could be some of the simulator parameters (for images generated from a simulator) and/or could be derived from high-level system (natural language) requirements. This is a challenging process requiring several iterations in collaboration with the domain experts. We obtained a list of 10 features: center-line, shadow, skid, position, heading, time-of-day, weather, visibility, intersection (junction) and objects (runway lights, birds, etc.) and values of interest for each feature respectively.

Data Analysis and Annotations We manually annotated a subset of 450 images from the test set with values for each feature. An initial data-coverage

Table 1: Rules for TaxiNet: d: annotated dataset, $\#d$: total number of instances for that feature value in d, R_d: recall (%) on d, P_v,R_v: precision (%) and recall (%) on validation set. Rules with highest R_d are shown.

Feature	Rule	#d	R_d	P_v	R_v
Center-line	$N_{3,9} <= 1.39 \wedge N_{3,9} > -0.98 \wedge N_{3,1} > -0.99$ $\wedge N_{3,4} > -0.99 \implies present$	202	92	93	100
	$N_{3,9} > 1.39 \wedge N_{3,6} <= -0.81 \implies absent$	25	40	100	12
Shadow	$N_{2,45} <= -0.75 \wedge N_{1,50} > -0.91$ $\wedge N_{1,9} <= -0.95 \implies present$	30	86	100	69.23
	$N_{2,4} <= -0.73 \wedge N_{2,3} > 0.06 \wedge N_{2,9} > -0.98 \implies absent$	200	94.5	97	100
Skid	$N_{2,8} <= -0.98 \wedge N_{2,10} <= 0.32 \implies dark$	40	52.5	94.44	43.5
	$N_{1,28} <= -0.93 \wedge N_{2,58} > -0.88 \implies no$	5	60	0	0
	$N_{2,8} > -0.997 \wedge N_{2,48} > -0.991 \wedge N_{2,42} <= -0.342$ $\wedge N_{2,25} <= 1.82 \implies light$	182	97.8	93.4	95
Position	$N_{2,2} > -0.99 \wedge N_{2,24} <= -0.3 \wedge N_{2,9} <= -1.19 \implies right$	101	90	92.3	95.09
	$N_{1,26} > -0.55 \wedge N_{1,20} <= -0.29 \wedge N_{1,52} <= -0.96 \implies left$	109	91	100	75.22
	$N_{3,6} > -0.17 \wedge N_{3,6} <= 0.45 \wedge N_{3,3} > -0.38 \wedge N_{3,7} <= -0.55$ $\wedge N_{3,0} <= 2.56 \wedge N_{3,5} <= -0.95 \implies on$	11	45	13.5	45.45
Heading	$N_{1,5} > 3.29 \wedge N_{1,90} <= -0.87 \wedge N_{1,81} <= -0.76 \implies away$	120	65	62.2	90.6
	$N_{1,5} <= 3.29 \wedge N_{1,37} > -0.84 \wedge N_{1,50} <= 8.22 \wedge N_{1,53} <= -0.39$ $\wedge N_{1,64} > -0.98 \wedge N_{1,45} <= -0.26 \wedge N_{1,34} <= 12.21 \implies towards$	102	83	73.9	16.5

Center-line Present   Center-line Absent   Shadow Present   Dark Skid

Fig. 2: Images satisfying rules for features

analysis of the distribution of the values for every feature across all the images, revealed many gaps. For instance, there were only day-time images, with only cloudy weather and all the images had high visibility. Also apart from runway lights, there were no images with any other objects on the runway. The analysis proved already useful, providing feedback to the experts with regard to the type of images that need to be added to improve the training and testing of the model.

Extracting Feature Rules We invoke Algorithm 2.1 to obtain rules in terms of the values of the neurons at the three dense layers of the network. Note that for each feature, we mined a separate rule for every value of interest. We used half of the annotated set of 450 images for extraction (d in Algorithm 2.1) and the remaining for validation of the rules. There are multiple rules extracted for each feature; each rule is associated with a support value (# of instances in d satisfying the rule) and has 100% precision on them since we only extract pure rules. The results are summarized in Table 1, indicating some high-quality rules (for "center-line present" , "shadow present" , "light skid", "position left", "position right"), measured on the validation set.

Figure 2 displays some of the images satisfying different rules. The corresponding heat maps were created by computing the image pixels impacting the neurons in the feature rule [7]. Note that for the "center-line present" rule, the part of the image impacting the rule (highlighted in red) is the center-line, indicating that indeed the rules identify the feature. On the other hand, in the absence of the center-line, it is unclear what information is used by the model (and the image leads to error). The heatmaps for the shadow and skid also correctly highlight the part of the image with the shadow of the nose and the skid marks. We used such visualization techniques to further validate the rules.

Labeling New Data The rules extracted based on a small set of manually annotated data can be leveraged to annotate a much larger data set. We used the rules for center-line (present/absent) to label all of the test data (2000 images). We chose the rule with highest R_d for the experiments. However, more rules could be chosen to increase coverage. 1822 of the images satisfied the rule for "center-line present" and 79 images for "center-line absent". We visually checked some of the images to estimate the accuracy of the labelling. We similarly annotated more images for the shadow and skid features. These new labels enable further data-coverage analysis over the train and test datasets.

Feature-Guided Analysis We performed preliminary experiments to demonstrate the potential of feature-guided analyses. We first calculated the model accuracy (MAE) on subsets of the data labelled with the feature present and absent respectively. We also determined the % of inputs in the respective subsets violating the correctness property. The results are summarized in Table 2.

Table 2: Feature-Guided Analysis Results

Rule	MAE CTE	MAE HE	errors
"center-line present"	0.36	1.63	45%
"center-line absent"	0.62	2.68	75%
"shadow present"	0.66	2.23	42%
"shadow absent"	0.34	1.55	7%
"dark skid"	0.43	1.84	52%
"light or no skid"	0.33	1.49	42%

These results can be used by developers to better understand and debug the model behavior. For instance, the model accuracy computed for the subsets with "shadow present" and "dark skid", respectively, is poor and also a high % of the respective inputs violate the correctness property. This information can be used by developers to retrieve more images with shadows and dark skids, to retrain the model and improve its performance. The extracted rules can be leveraged to automate the retrieval.

Furthermore, we observe that in the absence of the center-line feature, the model has difficulty in making correct predictions. This is not surprising, as the presence of the center-line can be considered as a (rudimentary) input requirement for the center-line tracking application. Indeed, in the absence of the center-line it is hard to envision how the network can estimate correctly the airplane position from it. The network may use other clues on the runway, leading to errors. We can thus consider the presence of the center-line feature as part of the ODD for the application. The rules for the center-line feature can be deployed as a *run-time monitor* to either pass inputs satisfying the rules for "present" or reject those that satisfy the rules for "absent", ensuring that the model operates in the safe zone as defined by the ODD, and at the same time increasing its accuracy.

We also experimented with generating rules to explain correct and incorrect behavior in terms of *combinations* of features such as: $(center - line \; present) \land$

Table 3: Rules for YOLOv4-Tiny (same metrics as in Table 1).

Feature	Rule	Metrics			
		#d	R_d	P_v	R_v
pedestrian.moving	pre(21 *terms*) $\implies$ *present*	1110	48	72	29
	pre(15 *terms*) $\implies$ *absent*	894	40	74	29
vehicle.parked	pre(10 *terms*) $\implies$ *present*	890	25	71	20
	pre(19 *terms*) $\implies$ *absent*	1114	43	70	32
pedestrian	pre(25 *terms*) $\implies$ *present*	1375	57	70	35
	pre(14 *terms*) $\implies$ *absent*	629	41	77	22
vehicle	pre(20 *terms*) $\implies$ *present*	1616	75	91	59
	pre(11 *terms*) $\implies$ *absent*	388	50	69	31

(shadow absent) $\land$ *(on position)* $\implies$ *correct*, and $\neg$*(center − line present)* $\land$ *(heading away)* $\land$ *(position right)* $\implies$ *incorrect*. [1]. These rules could be further used by developers to better understand and debug the model behavior.

4.2   Object Detection with YOLOv4-Tiny

We conducted another case study with a more challenging network, an object detector, to evaluate the quality of the extracted feature representations. For this study, we use the nuImages dataset, a public large-scale dataset for autonomous driving [1,6]. It contains 93000 images collected while driving around in actual cities. To facilitate computer vision tasks such as object detection for autonomous driving, each image comes labeled with 2d bounding boxes and the corresponding object labels (from one of 23 object classes). Each labeled object also comes with additional attribute annotations. For instance, the objects labeled *vehicle* carry additional annotations like *vehicle.moving*, *vehicle.stopped*, and *vehicle.parked*. Overall, the dataset has 12 categories of additional attribute annotations. We trained a YOLOv4-Tiny object detection model [14,2] on this dataset. YOLOv4-Tiny has 37 layers with 21 convolutional layers and 2 YOLO layers.

We leveraged the attribute annotations associated with each object as the feature labels (thus no manual labeling was necessary). For extracting feature representations, we run Algorithm 2.1 on a subset of 2000 images from the nuImages dataset, and then evaluate the extracted representations on a separate validation set of 2000 images.

Table 3 describes our results. We used layer 28 of the YOLOv4-Tiny model to extract the feature representations. For brevity, we only report the number of terms in the rule precondition, i.e., the number of neurons that appeared in the constraints, instead of describing the exact rule in Table 3. Note that layer 28 has 798720 neurons. Strikingly, the extracted rules only have between 10 to 25 terms in their preconditions, and yet achieve precision (P_v) between $69 - 74\%$. The recall (R_v) values are also encouraging, and can be improved further by

---

[1] The procedure to generate these rules has been omitted for brevity.

considering more than one rule for each feature value (here, we only consider pure rules with the highest recall R_d on dataset d used for feature extraction).

4.3   Challenges and Mitigations

Identifying relevant features is non-trivial and requires refinement and extensive discussions with domain experts. The feature annotations may need to be provided manually which is expensive and error-prone. However, we only need a small annotated dataset to extract the representations, which can be used to further annotate unlabeled data. The extracted rules may be incorrect (e.g., due to unbalanced annotated data). We mitigate by carefully validating them using a separate validation set and visualization techniques. It could also be that the network did not learn some important features. To address the issue, in future work, we plan to investigate neuro-symbolic approaches to build networks that are aware of high-level features and satisfy (by construction) the safety requirements.

5   Related Work

There is growing interest in developing software engineering approaches for machine learning in general, and neural networks specially, investigating requirements for neural networks [3], automated testing [16], debugging and fault localization [8], to name a few. Our work contributes with a feature-centric view of neural network behavior that links high-level requirements with the internal logic of the trained models to enable better testing and analysis of neural networks.

A closely related work [18] uses high-level features to guide neural network analysis. However, the features are extracted from input images, not from the internal neural network representation. Further, the work only considers testing, not other software engineering activities.

Our work is also related to concept analysis [17,11,15,13] which seeks to develop explanations of deep neural network behavior in terms of concepts specified by users. We propose to use high-level features for multiple software engineering activities, which go beyond explanations. Moreover, the use of decision tree learning makes our representations relatively cheap to extract. Note that there are other works that use decision tree learning to distill neural network input-output behavior, e.g., [5]; however none of them extract high-level features from the network's internal representation.

6   Conclusion

We proposed to extract high-level feature representations related to domain-specific requirements to enable analysis and explanation of neural network behavior. We presented initial empirical evidence in support of our ideas. In future work, we plan to further investigate meaningful requirements for neural networks and effective techniques for checking them. We also plan to apply Marabou [10] for the verification of safety properties expressed in terms of high-level features. Finally, we plan to investigate neuro-symbolic techniques to develope high-assurance neural network models.

References

1. nuimages, https://www.nuscenes.org/nuimages
2. Yolov4-tiny, https://github.com/WongKinYiu/PyTorch_YOLOv4
3. Ashmore, R., Calinescu, R., Paterson, C.: Assuring the machine learning lifecycle: Desiderata, methods, and challenges. ACM Comput. Surv. **54**(5), 111:1–111:39 (2021). https://doi.org/10.1145/3453444, https://doi.org/10.1145/3453444
4. Beland, S., Chang, I., Chen, A., Moser, M., Paunicka, J.L., Stuart, D., Vian, J., Westover, C., Yu, H.: Towards assurance evaluation of autonomous systems. In: IEEE/ACM International Conference On Computer Aided Design, ICCAD 2020, San Diego, CA, USA, November 2-5, 2020. pp. 84:1–84:6. IEEE (2020). https://doi.org/10.1145/3400302.3415785, https://doi.org/10.1145/3400302.3415785
5. Bondarenko, A., Aleksejeva, L., Jumutc, V., Borisov, A.: Classification tree extraction from trained artificial neural networks. Procedia Computer Science **104**, 556–563 (2017). https://doi.org/https://doi.org/10.1016/j.procs.2017.01.172, https://www.sciencedirect.com/science/article/pii/S1877050917301734, iCTE 2016, Riga Technical University, Latvia
6. Caesar, H., Bankiti, V., Lang, A.H., Vora, S., Liong, V.E., Xu, Q., Krishnan, A., Pan, Y., Baldan, G., Beijbom, O.: nuscenes: A multimodal dataset for autonomous driving. In: Proceedings of the IEEE/CVF conference on computer vision and pattern recognition. pp. 11621–11631 (2020)
7. Chattopadhay, A., Sarkar, A., Howlader, P., Balasubramanian, V.N.: Grad-cam++: Generalized gradient-based visual explanations for deep convolutional networks. In: 2018 IEEE Winter Conference on Applications of Computer Vision (WACV). pp. 839–847. IEEE (2018)
8. Fahmy, H.M., Pastore, F., Briand, L.C.: HUDD: A tool to debug dnns for safety analysis. In: 44th 2022 IEEE/ACM International Conference on Software Engineering: Companion Proceedings, ICSE Companion 2022, Pittsburgh, PA, USA, May 22-24, 2022. pp. 100–104. IEEE (2022). https://doi.org/10.1109/ICSE-Companion55297.2022.9793750, https://doi.org/10.1109/ICSE-Companion55297.2022.9793750
9. Frew, E., McGee, T., Kim, Z., Xiao, X., Jackson, S., Morimoto, M., Rathinam, S., Padial, J., Sengupta, R.: Vision-based road-following using a small autonomous aircraft. In: 2004 IEEE Aerospace Conference Proceedings (IEEE Cat. No.04TH8720). vol. 5, pp. 3006–3015 Vol.5 (2004). https://doi.org/10.1109/AERO.2004.1368106
10. Katz, G., Huang, D.A., Ibeling, D., Julian, K., Lazarus, C., Lim, R., Shah, P., Thakoor, S., Wu, H., Zeljić, A., et al.: The marabou framework for verification and analysis of deep neural networks. In: International Conference on Computer Aided Verification. pp. 443–452. Springer (2019)
11. Kim, B., Wattenberg, M., Gilmer, J., Cai, C., Wexler, J., Viegas, F., sayres, R.: Interpretability beyond feature attribution: Quantitative testing with concept activation vectors (TCAV). In: Dy, J., Krause, A. (eds.) Proceedings of the 35th International Conference on Machine Learning. Proceedings of Machine Learning Research, vol. 80, pp. 2668–2677. PMLR (10–15 Jul 2018), https://proceedings.mlr.press/v80/kim18d.html

12. Olah, C., Cammarata, N., Schubert, L., Goh, G., Petrov, M., Carter, S.: Zoom in: An introduction to circuits. Distill (2020). `https://doi.org/10.23915/distill.00024.001`, https://distill.pub/2020/circuits/zoom-in
13. Schwalbe, G.: Concept embedding analysis: A review (2022). `https://doi.org/10.48550/ARXIV.2203.13909`, `https://arxiv.org/abs/2203.13909`
14. Wang, C.Y., Bochkovskiy, A., Liao, H.Y.M.: Scaled-yolov4: Scaling cross stage partial network. In: Proceedings of the IEEE/cvf conference on computer vision and pattern recognition. pp. 13029–13038 (2021)
15. Yeh, C.K., Kim, B., Ravikumar, P.: Human-centered concept explanations for neural networks. In: Neuro-Symbolic Artificial Intelligence: The State of the Art, pp. 337–352. IOS Press (2021)
16. Zhang, M., Zhang, Y., Zhang, L., Liu, C., Khurshid, S.: Deeproad: Gan-based metamorphic testing and input validation framework for autonomous driving systems. In: Huchard, M., Kästner, C., Fraser, G. (eds.) Proceedings of the 33rd ACM/IEEE International Conference on Automated Software Engineering, ASE 2018, Montpellier, France, September 3-7, 2018. pp. 132–142. ACM (2018). `https://doi.org/10.1145/3238147.3238187`, https://doi.org/10.1145/3238147.3238187
17. Zhou, B., Sun, Y., Bau, D., Torralba, A.: Interpretable basis decomposition for visual explanation. In: Proceedings of the European Conference on Computer Vision (ECCV). pp. 119–134 (2018)
18. Zohdinasab, T., Riccio, V., Gambi, A., Tonella, P.: Efficient and effective feature space exploration for testing deep learning systems. ACM Trans. Softw. Eng. Methodol. (jun 2022). `https://doi.org/10.1145/3544792`, `https://doi.org/10.1145/3544792`, just Accepted

JavaBIP meets VerCors: Towards the Safety of Concurrent Software Systems in Java*

Simon Bliudze[1] , Petra van den Bos[2] , Marieke Huisman[2] ,
Robert Rubbens[2](✉) , and Larisa Safina[1]

[1] Univ. Lille, Inria, CNRS, Centrale Lille, UMR 9189 CRIStAL, 59000 Lille, France
{simon.bliudze,larisa.safina}@inria.fr
[2] Formal Methods and Tools, University of Twente, Enschede, The Netherlands
{p.vandenbos,m.huisman,r.b.rubbens}@utwente.nl

Abstract. We present "Verified JavaBIP", a tool set for the verification
of JavaBIP models. A JavaBIP model is a Java program where classes
are considered as components, their behaviour described by finite state
machine and synchronization annotations. While JavaBIP guarantees execution progresses according to the indicated state machines, it does not
guarantee properties of the data exchanged between components. It also
does not provide verification support to check whether the behaviour of
the resulting concurrent program is as (safe as) expected. This paper
addresses this by extending the JavaBIP engine with run-time verification support, and by extending the program verifier VerCors to verify JavaBIP models deductively. These two techniques complement each
other: feedback from run-time verification allows quicker prototyping of
contracts, and deductive verification can reduce the overhead of run-time
verification. We demonstrate our approach on the "Solidity Casino" case
study, known from the VerifyThis Collaborative Long Term Challenge.

1 Introduction

Modern software systems are inherently concurrent: they consist of multiple
components that run simultaneously and share access to resources. Component
interaction leads to resource contention, and if not coordinated properly, can
compromise safety-critical operations. The concurrent nature of such interactions
is the root cause of the sheer complexity of the resulting software [9]. Model-
based coordination frameworks such as Reo [5] and BIP [6] address this issue by
providing models with a formally defined behaviour and verification tools.

JavaBIP [10] is an open-source Java implementation of the BIP coordination mechanism. It separates the application model into *component behaviour*,
modelled as Finite State Machines (FSMs), and *glue*, which defines the possible stateless interactions among components in terms of synchronisation constraints. The overall behaviour of an application is to be enforced at run time

---

* L. Safina and S. Bliudze were partially supported by ANR Investissements d'avenir (ANR-16-
IDEX-0004 ULNE) and project NARCO (ANR-21-CE48-0011). P. van den Bos, M. Huisman and
R. Rubbens were supported by the NWO VICI 639.023.710 Mercedes project.

L. Lambers and S. Uchitel (Eds.): FASE 2023, LNCS 13991, pp. 143–150, 2023.
https://doi.org/10.1007/978-3-031-30826-0_8

by the framework's engine. Unlike BIP, JavaBIP does not provide automatic code generation from the provided model; instead it realises the coordination of existing software components in an exogenous manner, relying on component annotations that provide an abstract view of the software under development.

To model component behaviour, methods of a JavaBIP program are annotated with FSM transitions. These annotated methods model the actions of the program components. Computations are assumed to be terminating and non-blocking. Furthermore, side-effects are assumed to be either represented by the change of the FSM state, or to be irrelevant for the system behaviour. Any correctness argument for the system depends on these assumptions. A limitation of JavaBIP is that it does not guarantee that these assumptions hold. This paper proposes a joint extension of JavaBIP and VerCors [11] providing such guarantees about the implementation statically and at run time.

VerCors [11] is a state-of-the-art deductive verification tool for concurrent programs that uses permission-based separation logic [3]. This logic is an extension of Hoare logic that allows specifying properties using contract annotations. These contract annotations include permissions, pre- and postconditions and loop invariants. VerCors automatically verifies programs with contract annotations. To verify JavaBIP models, we (i) extend JavaBIP annotations with verification annotations, and (ii) adapt VerCors to support JavaBIP annotations. VerCors was chosen for integration with JavaBIP because it supports multi-threaded Java, which makes it straightforward to express JavaBIP concepts in its internal representation. To analyze JavaBIP models, VerCors transforms the model with verification annotations into contract annotations, leveraging their structure as specified by the FSM annotations and the glue.

For some programs VerCors requires extra contract annotations. This is generally the case with `while` statements and when recursive methods are used. To enable properties to be analysed when not all necessary annotations are added yet, we extend the JavaBIP engine with support for run-time verification. During a run of the program, the verification annotations are checked for that specific program execution at particular points of interest, such as when a JavaBIP component executes a transition. The run-time verification support is set up in such a way that it ignores any verification annotations that were already statically verified, reducing the overhead of run-time verification.

This paper presents the use of deductive and run-time verification to prove assumptions of JavaBIP models. We make the following contributions:

- We extend regular JavaBIP annotations with pre- and postconditions for transitions and invariants for components and states. This allows checking design assumptions, which are otherwise left implicit and unchecked.
- We extend VerCors to deductively verify a JavaBIP model, taking into account its FSM and glue structure.
- We add support for run-time verification to the JavaBIP engine.
- We link VerCors and the JavaBIP engine such that deductively proven annotations need not be monitored at run-time.
- Finally, we demonstrate our approach on a variant of the Casino case study from the VerifyThis Collaborative Long Term Challenge.

Tool binaries and case study sources are available through the artefact [7].

2   Related Work

There are several approaches to analyse behaviours of abstract models in the literature. Bliudze et al. propose an approach allowing verification of infinite state BIP models in the presence of data transfer between components [8]. Abdellatif et al. used the BIP framework to verify Ethereum smart contracts written in Solidity [1]. Mavridou et al. introduce the VeriSolid framework, which generates Solidity code from verified models [13]. André et al. describe a workflow to analyse Kmelia models [4]. They also describe the COSTOTest tool, which runs tests that interact with the model. Thus, these approaches do not consider verification of model implementation, which is what we do with Verified JavaBIP. Only COSTOTest establishes a connection between the model and implementation, but it does not guarantee memory safety or correctness.

There is also previous work on combining deductive and runtime verification. The following discussion is not exhaustive. Generally, these works do not support concurrent Java and JavaBIP. Nimmer et al. infer invariants with Daikon and check them with ESC/Java [14]. However, they do not check against an abstract model, and the results are not used to optimize execution. Bodden et al. and Stulova et al. optimize run-time checks using static analysis [12,16]. However, Stulova et al. do not support state machines, and Bodden et al. do not support data in state machines. The STARVOORS tool by Ahrendt et al. is comparable to Verified JavaBIP [2]. Some minor differences include the type of state machine used, and how Hoare triples are expressed. The major difference is that it is not trivial to support concurrency in STARVOORS. VerCors and Verified JavaBIP use separation logic, which makes concurrency support straightforward.

3   JavaBIP and Verification Annotations

JavaBIP annotations capture the FSM specification and describe the behaviour of a component. They are attached to classes, methods or method parameters, and were first introduced by Bliudze et al [10]. Listing 1 shows an example of JavaBIP annotations. @ComponentType indicates a class is a JavaBIP component and specifies its initial state. In the example this is the WAITING state. @Port declares a transition label. Method annotations include @Transition, @Guard and @Data. @Transition consists of a port name, start and end states, and optionally a guard. The example transition goes from WAITING to PINGED when the PING port is triggered. The transition has no guard so it may always be taken. @Guard declares a method which indicates if a transition is enabled. @Data either declares a getter method as outgoing data, or a method parameter as incoming data. Note that the example does not specify when ports are activated. This is specified separately from the JavaBIP component as glue [10].

We added component invariants and state predicates to Verified JavaBIP as class annotations. @Invariant(expr) indicates expr must hold after each component state change. @StatePredicate(state, expr) indicates expr must hold in state state. Pre- and postconditions were also added to the @Transition annotation. They have to hold before and after execution of the transition. @Pure

```
1  @Port(name = PING, type = PortType.enforceable)
2  @ComponentType(initial = WAITING, name = ECHO_SPEC)
3  public class Echo {
4    @Transition(name = PING, source = WAITING, target = PINGED)
5    public void ping() { System.out.println(this + ": pong");}}
```

Listing 1. Example of a minimal pinging component in JavaBIP

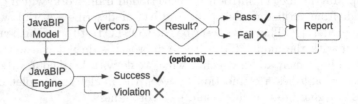

Fig. 1. Verified JavaBIP architecture. Ellipse boxes represent analysis or execution.

indicates that a method is side-effect-free, and is used with @Guard and @Data. Annotation arguments should follow the grammar of Java expressions. We do not support lambda expressions, method references, switch expressions, new, instanceOf, and wildcard arguments. In addition, as VerCors does not yet support Java features such as generics and inheritance, models that use these cannot be verified. These limitations might be lifted in the future.

4 Architecture of Verified JavaBIP

The architecture of Verified JavaBIP is shown in Figure 1. The user starts with a JavaBIP model, optionally with verification annotations. The user then has two choices: verify the model with VerCors, or execute it with the JavaBIP Engine.

We extended VerCors to transform the JavaBIP model into the VerCors internal representation, Common Object Language (COL). An example of this transformation is given in Listing 2. If verification succeeds, the JavaBIP model is memory safe, has no data races, and the components respect the properties specified in the verification annotations. In this case, no extra run-time verification is needed. If verification fails, there are either memory safety issues, components violate properties, or the prover timed out. In the first case, the user needs to change the program or annotations and retry verification with VerCors. This is necessary because memory safety properties cannot be checked with the JavaBIP engine, and therefore safe execution of the JavaBIP model is not guaranteed. In the second and third case, VerCors produces a verification report with the verification result for each property.

We extended the JavaBIP engine with run-time verification support. If a verification report is included with the JavaBIP model, the JavaBIP engine uses it to only verify at run-time the verification annotations that were not verified deductively. If no verification report is included, the JavaBIP engine verifies all verification annotations at run time.

```
@Transition(name=PING,source=PING,target=PING,guard=HAS_PING)
public void ping() { pingsLeft--; }
```

```
requires PING_state_predicate() && hasPing();
ensures PING_state_predicate();
public void ping() { pingsLeft--; }
```

Listing 2. Top: example of a transition in JavaBIP. Bottom: internal representation of `ping` after encoding JavaBIP semantics.

5   Implementation of Verified JavaBIP

This section briefly discusses relevant implementation details for Verified JavaBIP.

Run-time verification in the JavaBIP engine is performed by checking component properties after component construction, and before and after transitions. For example, before the JavaBIP engine executes a transition, it checks the component invariant, the state invariant, and the precondition of the transition. When a property is violated, either execution is terminated or a warning is printed, depending on how the user configured the JavaBIP engine. We expect runtime verification performance to scale linearly, as properties can be checked individually. We have not measured the impact of the use of reflection in the JavaBIP engine.

For deductive verification the JavaBIP semantics is encoded into COL. We describe this with an example. The top part of Listing 2 shows the `ping` method, where `@Transition` indicates a transition from `PING` to `PING`. The guard indicates that the transition is allowed if there is a ping. `HAS_PING` refers to a method annotated with `@Guard(name=HAS_PING)`, which returns `pingsLeft >= 1`.

The bottom part of Listing 2 shows the COL representation of the `ping` method after encoding the JavaBIP semantics. Line 1 states the precondition, line 2 the postcondition. `PING_state_predicate()` refers to the `PING` state predicate, which constrains the values of the class fields. By default it is just `true`. Since the predicate is both a pre- and a postcondition, it is assumed at the start of the method, and needs to hold at the end of the method. `hasPing()` is the method with the `@Guard` annotation for the `HAS_PING` label. The method is called directly in the COL representation. We have implemented such a transformation of JavaBIP to COL for each JavaBIP construct.

To prove memory safety, we extended VerCors to generate permissions. This ensures verification in accordance with the Java memory model. Currently, each component owns the data of all its fields. This works for JavaBIP models that do not share data between components. For other models, a different approach might be necessary, e.g. VerCors taking into account permissions annotations provided by the user. For more info about permissions, we refer the reader to [3].

Finally, scalability of deductive verification of JavaBIP models could be a point of future work, as the number of proof obligations scales quadratically in the number of candidate transitions of a synchronization.

6   VerifyThis Casino and Verified JavaBIP

We illustrate Verified JavaBIP with the Casino case study adapted from [17]. We discuss the case study and its verification. The case study sources and Verified JavaBIP sources and binaries are included in the artefact [7].

The model uses three component types: player, operator, and casino. The model supports multiple players and casinos, but each casino has only one operator. Players bet on the result of a coin flip. The casino pays out twice for a correct guess, and keeps the money otherwise. The casino contains the pot balance and money reserved for the current bet. The operator can add to or withdraw money from the casino pot based on a local copy of the casino pot.

We have added several invariants to this model. The purse of every player, the casino pot, its operator copy, the wallet of the operator, and the placed bet must all be non-negative, as the model does not support debts. If no bet is placed, it must be zero. These properties are defined as `@Invariant` or `@StatePredicate` annotations on the components in the model.

One problem with the model is that the player can win more than the casino pot contains, because there are no restrictions on how much the player can bet. The problem is detected by both deductive and run-time verification. VerCors cannot prove that the casino pot is non-negative, which is part of the casino invariant, after the `PLAYER_WIN` transition. The JavaBIP engine detects it, but is not guaranteed to because the model has some non-determinism. For example, if no player ever wins the problem is not detected by run-time verification.

There are several solutions. First, the user can choose to always enable run-time verification, such that the execution is always safe. This might be acceptable depending on the performance penalty of run-time verification. Second, guards can be added to restrict model behaviour. For example, `PLACE_BET` could require `bet <= pot`. However, in general, adding guards might introduce deadlocks. Third, a solution is to refactor the model to avoid the problem. For example, the casino could limit how much the player can bet. This introduces no extra run-time checks, however, in general the behaviour of the model will change.

7   Conclusions and Future Work

We presented Verified JavaBIP, a tool set for verifying the assumptions of JavaBIP models and their implementations. The tool set extends the original JavaBIP annotations for verification of functional properties. Verified JavaBIP supports deductive verification using VerCors, and run-time verification using the JavaBIP engine. Only properties that could not be verified deductively are checked at runtime. In the demonstration we automatically detect a problem on the Casino case study using Verified JavaBIP.

There are several directions for future work. First, support for checking memory safety could be extended by supporting data sharing between components. Second, we want to investigate run-time verification of memory safety. Third, more experimental evaluation can be done on the capabilities and performance of Verified JavaBIP. Fourth and finally, we want to investigate run-time verification of safety properties of the JavaBIP model beyond invariants.

References

1. Abdellatif, T., Brousmiche, K.L.: Formal verification of smart contracts based on users and blockchain behaviors models. In: 9th IFIP International Conference on New Technologies, Mobility and Security (NTMS), pp. 1–5. IEEE (Feb 2018). https://doi.org/10.1109/NTMS.2018.8328737

2. Ahrendt, W., Chimento, J.M., Pace, G.J., Schneider, G.: Verifying data- and control-oriented properties combining static and runtime verification: theory and tools. Form. Methods Syst. Des. **51**(1), 200–265 (Aug 2017). https://doi.org/10.1007/s10703-017-0274-y

3. Amighi, A., Hurlin, C., Huisman, M., Haack, C.: Permission-based separation logic for multithreaded Java programs. Logical Methods in Computer Science **11**(1) (Feb 2015). https://doi.org/10.2168/LMCS-11(1:2)2015

4. André, P., Attiogbé, C., Mottu, J.M.: Combining techniques to verify service-based components (Sep 2022), https://www.scitepress.org/Link.aspx?doi=10.5220/0006212106450656, [Online; accessed 26. Sep. 2022]

5. Arbab, F.: Reo: A channel-based coordination model for component composition. Mathematical Structures in Computer Science **14**(3), 329–366 (2004). https://doi.org/10.1017/S0960129504004153

6. Basu, A., Bozga, M., Sifakis, J.: Modeling heterogeneous real-time components in BIP. In: 4th IEEE Int. Conf. on Software Engineering and Formal Methods (SEFM06). pp. 3–12 (Sep 2006). https://doi.org/10.1109/SEFM.2006.27, invited talk

7. Bliudze, S., van den Bos, P., Huisman, M., Rubbens, R., Safina, L.: Artefact of: JavaBIP meets VerCors: Towards the Safety of Concurrent Software Systems in Java (2023). https://doi.org/10.4121/21763274

8. Bliudze, S., Cimatti, A., Jaber, M., Mover, S., Roveri, M., Saab, W., Wang, Q.: Formal verification of infinite-state BIP models. In: Finkbeiner, B., Pu, G., Zhang, L. (eds.) Automated Technology for Verification and Analysis. pp. 326–343. Springer International Publishing, Cham (2015). https://doi.org/10.1007/978-3-319-24953-7_25

9. Bliudze, S., Katsaros, P., Bensalem, S., Wirsing, M.: On methods and tools for rigorous system design. Int. J. Softw. Tools Technol. Transf. **23**(5), 679–684 (2021). https://doi.org/10.1007/s10009-021-00632-0

10. Bliudze, S., Mavridou, A., Szymanek, R., Zolotukhina, A.: Exogenous coordination of concurrent software components with JavaBIP. Software: Practice and Experience **47**(11), 1801–1836 (Apr 2017). https://doi.org/10.1002/spe.2405

11. Blom, S., Darabi, S., Huisman, M., Oortwijn, W.: The VerCors tool set: Verification of parallel and concurrent software. In: IFM. Lecture Notes in Computer Science, vol. 10510, pp. 102–110. Springer (2017), https://link.springer.com/chapter/10.1007/978-3-319-66845-1_7

12. Bodden, E., Lam, P., Hendren, L.: Partially Evaluating Finite-State Runtime Monitors Ahead of Time. ACM Trans. Program. Lang. Syst. **34**(2), 1–52 (Jun 2012). https://doi.org/10.1145/2220365.2220366

13. Mavridou, A., Laszka, A., Stachtiari, E., Dubey, A.: VeriSolid: Correct-by-design smart contracts for Ethereum. In: Financial Cryptography and Data Security, pp. 446–465. Springer, Cham, Switzerland (Sep 2019). https://doi.org/10.1007/978-3-030-32101-7_27

14. Nimmer, J.W., Ernst, M.D.: Static verification of dynamically detected program invariants: Integrating Daikon and ESC/Java. Electronic Notes in Theoretical Computer Science **55**(2), 255–276 (2001). https://doi.org/https://doi.org/10.

1016/S1571-0661(04)00256-7, RV'2001, Runtime Verification (in connection with CAV '01)

15. Solidity team: Solidity programming language, https://soliditylang.org/, (Accessed at: 2022-10-21)

16. Stulova, N., Morales, J.F., Hermenegildo, M.V.: Reducing the overhead of assertion run-time checks via static analysis. In: PPDP '16, pp. 90–103. Association for Computing Machinery (Sep 2016). https://doi.org/10.1145/2967973.2968597

17. VerifyThis collaborative long-term verification challenge: The Casino example, https://verifythis.github.io/casino/, (Accessed at: 2022-10-12)

Model-based Player Experience Testing with Emotion Pattern Verification

Saba Gholizadeh Ansari[1]([✉])(iD), I. S. W. B. Prasetya[1](iD) Davide Prandi[2], Fitsum Meshesha Kifetew[2], Mehdi Dastani[1], Frank Dignum[3], and Gabriele Keller[1]

[1] Utrecht University, Utrecht, The Netherlands, s.gholizadehansari@uu.nl
[2] Fondazione Bruno Kessler, Trento, Italy
[3] Umeå University, Umeå, Sweden

Abstract. Player eXperience (PX) testing has attracted attention in the game industry as video games become more complex and widespread. Understanding players' desires and their experience are key elements to guarantee the success of a game in the highly competitive market. Although a number of techniques have been introduced to measure the emotional aspect of the experience, automated testing of player experience still needs to be explored. This paper presents a framework for automated player experience testing by formulating emotion patterns' requirements and utilizing a computational model of players' emotions developed based on a psychological theory of emotions along with a model-based testing approach for test suite generation. We evaluate the strength of our framework by performing mutation test. The paper also evaluates the performance of a search-based generated test suite and LTL model checking-based test suite in revealing various variations of temporal and spatial emotion patterns. Results show the contribution of both algorithms in generating complementary test cases for revealing various emotions in different locations of a game level.

Keywords: automated player experience testing, agent-based testing, model-based testing, models of emotion

1 Introduction

Player experience (PX) testing has become an increasingly critical aspect of game development to assist game designers in realistically anticipating the experience of game players in terms of enjoyment [17], flow [46] and engagement [31]. While functional testing is intended to test the functionality of the game [38], the PX testing verifies whether emotions and psychology of players shaped during the interaction with the game are close to the design intention. This helps game designers in early development stages to identify design issues leading to game abandon, improve the general experience of players and even invoke certain experience during the game-play [53,3,25]. Let us also clarify that 'usability' is a concept in the broad domain of PX testing, but not the only concept. Usability

L. Lambers and S. Uchitel (Eds.): FASE 2023, LNCS 13991, pp. 151–172, 2023.
https://doi.org/10.1007/978-3-031-30826-0_9

tests are designed to address issues that can lead to degrading the human performance during the game-play [10], whereas PX can target the emotional experience of a player which eventually influences the success or failure of a game in the market [1]. This has led to the emergence of *Games User Research* (GUR) as an approach to gain insights into PX which is tied to human-computer-interaction, human factors, psychology and game development [14].

Validating a game design relies either on trained PX testers or acquiring information directly from players with methods such as interviews, questionnaires and physiological measurements [40,37], which are labour-intensive, costly and not necessarily representing all users profiles and their emotions. Moreover, such tests need to be repeated after every design change to assure the PX is still aligned with the design intention. Thus, GUR researchers have turned into developing AI-based PX testing methods. In particular, agent-based testing has attracted attention because it opens new rooms for automated testing of PX by imitating players while keeping the cost of labour and re-applying the tests low.

There exist appraisal theories of emotions that address the elicitation of emotions and their impact on emotional responses. They indicate that emotions are elicited by appraisal evaluation of events and situations [33]. Ortony, Clore, and Collins (**OCC**) theory [43] is one of several widely known appraisal theories in cognitive science that is also commonly used in modeling emotional agents [15,9,47,42,12]. Despite the influence of emotions on forming the experience of players [39,13], this approach has not been employed in PX testing [6].

In our automated PX testing approach, we opt for a model-driven approach to model emotions. Theoretical models of human cognition, used for decades in cognitive psychology, provide a more coherent outlook of cognitive processes. In contrast, applying a data-driven (machine learning) approach is greatly constrained by the availability of experimental data. Inferring a cognitive process from limited experimental data is an ill-posed problem [5] because such a process is subjective. Individuals can evaluate the same event differently due to age, gender, education, cultural traits, etc. For example, when a romantic relationship ends, some individuals feel sadness, others anger, and some even experience relief [48]. However, according to appraisal theories of emotions, common patterns can be found in emergence of the same emotion. These patterns are given as a structure of emotions by the aforementioned OCC. Thus, a model-driven approach derived form a well-grounded theory of emotions such as OCC, is sensible when access to a sufficient data is not possible.

In this paper, we present an agent-based player experience testing framework that allows to express emotional requirements as patterns and verify them on executed test suites generated by *model-based testing* (MBT) approach. The framework uses a computational model of emotions based on OCC theory [21] to generate the emotional experience of agent players. Comparing to [21], this paper contributes to expressing emotion patterns' requirements and generating covering test suites for verifying patterns on a game level. We show such a framework allows game designers to verify the emotion patterns' requirements and gain insight on emotions the game induce, over time and over space.

Revealing such patterns requires a test suite that can trigger enough diversity in the game behavior and as a result in the evoked emotions. This is where the model-based testing approach with its fast test suites generation can contribute. In this paper, we employ an *extended finite state machine* (EFSM) model [18] that captures all possible game play behaviors serving as a subset of human behaviors, at some level of abstraction. We use a *search based algorithm* (SB) for testing, more precisely *multi objective search algorithm* (MOSA) [44], and *linear temporal logic* (LTL) for *model checking* (MC) [8,11] as two model-based test suite generation techniques to investigate the ability of each generated test suite in revealing variations of emotion e.g absence of an emotion in a corridor. We apply test-cases distance metric to measure test suites' diversity and the distance between SB and MC test suites. Results on our 3D game case study shows that SB and MC, due to their different techniques for test generation, produce distinctive test cases which can identify different variations of emotions over space and time, that cannot be identified by just one of the test suites.

The remainder of this paper is organized as follows. Section 2 explains the computational model of emotions and the model-based testing approach. Section 3 presents the PX framework architecture. Section 4 describes our methodology of expressing PX requirements using emotion patterns, test suites diversity measurement, and the overall PX testing algorithm. Section 5 shows an exploratory case study to demonstrate the emotion pattern verification using model-based testing along with an investigation on results of SB and MC test suite generation techniques. Mutation testing is also addressed in this section to evaluate the strength of the proposed approach. Section 6 gives an overview of related work. Finally, Section 7 proposes future work and concludes the paper.

2   Preliminaries

This section summarizes the OCC computational model of emotions [21] and the model-based testing as key components of our PX framework.

2.1   Computational Model of Emotions

Gholizadeh Ansari et al. [21] introduces a transition system to model goal-oriented emotions based on a cognitive theory of emotions called OCC. The OCC theory gives a structure for 22 emotion types, viewed as cognitive processes where each emotion type is elicited under certain conditions. The structure is constructed based on the appraisal theory which is validated with a series of experiments in psychology [50,16,49]. The appraisal conditions, exist in the OCC, are modeled formally in [21] for six goal-oriented emotion types (ety), namely: hope, joy, satisfaction, fear, distress, and disappointment for a single agent simulations where the agent's emotional state changes only by game dynamism expressed through events to the agent. A game is treated as an environment that discretely produces events triggered by the agent's actions or environmental dynamism such as hazards. The event *tick* represents the passage of time. The emotion model of an agent is defined as a 7-tuple transition system M:

$$(S, s_0, G, E, \delta, Des, Thres)$$

- G is a set of goals, that the agent wants to achieve; each is a pair $\langle id, x \rangle$ of a unique id and significance degree.
- S is the set of M's possible states; each is a pair $\langle K, Emo \rangle$:
  - K is a set of propositions the agent believes to be true. It includes, for each goal g, a proposition $status(g, p)$ indicating if g has been achieved or failed, and a proposition $\mathbf{P}(g, v)$ with $v \in [0..1]$, stating the agent's current belief on the likelihood of reaching this goal.
  - Emo is the agent's emotional state represented by a set of active emotions, each is a tuple $\langle ety, w, g, t_0 \rangle$, ety is the emotion type, w is the intensity of the emotion respecting a goal g, and triggered time t_0.
- $s_0 \in S$ is the agent's initial state.
- E specifies the types of events the agent can experience.
- δ is M's state transition function; to be elaborated later.
- Des is an appraisal function; $Des(K, e, g)$ expresses the desirability, as a numeric value, of an event e with respect to achieving a goal g, judged when the agent believes K. OCC theory has more appraisal factors [43], but only desirability matters for aforementioned types of emotion [21].
- $Thres$: thresholds for activating every emotion type.

The **transition function** δ updates the agent's state $\langle K, Emo \rangle$, triggered by an incoming event $e \in E$ as follows:

$$\langle K , Emo \rangle \xrightarrow{e} \langle K' , \overbrace{newEmo(K, e, G) \oplus decayed(Emo)}^{\text{updated emotion } Emo'} \rangle$$

- $K' = e(K) \setminus H$, where $e(K)$ is the updated beliefs of the agent when K is exposed to e; these may include updates on goals' likelihood and their status. H is the set of likelihoods of goals that are achieved or failed; this information is no longer needed and removed from $e(K)$.
- $Emo' = newEmo(K, e, G) \oplus decayed(Emo)$, where $newEmo(K, e, G)$ and $decayed(Emo)$ are *newly* activated emotions and the still active emotions that decay over time. The operator $\oplus$ merges them after applying some constraints [21].

Emotion activation. One or multiple emotions can be activated by an incoming event (except *tick*). This is formulated as follows:

$$newEmo(K, e, G) = \{\langle ety, g, w, t \rangle \mid ety \in Etype, \ g \in G, w = \mathcal{E}_{ety}(K, e, g) > 0\} \quad (1)$$

where w is the intensity of the emotion ety towards the goal $g \in G$ and t is the current system. Upon an incoming event, the above function is called to check the occurrence of new emotions as well as re-stimulation of existing emotions in

Emo for every $g \in G$. $\mathcal{E}_{ety}(K, e, g)$ internally calculates an activation potential value and compares it to a threshold $Thres_{ety}$; a new emotion is only triggered if the activation potential value exceeds the threshold. These thresholds might vary according to players' characters and their moods. For instance, when a person is in a good mood, their threshold for activating negative emotions go up which conveys they become more tolerant before feeling negative-valenced emotions. There is also a memory (*emhistory*) of activated emotions in the past for some reasonable time frame. This is maintained implicitly in the emotions' activation functions. The activation function of each emotion, based on provided definitions in the OCC theory, is as bellows, where x, v and v' refer to the goal's importance, the goal likelihood in previous and the new state respectively.

$$- \mathcal{E}_{Hope}(K, e, g) = \overbrace{v' * x}^{\text{activation intensity}} - Thres_{Hope}$$
$$\underbrace{}_{\text{activation potential}}$$

provided $g = \langle id, x \rangle \in G$, $\mathbf{P}(g, v) \in K$, $\mathbf{P}(g, v') \in e(K)$, and $v < v' < 1$.

$- \mathcal{E}_{Fear}(K, e, g) = (1 - v') * x - Thres_{Fear}$, provided $g = \langle id, x \rangle \in G$, $\mathbf{P}(g, v) \in K$, $\mathbf{P}(g, v') \in e(K)$, and $0 < v' < v$.

$- \mathcal{E}_{Joy}(K, e, g) = Des(K, e, g) - Thres_{Joy}$, provided $g \in G$, $\mathbf{P}(g, 1) \in e(K)$, and $Des(K, e, g) > 0$.

$- \mathcal{E}_{Distress}(K, e, g) = |Des(K, e, g)| - Thres_{Distress}$, provided $g \in G$, $\mathbf{P}(g, 0) \in e(K)$, and $Des(K, e, g) < 0$.

$- \mathcal{E}_{Satisfaction}(K, e, g) = x - Thres_{Satisfaction}$, provided that $g = \langle id, x \rangle \in G$, $status(g, achieved) \in e(K)$, and both $\langle Hope, g \rangle, \langle Joy, g \rangle \in emhistory$.

$- \mathcal{E}_{Disappointment}(K, e, g) = x - Thres_{Disappointment}$, provided $g = \langle id, x \rangle \in G$, $status(g, failed) \in e(K)$, and both $\langle Hope, g \rangle, \langle Distress, g \rangle \in emhistory$.

Emotion decay. An emotion intensity in *Emo* declines over time, triggered by *tick* events. This is formulated with a decay function over intensity as follows:

$$decayed(Emo) = \{\langle ety, g, w', t_0 \rangle \mid \langle ety, g, w, t_0 \rangle \in Emo, \ w' = \mathsf{decay}_{ety}(w_0, t_0) > 0\} \quad (2)$$

where w_0 is the initial intensity of *ety* for the goal g at time t_0; this is stored in *emhistory*. decay_{ety} which is a decay function defined as an inverse exponential function over the peak of intensity (w_0) at time t_0.

2.2   Model-based Testing with EFSM

Since automated testing is a major challenge for the game industry due to the complexity and hugeness of games' interaction space, a recent development is to apply a model-based approach for test generation. [30,52,18]. For this purpose, an extended finite state machine (EFSM) M can be used which is a finite state machine (FSM), extended with a set V of *context variables* that allows the machine to have richer concrete states than the abstract states of its base FSM

[2]. Transitions t in M take the form $n \xrightarrow{l/g/\alpha} n'$ where n and n' are source and destination abstract states of the transition, l is a label, g is a predicate over V that guards the transition, and α is a function that updates the variables in V.

Figure 1 shows an example of a small level in a game called *Lab recruits* [4] which is the case study of this paper as well. A *Lab recruits* level is a maze with a set of rooms and interactive objects, such as doors and buttons. A level might also contain fire hazards The player's goal is to reach the object gf0. Access to it is guarded by door₃, so reaching it involves opening the door using a button, which in turn is in a different room, guarded by another door, and so on. Ferdous et al. [18] employs a combined search-based and model-based testing for functional bug detection in this game using EFSM model (Figure 1). In the model, all interactable objects are EFSM states: doors (3), buttons (4), and the goal object gf0. For each door$_i$, d$_i$p and d$_i$m are introduced to model the two sides of the door. The model has three context variables representing the state of each door (open/close). A solid edged transition on the model is unguarded, modelling the agent's trip from one object to another without walking through a door. A dotted transition models traversing through a door when the door is open. A dashed self loop transition models pressing a button; it toggles the status of the doors connected to the pressed button. Notice that the model captures the logical behavior of the game. It abstracts away the physical shape of the level, which would otherwise make the model more complicated and prone to changes during development. Given such a model, *abstract test cases* are constructed as sequences of consecutive transitions in the model. This paper will extend the EFSM model-based testing approach [18] for player experience testing.

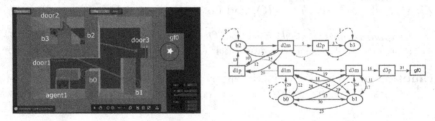

Fig. 1: A game level in the Lab Recruits game and its EFSM model [18].

3   PX Testing Framework

The proposed *automated PX testing framework* aims to aid game designers for PX assessment of their games by providing information on the time and place of emerged emotions and their patterns which would ultimately determine the general experience of player. E.g. if these patterns do not fulfill design intentions, game properties can be altered and testing process can be repeated.

---

[4] https://github.com/iv4xr-project/labrecruits

Figure 2 shows the general architecture of the framework. There are four main components: a *Model-based Testing* component for generating tests, the *Model of Emotions* component implements the computational model of emotions from Section 2.1, an Aplib *basic test agent* [45] for controlling the in-game player-character, and the *PX Testing Tool* as an interface for a game designer towards the framework. The designer needs to provide these inputs, see ① in Figure 2:

- An EFSM that abstractly models the functional behavior of the game.
- A selection of game events that have impacts on the player's emotions (e.g. defeating an enemy, acquiring gold).
- Characteristics that the designer wants to address in the agent to resemble a certain type of players, such as: a player's goals and their priorities, the player's initial mood and beliefs before playing the game, and the desirability of incoming events for the player. E.g. a player might experience a high level of positive emotions on defeating an enemy, while for another player who prefers to avoid conflicts, acquiring a gold bar could be more desirable.

Given the EFSM model, the *Model-based testing* component, ② in Figure 2, generates a test suite consisting of abstract test cases to be executed on the game under test (GUT). The test generation approach is explained in Section 4.1. Due to the abstraction of the model, emotion traces cannot be obtained from pure on-model executions. They require the executions of the test cases on the GUT. An adapter is needed to convert the abstract test cases into actual instructions for the GUT. The Aplib basic test agent does this conversion.

Attaching the *Model of Emotions* to the *basic test agent* creates an *emotional test agent*, ③ in Figure 2, which is able to simulate emotions based on incoming events. Via a plugin, the emotional test agent is connected to the GUT. Each test case of the test suite is then given to the agent for execution. The agent computes its emotional state upon observing events and records it in a *trace* file. Finally, when the whole test suite is executed, the *PX Testing Tool* analyzes the traces to verify given emotional requirements and provide heat-maps and timeline graphs of emotions for the given level (④ in Figure 2).

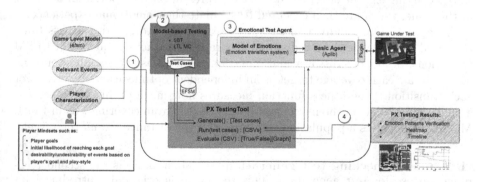

Fig. 2: Automated PX testing framework architecture.

4   Methodology

This section describes the framework's model-based test generation techniques and our approach to measure a test suite's diversity. Then, our approach for expressing emotion pattern requirements and verifying them are explained.

4.1   Test Suite Generation

A test generation algorithm is applied to produce abstract test cases from a model with respect to a given coverage criterion. From now on, we refer to these abstract test cases simply as test cases. In our context, game designers can evaluate the game experience by evaluating emerging emotional experience through various paths to the game's goal. So, a proper test suite needs to cover various variations of player behavior to expose various emotion patterns. Here, we aim at graph-based coverage, such as transition coverage. However, since the model of emotions from Section 2.1 is goal-oriented, some adjustment is needed:

Definition 1. *Transition-goal coverage over an EFSM model M with respect to a goal state g is a requirement to cover all transitions in M, where a transition t is covered by a test case if its execution passes t and terminates in g.*

Given the above definition, the PX framework uses the following complementary test generation approaches; one is stochastic and the other is deterministic.

Search Based Test generation Search based testing (SBT) formulates testing problems as an optimization problem in which a search algorithm is used to find an optimized solution, in the form of a test suite, that satisfies a given test adequacy criterion encoded as a fitness function [36]. Meta-heuristic algorithms such as genetic algorithm [23] and tabu [22,26] are commonly used for this. Our framework uses an open source library EvoMBT [18] that comes with several state of the art search algorithms e.g. MOSA [44]. We utilize this to produce a test suite satisfying e.g. the criterion in Def.1 to represent players' potential behavior in the game, which are then executed to simulate their emotional experience.

To apply MOSA, individual encoding, search operators and a fitness function need to be defined. An individual I is represented as a sequence of EFSM transitions. Standard crossover and mutation are used as the search operators. MOSA treats each coverage target as an independent optimisation objective. For each transition t, the fitness function measures how much of an individual I is actually executable on the model and how close it is from covering t as in Def.1. MOSA then evolves a population that minimize the distances to *all* the targets.

LTL model checking test generation Model checking is the second technique we use for test generation. This technique is originally introduced for automated software verification that takes a finite state model of a program as an input to check whether given specifications hold in the model [8]. Such specifications can be formulated in e.g. LTL which is a powerful language for expressing system properties over time. When the target formula is violated, a model checker produces a counter example in the form of an execution trace to help debugging the model. This ability is exploited for producing test cases by encoding coverage targets as negative formulas, and converting the produced counter examples to test cases [4,11,20]. We use this to generate test suites satisfying the coverage criterion in Def.1, encoded as an LTL properties. For each transition $t : n_1 \rightarrow n_2$ in the EFSM model, the transition-goal coverage requirement to cover t is encoded as the following LTL formula:

$$\phi_t = \neg g \, \mathcal{U} \, (n_1 \wedge \mathcal{X}(n_2 \wedge \neg g \, \mathcal{U} \, g))$$

where g is the goal state like gf0 in Figure 1. The model checking algorithm checks whether $\neg \phi_t$ is valid on the EFSM model using depth-first traversal [29]. If it is not, a counter example is produced that visits t and terminates in g. An extra iteration is added to find the shortest covering test case.

4.2   Test Suite Diversity

Diversity is an approach to measure the degree of variety of the control and data flow in software or a game[41]. We use this approach to measure the diversity of test suites obtained from the generators in Section 4.1. A test suite's diversity degree is the average distance between every pair of distinct test cases, which can be measured in e.g. the Jaro distance metric. For a test case tc, let $\overline{tc}$ and $|\overline{tc}|$ be its string representation and its length respectively. The Jaro distance between two test cases of tc_i and tc_j is calculated as follows:

$$Dis_{Jaro}(tc_i, tc_j) = \begin{cases} 1 & , \text{if } m = 0 \\ 1 - \frac{1}{3}(\frac{m}{|tc_i|} + \frac{m}{|tc_j|} + \frac{m-t}{m}) & , \text{if } m \neq 0 \end{cases} \quad (3)$$

where m is the number of matching symbols in two strings whose distance is less than $\lfloor |\overline{tc_i}|/2 \rfloor$, assuming $\overline{tc_i}$ is the longer string; and t is half of the number of transpositions. Then, the diversity of a test suite TS is a summation of distances between every pair of distinct test cases, divided by the number such pairs:

$$Div_{avg}(TS) = \frac{\sum_{i=1}^{|TS|} \sum_{j=i+1}^{|TS|} Dis_{Jaro}(tc_i, tc_j)}{\frac{|TS| * (|TS|-1)}{2}} \quad (4)$$

where $|TS|$ is TS' size. Additionally, if TS_1 and TS_2 are two test suites, the average distance between them is:

$$Dis_{avg}(TS_1, TS_2) = \frac{\sum_{tc_i \in TS_1, tc_j \in TS_2} Dis_{Jaro}(tc_i, tc_j)}{|TS_1| * |TS_2|} \quad (5)$$

This is used in Section 5 to measure the distance between the test suites generated by the two approaches (Section 4.1) provided by our framework, along with their complementary effects on revealing different emotion patterns.

4.3   Emotion Patterns' Requirements and Heat-maps

In Section 2.1, we described the emotion model of an agent. When the agent executes a test case, it produces a trace of its emotion state over time. Such a *trace* is a sequence of tuples (t, p, Emo) where t is a timestamp, Emo is the agent emotion state at time t, and p is its position. Running a test suite produces a set of such traces. We define *emotion patterns* to capture the presence or absence of an emotional experience in a game. Such a pattern is expressed by a string of symbols, each representing the *stimulation*, or lack of a certain emotion type.

Definition 2. *An emotion pattern is a sequence of stimulations e or $\neg e$, where e is one of the symbols H, J, S, F, D and P. Each represents the stimulation of respectively hope, joy, satisfaction, fear, distress, and disappointment.*

A single pattern such as F represents the stimulation of the corresponding emotion, in this case fear. We will restrict ourselves to simply mean that this stimulation occurs, without specifying e.g. when it happens exactly, nor for how long it is sustained. A negative single pattern such as $\neg F$ represents the absence of stimulation, in this case fear. A pattern is a sequence of one or more single patterns, specifying in what order the phenomenon that each single pattern describes is expected to occurs. Patterns provide a simple, intuitive, but reasonably expressive way to express PX. For example, the pattern JFS is satisfied by traces where the agent at some point becomes satisfied (S) after a stimulation of joy (J), but in between it also experiences a stimulation of fear at least once. Another example is $J\neg FS$ when there is no stimulation of fear between J and S. The presence of this pattern indicates the presence of a 'sneak' route, where a goal is achievable without the player has to fight enough for it.

As a part of PX *requirements*, developers might insist on presence or absence of certain patterns. More precisely, given a pattern p, we can pose these types of requirements: $Sat(p)$ requires that at least one execution of the game under test satisfies p; $UnSat(p)$ requires that $Sat(p)$ does not hold; and $Valid(p)$ requires that all executions satisfy p. In the context of testing, we will judge this by executions of the test cases in the given test suite TS.

Heat-maps Whereas above we discuss emotion patterns over *time*, a heat-map shows patterns over *space*. Assuming the visitable parts of a game level form a 2D surface, we can divide it into small squares of $u \times u$. Given a position p and a square s, we can check if $p \in s$. Given a trace τ, let $Emo(s) = \{Emo \mid (t, p, Emo) \in \tau, \ p \in s\}$: the set of emotions, that occur in the square s. This can be aggregated by a function $aggr$ that maps $Emo(s)$ to $\mathbf{R}$. An example of an aggregator is the function max_e that calculates the maximum of a specific emotion e (e.g. hope). Section 5 will show some examples. Such maps can be analyzed against requirements, e.g. that the aggregate values in certain areas should be of a certain intensity. We can also create an aggregated heat-map of an entire test suite by merging the traces of its test cases into a single trace, and then calculate the map from the combined trace. Finally, the overall methodology of our PX testing is summarized in Algorithm 1.

4.4 PX Framework Implementation

The test agent is implemented using APlib Java library [45]. It has a BDI architecture [27] with a novel goal and tactical programming layer. We use JOCC library [21] for modeling emotions. To facilitate the model-based testing, we integrate EvoMBT[18]. It generates abstract test suites from an EFSM model, utilizing EvoSuite [19] for search-based test generation. An implementation of LTL model checking algorithm is employed to produce model checking-based test suites. The framework and its data will be available for public use.

Algorithm 1 *The Execution of automated PX Testing Algorithm.*

Input: EFSM M, coverage criterion C,
configuration parameters $Config$ for test generator,
and emotion pattern requirements' list R.
Output: Emotion traces, Heat-maps of emotions,
and the verification of requirements' ($true/false$).

1: **procedure** EXEC($M, C, Config, R$)
2:    $TS_{abstract} \leftarrow$ TSGENERATE($M, C, Config$)
3:    $TS_{concrete} \leftarrow$ TRANSLATE($TS_{abstract}$)
4:    Configure an emotional test agent A
5:    $traces_{emotion} \leftarrow \emptyset$
6:    **for all** test cases $tc \in TS_{concrete}$ **do**
7:        $\tau \leftarrow A$ executes tc on the SUT
8:        $traces_{emotion} \leftarrow traces_{emotion} \cup \{\tau\}$
9:    **end for**
10:    $Hmaps \leftarrow$ GENERATEHEAT-MAPS($traces_{emotion}$)
11:    $Vresult \leftarrow \{ (r, \text{VERIFY}(r)) \mid r \in R \}$
12:    **return** ($traces_{emotions}, Hmaps, Vresults$)
13: **end procedure**

---

5 Case Study

This section presents an exploratory case study conducted to investigate the use of a model-based PX testing framework[5] for verifying emotion requirements in a game-level and to investigate the difference between the search based generated test suite and the model checker generated test suites on revealing emotion patterns. Finally, we run mutation testing to evaluate the strength of our framework.

5.1 Experiment Configuration

Figure 3 shows a test level called *Wave-the-flag* in the Lab Recruits, a configurable 3D game, designed for AI researchers to define their own testing problems. It is a medium sized level, consisting of a 1182 m^2 navigable virtual floor, 8 rooms, 12 buttons, and 11 doors. Its EFSM model consists of 35 states and 159 transitions. The player starts in the room marked green at the top, and must find a 'goal flag' gf0 marked red in the bottom room to finish the level. Doors and buttons form a puzzle in the game. A human player needs to disclose the connections between buttons and doors to open a path through

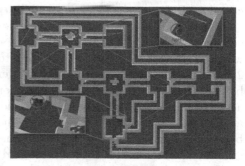

Fig. 3: *Wave-the-flag* level.

---

[5] https://doi.org/10.5281/zenodo.7506758

the maze to reach the aforementioned goal flag in a timely manner. The player can earn points by opening doors and lose health in case of passing fire flames. For the test agent, the latter is also observable as an event called *Ouch*. If the player runs out of health, it loses the game. The player also has no prior knowledge about the position of doors, buttons and the goal flag, nor the knowledge on which buttons open which doors. Since there are multiple paths to reach the target, depending on the path that the player chooses to explore, it might be able to reach the goal without health loss, at one end of spectrum, or it can end up dead at the other end. The EFSM model (not shown) of the *Wave-the-flag* level is constructed similar to the running example in section 2.2. To add excitement, *Wave-the-flag* also contains fire flames. However, these flames are not included into the EFSM model because the placement and amount of these objects are expected to change frequently during development. Keeping this information in the EFSM model would force the designer to constantly update the model after each change in flames. Thus, similar to the running example, the EFSM model contains doors, buttons and goal flags.

In addition to the EFSM model, we need to characterize a player to do PX testing (① in Figure 2). Table 1 shows basic characteristics of a player, defined with a set of parameters, to configure the emotion model of the agent before the execution. The level designer determines values of these parameters. After the execution of the model, we asked the designer to check the plausibility their values by checking the emotional heat-map results. The designer checked randomly selected number of test cases with their generated emotional heat maps to check the occurrence of emotions are reasonable. Thus, the utilized values for the following experiment is confirmed reasonable by the designer. Moreover, The likelihood of reaching the goal gf0 is set to 0.5 in the initial state to model a player who initially feels unbiased towards the prospect of finishing the level. Thus, the agent feels an equal level w of hope and fear at the beginning.

5.2   PX Testing Evaluation

Test suites are generated from the EFSM model using LTL model checking (MC) and the search-based (SB) approach with the full transition-goal coverage criterion (Def.1) named as TS_{SB} and TS_{MC}, both with 60 seconds time budget.

Abstract test suite characteristics. Our reason for using multiple test generation algorithms is to improve the diversity of the generated test cases, which in turn would improve our ability to reveal more emotion patterns. Table 2 shows the basic characteristics of the generated test suites. Due its stochastic behavior, the search-based (SB) generation is repeated 10 times, and then averaged. The SB algorithm manages to provide full transition-goal coverage with, in average, 54.6 test cases ($\sigma = 7.8$), with the average diversity of 0.192 ($\sigma = 0.03$) between test cases in a test suite. The model checker (MC) always satisfies the criterion with 74 test cases and average diversity of 0.113. The higher diversity of SB test suites (TS_{SB}) can be explained through the stochastic nature of the search algorithm. Table 2 also shows the length of the shortest and longest test cases. While SB manages to find a shorter test case with only 17.7 transitions

Table 1: *Configuration of Player Characterization. G is the agent's goal set; it has one goal for this level, namely reaching the goal-flag $gf0$, s_0 is the emotion model's initial state, a set of relevant events (E) needs to be defined by the designers: DoorOpen event, triggered when a new door gets open, is perceived as increasing the likelihood of reaching $gf0$ by v_1 in the model, Ouch event, that notifies fire burn, is perceived as declining the likelihood of reaching $gf0$ by v_2, GoalInSight event, triggered at the first time the agent observes the goal $gf0$ in its vicinity , is modelled as making the agent believes that the likelihood of reaching the goal becomes certain (1), and finally GoalAccomplished event is triggered when the goal $gf0$ is accomplished. Des reflects the desirability/undesirability of each event with respect to the goal and Thres is the emotions' activation thresholds. x, v_i, and y_i are constants determined by the designer.*

Parameter	Value
G	$g = < gf0, x > \in G$
s_0	$likelihood(gf0, 0.5) \in K_0$, $Emo_0 = \{< Hope, gf0, w, 0 >, < Fear, gf0, w, 0 >\}$
E	$= \{DoorOpen, Ouch, GoalInSight, GoalAccomplished\}$ on $DoorOpen$ event: $likelihood(gf0, +v_1)$, on fire burn in $Ouch$ event: $likelihood(gf0, -v_2)$, on $GoalInSight$ event: $likelihood(gf0, 1)$.
Des	$Des(K, DoorOpen, gf0) = +y_1$, $Des(K, Ouch, gf0) = -y_2$, $Des(K, GoalInSight, gf0) = +y_3$
$Thres$	0

in average, its longest test case has in average 74.25 transitions. Finally, the last row in Table 2 indicates the difference between SB and MC test suites. The distance between two test suites is measured for every generated TS_{SB} using Equation 5 which brings about 0.214 ($\sigma = 0.024$) distance in average between test cases of the two suites. Later, we investigate whether such a difference can lead to differences at the execution level in emotion patterns.

Table 2: *Characteristics of LTL-model checking-based and search-based test suites with respect to the same coverage criterion.*

Test suite	size	$Div_{avg}(TS_i)$	Shortest tc	longest tc
TS_{MC}	74	0.113	23	45
$TS_{SB_{avg}}$	54.6	0.192	17.7	74.25
$Div_{avg}(TS_{MC}, TS_{SB})$	128.6		0.214	

Evaluation of emotional heat-maps. Inspecting the emerging emotions requires real execution of test cases on the game under test. The execution of TS_{MC} with 74 test cases and the TS_{SB} with the average 54.5 test cases took 11,894 seconds and 10,201 respectively in the game. After the executions, the automated PX testing framework produces a heat-map of emotions for every test case to give spatial information about the intensity of the emotion at each location in the game. Unlike [21] which only produces heat-maps of emotions for a single pre-defined navigation path, Figure 4 shows the *aggregated* heat map visualization of some selected emotions, evoked during the execution of *all* test cases in TS_{MC} and a randomly chosen TS_{SB} suite from the previously generated 10 TS_{SB} suites, with the square size $u=1$ and max_e as the aggregation function. So, the maps show the maximum intensity on a given spot over the whole execution of the corresponding test suite. The brighter color shows the higher intensity of an emotion. In this case, the bright yellow represents the highest emotional intensity in heat maps. The heat maps of hope, joy and satisfaction for these test suites show quite similar spatial information (only hope and joy are shown in Figure 4). However, TS_{MC} generally shows a higher level of hope during the game-play (Figures 4a and 4b). So, if the designer verifies his level on the presence and spatial distribution of intensified hope through the level, the test cases produced by TS_{MC} can expose these attributes better. This can be explained by the model checker setup to find shortest test cases; some can then open the next door sooner, raising hope before its intensity decays too much.

The maps also show a difference in the spatial coverage of TS_{SB} and TS_{MC} (marked green in Figures 4a and 4b). The transition that traverses the corridor is present in TS_{MC}, but when the corresponding abstract test case is transformed into an executable test case for APlib test agent, they also incorporate optimization. So, it finds a more optimized way for execution by skipping the transition that actually passes the corridor towards the room, if the next transition is to traverse back along same corridor. The corridor is, however, covered by TS_{SB}.

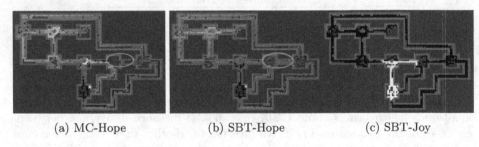

(a) MC-Hope   (b) SBT-Hope   (c) SBT-Joy

Fig. 4: Heat-map visualization of positive emotions for SBT and MC test suites.

The most striking differences between TS_{SB} and TS_{MC} are revealed in their negative emotions' heat-maps (Figure 5). Most places that are marked black as distress-free by executed TS_{MC} (Figure 5a) are actually highly distressful positions for some test cases of TS_{SB}. The presence of distress might be the intended player experience, whereas its absence in certain places might actually be undesirable. Upon closer inspection of individual test cases, it turns out that the test cases of TS_{SB} that pass e.g. the red regions in Figure 5a and 5b always show distress in the marked corridor, whereas one test case in TS_{MC} manages to find a 'sneak route' that passes the corridor without distress, and finishes the level successfully. Thus, if the designer is looking for the possibility of absence of distress in the sneak corridor, inspection of TS_{SB} would not suffice. The heat-maps of disappointment reveals another difference. While TS_{MC} only finds one location where the agent dies and feels disappointed, TS_{SB} manages to find 3 more locations in the level with the disappointment state (Figure 5c).

The main reason behind those differences is that a sequence of transitions results in experiencing an emotion in the agent, not just a single transition. Furthermore, emotions intensity has a residual behavior which means a sequence of transitions and behavior might result in an emotion which still remains in the agent emotional state after some time. Thus, providing state coverage or the transition-coverage criterion does not in itself suffice to manage revealing possible emotions and their patterns. The variation of transitions and their order in a test case can resemble the different player behaviors during the game-play that their outcomes ultimately form the player emotional experience. Therefore, finding a proper test suite that can capture the distributions of theses emotions with test cases exhibiting the presence or absence of emotions in various locations is challenging. As remarked before, due to the stochastic nature of its algorithm, the search algorithm produces more diverse test suite than the LTL model checker, and hence can increase the chance of revealing more variation of emotions in different locations of the level. However, our experiments show the model checker does provide useful complementary test cases, e.g. for finding corner cases which can be covered only by the model checker that were missed by SB. All mentioned differences can explain the 0.20 distant difference between TS_{MC} and TS_{SB}.

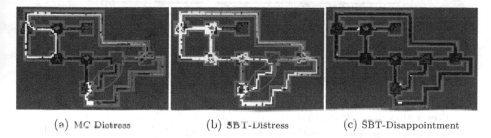

(a) MC Distress   (b) SBT-Distress   (c) SBT-Disappointment

Fig. 5: Heat-map visualization of negative emotions for SBT and MC test suites.

Checking emotion pattern requirements. The PX testing framework is also capable of verifying emotion requirements using patterns as defined in Definition 2 format based on stimulation of emotions. These patterns are verified by inspecting the order in which different emotions are stimulated, as recorded in the trace files. Although there are numerous combinations of emotions, only some of them matter for the designer to check. As a requirement, recall that a pattern can be posed as an existential requirement, i.e. $Sat(p)$, or need to happen for all game-plays, i.e. $Valid(p)$ or need to unwitnessed for all game-plays, i.e. $USat(p)$. It is also essential to clarify that the choice of which emotion patterns are to be required can vary among game-levels, as expectations on the occurrences of patterns depend on the design goal. E.g. a game level with $Sat(DHS)$ would provide at least one thrilling game-play. But if it is intended to be an easy level for beginners, the designer might insist on $UnSat(DHS)$ instead. We have collected a number of emotion pattern requirements from the designer of the *Wave-the-flag* level; these are shown in the upper part of Table 3. The main expectation of the designer is to ensure that the designed level is enjoyable by experiencing different positive as well as negative emotions during the game-play and to avoid the player to get bored by interpreting boredom as absence of active emotions in the agent emotional state for some time. As can be seen in Table 3, while most requirements are verified during the test, there are requirements like $Sat(J\neg S)$ that are failed. This requirement indicates the designer expects at least one execution path that joy is stimulated at least once thought the execution, but the agent never reaches the goal with satisfaction. Having Sat patterns failed to be witnessed, or $UnSat$ patterns that are witnessed, assist the designer to alter their game level and run the agent through the level again. For example, here, the fail on $Sat(J\neg S)$ is an indication that the designer needs to put some challenging objects like fire or enemies in the vicinity of the goal $gf0$.

Table 3: *Emotion pattern check with TS_{MC} and TS_{SB}. H= hope, F= fear, J= joy, D= distress, S= satisfaction, P = disappointment and $\neg X$ = absence of emotion X.*

Emotion patterns	TS_{MC}	TS_{SB}
$Sat(\neg DS)$	✔	✔
$UnSat(\neg FS)$	✔	✔
$Sat(J\neg S)$	✗	✗
$UnSat(JD)$	✔	✔
$Sat(JFS)$	✔	✔
$Sat(DHP)$	✔	✔
$Sat(DHS)$	✔	✔
$Sat(DH\neg DS)$	✗	✔
$Sat(FDHFJ)$	✗	✔
$Sat(HFDDDHFJ)$	✗	✔
$Sat(FDDHFP)$	✗	✗
Emotion patterns length=2	101/144 (70.2%)	101/144 (70.2%)
Emotion patterns length=3	88/150 (58.6%)	88/150 (58.6%)
Emotion patterns length=4	71/164 (43.2%)	72/164 (43.9%)
Emotion pattern length=5	60/177 (33.8%)	61/177 (34.4%)

Table 3 also shows the similar ratio of the pairwise combination of emotions over various $Sat(p)$ for the pattern p between length 2-5 by the TS_{SB} and the TS_{MC}, indicating that both test suites can perform well to detect Sat-type emotion patterns. However, there the last three patterns in Table 3 are covered by TS_{SB} but missed by TS_{MC}. Thus, they are complementary, which makes it reasonable to use both test suites for verifying emotion pattern requirements.

5.3   Mutation Testing Evaluation

Mutation testing [32] is a technique to evaluate the quality of test suites in detecting faults, represented by faulty variants ('mutants') of the target program generated through a set of mutation operators. Here, we use this to evaluate the strength of our PX testing approach. In the procedure, we use a corrected *Wave-the-flag* level ('original' level), satisfying all the emotion pattern requirements we posed in Table 3. Mutations are applied on the original's level definition file to produce mutants (one mutation per mutant). An example of a mutation is to remove all fire flames from a certain zone in the level; Table 4 lists the used mutation operators. A mutant represents an alternate design of the level, maintaining the level's logic, but may induce different PX. To apply the mutations, the game level is divided to 16 zones of about equal size. We apply the mutation operators on each zone. Every mutant is labeled with the applied mutation operator and z_x_y where (x, y) specifies the bottom-left corner of the zone on which the mutation is applied. After dropping mutations that do not change the level's properties, we obtain 20 distinct mutants, from which we randomly choose 10 mutants for execution. We re-run both TS_{MC} and TS_{SB} test suites on each mutant. A mutant is automatically killed when the correctness of a specification is judged differently from the original results. Table 5 shows that 8 of the 10 randomly selected mutants are killed. Remaining mutants are not killed because emotion requirements might not be distinctive enough to kill them too.

Table 4: *Mutation operators*

Code	Description
RF	Remove fire
RW2WF	Relocate fire between walls
RMRF	Relocate fire in middle of a room
AMRF	Add fire in middle of a room
AW2WF	Add fire between walls

Table 5: *Kill matrix of the mutants.*

Emotion patterns	Original	$RF\_z.0.51$	$RF\_z.48.17$	$RF\_z.0.51$	$RMRF\_z.24.0$	$RW2WF\_z.0.34$	$RW2WF\_z.24.51$	$RW2WF\_z.48.0$	$RW2WF\_z.48.17$	$AMRF\_z.24.51$	$AW2WF\_z.72.34$
$Sat(\neg DS)$	✔	✔	✔	✔	✔	✔	✔	✔	✔	✔	✔
$UnSat(\neg FS)$	✔	✗	✔	✔	✔	✔	✔	✔	✔	✔	✔
$Sat(J\neg S)$	✔	✔	✔	✗	✔	✔	✗	✗	✔	✗	✔
$UnSat(JD)$	✔	✔	✔	✔	✔	✔	✔	✔	✗	✔	✔
$Sat(JFS)$	✔	✔	✔	✔	✔	✔	✔	✔	✔	✔	✔
$Sat(DHP)$	✔	✔	✔	✔	✔	✔	✔	✔	✔	✔	✔
$Sat(DHS)$	✔	✔	✔	✔	✔	✔	✔	✔	✔	✔	✔
$Sat(DH\neg DS)$	✔	✔	✔	✔	✔	✔	✔	✔	✔	✔	✔
$Sat(FDHFJ)$	✔	✗	✔	✔	✔	✔	✔	✔	✔	✔	✔
$Sat(HFDDDHFJ)$	✔	✗	✔	✔	✔	✔	✔	✗	✔	✔	✔
$Sat(FDDHFP)$	✔	✗	✗	✗	✔	✔	✔	✔	✗	✔	✔

Threat to Validity. The designed character in Player Characterization, the selected coverage criterion for test generation to verify $UnSat$ specifications, and the small number of mutation testing assessments due to the computational cost are internal threats to the validity of the work. In terms of external threats, performing the experiment on one level is not safe to be generalized.

6 Related Work

A number of research has been conducted on automated play testing to reduce the cost of repetitive and labor-intensive functional testing tasks in video games [35,54]. In particular, agent based testing has been a subject of recent research to play and explore the game space on behalf of human players for testing purposes. Ariyurek et al. [7] introduces Reinforcement Learning (RL) and Monte Carlo Tree Search (MCTS) agents to detect bugs in video games automatically. Stahlke et al. [51] presents a basis for a framework to model player's memory and goal-oriented decision-making to simulate human navigational behavior for identifying level design issues. The framework creates an AI-agent that uses a path finding heuristic to navigate a level, optimized by a given player characteristics such as level of experience and play-style. Zhao et al. [55] intend to create agents with human-like behavior for balancing games based on skill and play-styles. These parameters are measured using introduced metrics to help training the agents in four different case studies to test the game balance and to imitate players with different play-styles. Gordillo et al. [24] addresses the game state coverage problem in play-testing by introducing a curiosity driven reinforcement learning agent for a 3D game. The test agent utilizes proximal policy optimization (PPO) with a curiosity factor reflected on the RL reward function with frequency of a game state visit. Pushing the agent to have the exploratory behaviour provides a better chance to explore unseen states for bugs.

Among game model-based testing, Iftikhar et al. [30] applies it on *Mario Brothers* game for functional testing. The study uses UML states machine as a game model for test case generation which manages to reveal faults. Ferdous et al. [18] employs combined search-based and model-based testing for automated play-testing using an EFSM. Search algorithms are compared regarding the model coverage and bug detection. Note that while an EFSM provides paths through a game, it can not reveal the experience of a player who navigates the path.

Despite some research on modeling human players and their behavior in agents for automated functional play testing, there are a few research on automation of PX evaluation. Holmgard et al. [28] propose to create procedural personas or player characteristics for test agent to help game designers to develop game contents and desirable level design for different players. The research proposes to create personas in test agents using MCTS with evolutionary computation for node selection. The result on *MiniDungeons 2* game shows how different personas brings about different behavior in response to game contents which can be seen as different play-styles. Lee et al. [34] investigate a data-driven cognitive model of human performance in moving-target acquisition to estimate the game difficulty for different players with different skill level. There is limited research on the emotion prediction and its usage for automation of PX evaluation. Gholizadeh et al. [21] introduce an emotional agent using a formal model of OCC emotions and propose the potential use of such an agent for PX assessment. However, the approach lacks automated path planning and reasoning, and hence it cannot do automated gameplay. Automatic coverage of game states and collecting all emerging emotions are thus not supported which are addressed in this paper.

7 Conclusion & Future work

This paper presented a framework for automated player experience testing, in particular automated verification of emotion requirement, using a computational model of emotions and model-based test generation targeting a subset of human players' behaviors. We presented a language for emotion patterns to capture emotion requirements. We also investigated the complementary impact of different test generation techniques on verifying spatial and temporal emotion patterns.

Future work. The explained language is able to capture complex patterns with the temporal order of emotions' stimulations in the framework. However, it cannot capture spatial behavior of emotions, such as differences in the heatmaps. Generally, combining spatial and temporal aspects to verify emotion requirements in specific areas and time intervals would give a more refined way to assess the emotional experience. How to capture this into formal patterns is still an open question. Investigating the application of our approach in empirical case studies with human players is future work.

References

1. Agarwal, A., Meyer, A.: Beyond usability: evaluating emotional response as an integral part of the user experience. In: CHI'09 Extended Abstracts on Human Factors in Computing Systems, pp. 2919–2930. ACM New York, NY, USA (2009)
2. Alagar, V., Periyasamy, K.: Extended finite state machine. In: Specification of software systems, pp. 105–128. Springer (2011)
3. Alves, R., Valente, P., Nunes, N.J.: The state of user experience evaluation practice. In: Proceedings of the 8th Nordic Conference on Human-Computer Interaction: Fun, Fast, Foundational. pp. 93–102 (2014)
4. Ammann, P.E., Black, P.E., Majurski, W.: Using model checking to generate tests from specifications. In: Proceedings second international conference on formal engineering methods (Cat. No. 98EX241). pp. 46–54. IEEE (1998)
5. Anderson, J.R.: Arguments concerning representations for mental imagery. Psychological review **85**(4), 249 (1978)
6. Ansari, S.G.: Toward automated assessment of user experience in extended reality. In: 2020 IEEE 13th international conference on software testing, validation and verification (ICST). pp. 430–432. IEEE (2020)
7. Ariyurek, S., Betin-Can, A., Surer, E.: Automated video game testing using synthetic and humanlike agents. IEEE Transactions on Games **13**(1), 50–67 (2019)
8. Baier, C., Katoen, J.P.: Principles of model checking. MIT press (2008)
9. Bartneck, C.: Integrating the occ model of emotions in embodied characters. In: Proceeding of the Workshop on Virtual Conversational Characters: Applications, Methods, and Research Challenges (2002)
10. Devan, N.: What is the difference between the purpose of usability and user experience evaluation methods. In: Proceedings of the Workshop UXEM. vol. 9, pp. 1–4. Citeseer (2009)
11. Callahan, J., Schneider, F., Easterbrook, S., et al.: Automated software testing using model checking. In: Proceedings 1996 SPIN workshop. vol. 353. Citeseer (1996)
12. Demeure, V., Niewiadomski, R., Pelachaud, C.: How is believability of a virtual agent related to warmth, competence, personification, and embodiment? Presence **20**(5), 431–448 (2011)
13. Desmet, P., Hekkert, P.: Framework of product experience. International journal of design **1**(1) (2007)
14. Drachen, A., Mirza-Babaei, P., Nacke, L.E.: Games user research. Oxford University Press (2018)
15. Elliott, C.D.: The affective reasoner: a process model of emotions in a multiagent system. Ph.D. thesis, Northwestern University (1992)
16. Ellsworth, P.C., Smith, C.A.: From appraisal to emotion: Differences among unpleasant feelings. Motivation and emotion **12**(3), 271–302 (1988)
17. Fang, X., Chan, S., Brzezinski, J., Nair, C.: Development of an instrument to measure enjoyment of computer game play. INTL. Journal of human–computer interaction **26**(9), 868–886 (2010)
18. Ferdous, R., Kifetew, F., Prandi, D., Prasetya, I., Shirzadehhajimahmood, S., Susi, A.: Search-based automated play testing of computer games: A model-based approach. In: International Symposium on Search Based Software Engineering. pp. 56–71. Springer (2021)
19. Fraser, G., Arcuri, A.: Evosuite: automatic test suite generation for object-oriented software. In: Proceedings of the 19th ACM SIGSOFT symposium and the 13th European conference on Foundations of software engineering. pp. 416–419 (2011)

20. Gargantini, A., Heitmeyer, C.: Using model checking to generate tests from requirements specifications. In: Software Engineering—ESEC/FSE'99. pp. 146–162. Springer (1999)
21. Gholizadeh Ansari, S., Prasetya, I.S.W.B., Dastani, M., Dignum, F., Keller, G.: An appraisal transition system for event-driven emotions in agent-based player experience testing. In: Engineering Multi-Agent Systems: 9th International Workshop, EMAS 2021, Virtual Event, May 3–4, 2021, Revised Selected Papers. pp. 156–174. Springer Nature (2021)
22. Glover, F.: Tabu search—part i. ORSA Journal on computing 1(3), 190–206 (1989)
23. Goldberg, D.E.: Genetic algorithms. Pearson Education India (2006)
24. Gordillo, C., Bergdahl, J., Tollmar, K., Gisslén, L.: Improving playtesting coverage via curiosity driven reinforcement learning agents. arXiv preprint arXiv:2103.13798 (2021)
25. Guckelsberger, C., Salge, C., Gow, J., Cairns, P.: Predicting player experience without the player. an exploratory study. In: Proceedings of the Annual Symposium on Computer-Human Interaction in Play. pp. 305–315 (2017)
26. Harman, M., Jones, B.F.: Search-based software engineering. Information and software Technology 43(14), 833–839 (2001)
27. Herzig, A., Lorini, E., Perrussel, L., Xiao, Z.: BDI logics for BDI architectures: old problems, new perspectives. KI-Künstliche Intelligenz 31(1) (2017)
28. Holmgård, C., Green, M.C., Liapis, A., Togelius, J.: Automated playtesting with procedural personas through mcts with evolved heuristics. IEEE Transactions on Games 11(4), 352–362 (2018)
29. Holzmann, G.J.: The model checker spin. IEEE Transactions on software engineering 23(5), 279–295 (1997)
30. Iftikhar, S., Iqbal, M.Z., Khan, M.U., Mahmood, W.: An automated model based testing approach for platform games. In: 2015 ACM/IEEE 18th International Conference on Model Driven Engineering Languages and Systems (MODELS). pp. 426–435. IEEE (2015)
31. Jennett, C., Cox, A.L., Cairns, P., Dhoparee, S., Epps, A., Tijs, T., Walton, A.: Measuring and defining the experience of immersion in games. International journal of human-computer studies 66(9), 641–661 (2008)
32. Jia, Y., Harman, M.: An analysis and survey of the development of mutation testing. IEEE transactions on software engineering 37(5), 649–678 (2010)
33. Lazarus, R.S., Folkman, S.: Stress, appraisal, and coping. Springer publishing company (1984)
34. Lee, I., Kim, H., Lee, B.: Automated playtesting with a cognitive model of sensorimotor coordination. In: Proceedings of the 29th ACM International Conference on Multimedia. pp. 4920–4929 (2021)
35. Lewis, C., Whitehead, J., Wardrip-Fruin, N.: What went wrong: a taxonomy of video game bugs. In: Proceedings of the fifth international conference on the foundations of digital games. pp. 108–115 (2010)
36. McMinn, P.: Search-based software test data generation: a survey. Software testing, Verification and reliability 14(2), 105–156 (2004)
37. Mirza-Babaei, P., Nacke, L.E., Gregory, J., Collins, N., Fitzpatrick, G.: How does it play better? exploring user testing and biometric storyboards in games user research. In: Proceedings of the SIGCHI conference on human factors in computing systems. pp. 1499–1508 (2013)
38. Myers, G.J., Sandler, C., Badgett, T.: The art of software testing. John Wiley & Sons (2011)

39. Nacke, L., Lindley, C.A.: Flow and immersion in first-person shooters: measuring the player's gameplay experience. In: Proceedings of the 2008 conference on future play: Research, play, share. pp. 81–88 (2008)
40. Nacke, L.E.: Games user research and physiological game evaluation. In: Game user experience evaluation, pp. 63–86. Springer (2015)
41. Nikolik, B.: Test diversity. Information and Software Technology 48(11), 1083–1094 (2006)
42. Ochs, M., Pelachaud, C., Sadek, D.: An empathic virtual dialog agent to improve human-machine interaction. In: Proceedings of the 7th international joint conference on Autonomous agents and multiagent systems-Volume 1. pp. 89–96 (2008)
43. Ortony, A., Clore, G., Collins, A.: The cognitive structure of emotions. cam (bridge university press. Cambridge, England (1988)
44. Panichella, A., Kifetew, F.M., Tonella, P.: Automated test case generation as a many-objective optimisation problem with dynamic selection of the targets. IEEE Transactions on Software Engineering 44(2), 122–158 (2017)
45. Prasetya, I., Dastani, M., Prada, R., Vos, T.E., Dignum, F., Kifetew, F.: Aplib: Tactical agents for testing computer games. In: International Workshop on Engineering Multi-Agent Systems. pp. 21–41. Springer (2020)
46. Procci, K., Singer, A.R., Levy, K.R., Bowers, C.: Measuring the flow experience of gamers: An evaluation of the dfs-2. Computers in Human Behavior 28(6), 2306–2312 (2012)
47. Reilly, W.S.: Believable social and emotional agents. Tech. rep., Carnegie-Mellon Univ Pittsburgh pa Dept of Computer Science (1996)
48. Roseman, I.J., Smith, C.A.: Appraisal theory. Appraisal processes in emotion: Theory, methods, research pp. 3–19 (2001)
49. Roseman, I.J., Spindel, M.S., Jose, P.E.: Appraisals of emotion-eliciting events: Testing a theory of discrete emotions. Journal of personality and social psychology 59(5), 899 (1990)
50. Smith, C.A., Ellsworth, P.C.: Patterns of cognitive appraisal in emotion. Journal of personality and social psychology 48(4), 813 (1985)
51. Stahlke, S.N., Mirza-Babaei, P.: Usertesting without the user: Opportunities and challenges of an ai-driven approach in games user research. Computers in Entertainment (CIE) 16(2), 1–18 (2018)
52. Utting, M., Legeard, B.: Practical model-based testing: a tools approach. Elsevier (2010)
53. Vermeeren, A.P., Law, E.L.C., Roto, V., Obrist, M., Hoonhout, J., Väänänen-Vainio-Mattila, K.: User experience evaluation methods: current state and development needs. In: Proceedings of the 6th Nordic conference on human-computer interaction: Extending boundaries. pp. 521–530 (2010)
54. Zarembo, I.: Analysis of artificial intelligence applications for automated testing of video games. In: ENVIRONMENT. TECHNOLOGIES. RESOURCES. Proceedings of the International Scientific and Practical Conference. vol. 2, pp. 170–174 (2019)
55. Zhao, Y., Borovikov, I., de Mesentier Silva, F., Beirami, A., Rupert, J., Somers, C., Harder, J., Kolen, J., Pinto, J., Pourabolghasem, R., et al.: Winning is not everything: Enhancing game development with intelligent agents. IEEE Transactions on Games 12(2), 199–212 (2020)

Opportunistic Monitoring of Multithreaded Programs

Chukri Soueidi[✉][iD], Antoine El-Hokayem [iD], and Yliès Falcone [iD]

Univ. Grenoble Alpes, CNRS, Inria, Grenoble INP, LIG, 38000 Grenoble, France
{chukri.soueidi,antoine.el-hokayem,
ylies.falcone}@univ-grenoble-alpes.fr

Abstract. We introduce a generic approach for monitoring multithreaded programs online leveraging existing runtime verification (RV) techniques. In our setting, monitors are deployed to monitor specific threads and only exchange information upon reaching synchronization regions defined by the program itself. They use the opportunity of a lock in the program, to evaluate information across threads. As such, we refer to this approach as opportunistic monitoring. By using the existing synchronization, our approach reduces additional overhead and interference to synchronize at the cost of adding a delay to determine the verdict. We utilize a textbook example of readers-writers to show how opportunistic monitoring is capable of expressing specifications on concurrent regions. We also present a preliminary assessment of the overhead of our approach and compare it to classical monitoring showing that it scales particularly well with the concurrency present in the program.

1 Introduction

Guaranteeing the correctness of concurrent programs often relies on dynamic analysis and verification approaches. Some approaches target generic concurrency errors such as data races [29, 37], deadlocks [11], and atomicity violations [28, 47, 57]. Others target behavioral properties such as null-pointer dereferences [27], and typestate violations [36, 38, 55] and more generally order violations with runtime verification [42]. In this paper, we focus on the runtime monitoring of general *behavioral* properties targeting violations that cannot be traced back to classical concurrency errors.

Runtime verification (RV) [9, 24, 25, 34, 42], also known as runtime monitoring, is a lightweight formal method that allows checking whether a run of a system respects a specification. The specification formalizes a behavioral property and is written in a suitable formalism based for instance on temporal logic such as LTL or finite-state machines [1, 45]. Monitors are synthesized from the specifications, and the program is instrumented with additional code to extract events from the execution. These extracted events generate the trace, which is fed to the monitors. From the monitor perspective, the program is a black box and the trace is the sole system information provided.

To model the execution of a concurrent program, verification techniques choose their trace collection approaches differently based on the class of targeted properties. When properties require reasoning about concurrency in the program, causality must be established during trace collection to determine the *happens-before* [40] relation between events. Data race detection techniques [29, 37] for instance require the causal ordering to check for concurrent accesses to shared variables; as well as predictive approaches targeting behavioral properties such as [19, 38, 55] in order to explore other

© The Author(s) 2023
L. Lambers and S. Uchitel (Eds.): FASE 2023, LNCS 13991, pp. 173–194, 2023.
https://doi.org/10.1007/978-3-031-30826-0_10

feasible executions. Causality is best expressed as a partial order over events. Partial orders are compatible with various formalisms for the behavior of concurrent programs such as weak memory consistency models [2,4,46], Mazurkiewicz traces [32,48], parallel series [43], Message Sequence Charts graphs [49], and Petri Nets [50]. However, while the program behaves non-sequentially, its observation and trace collection is sequential. Collecting partial order traces often relies on vector clock algorithms to timestamp events [3,16,47,53] and requires blocking the execution to collect synchronization actions such as locks, unlocks, reads, and writes. Hence, existing techniques that can reason on concurrent events are expensive to use in an online monitoring setup. Indeed, many of them are often intended for the design phase of the program and not in production environments (see Section 5).

Other monitoring techniques relying on total-order formalisms such as LTL and finite state machines require linear traces to be fed to the monitors. As such they immediately capture linear traces from a concurrent execution without reestablishing causality. Most of the top[1] existing tools for the online monitoring of Java programs, these include tools such as Java-MOP [18, 30] and Tracematches [5], provide multithreaded monitoring support using one or more of the following *two* modes. The *per-thread* mode specifies that monitors are only associated with a given thread, and receive all events of the given thread. This boils down to doing classical RV of single-threaded programs, assuming each thread is an independent program. In this case, monitors are unable to check properties that involve events across threads. The *global* monitoring mode spawns a global monitor and ensures that the events from different threads are fed to a central monitor atomically, by utilizing locks, to avoid data races. As such, the monitored program execution is *linearized* so that it can be processed by the monitors. In addition to introducing additional synchronization between threads inhibiting parallelism, this monitoring mode forces events of interest to be totally ordered across the entire execution, which oversimplifies and ignores concurrency.

Figure 1 illustrates a high-level view of a concurrent execution fragment of *1-Writer 2-Readers*, where a writer thread writes to a shared variable, and two other reader threads read from it. The reader threads share the same lock and can read concurrently once one of them acquires it, but no thread can write nor read while a write is occurring. We only depict the read/write events and omit lock acquires and releases for brevity. In this execution, the writer acquires the lock first and writes (event 1), then after one of the reader threads acquires the lock, they both concurrently read. The first reader performs 3 reads (events 2, 4, and 5), while the second reader performs 2 reads (events 3 and 6), after that the writer acquires the lock and writes again (event 7). A user

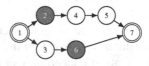

Fig. 1: Execution fragment of *1-Writer 2-Readers*. Double circle: `write`, normal: `read`. Numbers distinguish events. Events 2 and 6 (shaded) are example concurrent events.

---

[1] Based on the first three editions of the Competition on Runtime Verification [7,8,26,52].

may be interested in the following behavioral property: *"Whenever a writer performs a write, all readers must at least perform one read before the next write"*. Note that the execution here has no data races nor a deadlock, and techniques focusing on generic concurrency properties are not suitable for the property. Monitoring of this (partial) concurrent execution with both previously mentioned modes presents restrictions. For *per-thread* monitoring, since each of the readers is a thread, and the writer itself is a thread, it cannot check any specification that refers to an interaction between them. For *global* monitoring, it imposes an additional lock operation to send each read event to the monitor, introducing additional synchronization and suppressing the concurrency of the program.

A central observation we made is that when the program is free from generic concurrency errors such as data races and atomicity violations, a monitoring approach can be opportunistic and utilize the available synchronization in the program to reason about high-level behavioral properties. In the previous example, we know that reads and writes are guarded by a lock and do not execute concurrently (assuming we checked for data races). We also know that the relative ordering of the reads between themselves is not important to the property as we are only interested in counting that they all read the latest write. As such, instead of blocking the execution at each of the 7 events to safely invoke a global monitor and check for the property, we can have thread-local observations and only invoke the global monitor once either one of the readers acquires the lock or when the writer acquires it (only 3 events). As such, in this paper, we propose an approach to opportunistic runtime verification. We aim to (i) provide an approach that enables users to arbitrarily reason about concurrency fragments in the program, (ii) be able to monitor properties *online* without the need to record the execution, (iii) utilize the existing tools and formalism prevalent in the RV community, and (iv) do so efficiently without imposing additional synchronization.

We see our contributions as follows. We present a generic approach to monitor lock-based multithreaded programs that enable the re-use of the existing tools and approaches by bridging *per-thread* and *global* monitoring. Our approach consists of a two-level monitoring technique where at both levels existing tools can be employed. At the first level, a thread-local specification checks a given property on the thread itself, where events are totally ordered. At the second level, we define *scopes* which delimit concurrency regions. Scopes rely on operations in the program guaranteed to follow a total order. The guarantee is ensured by the platform itself, either the program model, the execution engine (JVM in our case), or the compiler. We assume that scopes execute atomically at runtime. Upon reaching the totally ordered operations, a scope monitor utilizes the result of all thread-local monitors executed in the concurrent region to construct a scope state, and perform monitoring on a sequence of such states. Our approach can be seen as a combination of performing global monitoring at the level of scope (for our example, we utilize lock acquires) and per-thread monitoring for active threads in the scope. Thus, we allow per-thread monitors to communicate their results when the program synchronizes. This approach relies on existing ordered operations in the program. However, it incurs minimal interference and overhead as it does not add additional synchronization, namely locks, between threads in order to collect a trace.

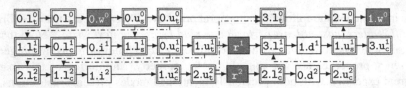

Fig. 2: Concurrent execution fragment of 1-Writer 2-Readers. Labels l, u, w, r indicate respectively: lock, unlock, write, read. Actions with a double border indicate actions of locks. The read and write actions are filled to highlight them.

2   Modeling the Program Execution

We are concerned with an abstraction of a concurrent execution, we focus on a model that can be useful for monitoring the behavioral properties. We choose the smallest observable execution step done by a program and refer to it as an *action*; for instance a method call or write operation.

Definition 1 (Action). *An action is a tuple* $\langle \text{lbl}, \text{id}, \text{ctx} \rangle$, *where:* lbl *is a label,* id *is a unique identifier, and* ctx *is the context of the action.*

The label captures an instruction name, function name, or specific task information depending on the granularity of actions. Since the action is a runtime object, we use id to distinguish two executions of the same syntactic element. Finally, the context (ctx) is a set containing dynamic contexts such as a thread identifier (threadid), process identifier (pid), resource identifier (resid), or a memory address. We use the notation $\text{id.lbl}_{\text{resid}}^{\text{threadid}}$ to denote an action, omit resid when absent, and id when there is no ambiguity. Furthermore, we use the notation a.threadid for a given action a to retrieve the thread identifier in the context, and a.ctx(key) to retrieve any element in the context associated with key.

Definition 2 (Concurrent Execution). *A concurrent execution is a partially ordered set of actions, that is a pair* $\langle \mathbb{A}, \rightarrow \rangle$, *where* $\mathbb{A}$ *is a set of actions and* $\rightarrow \subseteq \mathbb{A} \times \mathbb{A}$ *is a partial order over* $\mathbb{A}$.

Two actions a_1 and a_2 are related (i.e., $\langle a_1, a_2 \rangle \in \rightarrow$) if a_1 happens before a_2.

Example 1 (Concurrent fragment for 1-Writer 2-Readers.). Figure 2 shows another concurrent execution fragment for *1-Writer 2-Readers* introduced in Sec. 1. The concurrent execution fragment contains all actions performed by all threads, along with the partial order inferred from the synchronization actions such as locks and unlocks (depicted with dashed boxes). Recall that a lock action on a resource synchronizes with the latest unlock if it exists. This synchronization is depicted by the dashed arrows. We have three locks: test for readers (t), service (s), and readers counter (c). Lock t checks if any reader is currently reading, and this lock gives preference to writers. Lock s is used to regulate access to the shared resource, it can be either obtained by readers or one writer. Lock c is used to regulate access to the readers counter, it only synchronizes readers. In this concurrent execution, first, the writer thread acquires the lock and writes on a shared variable whose resource identifier is omitted for brevity. Second, the readers acquire the lock s and perform a read on the same variable. Third, the writer performs a second write on the variable.

In RV, we often do not capture the entire concurrent execution but are interested in gathering a *trace* of the relevant parts of it. In our approach, a trace is also a concurrent execution defined over a subset of actions. Since the trace is the input to any RV technique, we are interested in relating a trace to the concurrent execution, while focusing on a subset of actions. For this purpose, we introduce the notions of *soundness* and *faithfulness*. We first define the notion of *trace soundness*. Informally, a concurrent execution is a sound trace if it does not provide false information about the execution.

Definition 3 (Trace Soundness). *A concurrent trace* $tr = \langle \mathbb{A}_{tr}, \to_{tr} \rangle$ *is said to be a sound trace of a concurrent execution* $e = \langle \mathbb{A}, \to \rangle$ *(written* $\mathrm{snd}(e, tr)$*) iff (i)* $\mathbb{A}_{tr} \subseteq \mathbb{A}$ *and (ii)* $\to_{tr} \subseteq \to$.

Intuitively, to be sound, a trace (i) should not capture an action not found in the execution, and (ii) should not relate actions that are unrelated in the execution. While a sound trace provides no incorrect information on the order, it can still be missing information about the order. In this case, we want to also express the ability of a trace to capture all relevant order information. Informally, a *faithful trace* contains all information on the order of events that occurred in the program execution.

Definition 4 (Trace Faithfulness). *A concurrent trace* $tr = \langle \mathbb{A}_{tr}, \to_{tr} \rangle$ *is said to be faithful to a concurrent execution* $e = \langle \mathbb{A}, \to \rangle$ *(written* $\mathrm{faith}(e, tr)$*) iff* $\to_{tr} \supseteq (\to \cap \mathbb{A}_{tr} \times \mathbb{A}_{tr})$.

3 Opportunistic Monitoring

We start with distinguishing threads and events from the execution. We then define scopes that allow us to reason about properties over concurrent regions. We then devise a generic approach to evaluate scope properties and perform monitoring.

3.1 Managing Dynamic Threads and Events

Threads are typically created at runtime and have a unique identifier. We denote the set of all thread ids by TID. They are subject to change from one execution to another, and it is not known in advance how many threads will be spawned during the execution. As such, it is important to design specifications that can handle threads dynamically.

Distinguishing Threads To allow for a dynamic number of threads, we first denote thread types $\mathbb{T}$, to distinguish threads that are relevant to the specification. For example, the set of thread types for *readers-writers* is $\mathbb{T}_{rw} = \{\mathrm{reader}, \mathrm{writer}\}$. By using thread types, we can define properties for specific types regardless of the number of threads spawned for a given type. In order to assign a type to a thread in practice, we distinguish a set of actions $\mathbb{S} \subseteq \mathbb{A}$ called "spawn" actions. For example in *readers-writers*, we

can assign the spawn action of a reader (resp. writer) to be the method invocation of
Reader.run (Writer.run). Function spawn : $\mathbb{S} \to \mathbb{T}$, assigns a thread type to a spawn
action. The threads that match a given type are determined based on the spawn action(s)
present during the execution. We note that a thread can have multiple types. To reference
all threads assigned a given type, we use function pool : $\mathbb{T} \to 2^{\text{TID}}$. That is, given a
type t, a thread with *threadid tid*, we have $tid \in \text{pool}(t)$ iff $\exists a \in \mathbb{S} : \text{spawn}(a) =
t \wedge a.\text{threadid} = tid$. This allows a thread to have multiple types so that properties
operate on different events in the same thread.

Events As properties are defined over events, actions are typically abstracted into
events. As such, we define for each thread type $t \in \mathbb{T}$, the alphabet of events: $\mathbb{E}_t$. Set $\mathbb{E}_t$
contains all the events that can be generated from actions for the particular thread type
$t \in \mathbb{T}$. The empty event $\mathcal{E}$ is a special event that indicates that no events are matched.
Then, we assume a total function $\text{ev}_t : \mathbb{A} \to \{\mathcal{E}\} \cup \mathbb{E}_t$. The implementation of ev relies on the specification formalism used, it is capable of generating events based on the
context of the action itself. For example, the conversion can utilize the runtime context
of actions to generate parametric events when needed. We illustrate a function ev that
matches using the label of an action in Ex. 2.

Example 2 (Events.). We identify for *readers-writers* (Ex. 1) two thread types: $\mathbb{T}_{rw} \overset{\text{def}}{=}$
$\{\text{reader}, \text{writer}\}$. We are interested in the events $\mathbb{E}_{\text{reader}} \overset{\text{def}}{=} \{\text{read}\}$, and $\mathbb{E}_{\text{writer}} \overset{\text{def}}{=}$
$\{\text{write}\}$. For a specification at the level of a given thread, we have either a reader or a
writer, and the event associated with the reader (resp. writer) is read (resp. write).

$$
\text{ev}_{\text{reader}}(a) \overset{\text{def}}{=} \begin{cases} \text{read} & \text{if } a.\text{lbl} = \text{``r''}, \\ \mathcal{E} & \text{otherwise} \end{cases} \qquad \text{ev}_{\text{writer}}(a) \overset{\text{def}}{=} \begin{cases} \text{write} & \text{if } a.\text{lbl} = \text{``w''}, \\ \mathcal{E} & \text{otherwise}. \end{cases}
$$

3.2 Scopes: Properties Over Concurrent Regions

We now define the notion of *scope*. A scope defines a projection of the concurrent
execution to delimit concurrent regions and allow verification to be performed at the
level of regions instead of the entire execution.

Synchronizing Actions A scope s is associated with a synchronizing predicate $\text{sync}_s :
\mathbb{A} \to \mathbb{B}_2$ which is used to determine *synchronizing actions* (SAs). The set of synchroniz-
ing actions for a scope s is defined as: $\text{SA}_s = \{a \in \mathbb{A} \mid \text{sync}_s(a) = \top\}$. SAs constitute
synchronization points in a concurrent execution for multiple threads. A valid set of
SAs is such that there exists a total order on all actions in the set (i.e., no two SAs can
occur concurrently). As such SAs are sequenced and can be mapped to indices. Func-
tion $\text{idx}_s : \text{SA}_s \to \mathbb{N} \setminus \{0\}$ returns the index of a synchronizing action. For convenience,
we map them starting at 1, as 0 will indicate the initial state. We denote by $|\text{idx}_s|$ the
length of the sequence.

Scope Region A scope region selects actions of the concurrent execution delimited by two successive SAs. We define two "special" synchronizing actions: begin, end $\in \mathbb{A}$ common to all scopes that are needed to evaluate the first and last region. The actions refer to the beginning and end of the concurrent execution, respectively.

Definition 5 (Scope Regions). *Given a scope s and an associated index function* idx_s : $\text{SA}_s \to \mathbb{N}\backslash\{0\}$*, the scope regions are given by function* $\mathcal{R}_s : \text{codom}(\text{idx}_s)\cup\{0, |\text{idx}_s|+1\} \to 2^{\mathbb{A}}$*, defined as:*

$$\mathcal{R}_s(i) \stackrel{\text{def}}{=} \begin{cases} \{a \in \mathbb{A} \mid \langle a', a \rangle \in \to \wedge \langle a, a'' \rangle \in \to \wedge \text{issync}(a', i-1) & \text{if } 1 \leq i \leq |\text{idx}_s|, \\ \quad \wedge \text{issync}(a'', i)\} \\ \{a \in \mathbb{A} \mid \langle a', a \rangle \in \to \wedge \langle a, \text{end} \rangle \in \to \wedge \text{issync}(a', i-1)\} & \text{if } i = |\text{idx}_s|+1, \\ \{a \in \mathbb{A} \mid \langle \text{begin}, a \rangle \in \to \wedge \langle a, a'' \rangle \in \to \wedge \text{issync}(a'', 1)\} & \text{if } i = 0, \\ \emptyset & \text{otherwise} \end{cases}$$

where: $\text{issync}(a, i) \stackrel{\text{def}}{=} (\text{sync}_s(a) = \top \wedge \text{idx}_s(a) = i)$.

$\mathcal{R}_s(i)$ is the i-th scope region, the set of all actions that happened between the two synchronizing actions a and a', where $\text{idx}_s(a) = i$ and $\text{idx}_s(a') = i+1$ taking into account the start and end of a program execution (i.e., actions begin and end, respectively).

Example 3 (Scope regions). For *readers-writers* (Ex. 1), we consider the resource service lock (s) to be the one of interest, as it delimits the concurrent regions that allow either a writer to write or readers to read. We label the scope by res for the remainder of the paper. The synchronizing predicate sync_{res} selects all actions with label l (lock acquire) and with the lock id s present in the context of the action. The obtained sequence of SAs is $0.1_s^0 \cdot 1.1_s^1 \cdot 2.1_s^0$. The value of idx_{res} for each of the obtained SAs is respectively 1, 2, and 3. Every lock acquire delimits the regions of the concurrent execution. The region $k+1$ includes all actions between the two lock acquires 0.1_s^0 and 1.1_s^1. That is, $\mathcal{R}_{\text{res}}(k+1) = \{0.w^0, 0.u_s^0, 0.u_t^0, 1.1_t^1, 0.1_c^1, 0.i^1\}$. The region $k+2$ contains two concurrent reads: r^1, r^2.

Definition 6 (Scope fragment). *The scope fragment associated with a scope region* $\mathcal{R}_s(i)$ *is defined as* $\mathcal{F}_s(i) \stackrel{\text{def}}{=} \langle \mathcal{R}_s(i), \to \cap \mathcal{R}_s(i) \times \mathcal{R}_s(i) \rangle$.

Proposition 1 (Scope fragment preserves order). *Given a scope s, we have:* $\forall i \in \text{dom}(\mathcal{R}_s(i)) : \text{snd}(\langle \mathbb{A}, \to \rangle, \mathcal{F}_s(i)) \wedge \text{faith}(\langle \mathbb{A}, \to \rangle, \mathcal{F}_s(i))$.

Proposition 1 states that for a given scope, any fragment (obtained using $\mathcal{F}_s$) is a sound and faithful trace of the concurrent execution. This is ensured by construction using Definitions 5 and 6 which follow the same principles of the definitions of soundness (Definition 3) and faithfulness (Definition 4).

Remark 1. In this paper, scopes regions are defined by the user by selecting the synchronizing predicate as part of the specification. Given a property, regions should delimit events whose order is important for a property. For instance, for a property specifying that *"between each write, at least one read should occur"*, the scope regions should delimit read versus write events. Delimiting the read events themselves, performed by

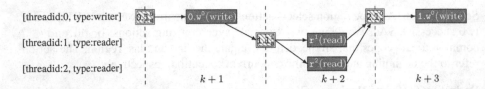

[threadid:0, type:writer]

[threadid:1, type:reader]

[threadid:2, type:reader]

$k+1$ $k+2$ $k+3$

Fig. 3: Projected actions using the scope and local properties of 1-Writer 2-Readers. The action labels l, w, r indicate respectively the following: lock, write, and read. Filled actions indicate actions for which function ev for the thread type returns an event. Actions with a pattern background indicate the SAs for the scope.

different threads, is not significant. How to analyze the program to find and suggest scopes for the user that are suitable for monitoring a given property is an interesting challenge that we leave for future work. Moreover, we assume the program is properly synchronized and free from data races.

Local Properties In a given scope region, we determine properties that will be checked locally on each thread. A thread-local monitor checks a local property independently for each given thread. These properties can be seen as the analogous of *per-thread* monitoring applied between two SAs. For a specific thread, we have a guaranteed total order on the local actions being formed. This ensures that local properties are compatible and can be checked with existing RV techniques and formalisms. We refer to those properties as *local properties*.

Definition 7 (Local property). *A local property is a tuple* $\langle$type, EVS, RT, eval$\rangle$ *with:*

- type $\in \mathbb{T}$ *is the thread type to which the local property applies;*
- EVS $\subseteq \mathbb{E}_{\text{type}}$ *is a subset of (thread type) events relevant to the property evaluation;*
- RT *is the resulting type of the evaluation (called* return type*); and*
- eval $: (\mathbb{N} \to \text{EVS}) \to \text{RT}$ *is the evaluation function of the property, taking as input a sequence of events, and returning the result of the evaluation.*

We use the dot notation: for a given property prop $= \langle$type, EVS, RT, eval$\rangle$ we use prop.type, prop.EVS, prop.RT, and prop.eval respectively.

Example 4 (At least one read). The property "at least one read", defined for the thread type reader, states that a reader must perform at least one read event. It can be expressed using the classical LTL$_3$ [10] (a variant of linear temporal logic with finite-trace semantics commonly used in RV) as $\varphi_{1r} \stackrel{\text{def}}{=} \mathbf{F}(\text{read})$ using the set of atomic propositions {read}. Let $\text{LTL3}_\varphi^{\text{AP}}$ denote the evaluation function of LTL$_3$ using the set of atomic propositions AP and a formula φ, and let $\mathbb{B}_3 = \{\top, \bot, ?\}$ be the truth domain where ? denotes an inconclusive verdict. To check on readers, we specify it as the local property: $\langle$reader, {read}, $\mathbb{B}_3$, $\text{LTL3}_{\varphi_{1r}}^{\{\text{read}\}}\rangle$. Similarly, we can define the local specification for at least one write.

Scope Trace To evaluate a local property, we restrict the trace to the actions of a given thread contained within a scope region. A scope trace is analogous to acquiring the trace for *per-thread* monitoring [5, 30] in a given scope region (see Definition 5). The scope trace is defined as a projection of the concurrent execution, on a specific thread, selecting actions that fall between two synchronizing actions.

Definition 8 (**Scope trace**). *Given a local property* $p = \langle type, EVS, RT, eval \rangle$ *in a scope region* $\mathcal{R}_s$ *with index* i, *a scope trace is obtained using the projection function* proj, *which outputs the sequence of actions of length* n *for a given thread with* tid $\in$ TID *that are associated with events for the property. We have:* $\forall \ell \in [0, n]$

$$\text{proj}(\text{tid}, i, p, \mathcal{R}_s) \stackrel{\text{def}}{=} \begin{cases} \text{filter}(a_0) \cdot \ldots \cdot \text{filter}(a_n) & \text{if } i \in \text{dom}(\mathcal{R}_s) \wedge \text{tid} \in \text{pool}(type), \\ \mathcal{E} & \text{otherwise,} \end{cases}$$

$$\text{with: filter}(a_\ell) \stackrel{\text{def}}{=} \begin{cases} e & \text{if } \text{ev}_{type}(a_\ell) \in \text{EVS} \\ \mathcal{E} & \text{otherwise,} \end{cases}$$

where $\cdot$ *is the sequence concatenation operator (such that* $a \cdot \mathcal{E} = \mathcal{E} \cdot a = a$*), with* $(\forall j \in [1, n] : \langle a_{j-1}, a_j \rangle \in \rightarrow) \wedge (\forall k \in [0, n] : a_k \in \mathcal{R}_s(i) \wedge a_k.\text{threadid} = \text{tid})$.

For a given thread, the scope trace filters the actions associated with an event for the local property (i.e., $\text{ev}_{type}(a_\ell) \in \text{EVS}$) of a scope region. It includes only actions that are associated with the thread that has the correct type associated with the local specification (i.e., tid $\in$ pool(type)). While the scope trace is obtained using projection, it is still needed to convert actions to events to later evaluate local properties, to do so we generate the sequence of events associated with the actions in the projected trace. That is, for a given action a in the sequence, we output $\text{ev}_{type}(a_\ell)$, we denote the generated sequence as evs(proj(tid, i, p, $\mathcal{R}_s$)).

Example 5 (Scope trace). Figure 3 illustrates the projection on the scope regions defined using the resource lock (Ex. 3) for each of the 1 writer and 2 reader threads, where the properties "at least one write" or "at least one read" (Example 4) apply. We see the scope traces for region $k + 1$ are respectively $0.w^0, \mathcal{E}, \mathcal{E}$ for the threads with thread ids 0, 1, and 2 respectively. For that region, we can now evaluate the local specification independently for each thread on the resulting traces by converting the sequences of events: write, $\mathcal{E}, \mathcal{E}$ for each of the scope traces.

Proposition 2 (proj **preserves per-thread order**). *Given a scope* s, *a thread with threadid* tid, *and a local property* p, *we have:*
$$\forall i \in \text{dom}(\mathcal{R}_s) : \text{snd}(\langle \mathbb{A}, \rightarrow \rangle, \text{proj}(\text{tid}, i, p, \mathcal{R}_s)) \wedge \text{faith}(\langle \mathbb{A}, \rightarrow \rangle, \text{proj}(\text{tid}, i, p, \mathcal{R}_s)).$$

Proposition 2 is guaranteed by construction (from Definition 8), ensuring that projection function proj does not produce any new actions and does not change any order information from the point of view of a given thread. We also note the assumption that for a single thread, all its actions are totally ordered, and therefore we capture all possible order information for the actions in the scope region. Finally, the function filter only suppresses actions that are not relevant to the property, without adding or re-ordering actions. The sequence of events obtained using the function evs also follows the same order.

Scope State A scope state aggregates the result of evaluating all local properties for a given scope region. To define a scope state, we consider a scope s, with a list of local properties $\langle \text{prop}_0, \ldots, \text{prop}_n \rangle$ of return types respectively $\langle \text{RT}_0, \ldots, \text{RT}_n \rangle$. Since a local specification can apply to an arbitrary number of threads during the execution, for each specification we create the type as a dictionary binding a *threadid* to the return type (represented as a total function). We use the type na to determine a special type indicating the property does not apply to the thread (as the thread type does not match the property). We can now define the return type of evaluating all local properties as $\text{RI} \stackrel{\text{def}}{=} \langle \text{TID} \rightarrow \{\text{na}\} \cup \text{RT}_0, \ldots, \text{TID} \rightarrow \{\text{na}\} \cup \text{RT}_n \rangle$. Function $\text{state}_s : \text{RI} \rightarrow \mathbb{I}_s$ processes the result of evaluating local properties to create a scope state in $\mathbb{I}_s$.

Example 6 (Scope state). We illustrate the scope state by evaluating the properties "at least one read" (p_r) and "at least one write" (p_w) (Ex. 4) on scope region $k + 2$ in Fig. 3. We have $\text{TID} = \{0, 1, 2\}$, we determine for each reader the trace (being (read) for both), and the writer being empty (i.e. no write was observed). As such for property p_r (resp. p_w), we have the result of the evaluation $[0 \mapsto \text{na}, 1 \mapsto \top, 2 \mapsto \top]$ (resp. $[0 \mapsto ?, 1 \mapsto \text{na}, 2 \mapsto \text{na}]$). We notice that for property p_r, the thread of type writer evaluates to na, as it is not concerned with the property.

We now consider the state creation function state_s. We consider the following atomic propositions activereader, activewriter, allreaders, and onewriter that indicate respectively: at least one thread of type reader performed a read, at least one thread of type writer performed a write, all threads of type reader ($|\text{pool}(\text{reader})|$) performed at least a read, and at most one thread of type writer performed a write. The scope state in this case is a list of 4 boolean values indicating each atomic proposition respectively. As such by counting the number of threads associated with $\top$, we can compute the Boolean value of each atomic proposition. For region $k + 2$, we have the following state: $\langle \top, \bot, \top, \bot \rangle$. We can establish a total order of scope states. For $k + 1$, $k + 2$ and $k + 3$, we have the sequence $\langle \bot, \top, \bot, \top \rangle \cdot \langle \top, \bot, \top, \bot \rangle \cdot \langle \bot, \top, \bot, \top \rangle$.

We are now able to define formally a scope by associating an identifier with a synchronizing predicate, a list of local properties, a spawn predicate, and a scope property evaluation function. We denote by SID the set of scope identifiers.

Definition 9 (Scope). *A scope is a tuple* $\langle \text{sid}, \text{sync}_{\text{sid}}, \langle \text{prop}_1, \ldots, \text{prop}_n \rangle, \text{state}_{\text{sid}}, \text{seval}_{\text{sid}} \rangle$, *where:*

- sid $\in$ SID *is the scope identifier;*
- $\text{sync}_{\text{sid}} : \mathbb{A} \rightarrow \mathbb{B}_2$ *is the synchronizing predicate that determines SAs;*
- $\langle \text{prop}_0, \ldots, \text{prop}_n \rangle$ *is a list of local properties (Definition 7);*
- $\text{state}_{\text{sid}} : \langle \text{TID} \rightarrow \{\text{na}\} \cup \text{prop}_0.\text{RT}, \ldots, \text{TID} \rightarrow \{\text{na}\} \cup \text{prop}_n.\text{RT} \rangle \rightarrow \mathbb{I}_s$ *is the scope state creation function;*
- $\text{seval}_{\text{sid}} : \mathbb{N} \times \mathbb{I}_s \rightarrow \mathbb{O}$ *is the evaluation function of the scope property over a sequence of scope states.*

3.3 Semantics for Evaluating Scopes

After defining scope states, we are now able to evaluate properties on the scope. To evaluate a scope property, we first evaluate each local property for the scope region, we then use $\text{state}_{\text{sid}}$ to generate the scope state for the region. After producing the sequence of scope states, the function $\text{seval}_{\text{sid}}$ evaluates the property at the level of a scope.

Definition 10 (Evaluating a scope property). *Using the synchronizing predicate* sync_{sid}, *we obtain the regions* $\mathcal{R}_{\text{sid}}(i)$ *for* $i \in [0, m]$ *with* $m = |\text{idx}_{\text{sid}}| + 1$. *The evaluation of a scope property (noted* res*) for the scope* $\langle \text{sid}, \text{sync}_{\text{sid}}, \langle \text{prop}_0, \dots, \text{prop}_n \rangle, \text{state}_{\text{sid}}, \text{seval}_{\text{sid}} \rangle$ *is computed as:* $\forall tid \in \text{TID}, \forall j \in [0, n]$

$$\text{res} = \text{seval}_{\text{sid}}(\text{SR}_0 \cdot \dots \cdot \text{SR}_m), \text{ where } \text{SR}_i = \text{state}_{\text{sid}}(\langle \text{LR}_0^i, \dots, \text{LR}_n^i \rangle)$$

$$\text{LR}_j^i = \begin{cases} tid \mapsto \text{prop}_j.\text{eval}(\text{evs}(\text{proj}(tid, i, \text{prop}_j, \mathcal{R}_{\text{sid}}))) & \textit{if } tid \in \text{pool}(\text{prop}_j.\text{type}) \\ tid \mapsto \text{na} & \textit{otherwise} \end{cases}$$

Example 7 (Evaluating scope properties). We use LTL to formalize three scope properties based on the scope states from Ex. 6 operating on the alphabet {activereader, activewriter, allreaders, onewriter}:

- Mutual exclusion between readers and writers: $\varphi_0 \overset{\text{def}}{=}$ activewriter **XOR** activereader.
- Mutual exclusion between writers: $\varphi_1 \overset{\text{def}}{=}$ activewriter $\implies$ onewriter.
- All readers must read a written value: $\varphi_2 \overset{\text{def}}{=}$ activereader $\implies$ allreaders.

Therefore the specification is: $\mathbf{G}(\varphi_0 \wedge \varphi_1 \wedge \varphi_2)$. We recall that a scope state is a list of boolean values for the atomic propositions in the following order: activereader, activewriter, allreaders, and onewriter. The sequence of scope states from Ex. 6: $\langle \bot, \top, \bot, \top \rangle \cdot \langle \top, \bot, \top, \bot \rangle \cdot \langle \bot, \top, \bot, \top \rangle$ complies with the specification.

Correctness of Scope Evaluation We assume that the SAs selected by the user in the specification are totally ordered. This ensures that the order of the scope states is a total order, it is then by assumption sound and faithful to the order of the SAs. However, it is important to ensure that the actions needed to construct the state are captured faithfully and in a sound manner. We capture the partial order as follows: (1) actions of different threads are captured in a sound and faithful manner between two successive SAs (Proposition 1), and (2) actions of the same thread are captured in a sound and faithful manner for that thread (Proposition 2). Furthermore, we are guaranteed by Definition 10 that each local property evaluation function is passed to all actions relevant to the given thread (and no other). As such, for the granularity level of the SAs, we obtain all relevant order information.

Evaluating without resetting. We notice that in Definition 10 monitors on local properties are reset for each concurrency region. As such, they are unable to express properties that span multiple concurrency regions of the same thread. The semantics of function res conceptually focus on treating concurrency regions independently. However, we can account for elaborating the expressiveness of local properties by extending the alphabet for each local property with the atomic proposition sync which delimits the concurrency region. The proposition sync denotes that the scope synchronizing action has occurred, and adds it to the trace. We need to take careful consideration that threads may sleep and not receive any events during a concurrent region. For example, consider two threads waiting on a lock, when one thread gets the lock, the other will not. As such, to pass the sync event to the local specification of the sleeping thread requires we instrument very

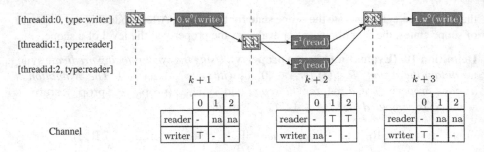

Fig. 4: Example of a scope channel for 1-Writer 2-Readers.

intrusively to account for that, a requirement we do not want to impose. Therefore, we add the restriction that local properties are only evaluated if at least one event relevant to the local property is encountered in the concurrency region (that is not the synchronization event). Using that consideration, we can define an evaluation that considers all events starting from concurrent region 0 up to i, and adding sync events between scopes (we omit the definition for brevity). This allows local monitors to account for synchronization, either to reset or check more expressive specifications such as "*a reader can read at most n times every m concurrency regions*", and "*writers must always write a value that is greater than the last write*".

3.4   Communicating Verdicts and Monitoring

We now proceed to describe how the monitors communicate their verdicts.

Scope channel. The *scope channel* stores information about the scope states during the execution. We associate each scope with a scope channel that has its own timestamp. The channel provides each thread-local monitor with an exclusive memory slot to write its result when evaluating local properties. Each thread can only write to its associated slot in the channel. The timestamp of the channel is readable by all threads participating in the scope but is only incremented by the scope monitor, as we will see.

Example 8 (Scope channel). Figure 4 displays the channel associated with the scope monitoring discussed in Ex. 6. For each scope region, the channel allows each monitor an exclusive memory slot to write its result (if the thread is not sleeping). The slots marked with a dash (-) indicate the absence of monitors. Furthermore, na indicates that the thread was given a slot, but it did not write anything in it (see Definition 10).

For a timestamp t, local monitors no longer write any information for any scope state with a timestamp inferior to t, this makes such states always consistent to be read by any monitor associated with the scope. While this is not in the scope of the paper, it allows monitors to effectively access past data of other monitors consistently.

Thread-local monitors. Each thread-local monitor is responsible for monitoring a local property for a given thread. Recall that each thread is associated with an identifier and a type. Multiple such monitors can exist on a given thread, depending on the needed properties to check. These monitors are spawned on the creation of the thread. It receives an event, performs checking, and can write its result in its associated scope channel at the current timestamp.

Scope monitors. Scope monitors are responsible for checking the property at the level of the scope. Upon reaching a synchronizing action by any of the threads associated with the scope, the given thread will invoke the scope monitor. The scope monitor relies on the scope channel (shared among all threads) to have access to all observations. Additional memory can be allocated for its own state, but it has to be shared among all threads associated with the scope. The scope monitor is invoked atomically after reaching the scope synchronizing action. First, it constructs the scope state based on the results of the thread-local monitors stored in the scope channel. Second, it invokes the verification procedure on the generated state. Finally, before completing, it increments the timestamp associated with the scope channel.

4   Preliminary Assessment of Overhead

We first opportunistically monitor *readers-writers*, using the specification found in Ex. 7. We then demonstrate our approach with classical concurrent programs[2].

4.1   Readers-Writers

Experiment setup. For this experiment, we utilize the standard LTL_3 semantics defined over the $\mathbb{B}_3$ verdict domain. As such, all the local and scope property types are $\mathbb{B}_3$. We instrument *readers-writers* to insert our monitors and compare our approach to global monitoring using a custom aspect written in AspectJ. In total, we have three scenarios: non-monitored, global, and opportunistic. In the first scenario (non-monitored), we do not perform monitoring. In the second and third scenarios, we perform global and opportunistic monitoring. We recall that global monitoring introduces additional locks at the level of the monitor for all events that occur concurrently. We make sure that the program is well synchronized and data race free with RVPredict [37].

Measures. To evaluate the overhead of our approach, we are interested in defining parameters to characterize concurrency regions found in *readers-writers*. We identify two parameters: the *number of readers* (nreaders), and the *width of the concurrency region* (cwidth). On the one hand, nreaders determines the maximum parallel threads that are verifying local properties in a given concurrency region. On the other hand, cwidth determines the number of reads each reader performs concurrently when acquiring the lock. Parameter cwidth is measured in number of read events generated. By increasing the size of the concurrency regions, we increase lock contention when multiple concurrent events cause a global monitor to lock. We use a number of writers equivalent to nreaders $\in \{1, 3, 7, 15, 23, 31, 63, 127\}$ and cwidth $\in \{1, 5, 10, 15, 30, 60, 100, 150\}$.

---

[2] The artifact for this paper is available [56].

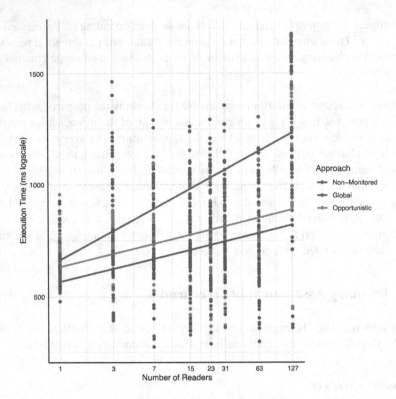

Fig. 5: Execution time for *readers-writers* for non-monitored, global, and opportunistic monitoring when varying the number of readers.

We perform a total of 100,000 writes and 400,000 reads, where reads are distributed evenly across readers. We measure the execution time (in ms) of 50 runs of the program for each of the parameters and scenarios.

Preliminary results. We report the results using the averages while providing the scatter plots with linear regression curves in Figures 5, and 6. Figure 5 shows the overhead when varying the number of readers (nreaders). We notice that for the base program (non-monitored), the execution time increases as lock contention overhead becomes more prominent and the JVM is managing more threads. In the case of global monitoring, as expected we notice an increasing overhead with the increase in the number of threads. As more readers are executing, the program is being blocked on each read which is supposed to be concurrent. For opportunistic, we notice a stable runtime in comparison to the original program as no additional locks are being used; only the delay to evaluate the local and scope properties. Figure 6 shows the overhead when varying the width of the concurrency region (cwidth). We observe that for the base program, the execution time decreases as more reads can be performed concurrently without contention on the shared resource lock. In the case of global monitoring, we also notice a slight decrease, while for opportunistic monitoring, we see a much greater decrease. By increasing the number of concurrent events in a concurrency region, we

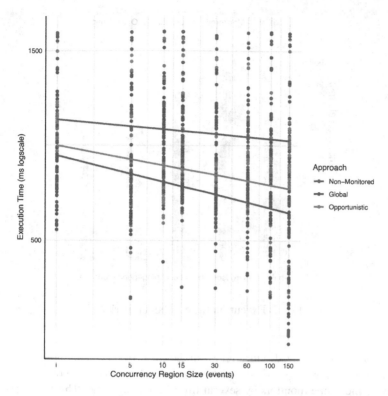

Fig. 6: Execution time varying the number of events in the concurrency region.

highlight the overhead introduced by locking the global monitor. We recall that a global monitor must lock to linearize the trace, and as such interferes with concurrency. This can be seen by looking at the two curves for global and opportunistic monitoring, we see that opportunistic closely follows the speedup of the non-monitored program, while global monitoring is much slower. For opportunistic monitoring, we expected a positive performance payoff when events in concurrency regions are dense.

4.2   Other Benchmarks

We target classical benchmarks that use different concurrency primitives to synchronize threads. We perform global and opportunistic monitoring and report our results using the averages of 100 runs in Figure 7. We use an implementation of the Bakery lock algorithm [39], for two threads *2-bakery* and n threads *n-bakery*. The algorithm performs synchronization using reads and writes on shared variables and guarantees mutual exclusion on the critical section. As such, we monitor the program for the *bounded waiting* property which specifies that a process should not wait for more than a limited number of turns before entering the critical section. For opportunistic monitoring, thread-local monitors are deployed on each thread to monitor if the thread acquires the critical section. Scope monitors check if a thread is waiting for more than n turns before entering the critical section. We notice slightly less overhead with opportunistic than global for

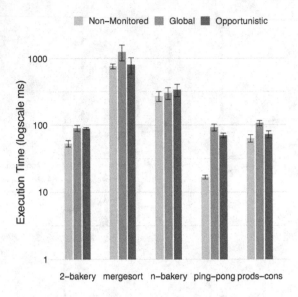

Fig. 7: Execution time of benchmarks.

2-bakery and more overhead with opportunistic on *n-bakery*. This is because of the small concurrency region (cwidth) which is equal to 1. As such, the overhead of evaluating local and scope monitors by several threads, having a cwidth of 1, exceeds the gain in performance achieved by our approach and hence not fitting for opportunistic monitoring.

We also monitor a textbook example of Ping-Pong algorithm [33] that is used for instance in databases and routing protocols. The algorithm synchronizes, using reads and writes on shared variables and busy waiting, between two threads producing events pi for the pinging thread and po for the pong thread. We monitor for the *alternation* property specified as $\varphi \stackrel{\text{def}}{=} (\text{ping} \implies \mathbf{X}\text{pong}) \wedge (\text{pong} \implies \mathbf{X}\text{ping})$. We also include a classic producer-consumer program from [35] which uses a concurrent FIFO queue using locks and conditions. We monitor the *precedence* property, which specifies the requirement that a consume (event c) is preceded by a produce (event p), expressed in LTL as $\neg c \mathbf{W} p$. For both above benchmarks, we observe less overhead when monitoring with opportunistic, since no additional locks are being enforced on the execution.

We also monitor a parallel mergesort algorithm which is a divide-and-conquer algorithm to sort an array. The algorithm uses the fork-join framework [41] which recursively splits the array into sorting tasks that are handled by different threads. We are interested in monitoring if a forked task is returning a correctly sorted array before performing a merge. The monitoring step is expensive and linear in the size of the array as it involves scanning it. For opportunistic, we use the joining of two subtasks as our synchronizing action and deploy scope monitors at all levels of the recursive hierarchy. We observe less overhead when monitoring with opportunistic than global monitoring, as concurrent threads do not have to wait at each monitoring step. This benchmark motivates us to further investigate other hierarchical models of computation where opportunistic RV can be used such as [22].

5 Related Work

We focus here on techniques developed for the verification of behavioral properties of multithreaded programs written in Java and refer to [12] for a detailed survey on tools covering generic concurrency errors. The techniques we cover typically analyze a trace to either *detect* or *predict* violations.

Java-MOP [18], Tracematches [5,13], MarQ [51], and LARVA [21] chosen from the RV competitions [8,26,52] are runtime monitoring tools for violation detection. These tools allow different specification formalisms such as finite-state machines, extended regular expressions, context-free grammars, past-time linear temporal logic, and Quantified Event Automata (QEA) [6]. Their specifications rely on a total order of events and require that a collected trace be linearized. They were initially developed to monitor single-threaded programs and later adapted to monitor multithreaded programs. As mentioned, to monitor global properties spanning multiple threads these techniques impose a lock on each event blocking concurrent regions in the program and forcing threads to synchronize. Moreover, they often produce inconsistent verdicts with the existence of concurrent events [23]. EnforceMOP [44] for instance, can be used to detect and enforce properties (deadlocks as well). It controls the runtime scheduler and blocks the execution of threads that might cause a property violation, sometimes itself leading to a deadlock.

Predictive techniques [19,31,38,54] reason about all feasible interleavings from a recorded trace of a single execution. As such, they need to establish the causal ordering between the actions of the program. These tools implement vector clock algorithms, such as [53], to timestamp events. The algorithm blocks the execution on each property event and also on all synchronizing actions such as reads and writes. Vector clock algorithms typically require synchronization between the instrumentation, program actions, and algorithm's processing to avoid data races [16]. jPredictor [19] for instance, uses sliced causality [17] to prune the partial order such that only relevant synchronization actions are kept. This is achieved with the help of static analysis and after recording at least one execution of the program. The tool is demonstrated on atomicity violations and data races; however, we are not aware of an application in the context of generic behavioral properties. RVPredict [37] develops a sound and maximal causal model to analyze concurrency in a multithreaded program. The correct behavior of a program is modeled as a set of logical constraints, thus restricting the possible traces to consider. Traces are ordered permutations containing both control flow operations and memory accesses and are constrained by axioms tailored to data race and sequential consistency. The theory supports any logical constraints to determine correctness, it is then possible to encode a specification on multithreaded programs as such. However, allowing for arbitrary specifications to be encoded while supported in the model, is not supported in the provided tool (RVPredict). In [27], the authors present ExceptioNULL that target null-pointer exceptions. Violations and causality are represented as constraints over actions, and the feasibility of violations is explored via an SMT constraint solver. GPredict [36] extends the specification formalism past data races to target generic concurrency properties. GPredict presents a generic approach to reason about behavioral properties and hence constitutes a monitoring solution when concurrency is present. Notably, GPredict requires specifying thread identifiers explicitly in the specification. This makes specifications with multiple threads to become extremely verbose; unable to handle a dynamic number of threads. For example, in the case of *readers-writers*, adding extra readers or writers requires rewriting the specification and combining events to specify each new thread. The approach behind GPredict can also be extended to become more expressive, e.g. to support counting events to account for fairness in a concurrent setting. Furthermore, GPredict relies on recording a trace of a program before performing an offline analysis to determine concurrency errors [36]. In addition to being incomplete due to the possibility of not getting results from the constraint solver, the analysis from GPredict might also miss some order relations between events resulting in false positives. In general, the presented predictive tools are often designed to be used offline and unfortunately, many of them are no longer maintained.

In [14,15], the authors present monitoring for *hyperproperties* written in alternation-free fragments of HyperLTL [20]. Hyperproperties are specified over sets of execution traces instead of a single trace. In our setup, each thread is producing its trace and thus scope properties we monitor can be expressed in HyperLTL for instance. The time occurrence of events will be delimited by concurrency regions and thus traces will consist of propositions that summarize the concurrency region. We have yet to explore the applicability of specifying and monitoring hyperproperties within our opportunistic approach.

6   Conclusion and Perspectives

We introduced a generic approach for the online monitoring of multithreaded programs. Our approach distinguishes between thread-local properties and properties that span concurrency regions referred to as scopes (both types of properties can be monitored with existing tools). Our approach relies heavily on existing totally ordered operations in the program. However, by utilizing the existing synchronization, we can monitor online while leveraging both existing per-thread and global monitoring techniques. Finally, our preliminary evaluation suggests that opportunistic monitoring incurs a lower overhead in general than classical monitoring.

While the preliminary results are promising, additional work needs to be invested to complete the automatic synthesis and instrumentation of monitors. So far, splitting the property over local and scope monitors is achieved manually and scope regions are guaranteed by the user to follow a total order. Analyzing the program to find and suggest scopes suitable for splitting and monitoring a given property is an interesting challenge that we leave for future work. The program can be run, for instance, to capture its causality and recommend suitable synchronization actions for delimiting scope regions. Furthermore, the expressiveness of the specification can be increased by extending scopes to contain other scopes and adding more levels of monitors. This allows for properties that target not just thread-local properties, but also concurrent regions enclosed in other concurrent regions, thus creating a hierarchical setting.

References

1. Patterns in property specifications for finite-state verification home page. https://matthewbdwyer.github.io/psp/patterns.html, https://matthewbdwyer.github.io/psp/patterns.html

2. Adve, S.V., Gharachorloo, K.: Shared memory consistency models: a tutorial. Computer 29(12), 66–76 (Dec 1996)

3. Agarwal, A., Garg, V.K.: Efficient dependency tracking for relevant events in shared-memory systems. In: Proceedings of the Twenty-Fourth Annual ACM Symposium on Principles of Distributed Computing. p. 19–28. PODC '05, Association for Computing Machinery, New York, NY, USA (2005), https://doi.org/10.1145/1073814.1073818

4. Ahamad, M., Neiger, G., Burns, J.E., Kohli, P., Hutto, P.W.: Causal memory: definitions, implementation, and programming. Distributed Computing 9(1), 37–49 (Mar 1995)

5. Allan, C., Avgustinov, P., Christensen, A.S., Hendren, L., Kuzins, S., Lhoták, O., de Moor, O., Sereni, D., Sittampalam, G., Tibble, J.: Adding Trace Matching with Free Variables to AspectJ. In: Proceedings of the 20th Annual ACM SIGPLAN Conference on Object-oriented Programming, Systems, Languages, and Applications. pp. 345–364. OOPSLA '05, ACM (2005)

6. Barringer, H., Falcone, Y., Havelund, K., Reger, G., Rydeheard, D.E.: Quantified Event Automata: Towards Expressive and Efficient Runtime Monitors. In: Giannakopoulou, D., Méry, D. (eds.) FM 2012: Formal Methods - 18th International Symposium, Paris, France, August 27-31, 2012. Proceedings. Lecture Notes in Computer Science, vol. 7436, pp. 68–84. Springer (2012), https://doi.org/10.1007/978-3-642-32759-9_9

7. Bartocci, E., Bonakdarpour, B., Falcone, Y.: First international competition on software for runtime verification. In: Bonakdarpour, B., Smolka, S.A. (eds.) Runtime Verification - 5th International Conference, RV 2014, Toronto, ON, Canada, September 22-25, 2014. Proceedings. Lecture Notes in Computer Science, vol. 8734, pp. 1–9. Springer (2014)

8. Bartocci, E., Falcone, Y., Bonakdarpour, B., Colombo, C., Decker, N., Havelund, K., Joshi, Y., Klaedtke, F., Milewicz, R., Reger, G., Rosu, G., Signoles, J., Thoma, D., Zalinescu, E., Zhang, Y.: First international competition on runtime verification: rules, benchmarks, tools, and final results of CRV 2014. International Journal on Software Tools for Technology Transfer (Apr 2017)

9. Bartocci, E., Falcone, Y., Francalanza, A., Reger, G.: Introduction to runtime verification. In: Bartocci, E., Falcone, Y. (eds.) Lectures on Runtime Verification - Introductory and Advanced Topics, Lecture Notes in Computer Science, vol. 10457, pp. 1–33. Springer (2018)

10. Bauer, A., Leucker, M., Schallhart, C.: Runtime verification for ltl and tltl. ACM Trans. Softw. Eng. Methodol. 20(4), 14:1–14:64 (Sep 2011)

11. Bensalem, S., Havelund, K.: Dynamic deadlock analysis of multi-threaded programs. In: Proceedings of the First Haifa International Conference on Hardware and Software Verification and Testing. p. 208–223. HVC'05, Springer-Verlag, Berlin, Heidelberg (2005), https://doi.org/10.1007/11678779_15

12. Bianchi, F.A., Margara, A., Pezzè, M.: A survey of recent trends in testing concurrent software systems. IEEE Transactions on Software Engineering 44(8), 747–783 (2018)

13. Bodden, E., Hendren, L., Lam, P., Lhoták, O., Naeem, N.A.: Collaborative Runtime Verification with Tracematches. Journal of Logic and Computation 20(3), 707–723 (Jun 2010)

14. Bonakdarpour, B., Sanchez, C., Schneider, G.: Monitoring hyperproperties by combining static analysis and runtime verification. In: Leveraging Applications of Formal Methods, Verification and Validation. Verification: 8th International Symposium, ISoLA 2018, Limassol, Cyprus, November 5-9, 2018, Proceedings, Part II. p. 8–27. Springer-Verlag, Berlin, Heidelberg (2018), https://doi.org/10.1007/978-3-030-03421-4_2

15. Brett, N., Siddique, U., Bonakdarpour, B.: Rewriting-based runtime verification for alternation-free hyperltl. In: Proceedings, Part II, of the 23rd International Conference on Tools and Algorithms for the Construction and Analysis of Systems - Volume 10206. p. 77–93. Springer-Verlag, Berlin, Heidelberg (2017), https://doi.org/10.1007/978-3-662-54580-5_5

16. Cain, H.W., Lipasti, M.H.: Verifying sequential consistency using vector clocks. In: Proceedings of the Fourteenth Annual ACM Symposium on Parallel Algorithms and Architectures. p. 153–154. SPAA '02, Association for Computing Machinery, New York, NY, USA (2002), https://doi.org/10.1145/564870.564897

17. Chen, F., Roşu, G.: Parametric and sliced causality. In: Proceedings of the 19th International Conference on Computer Aided Verification. p. 240–253. CAV'07, Springer-Verlag, Berlin, Heidelberg (2007)

18. Chen, F., Roşu, G.: Java-MOP: A Monitoring Oriented Programming Environment for Java. In: Tools and Algorithms for the Construction and Analysis of Systems. pp. 546–550. Lecture Notes in Computer Science, Springer (Apr 2005)

19. Chen, F., Serbanuta, T.F., Rosu, G.: Jpredictor: A predictive runtime analysis tool for java. In: Proceedings of the 30th International Conference on Software Engineering. p. 221–230. ICSE '08, Association for Computing Machinery, New York, NY, USA (2008), https://doi.org/10.1145/1368088.1368119

20. Clarkson, M.R., Schneider, F.B.: Hyperproperties. J. Comput. Secur. 18(6), 1157–1210 (sep 2010)

21. Colombo, C., Pace, G.J., Schneider, G.: LARVA — Safer Monitoring of Real-Time Java Programs (Tool Paper). In: Hung, D.V., Krishnan, P. (eds.) Seventh IEEE International Conference on Software Engineering and Formal Methods, SEFM 2009, Hanoi, Vietnam, 23-27 November 2009. pp. 33–37. IEEE Computer Society (2009), https://doi.org/10.1109/SEFM.2009.13

22. Dean, J., Ghemawat, S.: Mapreduce: Simplified data processing on large clusters. Commun. ACM 51(1), 107–113 (jan 2008), https://doi.org/10.1145/1327452.1327492

23. El-Hokayem, A., Falcone, Y.: Can we monitor all multithreaded programs? In: Colombo, C., Leucker, M. (eds.) Runtime Verification - 18th International Conference, RV 2018, Limassol, Cyprus, November 10-13, 2018, Proceedings. Lecture Notes in Computer Science, vol. 11237, pp. 64–89. Springer (2018), https://doi.org/10.1007/978-3-030-03769-7_6

24. Falcone, Y., Havelund, K., Reger, G.: A tutorial on runtime verification. In: Broy, M., Peled, D.A., Kalus, G. (eds.) Engineering Dependable Software Systems, NATO Science for Peace and Security Series, D: Information and Communication Security, vol. 34, pp. 141–175. IOS Press (2013)

25. Falcone, Y., Krstic, S., Reger, G., Traytel, D.: A taxonomy for classifying runtime verification tools. In: Colombo, C., Leucker, M. (eds.) Runtime Verification - 18th International Conference, RV 2018, Limassol, Cyprus, November 10-13, 2018, Proceedings. Lecture Notes in Computer Science, vol. 23, pp. 241–262. Springer (2018)

26. Falcone, Y., Nickovic, D., Reger, G., Thoma, D.: Second international competition on runtime verification CRV 2015. In: Bartocci, E., Majumdar, R. (eds.) Runtime Verification - 6th International Conference, RV 2015 Vienna, Austria, September 22-25, 2015. Proceedings. Lecture Notes in Computer Science, vol. 9333, pp. 405–422. Springer (2015)

27. Farzan, A., Parthasarathy, M., Razavi, N., Sorrentino, F.: Predicting null-pointer dereferences in concurrent programs. In: Proceedings of the ACM SIGSOFT 20th International Symposium on the Foundations of Software Engineering. FSE '12, Association for Computing Machinery, New York, NY, USA (11 2012), https://doi.org/10.1145/2393596.2393651

28. Flanagan, C., Freund, S.N.: Atomizer: A dynamic atomicity checker for multithreaded programs. SIGPLAN Not. 39(1), 256–267 (jan 2004), https://doi.org/10.1145/982962.964023

29. Flanagan, C., Freund, S.N.: Fasttrack: Efficient and precise dynamic race detection. In: Proceedings of the 30th ACM SIGPLAN Conference on Programming Language Design and Implementation. p. 121–133. PLDI '09, Association for Computing Machinery, New York, NY, USA (2009), https://doi.org/10.1145/1542476.1542490

30. Formal Systems Laboratory: JavaMOP4 Syntax (2018), http://fsl.cs.illinois.edu/index.php/JavaMOP4_Syntax

31. Gao, Q., Zhang, W., Chen, Z., Zheng, M., Qin, F.: 2ndstrike: Toward manifesting hidden concurrency typestate bugs. In: Proceedings of the Sixteenth International Conference on Architectural Support for Programming Languages and Operating Systems. ASPLOS XVI, vol. 39, p. 239–250. Association for Computing Machinery, New York, NY, USA (mar 2011), https://doi.org/10.1145/1950365.1950394

32. Gastin, P., Kuske, D.: Uniform satisfiability problem for local temporal logics over Mazurkiewicz traces. Inf. Comput. 208(7), 797–816 (2010)

33. Gray, J., Reuter, A.: Transaction Processing: Concepts and Techniques. Morgan Kaufmann Publishers Inc., San Francisco, CA, USA, 1st edn. (1992)

34. Havelund, K., Goldberg, A.: Verify your runs. In: Meyer, B., Woodcock, J. (eds.) Verified Software: Theories, Tools, Experiments, First IFIP TC 2/WG 2.3 Conference, VSTTE 2005, Zurich, Switzerland, October 10-13, 2005, Revised Selected Papers and Discussions. Lecture Notes in Computer Science, vol. 4171, pp. 374–383. Springer (2005)

35. Herlihy, M., Shavit, N.: The Art of Multiprocessor Programming, Revised Reprint. Morgan Kaufmann Publishers Inc., San Francisco, CA, USA, 1st edn. (2012)

36. Huang, J., Luo, Q., Rosu, G.: Gpredict: Generic predictive concurrency analysis. In: 37th IEEE/ACM International Conference on Software Engineering, ICSE 2015, Volume 1. pp. 847–857 (2015)

37. Huang, J., Meredith, P.O., Rosu, G.: Maximal sound predictive race detection with control flow abstraction. SIGPLAN Not. 49(6), 337–348 (Jun 2014), https://doi.org/10.1145/2594291.2594315

38. Joshi, P., Sen, K.: Predictive typestate checking of multithreaded java programs. In: Proceedings of the 2008 23rd IEEE/ACM International Conference on Automated Software Engineering. p. 288–296. ASE '08, IEEE Computer Society, USA (2008), https://doi.org/10.1109/ASE.2008.39

39. Lamport, L.: A new solution of dijkstra's concurrent programming problem. Commun. ACM 17(8), 453–455 (aug 1974), https://doi.org/10.1145/361082.361093

40. Lamport, L.: Time, Clocks, and the Ordering of Events in a Distributed System. Commun. ACM 21(7), 558–565 (Jul 1978), https://doi.org/10.1145/359545.359563

41. Lea, D.: A java fork/join framework. In: Proceedings of the ACM 2000 Java Grande Conference, San Francisco, CA, USA, June 3-5, 2000. pp. 36–43 (2000), https://doi.org/10.1145/337449.337465

42. Leucker, M., Schallhart, C.: A brief account of runtime verification. The Journal of Logic and Algebraic Programming 78(5), 293–303 (May 2009)

43. Lodaya, K., Weil, P.: Rationality in algebras with a series operation. Inf. Comput. 171(2), 269–293 (2001)

44. Luo, Q., Rosu, G.: Enforcemop: A runtime property enforcement system for multithreaded programs. In: Proceedings of International Symposium in Software Testing and Analysis (ISSTA'13). pp. 156–166. ACM (July 2013)

45. Manna, Z., Pnueli, A.: A hierarchy of temporal properties (invited paper, 1989). In: Proceedings of the Ninth Annual ACM Symposium on Principles of Distributed Computing. p. 377–410. PODC '90, Association for Computing Machinery, New York, NY, USA (1990), https://doi.org/10.1145/93385.93442

46. Manson, J., Pugh, W., Adve, S.V.: The Java Memory Model. In: Proceedings of the 32nd ACM SIGPLAN-SIGACT Symposium on Principles of Programming Languages. pp. 378–391. POPL '05, ACM (2005)

47. Mathur, U., Viswanathan, M.: Atomicity Checking in Linear Time Using Vector Clocks, p. 183–199. Association for Computing Machinery, New York, NY, USA (2020), https://doi.org/10.1145/3373376.3378475

48. Mazurkiewicz, A.W.: Trace theory. In: Brauer, W., Reisig, W., Rozenberg, G. (eds.) Petri Nets: Central Models and Their Properties, Advances in Petri Nets 1986, Part II, Proceedings of an Advanced Course, Bad Honnef, Germany, 8-19 September 1986. Lecture Notes in Computer Science, vol. 255, pp. 279–324. Springer (1986)

49. Meenakshi, B., Ramanujam, R.: Reasoning about layered message passing systems. Computer Languages, Systems & Structures 30(3-4), 171–206 (2004)

50. Nielsen, M., Plotkin, G.D., Winskel, G.: Petri nets, event structures and domains, part I. Theor. Comput. Sci. 13, 85–108 (1981)

51. Reger, G., Cruz, H.C., Rydeheard, D.E.: MarQ: Monitoring at Runtime with QEA. In: Baier, C., Tinelli, C. (eds.) Tools and Algorithms for the Construction and Analysis of Systems - 21st International Conference, TACAS 2015, Held as Part of the European Joint Conferences on Theory and Practice of Software, ETAPS 2015, London, UK, April 11-18, 2015. Proceedings. Lecture Notes in Computer Science, vol. 9035, pp. 596–610. Springer (2015)

52. Reger, G., Hallé, S., Falcone, Y.: Third international competition on runtime verification - CRV 2016. In: Falcone, Y., Sánchez, C. (eds.) Runtime Verification - 16th International Conference, RV 2016, Madrid, Spain, September 23-30, 2016, Proceedings. Lecture Notes in Computer Science, vol. 10012, pp. 21–37. Springer (2016)

53. Rosu, G., Sen, K.: An instrumentation technique for online analysis of multithreaded programs. In: 18th International Parallel and Distributed Processing Symposium, 2004. Proceedings. pp. 268– (2004)

54. Sen, K., Rosu, G., Agha, G.: Runtime safety analysis of multithreaded programs. SIGSOFT Softw. Eng. Notes 28(5), 337–346 (Sep 2003), https://doi.org/10.1145/949952.940116

55. Serbanuta, T., Chen, F., Rosu, G.: Maximal causal models for sequentially consistent systems. In: Runtime Verification, Third International Conference, RV 2012, Istanbul, Turkey, September 25-28, 2012, Revised Selected Papers. pp. 136–150 (2012), https://doi.org/10.1007/978-3-642-35632-2_16

56. Soueidi, C., Falcone, Y.: Artifact Repostiory - Opportunistic Monitoring of Multithreaded Programs (1 2023), https://doi.org/10.6084/m9.figshare.21828570

57. Wang, L., Stoller, S.: Runtime analysis of atomicity for multithreaded programs. IEEE Transactions on Software Engineering 32(2), 93–110 (2006)

Parallel Program Analysis via Range Splitting

Jan Haltermann[1](✉)(ID)*, Marie-Christine Jakobs[2](ID), Cedric Richter[1](ID),
and Heike Wehrheim[1](ID)

[1] University of Oldenburg, Department of Computing Science, Oldenburg, Germany
{jan.haltermann,cedric.richter,heike.wehrheim}@uol.de
[2] Technical University of Darmstadt, Computer Science, Darmstadt, Germany
jakobs@cs.tu-darmstadt.de

Abstract. *Ranged symbolic execution* has been proposed as a way of
scaling symbolic execution by splitting the task of path exploration onto
several workers running in parallel. The split is conducted along path
ranges which – simply speaking – describe sets of paths. Workers can
then explore path ranges in parallel.

In this paper, we propose *ranged analysis* as the generalization of ranged
symbolic execution to arbitrary program analyses. This allows us to not
only parallelize a single analysis, but also run *different* analyses on different ranges of a program in parallel. Besides this generalization, we
also provide a novel *range splitting* strategy operating along loop bounds,
complementing the existing random strategy of the original proposal. We
implemented ranged analysis within the tool CPACHECKER and evaluated it on programs from the SV-COMP benchmark. The evaluation in
particular shows the superiority of loop bounds splitting over random
splitting. We furthermore find that compositions of ranged analyses can
solve analysis tasks that none of the constituent analysis alone can solve.

Keywords: Ranged Symbolic Execution, Cooperative Software Verification, Parallel Configurable Program Analysis

1 Introduction

Recent years have seen enormous progress in automatic software verification,
driven amongst others by annual competitions like SV-COMP [13]. Software verification tools employ a bunch of different techniques for analysis, like predicate
analysis, bounded model checking, k-induction, property-directed reachability, or
automata-based methods. As however none of these techniques is superior over
the others, today often a form of *cooperative verification* [24] is employed. The
idea of cooperative verification is to have different sorts of analyses cooperate on
the task of software verification. This principle has already been implemented
in various forms [16,19,33,59], in particular also as cooperations of testing and
verification tools [10,39,41,42]. Such cooperations most often take the form of se-

---

* This author was partially supported by the German Research Foundation (DFG) —
WE2290/13-1 (Coop).

L. Lambers and S. Uchitel (Eds.): FASE 2023, LNCS 13991, pp. 195–219, 2023.
https://doi.org/10.1007/978-3-031-30826-0_11

quential combinations, where one tool starts with the full task, stores its partial analysis result within some verification artefact, and the next tool then works on the remaining task. In contrast, *parallel* execution of different tools is in the majority of cases only done by *portfolio* approaches, simply running the different tools on the same task in parallel. One reason for using portfolios when employing parallel execution is the fact that it is unclear how to best split a program into parts on which different tools could work separately while still being able to join their partial results into one for the entire program.

With *ranged symbolic execution*, Siddiqui and Khurshid [86] proposed one such technique for splitting programs into parts. The idea of ranged symbolic execution is to scale symbolic execution by splitting path exploration onto several workers, thereby, in particular allowing the workers to operate in parallel. To this end, they defined so-called *path ranges*. A path range describes a set of program paths defined by two inputs to the program, where the path π_1 triggered by the first input is the lower bound and the path π_2 for the second input is the upper bound of the range. All paths in between, i.e., paths π such that $\pi_1 \leq \pi \leq \pi_2$ (based on some ordering $\leq$ on paths), make up a range. A worker operating on a range performs symbolic execution on paths of the range only. In their experiments, Siddiqui and Khurshid investigated one form of splitting via path ranges, namely by randomly generating inputs, which then make up a number of ranges.

In this paper, we generalize ranged symbolic execution to arbitrary analyses. In particular, we introduce the concept of a *ranged analysis* to execute an arbitrary analysis on a given range and compose different ranged analyses, which can then operate on different ranges in *parallel*. Also, we propose a novel *splitting strategy*, which generates ranges along loop bounds. We implemented ranged analysis in the software verification tool CPACHECKER [21], which already provides a number of analyses, all defined as configurable program analyses (CPAs). To integrate ranged analysis in CPACHECKER, we defined a new *range reduction* CPA, and then employed the built-in feature of analysis composition to combine it with different analyses. The thus obtained ranged analyses are then run on different ranges in parallel, using COVERITEAM [20] as tool for orchestration. We furthermore implemented two strategies for generating path ranges, our novel strategy employing loop bounds for defining ranges plus the original random splitting technique. A loop bound n splits program paths into ranges only entering the loop at most n times and ranges entering for more than n times[3].

Our evaluation on SV-COMP benchmarks [36] first of all confirms the results of Siddiqui and Khurshid [86] in that symbolic execution benefits from a ranged execution. Second, our results show that a loop-bound based splitting strategy brings an improvement over random splitting. Finally, we see that a composition of ranged analyses can solve analysis tasks that none of the (different) constituent analyses of a combination can solve alone.

---

[3] Such splits can also be performed on intervals on loop bounds, thereby generating more than two path ranges.

```
1  int mid(int x, int y, int z)
2  {
3    if (x < y)
4      {
5      if (y < z) return y;
6      else if (x < z) return z;
7      else return x ;
8      }
9      else if (x < z) return x;
10     else if (y < z) return z;
11     else return y;
12 }
```

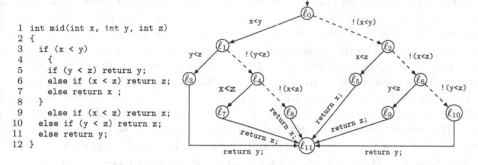

Fig. 1: Example program `mid` (taken from [86]) and its CFA

2   Background

We start by introducing some notations on programs, defining path ranges, and introducing configurable program analysis as implemented in CPACHECKER.

2.1   Program Syntax and Semantics

For the sake of presentation, we consider simple, imperative programs with a deterministic control-flow with one sort of variables (from some set $\mathcal{V}$) only[4]. Formally, we model a program by a *control-flow automaton* (CFA) $P = (L, \ell_0, G)$, where $L \subseteq Loc$ is a subset of the program locations Loc (the program counter values), $\ell_0 \in L$ represents the beginning of the program, and control-flow edges $G \subseteq L \times Ops \times L$ describe when which statements may be executed. Therein the set of statements Ops contains all possible statements, e.g., assume statements (boolean expressions over variables $\mathcal{V}$, denoted by $BExpr$), assignments, etc. We expect that CFAs originate from program code and, thus, control-flow may only branch at assume operations, i.e., CFAs $P = (L, \ell_0, G)$ are deterministic in the following sense. For all $(\ell, op', \ell'), (\ell, op'', \ell'') \in G$ either $op' = op'' \wedge \ell' = \ell''$ or op', op'' are assume operations and $op' \equiv \neg(op'')$. We assume that there exists an *indicator function* $B_P : G \to \{T, F, N\}$ that reports the branch direction, either N(one), T(rue), or F(alse). This indicator function assigns N to all edges without assume operations and for any two assume operations $(\ell, op', \ell'), (\ell, op'', \ell'') \in G$ with $op' \neq op''$ it guarantees $B_P((\ell, op', \ell')) \cup B_P((\ell, op'', \ell'')) = \{T, F\}$. Since CFAs are typically derived from programs and assume operations correspond to the two evaluations of conditions of e.g., if or while statements, the assume operation representing the true evaluation of the condition is typically assigned T. We will later need this indicator function for defining path orderings.

Figure 1 shows our example program `mid`, which returns the middle value of the three input values, and its CFA. For each condition of an if statement it contains one assume edge for each evaluation of the condition, namely solid edges labelled by the condition for entering the if branch after the condition evaluates

---

[4] Our implementation supports C programs.

to true and dashed edges labelled by the negated condition for entering the else branch after the condition evaluates to false, i.e., the negated condition evaluates to true. All other statements are represented by a single edge.

We continue with the operational semantics of programs. A program *state* is a pair (ℓ, c) of a program location $\ell \in L$ and a data state c from the set C of data states that assign to each variable $v \in V$ a value of the variable's domain. Program *execution paths* $\pi = (\ell_0, c_0) \xrightarrow{g_1} (\ell_1, c_1) \xrightarrow{g_2} \ldots \xrightarrow{g_n} (\ell_n, c_n)$ are sequences of states and edges such that (1) they start at the beginning of the program and (2) only perform valid execution steps that (a) adhere to the control-flow, i.e., $\forall 1 \leq i \leq n : g_i = (\ell_{i-1}, \cdot, \ell_i)$, and (b) properly describe the effect of the operations, i.e., $\forall 1 \leq i \leq n : c_i = sp_{op_i}(c_{i-1})$, where the strongest postcondition $sp_{op_i} : C \rightharpoonup C$ is a partial function modeling the effect of operation $op_i \in Ops$ on data states. Execution paths are also called *feasible* paths, and paths that fulfil properties (1) and (2a) but violate property (2b) are called *infeasible* paths. The set of all execution paths of a program P is denoted by $paths(P)$.

2.2   Path Ordering, Execution Trees, and Ranges

Our ranged analysis analyses sets of consecutive program execution paths. To specify these sets, we first define an *ordering* on execution paths. Given two program paths $\pi = (\ell_0, c_0) \xrightarrow{g_1} (\ell_1, c_1) \xrightarrow{g_2} \ldots \xrightarrow{g_n} (\ell_n, c_n)$ and $\pi' = (\ell'_0, c'_0) \xrightarrow{g'_1} (\ell'_1, c'_1) \xrightarrow{g'_2} \ldots \xrightarrow{g'_m} (\ell'_m, c'_m) \in paths(P)$, we define their order $\leq$ based on their control-flow edges. More specifically, edges with assume operations representing a true evaluation of a condition are smaller than the edges representing the corresponding false evaluation of that condition. Following this idea, $\pi \leq \pi'$ if $\exists\, 0 \leq k \leq n : \forall\, 1 \leq i \leq k : g_i = g'_i \wedge ((n = k \wedge m \geq n) \vee (m > k \wedge n > k \wedge B_P(g_{k+1}) = T \wedge B_P(g'_{k+1}) = F))$. An *execution tree* is a tree containing all execution paths of a program with the previously defined ordering, where nodes are labelled with the assume operations.

Based on the above ordering, we now specify ranges, which describe sets of consecutive program execution paths analysed by a ranged analysis and which are characterized by a left and right path that limit the range. Hence, a *range* $[\pi, \pi']$ is the set $\{\pi_r \in paths(P) \mid \pi \leq \pi_r \leq \pi'\}$[5]. To easily describe ranges that are not bound on the left or right, we use the special paths $\pi_\perp, \pi^\top \notin paths(P)$ which are smaller and greater than every path, i.e., $\forall \pi \in paths(P) : (\pi \leq \pi^\top) \wedge (\pi^\top \not\leq \pi) \wedge (\pi_\perp \leq \pi) \wedge (\pi \not\leq \pi_\perp)$. Consequently, $[\pi_\perp, \pi^\top] = paths(P)$.

As the program is assumed to be deterministic except for the input, a *test case* $\tau, \tau : V \to \mathbb{Z}$, which maps each input variable to a concrete value, describes exactly a single path π^6. We say that τ *induces* π and write this path as π_τ. Consequently, we can define a range by two induced paths, i.e., as $[\pi_{\tau_1}, \pi_{\tau_2}]$ for test cases τ_1 and τ_2. For the example program from Fig. 1, two example test cases are $\tau_1 = \{x : 0, y : 2, z : 1\}$ and $\tau_2 = \{x : 1, y : 0, z : 2\}$. Two such induced

---

[5] In [86], the range is formalized as $[\pi, \pi')$ but their implementation works on $[\pi, \pi']$.

[6] More concretely, test input τ describes a single maximal path and all its prefixes.

path are $\pi_{\tau_1} = (\ell_0, c_1) \xrightarrow{x<y} (\ell_1, c_1) \xrightarrow{!(y<z)} (\ell_4, c_1) \xrightarrow{x<z} (\ell_7, c_1) \xrightarrow{ret\ z} (\ell_{11}, c_1)$,
where $c_1 = [x \mapsto 0, y \mapsto 2, z \mapsto 1]$ and $\pi_{\tau_2} = (\ell_0, c_2) \xrightarrow{!(x<y)} (\ell_2, c_2) \xrightarrow{x<z}$
$(\ell_5, c_2) \xrightarrow{ret\ x} (\ell_{11}, c_2)$, where $c_2 = [x \mapsto 1, y \mapsto 0, z \mapsto 2]$.

2.3   Configurable Program Analysis

We will realize our ranged analysis using the *configurable program analysis* (CPA)
framework [17]. This framework allows one to define customized, abstract-inter-
pretation based analyses, i.e., it allows a selection of the abstract domain as well
as a configuration for exploration. For the latter, one defines when and how to
combine information and when to stop exploration. Formally, a CPA $\mathbb{A} = (D, \rightsquigarrow,$
merge, stop) consists of

- the *abstract domain* $D = (Loc \times C, (E, \top, \sqsubseteq, \sqcup), \llbracket \cdot \rrbracket)$, which is composed of
  a set $Loc \times C$ of program states, a join semi-lattice on the abstract states E
  as well as a concretization function, which fulfils that

$$\llbracket \top \rrbracket = Loc \times C \text{ and } \forall e, e' \in E : \llbracket e \rrbracket \cup \llbracket e' \rrbracket \subseteq \llbracket e \sqcup e' \rrbracket$$

- the *transfer relation* $\rightsquigarrow \subseteq E \times \mathcal{G} \times E$ defining the abstract semantics that
  safely overapproximates the program semantics, i.e.,

  $\forall e \in E, g \in Loc \times Ops \times Loc :$

$$\{s' \mid \exists \text{ valid execution step } s \xrightarrow{g} s' : s \in \llbracket e \rrbracket\} \subseteq \bigcup_{(e,g,e') \in \rightsquigarrow} \llbracket e' \rrbracket$$

- the *merge operator* merge $: E \times E \to E$ used to combine information that
  satisfies
  $$\forall e, e' \in E : e' \sqsubseteq \text{merge}(e, e')$$

- the *termination check* stop $: E \times 2^E \to \mathbb{B}$ that decides whether the exploration of an abstract state can be omitted and that fulfils
  $$\forall e \in E, E_{sub} \subseteq E : \text{stop}(e, E_{sub}) \implies \llbracket e \rrbracket \subseteq \bigcup_{e' \in E_{sub}} \llbracket e' \rrbracket$$

To run the configured analysis, one executes a meta reachability analysis, the
so-called CPA algorithm, configured by the CPA and provides an initial value
$e_{init} \in E$ which the analysis will start with. For details on the CPA algorithm,
we refer the reader to [17].

As part of our ranged analysis, we use the abstract domain and transfer
relation of a CPA $\mathbb{V}$ for *value analysis* [9] (also known as constant propaga-
tion or explicit analysis). An abstract state v of the value analysis ignores program locations and maps each variable to either a concrete value of its do-
main or $\top$, which represents any value. The partial order $\sqsubseteq_\mathbb{V}$ and the join
operator $\sqcup_\mathbb{V}$ are defined variable-wise while ensuring that $v \sqsubseteq_\mathbb{V} v' \Leftrightarrow \forall v \in$
$\mathcal{V} : v(v) = v'(v) \lor v'(v) = \top^7$ and $(v \sqcup_\mathbb{V} v')(v) = v(v)$ if $v(v) = v'(v)$ and
otherwise $(v \sqcup_\mathbb{V} v')(v) = \top$. The concretization of abstract state v contains

---
[7] Consequently, $\forall v \in \mathcal{V} : \top_\mathbb{V}(v) = \top$.

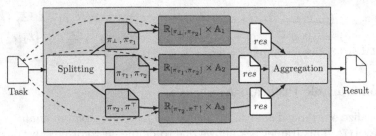

Fig. 2: Composition of three ranged analyses (in orange)

all concrete states that agree on the concrete variable values, i.e., $[\![v]\!]_V :=$ $\{(\ell, c) \in Loc \times C \mid \forall \mathbf{v} \in V : v(\mathbf{v}) = \top \lor v(\mathbf{v}) = c(\mathbf{v})\}$. If the values for all relevant variables are known, the transfer relation $\rightsquigarrow_V$ will behave like the program semantics. Otherwise, it may overapproximate the executability of a CFA edge and may assign value $\top$ if a concrete value cannot be determined.

To easily build ranged analysis instances for various program analyses, we modularize our ranged analysis into a ranged reduction and a program analysis. Technically, we will compose a ranged analysis from different CPAs using the concept of a *composite CPA* [17]. We demonstrate the composition for two CPAs. The composition of more than two CPAs works analogously or can be achieved by recursively composing two (composite) CPAs. A composite CPA $\mathbb{A}_\times = (D_\times, \rightsquigarrow_\times, \mathsf{merge}_\times, \mathsf{stop}_\times)$ of CPA $\mathbb{A}_1 = ((Loc \times C, (E_1, \top_1, \sqsubseteq_1, \sqcup_1), [\![\cdot]\!]_1), \rightsquigarrow_1, \mathsf{merge}_1, \mathsf{stop}_1)$ and CPA $\mathbb{A}_2 = ((Loc \times C, (E_2, \top_2, \sqsubseteq_2, \sqcup_2), [\![\cdot]\!]_2), \rightsquigarrow_2,$ $\mathsf{merge}_2, \mathsf{stop}_2)$ considers the product domain $D_\times = (Loc \times C, (E_1 \times E_2, (\top_1, \top_2),$ $\sqsubseteq_\times, \sqcup_\times), [\![\cdot]\!]_\times)$ that defines the operators elementwise, i.e., $(e_1, e_2) \sqsubseteq_\times (e_1', e_2')$ if $e_1 \sqsubseteq_1 e_1'$ and $e_2 \sqsubseteq_2 e_2'$, $(e_1, e_1) \sqcup_\times (e_1', e_2') = (e_1 \sqcup_1 e_1', e_2 \sqcup e_2')$, and $[\![(e_1, e_2)]\!] =$ $[\![e_1]\!]_1 \cap [\![e_2]\!]_2$. The transfer relation may be the product transfer relation or may strengthen the product transfer relation using knowledge about the other abstract successor. In contrast, $\mathsf{merge}_\times$ and $\mathsf{stop}_\times$ cannot be derived and must always be defined.

3   Composition of Ranged Analyses

In this section, we introduce the *composition of ranged analyses* as a generalization of ranged symbolic execution to arbitrary program analyses. The overall goal is to split the program paths into multiple disjoint ranges each of which is being analysed by a (different) program analysis. Therein, the task of a program analysis is to verify whether a program fulfils a given specification. Specifications are often given in the form of error locations, so that the task is proving the unreachability of error locations. The results for the verification task contain a *verdict* and potentially an additional witness (a justification or a concrete path violating the specification [14]). The verdict indicates whether the program fulfils the specification (verdict "true"), violates it (verdict "false") or if the analysis did not compute a result (verdict "unknown").

To ensure that an arbitrary program analysis operates on paths within a given range only, we employ *ranged analysis*. A ranged analysis is realized as

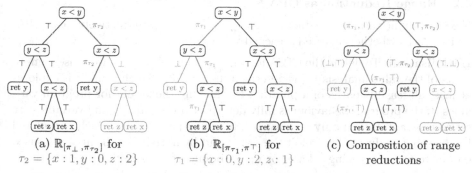

(a) $\mathbb{R}_{[\pi_\perp,\pi_{\tau_2}]}$ for $\tau_2 = \{x : 1, y : 0, z : 2\}$

(b) $\mathbb{R}_{[\pi_{\tau_1},\pi^\top]}$ for $\tau_1 = \{x : 0, y : 2, z : 1\}$

(c) Composition of range reductions

Fig. 3: Application of range reduction on the running example of Fig. 1

a composition of an arbitrary program analysis (a CPA) and a *range reduction* (also given as a CPA below) ensuring path exploration to stay within the range. Then, a *composition* of ranged analyses is obtained by (1) *splitting* the program into ranges, (2) then running several ranged analyses in parallel, and (3) at the end *aggregating* analysis results (see Fig. 2). Splitting is described in Sec. 4. For aggregation, we simply return the verdict "false" whenever one analysis returns "false", we return "unknown" whenever no analysis returns "false" and one analysis returns "unknown" or aborts, otherwise we return "true". We do not support aggregation of witnesses yet (but this could be realized similar to [70]).

3.1   Ranged Analysis

Next, we define ranged analysis as a CPA composition of the target program analysis and the novel range reduction. The range reduction decides whether a path is included in a range $[\pi_{\tau_1}, \pi_{\tau_2}]$ and limits path exploration to this range. We decompose the range reduction for $[\pi_{\tau_1}, \pi_{\tau_2}]$ into a composition of two specialized ranged reductions $\mathbb{R}_{[\pi_{\tau_1},\pi^\top]}$ and $\mathbb{R}_{[\pi_\perp,\pi_{\tau_2}]}$, which decide whether a path is in the range $[\pi_{\tau_1}, \pi^\top]$ and $[\pi_\perp, \pi_{\tau_2}]$, respectively. Since $[\pi_{\tau_1}, \pi_{\tau_2}] = [\pi_{\tau_1}, \pi^\top] \cap [\pi_\perp, \pi_{\tau_2}]$ and the composition stops the exploration of a path if one analysis returns $\perp$, the composite analysis $\mathbb{R}_{[\pi_{\tau_1},\pi_{\tau_2}]} = \mathbb{R}_{[\pi_\perp,\pi_{\tau_2}]} \times \mathbb{R}_{[\pi_{\tau_1},\pi^\top]}$ only explores paths that are included in both ranges (which are exactly the paths in $[\pi_{\tau_1}, \pi_{\tau_2}]$). Figure 3 depicts the application of range reduction to the example from Fig. 1, where the range reduction $\mathbb{R}_{[\pi_\perp,\pi_{\tau_2}]}$ is depicted in Fig. 3a and $\mathbb{R}_{[\pi_{\tau_1},\pi^\top]}$ in Fig. 3b and the composition of both range reductions in Fig. 3c. Finally, the ranged analysis of any arbitrary program analysis $\mathbb{A}$ in a given range $[\pi_{\tau_1}, \pi_{\tau_2}]$ can be represented as a composition:

$$\mathbb{R}_{[\pi_{\tau_1},\pi^\top]} \times \mathbb{R}_{[\pi_\perp,\pi_{\tau_2}]} \times \mathbb{A}$$

For $\mathbb{R}_{[\pi_{\tau_1},\pi_{\tau_2}]}$, we define $\mathsf{merge}_\times$ component-wise for the individual merge operators and $\mathsf{stop}_\times$ as conjunction of the individual stop operators. As soon as the range reduction decides that a path π is not contained in the range $[\pi_{\tau_1}, \pi_{\tau_2}]$ and returns $\perp$, the exploration of the path stops for all analyses defined in the composition.

3.2 Range Reduction as CPA

Next, we define the range reduction $\mathbb{R}_{[\pi_{\tau_1},\pi^\top]}$ ($\mathbb{R}_{[\pi_\perp,\pi_{\tau_2}]}$, respectively) as a CPA, which tracks whether a state is reached via a path in $[\pi_{\tau_1},\pi^\top]$ ($[\pi_\perp,\pi_{\tau_2}]$).

Initialisation. To define the CPAs for $\mathbb{R}_{[\pi_{\tau_1},\pi^\top]}$ and $\mathbb{R}_{[\pi_\perp,\pi_{\tau_2}]}$, we reuse components of the value analysis $\mathbb{V}$ (as described in Sec. 2.3). A value analysis explores at least all feasible paths of a program by tracking the values for program variables. If the program behaviour is fully determined (i.e., all (input) variables are set to constants), then only one feasible, maximal path exists, which is explored by the value analysis. We exploit this behaviour by initializing the analysis based on our test case τ (being a lower or upper bound of a range):

$$e_{INIT} = \begin{cases} v(x) = \tau(x) & \text{if } x \in dom(\tau), x \in \mathcal{V} \\ v(x) = \top & \text{otherwise} \end{cases}$$

In this case, all variables which are typically undetermined[8] and dependent on the program input have now a determined value, defined through the test case. As the behaviour of the program under the test case τ is now fully determined, the value analysis only explores a single path π_τ, which corresponds to the execution trace of the program given the test case. Now, as we are interested in all paths defined in a range and not only a single path, we adapt the value analysis as follows:

Lower Bound CPA. For the CPA range reduction $\mathbb{R}_{[\pi_{\tau_1},\pi^\top]}$ we borrow all components of the value analysis except for the transfer relation $\leadsto_{\tau_1}$. The transfer relation $\leadsto_{\tau_1}$ is defined as follows:

$$(v,g,v') \in \leadsto_{\tau_1} \text{ iff } \begin{cases} v = \top \land v' = \top, \text{or} \\ v \neq \top \land v' = \top \land B_P(g) = F \land (v,g,\perp) \in \leadsto_\mathbb{V}, \text{or} \\ v \neq \top \land (v' \neq \perp \lor B_P(g) \neq F) \land (v,g,v') \in \leadsto_\mathbb{V} \end{cases}$$

Note that $\top$ represents the value analysis state where no information on variables is stored and $\perp$ represents an unreachable state in the value analysis, which stops the exploration of the path. Hence, the second case ensures that $\mathbb{R}_{[\pi_{\tau_1},\pi^\top]}$ also visits the false-branch of a condition when the path induced by τ_1 follows the true-branch. Note that in case that $\leadsto_\mathbb{V}$ computes $\perp$ as a successor state for an assumption g with $B_P(g) = T$, the exploration of the path is stopped, as π_{τ_1} follows the false-branch (contained in the third case).

Upper Bound CPA. For the CPA range reduction $\mathbb{R}_{[\pi_\perp,\pi_{\tau_2}]}$ we again borrow all components of the value analysis except for the transfer relation $\leadsto_{\tau_2}$. The transfer relation $\leadsto_{\tau_2}$ is defined as follows:

$$(v,g,v') \in \leadsto_{\tau_2} \text{ iff } \begin{cases} v = \top \land v' = \top \\ v \neq \top \land v' = \top \land B_P(g) = T \land (v,g,\perp) \in \leadsto_\mathbb{V} \\ v \neq \top \land (v' \neq \perp \lor B_P(g) \neq T) \land (v,g,v') \in \leadsto_\mathbb{V} \end{cases}$$

The second condition now ensures that $\mathbb{R}_{[\pi_\perp,\pi_{\tau_2}]}$ also visits the true-branch of a condition when π_{τ_2} follows the false-branch.

---

[8] Assuming that randomness is controlled through an input and hence the program is deterministic.

3.3   Handling Underspecified Test Cases

So far, we have assumed that test cases are fully specified, i.e., contain values for all input variables, and the behaviour of the program is deterministic such that executing a test case τ follows a single (maximal) execution path π_τ. However, in practice, we observe that test cases can be underspecified such that a test case τ does not provide concrete values for all input variables. We denote by P_τ the *set* of all paths that are then induced by τ. In this case, we define:

$$[\pi_\perp, P_\tau] = \{\pi \mid \forall \pi' \in P_\tau : \pi \leq \pi'\} = \{\pi \mid \pi \leq \min(P_\tau)\}$$

and

$$[P_\tau, \pi^\top] = \{\pi \mid \exists \pi' \in P_\tau : \pi' \leq \pi\} = \{\pi \mid \min(P_\tau) \leq \pi\}$$

Interestingly enough, by defining $\pi_\tau = \min(P_\tau)$ for an underspecified test case τ we can handle the range as if τ would be fully specified.

4   Splitting

A crucial part of the ranged analysis is the generation of ranges, i.e., the splitting of programs into parts that can be analysed in parallel. The splitting has to either compute two paths or two test cases, both defining one range. Ranged symbolic execution [36] employs a random strategy for range generation (together with an online work stealing concept to balance work among different workers). For the work here, we have also implemented this random strategy, selecting random paths in the execution tree to make up ranges. In addition, we propose a novel strategy based on the number of loop unrollings. Both strategies are designed to work "on-the-fly" meaning that none requires building the full execution tree upfront, they rather only compute the paths or test cases that are used to fix a range. Next, we explain both strategies in more detail, especially how they are used to generate more than two ranges.

Bounding the Number of Loop Unrollings (LB). Given a *loop bound* $i \in \mathbb{N}$, the splitting computes the left-most path in the program that contains exactly i unrollings of the loop. If the program contains nested loops, each nested loop is unrolled for i times in each iteration of the outer loop. For the computed path, we (1) build its path formula using the strongest post-condition operator [46], (2) query an SMT-solver for satisfiability and (3) in case of an answer SAT, use the evaluation of the input variables in the path formula as one test case. In case that the path formula is unsatisfiable, we iteratively remove the last statement from the path, until a satisfying path formula is found. A test case τ determined in this way defines two ranges, namely $[\pi_\perp, \pi_\tau]$ and $[\pi_\tau, \pi^\top]$. In case that the program is loop-free, the generation of a test case fails and we generate a single range $[\pi_\perp, \pi^\top]$. In the experiments, we used the loop bounds 3 (called LB3) and 10 (called LB10) with two ranges each. To compute more than two ranges, we use intervals of loop bounds.

Generating Ranges Randomly (RDM). The second splitting strategy selects the desired number of paths randomly. At each assume edge in the program

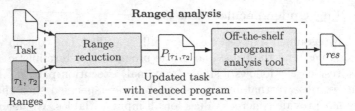

Fig. 4: Construction of a ranged analysis from an off-the-shelf program analysis

(either a loop head or an if statement), it follows either the true- or the false-branch with a probability of 50%, until it reaches a node in the CFA without successor. Again, we compute the path formula for that path and build a test case. This purely random approach is called RDM.

Selecting the true- or the false-branch with the same probability may lead to fairly short paths with few loop iterations. As the execution tree of a program is often not balanced, it rather grows to the left (true-branches). Thus, we used a second strategy based on random walks, which takes the true-branch with a probability of 90%. We call this strategy RDM9.

5   Implementation

To show the advantages of the composition of ranged analyses, especially the possibility of running conceptually different analyses on different ranges of a program, we realized the range reduction from Sec. 3.2 and the ranged analyses in the tool CPACHECKER [21]. The realization of the range reduction follows our formalization, i.e., it reuses elements from the value analysis, which are already implemented within CPACHECKER.

Due to the composite pattern, we can build a ranged analysis as composition of range reduction and any existing program analysis within CPACHECKER with nearly no effort. We can also use other (non CPA-based) off-the-shelf analyses by employing the construction depicted in Fig. 4: Instead of running the analysis in parallel with the range reduction CPA, we can build a sequential composition of the range reduction and the analysis itself. As off-the-shelf tools take programs as inputs, not ranges, we first construct a reduced program,which by construction only contains the paths within the given range. For this, we can use the existing residual program generation within CPACHECKER [19].

The composition of ranged analyses from Sec. 3 is realized using the tool COVERITEAM [20]. COVERITEAM allows building parallel and sequential compositions using existing program analyses, like the ones of CPACHECKER. We use COVERITEAM for the orchestration of the composition of ranged analyses. The implementation follows the structure depicted in Fig. 2 and also contains the AGGREGATION component. It is configured with the program analysis $A_1, \cdots, A_n$ and a splitting component. For splitting, we realized the splitters LB3, LB10, RDM and RDM9 in CPACHECKER. Each splitter generates test cases in the standardized XML-based TEST-COMP test case format[9]. In case that the splitter fails (e.g. LB3 cannot compute a test-case, if the program does not contain a loop) our implementation executes the analysis A_1 on the interval $[\pi_\perp, \pi^\top]$. For the evaluation, we used combinations of three existing program analyses within the ranged analysis, briefly introduced next.

Symbolic Execution. Symbolic execution [73] analyses program paths based on symbolic inputs. Here, states are pairs of a symbolic store, which describes variable values by formulae on the symbolic inputs, and a path condition, which tracks the executability of the path. Operations update the symbolic store and at branching points the path condition is extended by the symbolic evaluation of the branching condition. Furthermore, the exploration of a path is stopped when it reaches the program end or its path condition becomes unsatisfiable.

Predicate Analysis. We use CPACHECKER's standard predicate analysis, which is configured to perform model checking and predicate abstraction with adjustable block encoding [22] such that it abstracts at loop heads only. The required set of predicates is determined by counterexample-guided abstraction refinement [35], lazy refinement [64], and interpolation [63].

Bounded Model Checking. We use iterative bounded model checking (BMC). Each iteration inspects the behaviour of the CFA unrolled up to loop bound k and increases the loop bound in case no property violation was detected. To inspect the behaviour, BMC first encodes the unrolled CFA and the property in a formula using the unified SMT-based approach for software verification [15]. Thereafter, it checks the satisfiability of the formula encoding to detect property violations.

For the evaluation, we build four different basic configurations and employed our different range splitters: RA-2SE and RA-3SE which employ two resp. three instances of symbolic execution in parallel, RA-2BMC employing two instances of BMC and RA-SE-PRED that uses symbolic execution for the range $[\pi_\perp, \pi_\tau]$ and predicate analysis on $[\pi_\tau, \pi^\top]$ for some computed test input τ.

6   Evaluation

Siddiqui and Khurshid concentrated their evaluation on the issue of scaling, i.e., showing that a certain speed-up can be achieved by ranged execution [86]. More specifically, they showed that ranged symbolic execution can speed-up path exploration when employing ten workers operating on ranges in parallel. In contrast, our interest was not in scaling issues only, but also in the obtained verification results. We in particular wanted to find out whether a ranged analysis can obtain more results for verification tasks than analyses in isolation would achieve within the same resource limitations. Furthermore, our evaluation is

---

[9] https://gitlab.com/sosy-lab/test-comp/test-format/blob/testcomp22/doc/Format.md

different to [86] in that we limit the available CPU time, meaning that both analyses, the default analysis and the composition of ranged analyses, have the same resources and that we employ *different* analyses. Finally, we were interested in evaluating our novel splitting strategy, in particular in comparison to the existing random strategy. To this end, we studied the following research questions:

RQ1 Can a composition of ranged analyses, in particular our novel splitting strategy, increase the efficiency and effectiveness of symbolic execution?

RQ2 Can other analyses also benefit from using a composition of ranged analyses, in particular combinations of different analyses?

6.1   Evaluation Setup

All experiments were run on machines with an Intel Xeon E3-1230 v5 @ 3.40 GHz (8 cores), 33 GB of memory, and Ubuntu 20.04 LTS with Linux kernel 5.4.0. We use BENCHEXEC [23] for the execution of our experiments to increase the reproducibility of the results. In a verification run, a tool-configuration is given a task (a program plus specification) and computes either a proof (if the program fulfils the specification) or raises an alarm (if the specification is violated on the program). We limit each verification run to 15 GB of memory, 4 CPU cores, and 15 min of CPU time, yielding a setup that is comparable to the one used in SV-COMP. The evaluation is conducted on a subset of the SV-BENCHMARKS used in the SV-COMP and all experiments were conducted once. It contains in total 5 400 C-tasks from all sub-categories of the SV-COMP category reach-safety [36]. The specification for this category, and hence for these tasks, states that all calls to the function reach_error are unreachable. Each task contains a ground truth that contains the information, whether the task fulfils the specification (3 194 tasks) or not (2 206 tasks). All data collected is available in our supplementary artefact [60].

6.2   RQ 1: Composition of Ranged Analyses for Symbolic Execution

Evaluation Plan. To analyse the performance of symbolic execution in a composition of ranged analyses, we compare the effectiveness (number of tasks solved) and efficiency (time taken to solve a task) for the composition of ranged analyses with two and three ranged analyses each using a symbolic execution with one of the four splitters from Sec. 5 against symbolic execution standalone. For efficiency, we compare the consumed *CPU time* as well as the (real) time taken overall to solve the task (called *wall time*). The CPU time is always limited for the full configuration, s.t. an instance combining two ranged analyses in parallel has also only 900 s CPU time available, hence at most 450 s per ranged analysis. To achieve a fair comparison, we also executed symbolic execution in COVERITEAM, where we build a simple configuration that directly calls CPA-CHECKER running its symbolic execution.

Table 1: Number of correct and incorrect verdicts reported by SYMBEXEC and compositions of ranged analyses with symbolic executions using different splitters

| | correct | | | incorrect | | |
	overall	proof	alarm	add.	proof	alarm
SYMBEXEC	1 386	565	821	-	1	31
RA-2SE-LB3	**1487**	566	921	116	1	36
RA-2SE-LB10	1 464	567	897	92	1	37
RA-2SE-RDM	1 464	569	895	97	1	39
RA-2SE-RDM9	1 408	565	843	46	1	34
RA-3SE-LB	**1532**	563	969	181	1	35
RA-3SE-RDM	1 505	565	940	160	1	55
RA-3SE-RDM9	1 416	556	860	80	1	53

Effectiveness. Table 1 compares the verdicts of symbolic execution (SYMB-EXEC) and the configurations using a composition of ranged analyses with one range (and thus two analyses in parallel, called RA-2SE) or with two ranges (and three analyses, called RA-3SE). The table shows the number of overall correct verdicts reported (divided into the number of correct proofs and correct alarms), the number of correct verdicts additionally reported compared to SYMBEXEC as well as the number of incorrect proofs and alarms reported. First of all, we observe that all configurations using a composition of ranged analyses compute more correct verdicts than SYMBEXEC alone. We see the largest increase for RA-2SE-LB3, where 116 tasks are additionally solved. This increase comes nearly exclusively from the fact that RA-2SE-LB3 computes more correct alarms. The number of reported proofs does not change significantly, as SYMBEXEC and all configurations of the composition of ranged analyses both have to check the same number of paths in the program leading to a property violation (namely all) for being infeasible. Thus, all need to do "the same amount of work" to compute a proof. As the available CPU time is identical for both, the ranged analyses do not compute additional proofs by sharing work. In contrast, for computing an alarm, finding a single path that violates the specification suffices. Thus, using two symbolic execution analyses in parallel working on different parts of the program increases the chance of finding such a violating path. All configurations employing the composition of ranged analyses compute a few more false alarms. For these tasks, SYMBEXEC runs into a timeout and would also compute a false alarm, if its time limit would be increased.

For configurations using *three* symbolic executions in parallel, we used three splitters: RA-3SE-LB, which uses both loop-bound splitters in parallel, i.e., we have the ranges with less than three loop unrollings, three to ten loop unrollings and more than ten, and RA-3SE-RDM resp. RA-3SE-RDM9, which both employ the random splitting to generate two ranges. Again all configurations can compute more correct alarms compared to SYMBEXEC, even more than RA-2SE-LB3. Again, splitting the state space in even more parts that are analysed in parallel increases the chance to find an alarm.

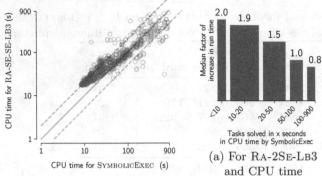

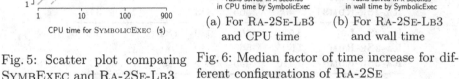

(a) For RA-2SE-LB3 and CPU time

(b) For RA-2SE-LB3 and wall time

Fig. 5: Scatter plot comparing SYMBEXEC and RA-2SE-LB3

Fig. 6: Median factor of time increase for different configurations of RA-2SE

Finally, when comparing the effectiveness of the different strategies employed to generate bounds, we observe that splitting the program using our novel component LB3 is more effective than using a randomly generated bound when using two and three symbolic execution analyses in parallel.

Efficiency. For comparing the efficiency of compositions of ranged analyses, we compare the CPU time and the wall time taken to compute a correct solution by SYMBEXEC and several configurations of ranged analysis. We excluded all tasks where the generation of the ranges fails, as SYMBEXEC and the composition of ranged analyses behave equally in these cases. In general, all configurations consume overall approximately as much CPU time as SYMBEXEC to solve all tasks and are even faster w.r.t. wall time. The scatter-plot in Fig. 5 visualizes the CPU time consumed to compute a result in a log-scale by SYMBEXEC (on the x-axis) and by RA-2SE-LB3 (on the y-axis), for tasks solved correctly by both analyses. It indicates that for tasks solved quickly, RA-2SE-LB3 requires more time than SYMBEXEC, as the points are most of the time above the diagonal, and that the difference gets smaller the longer the analyses run.

We present a more detailed analysis of the efficiency in Fig. 6a and 6b. Each of the bar-plots represents the median factor of the increase in the run time for tasks that are solved by SYMBEXEC within the time interval that is given on the x-axis. If for example SYMBEXEC solves all tasks in five CPU seconds and RA-2SE-LB3 in six CPU seconds, the factor would be 1.2, if SYMBEXEC takes five CPU seconds and RA-2SE-LB3 only three, the factor is 0.6. The width of the bars corresponds to the number of tasks within the interval. Figure 6a visualizes the comparison of the CPU time for RA-2SE-LB3 and SYMBEXEC. For RA-2SE-LB3, the median and average increase is 1.6 for all tasks. Taking a closer look, in the median it takes twice as long to solve tasks which are solved by SYMBEXEC within at most ten CPU seconds. Generating the ranges is done for the vast majority of all tasks within a few seconds. For tasks that can be solved in fewer than ten CPU seconds, the nearly constant factor for generating the ranges that is present in each run of RA-2SE-LB3 has a large impact on both

Table 2: Number of correct and incorrect verdicts reported by compositions of bounded model checking (upper half) and combinations of symbolic execution and predicate analysis (lower half) using different splitters

	overall	correct proof	alarm	add.	incorrect proof	alarm
BMC	2 534	930	1 604	-	0	68
Ra-2bmc-Lb3	2437	925	1 512	36	0	68
Ra-2bmc-Lb10	2 445	926	1 519	43	0	70
Ra-2bmc-Rdm	2 457	925	1 532	48	0	69
Ra-2bmc-Rdm9	**2505**	932	1 573	**48**	0	68
SymbExec	1 386	565	821	-	1	31
Pred	2 254	1 107	1 147	-	0	38
Ra-Se-Pred-Lb3	**2021**	913	1 108	30	0	40
Ra-Se-Pred-Lb10	2 021	911	1 110	36	0	38
Ra-Se-Pred-Rdm	1 643	534	1 109	27	1	40
Ra-Se-Pred-Rdm9	1 795	715	1 080	17	1	38

CPU and wall time taken. Most importantly, the impact gets smaller the longer the analyses need to compute the result (the factor is constantly decreasing). For tasks that are solved by SymbExec in more than 50 CPU seconds, Ra-2Se-Lb3 is as fast as SymbExec, for tasks solved in more than 100 CPU seconds it is 20% faster. As stated above, the CPU time consumed to computing a proof is not affected by parallelization. Thus, when only looking at the time taken to compute a proof, Ra-2Se-Lb3 takes as long as SymbExec after 50 CPU seconds. In contrast, Ra-2Se-Lb3 is faster for finding alarms in that interval. A more detailed analysis can be found in the artefact [60].

When comparing the wall time in Fig. 6b, the positive effect of the parallelization employed in all configurations of a composition of ranged analyses gets visible. Ra-2Se-Lb3 is faster than SymbExec, when SymbExec takes more than 20 seconds in real time to solve the task. To emphasize the effect of the parallelization, we used pre-computed ranges for Ra-2Se-Lb3. Now, Ra-2Se-Lb3 takes only the 1.1-fold wall time in the median compared to SymbExec, and is equally fast or faster for all tasks solved in more than ten seconds.

> The use of compositions of ranged analysis for symbolic execution increases its effectiveness for finding violations of the specification. Moreover, the real overall time consumed to compute the result is reduced for large or complex tasks due to the parallelization employed. We have hence reproduced the findings from [86] in a different setting.

6.3 RQ 2: Composition of Ranged Analyses for Other Analyses

Evaluation Plan. To investigate whether other analysis combinations benefit from a composition of ranged analyses, we evaluated two combinations: The first

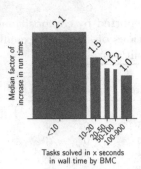
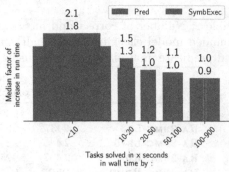

(a) For RA-2BMC-RDM9 and wall time   (b) For RA-SE-PRED-LB3 and wall time

Fig. 7: Median factor of time increase for different compositions of ranged analyses

uses two instances of BMC (RA-2BMC), the second one uses symbolic execution on the interval $[\pi_\perp, \pi_\tau]$ and predicate analysis on the range $[\pi_\tau, \pi^\top]$ (RA-SE-PRED). We are again interested in effectiveness and efficiency.

Results for BMC. The upper part of Tab. 2 contains the results for a composition of ranged analyses using two instances of BMC. In contrast to RA-2SE, RA-2BMC does not increase the number of overall correct verdicts compared to BMC. RA-2BMC-RDM9 computes 48 correct verdicts that are not computed by BMC, it also fails to compute the correct verdict in 77 cases solved by BMC. Both observations can mainly be explained from the fact that one analysis computes a result for a task where the other runs into a timeout. Again, we observe that the composition of ranged analyses computes additional alarms (here 36), as both ranged analyses search in different parts of the program.

When comparing the efficiency, we notice that the CPU time consumed to compute a result for RA-2BMC-RDM9 (and all other instances) is higher than for BMC. In average, the increase is 2.6, the median is 2.5, whereas the median increase for tasks solved in more than 100 CPU seconds by BMC is 1.1. For wall time, where we depict the increases in Fig. 7a, the median overall increase is 1.9. This high overall increase is caused by the fact that BMC can solve nearly 65% of all tasks within ten seconds wall time. Thus, the effect of computing the splitting has a big impact on the factor. For more complex or larger instances, where BMC uses more time, the wall time of RA-2BMC-RDM9 is comparable, for instances taking more than 100 seconds, both takes approximately the same time.

Results for Predicate Analysis and Symbolic Execution. Table 2 also contains the results for the compositions of ranged analyses using predicate analysis and symbolic execution in combination. Here, the column "add." contains the tasks that are neither solved by PRED nor SYMBEXEC. Both default analyses used in this setting have different strengths, as PRED solves 1 517 tasks not solved by SYMBEXEC, and SYMBEXEC 649 not solved by PRED. 737 tasks are solved by both analyses.

The most successful configuration of the composition of ranged analyses again uses LB3 for generating the ranges. In comparison to SYMBEXEC and PRED, RA-SE-PRED-LB3 computes 635 more overall correct verdicts than SYMBEXEC, but 233 fewer than PRED. It solves 430 tasks not solved by PRED and 918 tasks not solved by SYMBEXEC. Most important, it can compute 36 correct proofs and alarms that are neither found by PRED nor SYMBEXEC. The effect that tasks can be solved by the composition of ranged analyses that are not solvable by one or both instances lays in the fact that both analyses work only on a part of the program, making the verification problem easier. Unfortunately, the remaining part is sometimes still too complex for the analysis to be verified in the given time limit. Then, RA-SE-PRED-LB3 cannot compute a final result.

When evaluating the effectiveness of RA-SE-PRED-LB3, we need to compare it to both PRED and SYMBEXEC. Figure 7b compares the median factor of the wall time increase for PRED and SYMBEXEC. For both, we observe that the median increase factor of the wall time is high (2.1 for PRED and 1.6 for SYMB-EXEC) for tasks that are solved quickly (within ten seconds), but decreases for more complex tasks. For tasks that are solved with a wall time greater 100 s, RA-SE-PRED-LB3 takes approx. the same time as PRED, and is 10% faster than SYMBEXEC. Important to note that Fig. 7b does not include the situation that PRED or SYMBEXEC does not compute a solution but RA-SE-PRED-LB3 does. For the former questions, these cases happen rarely, for RA-SE-PRED-LB3 and SYMBEXEC it occurs for 918 tasks. RA-SE-PRED-LB3 needs in median 15 seconds wall time to compute a solution when PRED runs into a timeout and 52 seconds for SYMBEXEC, both would lead to an increase factor smaller than 0.1.

> In summary, BMC can partially benefit from using a composition of ranged analyses, although the effect is not as good as for symbolic execution. The use of predicate analysis and symbolic execution within a composition of ranged analyses increases the performance of the weaker performing analysis SYMBEXEC drastically, but slightly decreases the performance of the better performing predicate analysis. Again, LB3 is a good choice for splitting.

7 Related Work

Numerous approaches combine different verification techniques. Selective combinations [6,40,45,51,72,83,92] consider certain features of a task to choose the best approach for that task. Nesting approaches [3,4,25,26,30,32,49,82,84] use one or more approaches as components in a main approach. Interleaved approaches [1,2,5,10,42,50,55,58,62,68,75,78,90,97] alternate between different approaches that may or may not exchange information. Testification approaches [28,29,39,43,52,74,81] often sequentially combine a verification and a validation approach and prioritize or only report confirmed proofs and alarms. Sequential portfolio approaches [44,61] run distinct, independent analyses in sequence while parallel portfolio approaches [91,12,57,65,66,96] execute various, independent analyses in parallel. Parallel white-box combinations [7,9,37,38,54,56,59,79] run different approaches in parallel, which exchange information for the purpose of collaboration. Next, we discuss cooperation approaches that split the search space as we do.

A common strategy for dividing the search space in sequential or interleaved combinations is to restrict the subsequent verifiers to the yet uncovered search space, e.g., not yet covered test goals [12], open proof obligations [67], or yet unexplored program paths [8,10,19,31,33,41,42,47,53,71]. Some parallel combinations like CoDiDroid [80], distributed assertion checking [93], or the compositional tester sketched in conditional testing [12] decompose the verification statically into separate subtasks. Furthermore, some techniques split the search space to run different instances of the same analysis in parallel on different parts of the program. For example, conditional static analysis [85] characterizes paths based on their executed program branches and uses sets of program branches to describe the split. Concurrent bounded model checking techniques [69,77] split paths based on their thread interleavings. Yan et al. [95] dynamically split the input space if the abstract interpreter returns an inconclusive result and analyses the input partitions separately with the abstract interpreter. To realize parallel test-case generation, Korat [76] considers different input ranges in distinct parallel instances. Parallel symbolic execution approaches [82,86,87,88,89,94] and ranged model checking [48] split execution paths, thereby often partitioning the execution tree. The set of paths are characterized by input constraints [89], path prefixes [87,88], or ranges [82,86,94,48] and are either created statically from an initial shallow symbolic execution [87,88,89] or tests [82,86,94] or dynamically based on the already explored symbolic execution tree [27,34,82,86,98]. While we reuse the idea of splitting the program paths into ranges [82,86,94,48], we generalize the idea of ranged symbolic execution [82,86,94] to arbitrary analyses and in particular allow to combine different analyses. Furthermore, we introduce a new static splitting strategy along loop bounds.

8   Conclusion

Ranged symbolic execution scales symbolic execution by having several analysis instances ran on different ranges in parallel. In this paper, we have generalized this idea to arbitrary analyses by introducing and formalizing the notion of a *composition of ranged analyses*. We have moreover proposed and implemented a novel splitting component based on loop bounds. Our evaluation shows that a composition of ranged analyses can in particular increase the number of solved tasks. It furthermore demonstrates the superiority of the novel splitting strategy. As future work we see the incorporation of information sharing between analysis running in parallel.

Data Availability Statement. All experimental data and our open source implementation are archived and available in our supplementary artefact [60].

References

1. Albarghouthi, A., Gurfinkel, A., Chechik, M.: From under-approximations to over-approximations and back. In: Proc. TACAS. pp. 157–172. LNCS 7214, Springer (2012). https://doi.org/10.1007/978-3-642-28756-5_12

2. Avgerinos, T., Rebert, A., Cha, S.K., Brumley, D.: Enhancing symbolic execution with veritesting. In: Proc. ICSE. pp. 1083–1094. ACM (2014), https://doi.org/10.1145/2568225.2568293

3. Baars, A.I., Harman, M., Hassoun, Y., Lakhotia, K., McMinn, P., Tonella, P., Vos, T.E.J.: Symbolic search-based testing. In: Proc. ASE. pp. 53–62. IEEE (2011). https://doi.org/10.1109/ASE.2011.6100119

4. Baluda, M.: EvoSE: Evolutionary symbolic execution. In: Proc. A-TEST. pp. 16–19. ACM (2015), https://doi.org/10.1145/2804322.2804325

5. Beckman, N., Nori, A.V., Rajamani, S.K., Simmons, R.J.: Proofs from tests. In: Proc. ISSTA. pp. 3–14. ACM (2008). https://doi.org/10.1145/1390630.1390634

6. Beyer, D., Dangl, M.: Strategy selection for software verification based on boolean features: A simple but effective approach. In: Proc. ISoLA. pp. 144–159. LNCS 11245, Springer (2018). https://doi.org/10.1007/978-3-030-03421-4_11

7. Beyer, D., Dangl, M., Wendler, P.: Boosting k-induction with continuously-refined invariants. In: Proc. CAV. pp. 622–640. LNCS 9206, Springer (2015). https://doi.org/10.1007/978-3-319-21690-4_42

8. Beyer, D., Henzinger, T.A., Keremoglu, M.E., Wendler, P.: Conditional model checking: A technique to pass information between verifiers. In: Proc. FSE. ACM (2012). https://doi.org/10.1145/2393596.2303664

9. Beyer, D., Henzinger, T.A., Théoduloz, G.: Program analysis with dynamic precision adjustment. In: Proc. ASE. pp. 29–38. IEEE (2008). https://doi.org/10.1109/ASE.2008.13

10. Beyer, D., Jakobs, M.: CoVeriTest: Cooperative verifier-based testing. In: Proc. FASE. pp. 389–408. LNCS 11424, Springer (2019). https://doi.org/10.1007/978-3-030-16722-6_23

11. Beyer, D., Jakobs, M., Lemberger, T., Wehrheim, H.: Reducer-based construction of conditional verifiers. In: Proc. ICSE. pp. 1182–1193. ACM (2018), https://doi.org/10.1145/3180155.3180259

12. Beyer, D., Lemberger, T.: Conditional testing: Off-the-shelf combination of test-case generators. In: Proc. ATVA. pp. 189–208. LNCS 11781, Springer (2019). https://doi.org/10.1007/978-3-030-31784-3_11

13. Beyer, D.: Progress on software verification: SV-COMP 2022. In: TACAS. Lecture Notes in Computer Science, vol. 13244, pp. 375–402. Springer (2022). https://doi.org/10.1007/978-3-030-99527-0_20

14. Beyer, D., Dangl, M., Dietsch, D., Heizmann, M.: Correctness witnesses: exchanging verification results between verifiers. In: Proc. FSE. pp. 326–337. ACM (2016), https://doi.org/10.1145/2950290.2950351

15. Beyer, D., Dangl, M., Wendler, P.: A unifying view on SMT-based software verification. J. Autom. Reasoning 60(3), 299–335 (2018), https://doi.org/10.1007/s10817-017-9432-6

16. Beyer, D., Haltermann, J., Lemberger, T., Wehrheim, H.: Decomposing software verification into off-the-shelf components: An application to CEGAR. In: Proc. ICSE. ACM (2022). https://doi.org/10.1145/3510003.351006

17. Beyer, D., Henzinger, T.A., Théoduloz, G.: Configurable software verification: Concretizing the convergence of model checking and program analysis. In:

Proc. CAV. pp. 504–518. LNCS 4590, Springer (2007). https://doi.org/10.1007/978-3-540-73368-3_51

18. Beyer, D., Henzinger, T.A., Théoduloz, G.: Program analysis with dynamic precision adjustment. In: Proc. (ASE. pp. 29–38. IEEE (2008). https://doi.org/10.1109/ASE.2008.13

19. Beyer, D., Jakobs, M., Lemberger, T., Wehrheim, H.: Reducer-based construction of conditional verifiers. In: Proc. ICSE. pp. 1182–1193. ACM (2018). https://doi.org/10.1145/3180155.3180259

20. Beyer, D., Kanav, S.: Coveriteam: On-demand composition of cooperative verification systems. In: Proc. TACAS. LNCS, vol. 13243, pp. 561–579. Springer (2022). https://doi.org/10.1007/978-3-030-99524-9_31

21. Beyer, D., Keremoglu, M.E.: CPACHECKER: A tool for configurable software verification. In: Proc. CAV. pp. 184–190. LNCS 6806, Springer (2011), https://doi.org/10.1007/978-3-642-22110-1_16

22. Beyer, D., Keremoglu, M.E., Wendler, P.: Predicate abstraction with adjustable-block encoding. In: Proc. FMCAD. pp. 189–197. IEEE (2010), https://ieeexplore.ieee.org/document/5770949/

23. Beyer, D., Löwe, S., Wendler, P.: Reliable benchmarking: requirements and solutions. Int. J. Softw. Tools Technol. Transf. **21**(1), 1–29 (2019). https://doi.org/10.1007/s10009-017-0469-y

24. Beyer, D., Wehrheim, H.: Verification Artifacts in Cooperative Verification: Survey and Unifying Component Framework. In: Proc. ISoLA. LNCS, vol. 12476, pp. 143–167. Springer (2020). https://doi.org/10.1007/978-3-030-61362-4_8

25. Boldo, S., Filliâtre, J., Melquiond, G.: Combining coq and gappa for certifying floating-point programs. In: Proc. MKM. pp. 59–74. LNCS 5625, Springer (2009), https://doi.org/10.1007/978-3-642-02614-0_10

26. Braione, P., Denaro, G., Mattavelli, A., Pezzè, M.: Combining symbolic execution and search-based testing for programs with complex heap inputs. In: Proc. ISSTA. pp. 90–101. ACM (2017), https://doi.org/10.1145/3092703.3092715

27. Bucur, S., Ureche, V., Zamfir, C., Candea, G.: Parallel symbolic execution for automated real-world software testing. In: Proc. EuroSys. pp. 183–198. ACM (2011), https://doi.org/10.1145/1966445.1966463

28. Chebaro, O., Kosmatov, N., Giorgetti, A., Julliand, J.: Program slicing enhances a verification technique combining static and dynamic analysis. In: Proc. SAC. pp. 1284–1291. ACM (2012). https://doi.org/10.1145/2245276.2231980

29. Chen, T., Heo, K., Raghothaman, M.: Boosting static analysis accuracy with instrumented test executions. In: Proc. FSE. pp. 1154–1165. ACM (2021), https://doi.org/10.1145/3468264.3468626

30. Chowdhury, A.B., Medicherla, R.K., Venkatesh, R.: Verifuzz: Program aware fuzzing - (competition contribution). In: Proc. TACAS, part 3. pp. 244–249. LNCS 11429, Springer (2019). https://doi.org/10.1007/978-3-030-17502-3_22

31. Christakis, M., Müller, P., Wüstholz, V.: Guiding dynamic symbolic execution toward unverified program executions. In: Proc. ICSE. pp. 144–155. ACM (2016). https://doi.org/10.1145/2884781.2884843

32. Christakis, M., Eniser, H.F., Hermanns, H., Hoffmann, J., Kothari, Y., Li, J., Navas, J.A., Wüstholz, V.: Automated safety verification of programs invoking neural networks. In: Proc. CAV. pp. 201–224. LNCS 12759, Springer (2021), https://doi.org/10.1007/978-3-030-81685-8_9

33. Christakis, M., Müller, P., Wüstholz, V.: Collaborative verification and testing with explicit assumptions. In: Proc. FM. LNCS, vol. 7436, pp. 132–146. Springer (2012). https://doi.org/10.1007/978-3-642-32759-9_13

34. Ciortea, L., Zamfir, C., Bucur, S., Chipounov, V., Candea, G.: Cloud9: A software testing service. OSR **43**(4), 5–10 (2009), https://doi.org/10.1145/1713254.1713257
35. Clarke, E.M., Grumberg, O., Jha, S., Lu, Y., Veith, H.: Counterexample-guided abstraction refinement. In: Proc. CAV. pp. 154–169. LNCS 1855, Springer (2000), https://doi.org/10.1007/10722167_15
36. SV-Benchmarks Community: SV-Benchmarks (2022), https://gitlab.com/sosy-lab/benchmarking/sv-benchmarks/-/tree/svcomp22
37. Cousot, P., Cousot, R.: Systematic design of program-analysis frameworks. In: Proc. POPL. pp. 269–282. ACM (1979). https://doi.org/10.1145/567752.567778
38. Cousot, P., Cousot, R., Feret, J., Mauborgne, L., Miné, A., Monniaux, D., Rival, X.: Combination of abstractions in the ASTRÉE static analyzer. In: Proc. ASIAN'06. pp. 272–300. LNCS 4435, Springer (2008). https://doi.org/10.1007/978-3-540-77505-8_23
39. Csallner, C., Smaragdakis, Y.: Check 'n' crash: Combining static checking and testing. In: Proc. ICSE. pp. 422–431. ACM (2005). https://doi.org/10.1145/1062455.1062533
40. Czech, M., Hüllermeier, E., Jakobs, M., Wehrheim, H.: Predicting rankings of software verification tools. In: Proc. SWAN. pp. 23–26. ACM (2017). https://doi.org/10.1145/3121257.3121262
41. Czech, M., Jakobs, M., Wehrheim, H.: Just test what you cannot verify! In: Proc. FASE. LNCS, vol. 9033, pp. 100–114. Springer (2015). https://doi.org/10.1007/978-3-662-46675-9_7
42. Daca, P., Gupta, A., Henzinger, T.A.: Abstraction-driven concolic testing. In: Proc. VMCAI. pp. 328–347. LNCS 9583, Springer (2016). https://doi.org/10.1007/978-3-662-49122-5_16
43. Dams, D., Namjoshi, K.S.: Orion: High-precision methods for static error analysis of C and C++ programs. In: Proc. FMCO. pp. 138–160. LNCS 4111, Springer (2005). https://doi.org/10.1007/11804192_7
44. Dangl, M., Löwe, S., Wendler, P.: Cpachecker with support for recursive programs and floating-point arithmetic - (competition contribution). In: Proc. TACS. pp. 423–425. LNCS 9035, Springer (2015), https://doi.org/10.1007/978-3-662-46681-0_34
45. Demyanova, Y., Pani, T., Veith, H., Zuleger, F.: Empirical software metrics for benchmarking of verification tools. In: Proc. CAV. pp. 561–579. LNCS 9206, Springer (2015). https://doi.org/10.1007/978-3-319-21690-4_39
46. Dijkstra, E.W., Scholten, C.S.: Predicate Calculus and Program Semantics. Texts and Monographs in Computer Science, Springer (1990). https://doi.org/10.1007/978-1-4612-3228-5
47. Ferles, K., Wüstholz, V., Christakis, M., Dillig, I.: Failure-directed program trimming. In: Proc. ESEC/FSE. pp. 174–185. ACM (2017), http://doi.acm.org/10.1145/3106237.3106249
48. Funes, D., Siddiqui, J.H., Khurshid, S.: Ranged model checking. ACM SIGSOFT Softw. Eng. Notes **37**(6), 1–5 (2012), https://doi.org/10.1145/2382756.2382799
49. Galeotti, J.P., Fraser, G., Arcuri, A.: Improving search-based test suite generation with dynamic symbolic execution. In: Proc. ISSRE. pp. 360–369. IEEE (2013), https://doi.org/10.1109/ISSRE.2013.6698889
50. Gao, M., He, L., Majumdar, R., Wang, Z.: LLSPLAT: improving concolic testing by bounded model checking. In: Proc. SCAM. pp. 127–136. IEEE (2016), https://doi.org/10.1109/SCAM.2016.26

51. Gargantini, A., Vavassori, P.: Using decision trees to aid algorithm selection in combinatorial interaction tests generation. In: Proc. ICST. pp. 1–10. IEEE (2015), https://doi.org/10.1109/ICSTW.2015.7107442

52. Ge, X., Taneja, K., Xie, T., Tillmann, N.: Dyta: Dynamic symbolic execution guided with static verification results. In: Proc. ICSE. pp. 992–994. ACM (2011). https://doi.org/10.1145/1985793.1985971

53. Gerrard, M.J., Dwyer, M.B.: ALPACA: a large portfolio-based alternating conditional analysis. In: Proc. ICSE. pp. 35–38. IEEE / ACM (2019), https://doi.org/10.1109/ICSE-Companion.2019.00032

54. Godefroid, P., Klarlund, N., Sen, K.: DART: Directed automated random testing. In: Proc. PLDI. pp. 213–223. ACM (2005), https://doi.org/10.1145/1065010.1065036

55. Godefroid, P., Nori, A.V., Rajamani, S.K., Tetali, S.: Compositional may-must program analysis: Unleashing the power of alternation. In: Proc. POPL. pp. 43–56. ACM (2010). https://doi.org/10.1145/1706299.1706307, http://doi.acm.org/10.1145/1706299.1706307

56. Godefroid, P., Levin, M.Y., Molnar, D.A.: Automated whitebox fuzz testing. In: Proc. NDSS. The Internet Society (2008), http://www.isoc.org/isoc/conferences/ndss/08/papers/10_automated_whitebox_fuzz.pdf

57. Groce, A., Zhang, C., Eide, E., Chen, Y., Regehr, J.: Swarm testing. In: Proc. ISSTA. pp. 78–88. ACM (2012), https://doi.org/10.1145/2338965.2336763

58. Gulavani, B.S., Henzinger, T.A., Kannan, Y., Nori, A.V., Rajamani, S.K.: SYNERGY: A new algorithm for property checking. In: Proc. FSE. pp. 117–127. ACM (2006). https://doi.org/10.1145/1181775.1181790

59. Haltermann, J., Wehrheim, H.: CoVEGI: Cooperative Verification via Externally Generated Invariants. In: Proc. FASE. pp. 108–129. LNCS 12649, Springer (2021), https://doi.org/10.1007/978-3-030-71500-7_6

60. Haltermann, J., Jakobs, M., Richter, C., Wehrheim, H.: Replication package for article 'Parallel Program Analysis via Range Splitting' (Jan 2023). https://doi.org/10.5281/zenodo.7189816

61. Heizmann, M., Chen, Y., Dietsch, D., Greitschus, M., Hoenicke, J., Li, Y., Nutz, A., Musa, B., Schilling, C., Schindler, T., Podelski, A.: Ultimate automizer and the search for perfect interpolants - (competition contribution). In: Proc. TACAS. pp. 447–451. LNCS 10806, Springer (2018), https://doi.org/10.1007/978-3-319-89963-3_30

62. Helm, D., Kübler, F., Reif, M., Eichberg, M., Mezini, M.: Modular collaborative program analysis in OPAL. In: Proc. FSE. pp. 184–196. ACM (2020), https://doi.org/10.1145/3368089.3409765

63. Henzinger, T.A., Jhala, R., Majumdar, R., McMillan, K.L.: Abstractions from proofs. In: Proc. POPL. pp. 232–244. ACM (2004), https://doi.org/10.1145/964001.964021

64. Henzinger, T.A., Jhala, R., Majumdar, R., Sutre, G.: Lazy abstraction. In: Proc. POPL. pp. 58–70. ACM (2002), https://doi.org/10.1145/503272.503279

65. Holík, L., Kotoun, M., Peringer, P., Soková, V., Trtík, M., Vojnar, T.: Predator shape analysis tool suite. In: Proc. HVC. pp. 202–209. LNCS 10028 (2016), https://doi.org/10.1007/978-3-319-49052-6_13

66. Holzmann, G.J., Joshi, R., Groce, A.: Swarm verification. In: Proc. ASE. pp. 1–6. IEEE (2008). https://doi.org/10.1109/ASE.2008.9

67. Huster, S., Ströbele, J., Ruf, J., Kropf, T., Rosenstiel, W.: Using robustness testing to handle incomplete verification results when combining verification and testing

techniques. In: Proc. ICTSS. pp. 54–70. LNCS 10533, Springer (2017), https://doi.org/10.1007/978-3-319-67549-7_4

68. Inkumsah, K., Xie, T.: Improving structural testing of object-oriented programs via integrating evolutionary testing and symbolic execution. In: Proc. ASE. pp. 297–306. IEEE (2008), https://doi.org/10.1109/ASE.2008.40

69. Inverso, O., Trubiani, C.: Parallel and distributed bounded model checking of multi-threaded programs. In: Proc. PPoPP. pp. 202–216. ACM (2020), https://doi.org/10.1145/3332466.3374529

70. Jakobs, M.: $PART_{PW}$: From partial analysis results to a proof witness. In: Proc. SEFM. pp. 120–135. LNCS 10469, Springer (2017), https://doi.org/10.1007/978-3-319-66197-1_8

71. Jalote, P., Vangala, V., Singh, T., Jain, P.: Program partitioning: A framework for combining static and dynamic analysis. In: Proc. WODA. pp. 11–16. ACM (2006). https://doi.org/10.1145/1138912.1138916, http://doi.acm.org/10.1145/1138912.1138916

72. Jia, Y., Cohen, M.B., Harman, M., Petke, J.: Learning combinatorial interaction test generation strategies using hyperheuristic search. In: Proc. ICSE. pp. 540–550. IEEE (2015), https://doi.org/10.1109/ICSE.2015.71

73. King, J.C.: Symbolic execution and program testing. Commun. ACM **19**(7), 385–394 (1976), https://doi.org/10.1145/360248.360252

74. Li, K., Reichenbach, C., Csallner, C., Smaragdakis, Y.: Residual investigation: Predictive and precise bug detection. In: Proc. ISSTA. pp. 298–308. ACM (2012). https://doi.org/10.1145/2338965.2336789

75. Majumdar, R., Sen, K.: Hybrid concolic testing. In: Proc. ICSE. pp. 416–426. IEEE (2007), https://doi.org/10.1109/ICSE.2007.41

76. Misailovic, S., Milicevic, A., Petrovic, N., Khurshid, S., Marinov, D.: Parallel test generation and execution with Korat. In: Proc. ESEC/FSE. pp. 135–144. ACM (2007), https://doi.org/10.1145/1287624.1287645

77. Nguyen, T.L., Schrammel, P., Fischer, B., La Torre, S., Parlato, G.: Parallel bug-finding in concurrent programs via reduced interleaving instances. In: Proc. ASE. pp. 753–764. IEEE (2017). https://doi.org/10.1109/ASE.2017.8115686

78. Noller, Y., Kersten, R., Pasareanu, C.S.: Badger: Complexity analysis with fuzzing and symbolic execution. In: Proc. ISSTA. pp. 322–332. ACM (2018), http://doi.acm.org/10.1145/3213846.3213868

79. Noller, Y., Pasareanu, C.S., Böhme, M., Sun, Y., Nguyen, H.L., Grunske, L.: Hydiff: Hybrid differential software analysis. In: Proc. ICSE. pp. 1273–1285. ACM (2020), https://doi.org/10.1145/3377811.3380363

80. Pauck, F., Wehrheim, H.: Together strong: Cooperative android app analysis. In: Proc. ESEC/FSE. pp. 374–384. ACM (2019), https://doi.org/10.1145/3338906.3338915

81. Post, H., Sinz, C., Kaiser, A., Gorges, T.: Reducing false positives by combining abstract interpretation and bounded model checking. In: Proc. ASE. pp. 188–197. IEEE (2008). https://doi.org/10.1109/ASE.2008.29

82. Qiu, R., Khurshid, S., Pasareanu, C.S., Wen, J., Yang, G.: Using test ranges to improve symbolic execution. In: Proc. NFM. pp. 416–434. LNCS 10811, Springer (2018), https://doi.org/10.1007/978-3-319-77935-5_28

83. Richter, C., Hüllermeier, E., Jakobs, M., Wehrheim, H.: Algorithm selection for software validation based on graph kernels. JASE **27**(1), 153–186 (2020), https://doi.org/10.1007/s10515-020-00270-x

84. Sakti, A., Guéhéneuc, Y., Pesant, G.: Boosting search based testing by using constraint based testing. In: Proc. SSBSE. pp. 213–227. LNCS 7515, Springer (2012). https://doi.org/10.1007/978-3-642-33119-0_16

85. Sherman, E., Dwyer, M.B.: Structurally defined conditional data-flow static analysis. In: Proc. TACAS. pp. 249–265. LNCS 10806, Springer (2018), https://doi.org/10.1007/978-3-319-89963-3_15

86. Siddiqui, J.H., Khurshid, S.: Scaling symbolic execution using ranged analysis. In: Proc. SPLASH. pp. 523–536. ACM (2012), https://doi.org/10.1145/2384616.2384654

87. Singh, S., Khurshid, S.: Parallel chopped symbolic execution. In: Proc. ICFEM. pp. 107–125. LNCS 12531, Springer (2020), https://doi.org/10.1007/978-3-030-63406-3_7

88. Singh, S., Khurshid, S.: Distributed symbolic execution using test-depth partitioning. CoRR **abs/2106.02179** (2021), https://arxiv.org/abs/2106.02179

89. Staats, M., Pasareanu, S.S.: Parallel symbolic execution for structural test generation. In: Proc. ISSTA. pp. 183–194. ACM (2010), https://doi.org/10.1145/1831708.1831732

90. Stephens, N., Grosen, J., Salls, C., Dutcher, A., Wang, R., Corbetta, J., Shoshitaishvili, Y., Kruegel, C., Vigna, G.: Driller: Augmenting fuzzing through selective symbolic execution. In: Proc. NDSS. The Internet Society (2016), http://wp.internetsociety.org/ndss/wp-content/uploads/sites/25/2017/09/driller-augmenting-fuzzing-through-selective-symbolic-execution.pdf

91. Tschannen, J., Furia, C.A., Nordio, M., Meyer, B.: Usable verification of object-oriented programs by combining static and dynamic techniques. In: Proc. SEFM. pp. 382–398. LNCS 7041, Springer (2011), https://doi.org/10.1007/978-3-642-24690-6_26

92. Tulsian, V., Kanade, A., Kumar, R., Lal, A., Nori, A.V.: MUX: Algorithm selection for software model checkers. In: Proc. MSR. p. 132–141. ACM (2014), https://doi.org/10.1145/2597073.2597080

93. Yang, G., Do, Q.C.D., Wen, J.: Distributed assertion checking using symbolic execution. ACM SIGSOFT Softw. Eng. Notes **40**(6), 1–5 (2015), https://doi.org/10.1145/2830719.2830729

94. Yang, G., Qiu, R., Khurshid, S., Pasareanu, C.S., Wen, J.: A synergistic approach to improving symbolic execution using test ranges. Innov. Syst. Softw. Eng. **15**(3-4), 325–342 (2019). https://doi.org/10.1007/s11334-019-00331-9

95. Yin, B., Chen, L., Liu, J., Wang, J., Cousot, P.: Verifying numerical programs via iterative abstract testing. In: Proc. SAS. pp. 247–267. LNCS 11822, Springer (2019), https://doi.org/10.1007/978-3-030-32304-2_13

96. Yin, L., Dong, W., Liu, W., Wang, J.: Parallel refinement for multi-threaded program verification. In: Proc. ICSE. pp. 643–653. IEEE (2019), https://doi.org/10.1109/ICSE.2019.00074

97. Yorsh, G., Ball, T., Sagiv, M.: Testing, abstraction, theorem proving: Better together! In: Proc. ISSTA. pp. 145–156. ACM (2006). https://doi.org/http://doi.acm.org/10.1145/1146238.1146255

98. Zhou, L., Gan, S., Qin, X., Han, W.: Secloud: Binary analyzing using symbolic execution in the cloud. In: Proc. CBD. pp. 58–63. IEEE (2013), https://doi.org/10.1109/CBD.2013.31

Runtime Enforcement Using Knowledge Bases

Eduard Kamburjan[1]($\boxtimes$) and Crystal Chang Din[2]

[1] University of Oslo, Oslo, Norway
eduard@ifi.uio.no
[2] University of Bergen, Bergen, Norway
crystal.din@uib.no

Abstract. Knowledge bases have been extensively used to represent and reason about *static* domain knowledge. In this work, we show how to enforce domain knowledge about *dynamic processes* to guide executions at runtime. To do so, we map the execution trace to a knowledge base and require that this mapped knowledge base is always consistent with the domain knowledge. This means that we treat the *consistency* with domain knowledge as an invariant of the execution trace. This way, the domain knowledge guides the execution by determining the next possible steps, i.e., by exploring which steps are possible and rejecting those resulting in an inconsistent knowledge base. Using this invariant directly at runtime can be computationally heavy, as it requires to check the consistency of a large logical theory. Thus, we provide a transformation that generates a system which is able to perform the check only on the *past* events up to now, by evaluating a smaller formula. This transformation is transparent to domain users, who can interact with the transformed system in terms of the domain knowledge, e.g., to query computation results. Furthermore, we discuss different mapping strategies.

1 Introduction

Knowledge bases (KBs) are logic-based representations of both data and domain knowledge, for which there exists a rich toolset to query data and reason about data *semantically*, i.e., in terms of the domain knowledge. This enables domain users to interact with modern IT systems [39] without being exposed to implementation details, as well as to make their domain knowledge available for software applications. KBs are the foundation of many modern innovation drivers and key technologies: Applications range from Digital Twin engineering [31], over industry standards in robotics [23] to expert systems, e.g., in medicine [38].

The success story of KBs, however, is so far based on the use of domain knowledge about *static* data. The connection to transition systems and programs beyond Prolog-style logic programming has just begun to be explored. This is mainly triggered by tool support for developing applications that *use* KBs [7,13,28], in a type-safe way [29,32].

In this work, we investigate how one can use domain knowledge about dynamic processes and formalize knowledge about the order of computations to be performed. More concretely, we describe a runtime enforcement technique to use domain knowledge to *guide* the selection of rules in a transition system, for

L. Lambers and S. Uchitel (Eds.): FASE 2023, LNCS 13991, pp. 220–240, 2023.
https://doi.org/10.1007/978-3-031-30826-0_12

example to simulate behavior with respect to domain knowledge, a scenario that we use as a guiding example in this article, or to enforce compliance of business process models with respect to restrictions arising from the domain [41].

Approach. At the core, our approach considers the *execution trace* of a run, i.e., the sequence of rule applications, as a KB itself. As such, it can be combined with the KB that expresses the domain knowledge of *dynamic processes* (DKDP). The DKDP expresses knowledge about (partial) executions such that the execution trace must be consistent with it before and after every rule application. For example, in a simulation system for geology, the DKDP may express that a certain rock layer A is above a certain rock layer B and, thus, the event to deposit a layer must occur for B, before it occurs for A. Consistency with the DKDP forms a *domain invariant* for the trace of a system, i.e., a *trace property*.

To trigger a transition rule, we use a hypothetical execution step: the execution trace is extended with a potential event and the consistency of the extended trace against the DKDP is checked. However using this consistency invariant directly at run time can be computationally heavy, as it requires to check the consistency of a large logical theory. Thus, we give a transformation that removes the need for a hypothetical execution step and instead results in a transition system that evaluates a transformed condition on (1) the *existing* trace and (2) the parameters of the potentially extended event. This condition does not require domain-specific reasoning anymore. This transformation removes the need for hypothetical execution steps and DKDP can be used to guide *any* transition system, including languages based on structural operational semantics. For example, it is then possible to express the invariant checking as a guard for the rule that deposits layers (e.g., only deposit A if layer B has been deposited already).

It is crucial that this system is usable for both the domain user (who possesses the domain knowledge) and the programmer (that has to program the interaction with the domain knowledge), a requirement explicitly stressed by Corea et al. [16] for the use of ontologies in business process models. We, thus, carefully designed our framework to increase its usability: First, the reasoning (in the geology example above, from spatial properties of layers to temporal properties of events) is completely performed in the domain and needs not be handled by the transition system. I.e., the programmer must not perform reasoning over the KB in the program itself. Second, the DKDP is expressed over *domain events*, as the domain users do not have knowledge about implementation details, such as the state organization. Furthermore, the formalization of the DKDP should not be affected by the underlying implementation details such that the DKDP can be reused. The DKDP can reuse the aforementioned industry standards and established ontologies, as well as modeling languages and techniques from ontology engineering [17], such as OWL [42], which are established for domain modeling and more suitable for this task than correctness-focused temporal logics such as LTL [35]: The domain users must not be an expert in programming or verification to contribute to the system.

The transformation that replaces the need for a hypothetical execution step with a transition system evaluating a transformed condition is also transparent to the domain users. We say a transformed guarded rule is applicable if it would not violate consistency w.r.t. the DKDP. Lastly, we provide the domain users possibilities to query the final result, i.e., the KB of the final execution trace, and to explore possible simulations using the defined DKDP. Note that the mapping from trace to KB must not necessarily be designed manually: various (semi-) automatic mapping design strategies are discussed in the paper.

Contributions and Structure. Our main contributions are (1) a system that enforces domain knowledge to guide a transition system at runtime, and (2) a procedure that transforms such a transition system that uses consistency with domain knowledge as an invariant into a transition system using first-order guards over past events in a transparent way. We give preliminaries in Sec. 2 and present our running example in Sec. 3. We formalize our approach in Sec. 4 and give the transformation in Sec. 5, before we discuss (semi-)automatically generated mappings in Sec. 6. We discuss the mappings in Sec. 7 and related work in Sec. 8. Lastly, Sec. 9 concludes.

2   Preliminaries

We give some technical preliminaries for knowledge bases as well as transition systems, as far as they are needed for our runtime enforcement technique.

Definition 1 (Domain Knowledge of Dynamic Processes). Domain knowledge of dynamic processes *(DKDP) is the knowledge about events and changes.*

Example 1 (DKDP in Geology). DKDP describes knowledge about some temporal properties in a domain. In geology, for example, this may be the knowledge that a deposition of some geological layers in Cretaceous should happen after a deposition in Jurassic, because the Cretaceous is after the Jurassic. This can be deduced from, e.g., fossils found in the layers.

A description logic (DL) is a decidable fragment of first-order logic with suitable expressive power for knowledge representation [3]. We do not commit to any specific DL here, but require that for the chosen DL it is decidable to check consistency of a KB, which we define next. A knowledge base is a collection of DL axioms, over individuals (corresponding to first-order logic constants), *concepts*, also called classes (corresponding to first-order logic unary predicates) and *roles*, also called properties (corresponding to first-order logic binary predicates).

Definition 2 (Knowledge Base). *A knowledge base (KB) $\mathcal{K} = (\mathcal{R}, \mathcal{T}, \mathcal{A})$ is a triple of three sets of DL axioms, where the ABox $\mathcal{A}$ contains assertions over individuals, the TBox $\mathcal{T}$ contains axioms over concepts, and the RBox $\mathcal{R}$ contains axioms over roles. A KB is consistent if no contradiction follows from it.*

KBs can be seen as first-order logic theories, so we refrain from introducing them fully formally and introduce them by examples throughout the article. The Manchester syntax [25] is used for DL formulas in examples to emphasize that they model knowledge, but we treat them as first-order logic formulas otherwise.

Example 2. Continuing Exp. 1, the following axiom, expressing that Jurassic is before Cretaceous, is expressed by the following ABox axiom, where `Jurassic` and `Cretaceous` are individuals, while `before` is a role.

before(Jurassic, Cretaceous)

The following TBox axioms express that every layer with Stegosaurus fossils has been deposited during the Jurassic. The first two axioms define the concepts `StegoLayer` (the class of things having the value `Stegosaurus` as their `contains` role) and `JurassicLayer` (the class of things having the value `Jurassic` as their `during` role). The last axiom says that the class of things having the value `Stegosaurus` as their `contains` role is a subclass of `JurassicLayer`. [3] The bold literals are keywords, the literals `StegoLayer`, `JurassicLayer` denote concepts/classes, the literals `contains`, `during` denote roles/properties and the literals `Stegosaurus`, `Jurassic` denote individuals.

> StegoLayer **EquivalentTo** contains **value** Stegosaurus
> JurassicLayer **EquivalentTo** during **value** Jurassic
> StegoLayer **SubClassOf** JurassicLayer

The following RBox axioms express two constraints: The first line states that both `below` and `before` roles are asymmetric. The second line states that if a deposition is from an age before the age of another deposition, then it is below that deposition. Formally, the axiom expresses that the concatenation of the following three roles (a) the `during` role, (b) the `before` role, and (c) the inverse of the `during` role, is the sub-property of the `below` role. I.e., given an individual a, every individual b reachable from a following the chain `during`, `before` and the inverse of `during`, is also reachable by just `below`.

> **Asy**(below)   **Asy**(before)
> during **o** before **o** **inverse**(during) **SubPropertyOf** below

Knowledge based guiding can be applied to any transition system to leverage domain knowledge during execution. States are not the focus of our work, and neither is the exact form of the rules that specify the transition between states. For our purposes, it suffices to define states as terms, i.e., finite trees where each node is labeled with a name from a finite set of term symbols, and transition rules as transformations between schematic terms. State guards can be added but are omitted for brevity's sake.

Definition 3 (Terms and Substitutions). *Let Σ_T be a finite set of term labels and Σ_V a disjoint set of term variables. A term t is a finite tree, where each inner node is a term label and each leaf is either a term label or a term variable. The set of term variables in a term t is denoted $\Sigma(t)$. We denote the set of all terms with T. A substitution σ is a map from term variables to terms without term variables. The application of a substitution σ to a term t, with the usual semantics, is denoted $t\sigma$. In particular, if t contains no term variables, then $t\sigma = t$.*

---

[3] The first-order equivalent is $\forall x.\ \text{contains}(x, \text{Stegosaurus}) \rightarrow \text{during}(x, \text{Jurassic})$

Rewrite rules map one term to another by unifying a subterm with the head term. The matched subterm is then rewritten by applying the substitution to the body term. Normally one would have additional conditions on the transition rules, but these are not necessary to present semantical guiding.

Definition 4 (Term Rewriting Systems). *A transition rule in the term rewriting system has the form*

$$t_{\text{head}} \xrightarrow{r} t_{\text{body}}$$

Where r *is the name of the rule, and* $t_{\text{head}}, t_{\text{body}} \in T$ *are the head and body terms.*

A rule matches on a term t with $\Sigma(t) = \emptyset$, *if there is a subterm* t_s *of* t, *such that* $t_{\text{head}} = t_s\sigma$, *for a suitable substitution* σ. *A rule produces a term* t', *by matching on subterm* t_s *with substitution* σ, *and generating* t' *by replacing* t_s *in* t *by* $t_s\sigma'$, *where* σ' *is equal to* σ *for all* $v \in \Sigma(t_{\text{body}}) \cap \Sigma(t_{\text{head}})$ *and maps* $v \in \Sigma(t_{\text{head}}) \setminus \Sigma(t_{\text{body}})$ *to fresh term symbols. For production, we write*

$$t \xrightarrow{r,\sigma'} t'$$

3 A Scenario for Knowledge Based Guiding

To illustrate our approach, we continue with geology, namely with a simulator for deposition and erosion of geological layers. Such a simulator is used, e.g., for hydrocarbon exploration [20]. It contains domain knowledge about the type of fossils and the corresponding geological age, and connects spatial information about deposition layers with temporal information about their deposition. We started a formalization of the DKDP in Ex. 2 and expand it below.

The core challenge is that the simulator must make sure that it does not violate domain properties. This means that it cannot deposit a layer containing fossils from the Jurassic after depositing a layer containing fossils from the Cretaceous. This information is given by the domain users as an *invariant*, i.e., as knowledge that the execution must be consistent with at all times.

Programming with Knowledge Bases. Our model of computation is a set of rewrite rules on some transition structure. The sequence of rule applications, denoted *events*, forms the trace. DKDP constrains the extension of the trace. This realizes a clear separation of concerns between *declarative* data modelling and *imperative* programming with, in our case, transitions.

Example 3. Let us assume 4 rules: a rule `deposit` that deposits a layer without fossils, a rule `depositStego` that deposits a layer with Stegosaurus fossils, an analogous rule `depositTRex` that deposits a layer with Tyrannosaurus fossils, and a rule `erode` that removes the top layer of the deposition. One example reduction sequence, for some terms t_i and with substitutions omitted, is as follows:

$$t_0 \xrightarrow{\text{depositStego}} t_1 \xrightarrow{\text{erode}} t_2 \xrightarrow{\text{depositTRex}} t_3$$

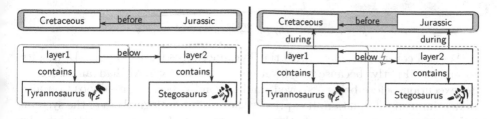

Fig. 1. Left: KB as generated. Right: Inferred KB to detect inconsistency.

which describes the rule application of `depositStego` on term t_0 following by the rule application of `erode` on term t_1 and then `depositTRex` on term t_2.

In the domain KB, we add an axiom expressing that the geological layer containing Stegosaurus fossils is deposited during the Jurassic, and that the geological layer containing Tyrannosaurus fossils is deposited during the Cretaceous.

Consider that rule `depositStego` may trigger on term t_3.

$$\ldots t_2 \xrightarrow{\text{depositTRex}} t_3 \xrightarrow[?]{\text{depositStego}}$$

This would violate the domain knowledge, as we can derive a situation, where a layer with Tyrannosaurus fossils is below a layer with Stegosaurus fossils, implying that the Cretaceous is before the Jurassic. This contradiction is captured by the knowledge base in Fig. 1. The domain knowledge DKDP should prevent this rule application at t_3 to happen. To achieve this, i.e., enforce domain knowledge at runtime, we must connect the trace with the KB. Specifically, we represent the trace as a KB itself, i.e., instead of operating on a KB, we record the events and generate a KB from a trace using a mapping.

For example, consider the left KB in Fig. 1. The upper part is (a part of) our DKDP about geological ages, while the lower part is the KB mapped from the trace. Together they form a KB. In the knowledge base of this example, we add one layer that contains Stegosaurus fossils for each `depositStego` event and analogously for `depositTRex` events. We also add the `below` relation between two layers, if their events are ordered. So, if we would execute `depositStego` after `depositTRex`, there would be two layers in the KB as shown in Fig. 1, with corresponding fossils, connected using the `below` relation. On the right, the KB is shown with the additional knowledge following from its axioms. In particular, we can deduce that layer2 must be below layer1 using the axioms from Sec. 2. This, in turn, makes the overall KB inconsistent, as `below` must be asymmetric.

We stress that consistency of the execution with the DKDP is a trace property, it is reasoning about the events that happen regardless of the current state. In our example, consider the situation, where the next event after t_3 rule `erode` triggers again, and then we consider rule `depositStego`. I.e., the following continuation of the trace

$$\dots t_2 \xrightarrow{\text{depositTRex}} t_3 \xrightarrow{\text{erode}} t_4 \xrightarrow[?]{\text{depositStego}}$$

We still consider the layer with the Tyrannosaurus fossils in our KB, despite its erosion. Firstly, because the layer may potentially have had an effect on the execution before being removed, and, secondly, because its deposition also models implicit information. It expresses the current geological era of the system, which cannot be reverted: at t_3 the system is in the Cretaceous, and while the depositStego models an action in the Jurassic – the trace would not represent a semantically sensible execution if the depositStego rule would be executed.

Fig. 2 illustrates the runtime enforcement of domain knowledge on traces in a more general setting. The execution itself is a reduction sequence over some terms t, where each rule application emits some event ev, e.g., name of the applied rule and matched subterms. A *mapping* μ is used to generate a KB from the trace. The knowledge base then contains (a) the DKDP, pictured as the shaded box, (b) the mapping of the trace so far, pictured as the unshaded box with solid frame, and (c) the potential next event, pictured as the dashed box. Additionally, new connections may be inferred.

The mapping from a trace to a KB matches the system formalized by the domain knowledge to the system used for *programming*, it is the interface between domain experts and the programmer. Indeed, the mapping allows the domain users to investigate program executions without being exposed to the implementation details. Given a fixed execution, the mapping can be applied to allow the domain users to query its results (in form of the trace) using domain vocabulary.

From the program's point of view, it defines an invariant over the trace, which must always hold: consistency with domain knowledge. While this saves the domain users from learning about the implementation, it poses two challenges to the programmer: first, the mapping must be developed additionally to the rules, and second, the invariant is not specific to the rules. The *extended* trace caused by the execution of one single event, must be checked against the full DKDP, which is not specific to any transition event. Instead of this computationally costly operation, we provide an alternative. For example, to ensure consistency when executing the rule depositStego, it suffices to evaluate the following formula on the *past* trace tr to check that depositTRex has not been executed yet: $\forall i \leq |tr|. \ tr[i] \neq \text{ev}(\text{depositTRex})$. The condition of a rule is specific to the corresponding transition action, instead of a general condition on all the rules.

After defining runtime enforcement of domain knowledge formally, we will return to these challenges and (a) discuss different mapping strategies, and especially the (semi-)automatic generation of mappings and (b) give a system that, for a big class of mappings, also derives local conditions.

4   Knowledge Guided Transition Systems

We now introduce runtime enforcement using KBs. To this end, we define the mapping of traces to KBs formally and give the transition system that uses this lifting for consistency checking. First, we define the notion of traces.

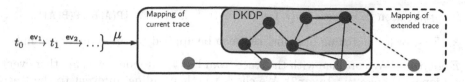

Fig. 2. Runtime enforcement of knowledge bases on traces.

Definition 5 (Execution Traces). *An* event *ev for a rule r and a substitution σ has the form $ev(r, \sigma)$, which we write as $ev(r, v_1 : t_1, \ldots, v_n : t_n)$, where $v_i : t_i$ are the pairs in σ. To record the sequence of an execution, we use* traces. *A* trace *is a finite sequence of events, where each event records the applied rule and the corresponding substitutions, if there are any.*

Example 4. The trace of the rule application in Ex. 3 is as follows, for suitable substitutions that all store the deposited or eroded layer in the variable v.

$$\Big\langle \text{ev}(\text{depositStego}, v : \text{layer0}), \text{ev}(\text{erode}, v : \text{layer0}), \text{ev}(\text{depositTRex}, v : \text{layer1}) \Big\rangle$$

To connect executions with knowledge bases, we define mappings that transform traces into knowledge bases, given a fixed vocabulary Σ.

Definition 6 (Mappings). *A Σ-mapping μ is a function from traces to knowledge bases over vocabulary Σ.*

The mapping is given by the user, who has to respect the signature of the KB formalizing the used domain knowledge. While we are not specific in the structure of the mapping in general, we introduce the notion of a *first-order matching mapping*, which allow for optimization and automatization.

Definition 7 (First-Order Matching Mapping). *A first-order matching mapping μ is defined by a set $\{\varphi_1 \mapsto_{N_1} ax_1, \ldots, \varphi_n \mapsto_{N_n} ax_n\}$, where each element has a first-order logic formula φ_i as its guard, a set of individuals N_i and some set ax_i of KB axioms as its body. We write $ax_i(N)$ to emphasize that a set of individuals N occur in $ax_i(N)$.*

The mapping is applied to a trace tr by adding all those bodies whose guard evaluates to true and replacing all members of N in ax_1 by fresh individual names:

$$\mu(tr) = \left(\bigcup_{tr \models \varphi_i} ax_i(N) \right) [N \text{ fresh}]$$

Where $A[N \text{ fresh}]$ substitutes all individuals in N with fresh names in A.

Example 5. Consider the following first-order matching mapping μ, for some role/property P and individuals A, B and C. The function $\text{rule}(ev)$ extracts the rule name from the given event ev.

$$\{\exists i.\ \text{rule}(tr[i]) \doteq r_1 \mapsto_\emptyset P(A, B), \quad \exists i.\ \text{rule}(tr[i]) \doteq r_2 \mapsto_\emptyset P(B, A),$$
$$\exists i.\ \text{rule}(tr[i]) \doteq r_3 \mapsto_\emptyset P(A, C), \quad \exists i.\ \text{rule}(tr[i]) \doteq r_4 \mapsto_\emptyset P(C, A)\}$$

Its application to a trace $\langle \mathsf{ev}(r_1), \mathsf{ev}(r_1), \mathsf{ev}(r_2) \rangle$ is the set $\{P(A, B), P(B, A)\}$.

First-order matching mapping can also be applied to our running example.

Example 6. We continue with the trace from Ex. 4, extended with another event $\mathsf{ev}(\mathsf{depositStego}, v : \mathsf{layer2})$. We check whether adding an event to the trace would result in a consistent KB by actually extending the trace for analysis. We call this a hypothetical execution step.

The following mapping, which must be provided by the user adds the spatial information about layers w.r.t. the fossils found within. The first-order logic formula at the guard of the mapping expresses that an event of $\mathsf{depositTRex}$ is found before the event of $\mathsf{depositStego}$ in the trace. Note that the given set of axioms from the mapping faithfully describes the *event structure of the trace*, i.e., the mapping could produce axioms which will cause inconsistency w.r.t. the domain knowledge: Together with the DKDP, we can see that the trace is mapped to an inconsistent knowledge base by adding 5 axioms. Note that we do not generate one layer for each deposition event during simulation, but only two specific ones, $\mathsf{Layer}(l_1)$ and $\mathsf{Layer}(l_2)$ in this case, for the relevant information. One can extend mapping rules for the different cases (for instance, $\mathsf{depositStego}$ before $\mathsf{depositTRex}$, only $\mathsf{depositTRex}$ events, etc.), or use a different mapping mechanism, which we discuss further in Sec. 6.

$$\exists l_1, l_2. \ \exists i_1, i_2.$$
$$tr[i_1] \doteq \mathsf{ev}(\mathsf{depositTRex}, v : l_1) \wedge tr[i_2] \doteq \mathsf{ev}(\mathsf{depositStego}, v : l_2) \wedge i_1 < i_2$$
$$\mapsto_{l_1, l_2}$$
$$\{\mathsf{Layer}(l_1), \mathsf{contains}(l_1, \mathsf{Tyrannosaurus}),$$
$$\mathsf{Layer}(l_2), \mathsf{contains}(l_2, \mathsf{Stegosaurus}), \mathsf{below}(l_1, l_2)\}$$

We stress again that we are interested in trace properties, a layer may still have had effects on the state despite being completely removed at one point (by an **erode** event). Thus, we must consider the *deposition event* of a layer to check the trace against the domain knowledge.

The guided transition systems extends the mapping of a basic transition system, by additionally ensuring that the trace *after* executing the rule would be mapped to a consistent knowledge base. This treats the domain knowledge as an invariant that is enforced, i.e., a transition is only allowed if it indeed preserves the invariant.

Definition 8 (Guided Transition System). *Given a set of rules $\mathcal{R}$, a mapping μ and a knowledge base $\mathcal{K}$, the guided semantics is defined as a transition system between pairs of terms t and traces tr. For each rule $r \in \mathcal{R}$, we have one guided rule (for consistency, cf. Def. 2):*

$$\mathbf{(kb)} \ \frac{t \xrightarrow{r,\sigma} t' \qquad ev = \mathsf{ev}(r, \sigma) \qquad \mu(tr \circ ev) \cup \mathcal{K} \text{ is consistent}}{(t, tr) \xrightarrow{r} (t', tr \circ ev)}$$

The set of traces generated by a rewrite system $\mathcal{R}$ from a starting term t_0 is denoted $\mathbf{H}(\mathcal{R}, \mu, \mathcal{K}, t_0)$. Execution always starts with the empty trace.

5   Well-Formedness and Optimization

The transition rule in Def. 8 uses the knowledge base directly to check consistency, and while this enables to integrate domain knowledge into the system directly, it also poses challenges from a practical point of view. First, the condition of the rule application is not specific to the change of the trace, and must check the consistency of the whole knowledge base, which can be computationally heavy. Second, the consistency check is performed at every step, for every potential rule application. Third, the trace must be mapped whenever it is extended. Which means the same mapping computation that has been performed in the previous step may be executed all over again.

To overcome these challenges, we provide a system that reduces consistency checking by using *well-formedness* guards, which only require to evaluate an expression over the trace without accessing the knowledge base. These guards are transparent to the domain users, the system behaves the same as with the consistency checks of the knowledge base. At its core, we use well-formedness predicates, which characterize the relation of domain knowledge and mappings.

Definition 9 (Well-Formedness). *A first-order predicate wf of a trace tr is a well-formedness predicate for some mapping μ and some knowledge base $\mathcal{K}$, if the following holds:*

$$\forall tr. \; wf(tr) \iff \mu(tr) \cup \mathcal{K} \text{ is consistent}$$

Using this definition we can slightly rewrite the rule of Def. 8: For every starting term t_0, the set of generated traces is the same if the rule of Def. 8 is replaced by the following one

$$(\text{wf}) \; \frac{t \xrightarrow{r,\sigma} t' \quad ev = \mathsf{ev}(r,\sigma) \quad wf(tr \circ ev)}{(t, tr) \xrightarrow{r} (t', tr \circ ev)}$$

For first-order matching mappings, we can generate the well-formedness predicate by testing all possible extensions of the knowledge base upfront and defining the guards of those sets that are causing inconsistency as non-well-formed.

Theorem 1. *Let μ be a first-order matching mapping for some knowledge base $\mathcal{K}$. Let $\mathrm{Ax} = \{ax_1, \ldots, ax_n\}$ be the set of all bodies in μ. Let Incons be the set of all subsets of Ax, such that for each $A \in \mathrm{Incons}$, $\bigcup_{a \in A} a \cup \mathcal{K}$ is inconsistent. Let guard_A be the set of guards corresponding to each body in A. The following predicate wf_μ is a well-formedness predicate for μ and $\mathcal{K}$.*

$$wf_\mu = \neg \bigvee_{A \in \mathrm{Incons}} \bigwedge_{\varphi \in \mathrm{guard}_A} \varphi$$

Example 7. We continue with Ex. 5. Consider a knowledge base $\mathcal{K}$ expressing that role P is asymmetric. The knowledge base becomes inconsistent if the first two or the last two axioms from μ are added to the knowledge base. Thus, the generated well-formedness predicate *wf* is the following

$$wf_\mu(tr) \equiv \neg\Big(\big((\exists i.\ \mathsf{rule}(tr[i]) \doteq \mathsf{r}_1) \wedge (\exists i.\ \mathsf{rule}(tr[i]) \doteq \mathsf{r}_2)\big)\vee$$
$$\big((\exists i.\ \mathsf{rule}(tr[i]) \doteq \mathsf{r}_3) \wedge (\exists i.\ \mathsf{rule}(tr[i]) \doteq \mathsf{r}_4)\big)\Big)$$

The above procedure has exponential complexity in the number of branches of the mapping. But as the superset of an inconsistent set is also inconsistent, it is not necessary to generate all the subsets. I.e., it suffices to consider the following set of minimal inconsistencies instead, which can be computed by testing for inconsistencies based on the sets ordered by $\subset$.

$$\mathtt{min\text{-}Incons} = \{A \mid A \in \mathtt{Incons} \wedge \forall A' \in \mathtt{Incons}.\ A' \neq A \rightarrow A' \not\subset A\}$$

If well-formedness is defined inductively, then we can give an even more specific transformation. The well-formedness predicate is inductive, if it checks well-formedness for each trace and its last event is equivalent to the evaluation of a formula over the trace, which is *specific* to the event. If this is the case, then each rule, which dictates the event, can have an own, highly specialized well-formedness guard, which further enhances efficiency.

Definition 10 (Inductive Well-Formedness). *A well-formedness predicate wf is* inductive [4] *for some set of rules $\mathcal{R}$ if there is a set of predicates wf_r for all rules $r \in \mathcal{R}$, such that wf can be written as an inductive definition:*

$$wf(\langle\rangle) \equiv \mathsf{true}$$
$$wf(tr \circ ev) \equiv wf(tr) \wedge \bigwedge_{r \in \mathcal{R}} \big((\mathsf{rule}(ev) \doteq r) \rightarrow wf_r(tr, ev)\big)$$

in which $wf_r(tr, ev)$ is the local well-formedness predicate specifically for rule r with the condition $\mathsf{rule}(ev) \doteq r$. The predicate wf_r forms the guard for rule r. Every well-formedness predicate is equivalent to an inductive well-formedness predicate by setting $wf_r(tr, ev) = wf(tr \circ ev)$, but we aim to give more specific predicates per rule.

Example 8. Finishing our geological system, we can give local well-formedness predicates for all rules. For example, we can define a specific guard for rule `depositStego` expressing that the deposition of a layer containing Stegosaurus fossil is not allowed if there is already a deposition of a layer containing Tyrannosaurus fossils captured in the trace tr up to now. Compare with the approach that the whole knowledge base needs to be checked, this proposed solution using

---

[4] Our well-formedness predicates are inspired by the ones used in verification of concurrent systems, where they characterize traces w.r.t. a specific concurrency model [21].

inductive well-formedness simplifies the complexity of analysis significantly. For instance, the rule for deposition does not need to concern with the ordering of the geological age.

$$wf_{\text{deposit}}(tr, \text{ev}(\text{deposit}, v : l)) \equiv wf_{\text{erode}}(tr, \text{ev}(\text{erode}, v : l)) \equiv \text{true}$$

$$wf_{\text{depositTRex}}(tr, \text{ev}(\text{depositTRex}, v : l)) \equiv \text{true}$$

$$wf_{\text{depositStego}}(tr, \text{ev}(\text{depositStego}, v : l)) \equiv \forall i \leq |tr|. \text{ rule}(tr[i]) \neq \text{depositTRex}$$

Definition 11 (Transition System using Well-Formedness). *Let wf be an inductive well-formedness predicate for a set of rules $\mathcal{R}$, some mapping μ, some knowledge base $\mathcal{K}$. We define the transformed guarded transition system with the following rule for each $r \in \mathcal{R}$.*

$$(\textbf{wf-r}) \; \frac{t \xrightarrow{r,\sigma} t' \qquad ev = \text{ev}(r, \sigma) \qquad wf_r(tr, ev)}{(t, tr) \xrightarrow{r} (t', tr \circ ev)}$$

The set of traces generated by this transition system from a starting term t_0 is denoted $\mathbf{G}(\mathcal{R}, wf, t_0)$. Execution always starts with the empty trace.

Note that (a) we do use a specific well-formedness predicate per rule, and that (b) we do *not* extend the trace tr in the premise as the rules in Def. 8 and Def. 9.

Theorem 2. *Let wf be an inductive well-formedness predicate for a set of rules $\mathcal{R}$, some mapping μ, some knowledge base $\mathcal{K}$. The guided system of Def. 8 and Def. 11 generate the same traces: $\forall t. \; \mathbf{H}(\mathcal{R}, \mu, \mathcal{K}, t) = \mathbf{G}(\mathcal{R}, wf, t)$*

We can also define determinism as terms of the inductive well-formedness. An inductive well-formedness predicate wf is deterministic, if for each trace tr and event ev, only one possible local well-formedness predicate $wf_r(tr, ev)$ holds.

Proposition 1 (Deterministic Well-Formedness). *An inductive well-formedness predicate wf with local well-formedness predicates $\{wf_r\}_{r \in \mathcal{R}}$ is deterministic, if*

$$\forall tr. \; \forall ev. \bigwedge_{r \in \mathcal{R}} \left(wf_r(tr, ev) \rightarrow \bigwedge_{\substack{r' \in \mathcal{R} \\ r' \neq r}} \neg wf_{r'}(tr, ev) \right)$$

For deterministic predicates, only one trace is generated: $|\mathbf{G}(\mathcal{R}, wf, t)| = 1$.

When the programmer designs the mapping, the focus is on mapping enough information to achieve *inconsistency*, to ensure that certain transition steps are not performed. If the same mapping is to be used to retrieve results from the computation, e.g., to query over the final trace, this may be insufficient. Next, we discuss mappings that preserve more, or all information from the trace.

6   (Semi-)Automatically Generated Mappings

The mappings we discussed so far require to be defined completely by the programmer and are used to extract a certain correct information from a trace, which is sufficient to enforce domain invariants at runtime. In this section, we introduce mappings which can be constructed (semi-)automatically to simplify the usage of domain invariants: The *transducing mappings* and *direct mappings* leverage the structure of the trace directly. A *transducing mapping* is constructed semi-automatically. It applies some manually defined mapping to each event and automatically connects every pair of consecutive events in a trace using the **next** role in KB. A *direct mapping* relates each event with its parameters and is constructed fully automatically. Both kinds of mappings are not only easier to use for the programmer, they can also be used by the domain users to access the results of the computation in terms of the domain.

A transducing mapping is semi-automatic in the sense that part of the mapping is pre-defined, and the programmer must only define a part of it, namely the mapping from a single event to a KB.

Formally, a transducing mapping consists of a function ι that generates unique individual names[5] per event and a user-defined function ϵ that maps every event to a KB.

Definition 12 (Transducing Mapping). *Let ι an injective function from natural numbers to individuals, and ϵ be a function from events to KBs. Let* **next** *be an asymmetric role. Given a trace* tr, *a transducing mapping* $\delta_{\iota,\epsilon}^{\texttt{next}}(tr)$ *is defined as follows. For simplicity, we annotate the index i of an event in tr directly.*

$$\delta_{\iota,\epsilon}^{\texttt{next}}(\langle\rangle) = \emptyset \qquad\qquad \delta_{\iota,\epsilon}^{\texttt{next}}(\langle\mathsf{ev}_i\rangle) = \epsilon(\mathsf{ev}_i)$$

$$\delta_{\iota,\epsilon}^{\texttt{next}}(\langle\mathsf{ev}_i,\mathsf{ev}_j\rangle \circ tr) = \epsilon(\mathsf{ev}_i) \cup \{\texttt{next}(\iota(i),\iota(j))\} \cup \delta_{\iota,\epsilon}^{\texttt{next}}(\langle\mathsf{ev}_j\rangle \circ tr)$$

in which the $\circ$ operator concatenates two traces. This approach is less demanding than to design an arbitrary mapping, as the structure of the sequence between each pair of consecutive events is taken care of by the **next** role and ι is trivial in most cases: one can just generate a fresh node with the number as part of its individual symbol. The programmer only has to provide a function ϵ for events.

Example 9. Our geology example can be reformulated with the following user-defined function ϵ_{geo}. Let ι_{geo} map every natural number i to the symbol layer_i:

$$\epsilon_{geo}(\mathsf{ev}_i(\mathsf{depositStego}, v\!:\!l)) = \{\texttt{contains}(\iota_{geo}(i),\mathsf{Stegosaurus}),\mathsf{Layer}(\iota_{geo}(i))\}$$

$$\epsilon_{geo}(\mathsf{ev}_i(\mathsf{depositTRex}, v\!:\!l)) = \{\texttt{contains}(\iota_{geo}(i),\mathsf{Tyrannosaurus}),\mathsf{Layer}(\iota_{geo}(i))\}$$

$$\epsilon_{geo}(\mathsf{ev}_i(\mathsf{deposit}, v\!:\!l)) = \{\texttt{contains}(\iota_{geo}(i),\mathsf{Nothing}),\mathsf{Layer}(\iota_{geo}(i))\}$$

$$\epsilon_{geo}(\mathsf{ev}_i(\mathsf{erode})) = \emptyset$$

Note that the function $\iota_{geo}(i)$ is used to generate new symbols for each event, which are then declared to be geological layers by the axiom $\mathsf{Layer}(\iota_{geo}(i))$. It

---

[5] If using the Resource Description Framework (RDF) [43] for the knowledge base, one requires fresh unique resource identifiers (URI).

generalizes the set of fresh names from first-order matching mappings in Def. 7. Based on this function definition, the example in Sec. 3 can be performed using the transducing mapping $\delta^{below}_{\iota_{geo}, \epsilon_{geo}}$. The connections between each pair of consecutive events in a trace, i.e., a layer is below another layer, is derived from the axioms in the domain knowledge and is added as additional axioms to the KB.

So far, the mappings of the trace to some information in terms of a specific domain are defined by the programmer. To further enhance the automation of the mapping construction, we give a *direct* mapping, that captures *all* information of a trace in a KB. More technically, the *direct* mapping directly expresses the trace structure using a special vocabulary, which captures domain knowledge about traces *themselves* and is independent from any application domain. We first define the domain knowledge about trace structure.

Definition 13 (Knowledge Base for Traces). *The knowledge base for traces contains the concept* Event *modeling events, the concept* Match *modeling one pair of variable and its matching terms, and the concept* Term *for terms. Furthermore, the functional property* appliesRule *connects events to rule names (as strings), the property* match *that connects the individuals for events with the individuals for matches (i.e., an event with the pairs $v : t$ of a variable and the term assigned to this variable), the property* var *that connects matches and variables (as strings), and* term *that connects matches and terms.*

We remind that KBs only support binary predicates and we cannot avoid formalizing the concept of a match, which connects three parts: event, variable and term. The direct mapping lessens the workload for the programmer further: it requires no additional input and can be done fully automatically. It is a predefined mapping for *all programs* and is defined by instantiating a transducing mapping using the **next** role and pre-defined functions ϵ_{direct} and ι_{direct} for ϵ and ι. Also, we must generate additional fresh individuals for the matches. The formal definition of the pre-defined functions for the direct mapping is as follows.

Definition 14 (Direct Mapping). *The direct mapping is defined as a transducing mapping $\delta^{next}_{\iota_{direct}, \epsilon_{direct}}$, where the function ι_{direct} maps every natural number i to an individual* ei. *The individuals* matchi_j *uniquely identify a match inside a trace for the jth variable of the ith event, and we regard variables as strings containing their names. Function ϵ_{direct} is defined as follows:*

$\epsilon_{direct}(ev_i(r, v_1 : t_1, \ldots, v_n, t_n)) =$

$\{$Event$(\iota_{direct}(i)),$ appliesRule$(\iota_{direct}(i), r)\} \cup$

$\bigcup_{j \leq n} (\{$match$(\iota_{direct}(i), $matchi_j$),$ var$($matchi_j$, v_j),$ term$($matchi_j$, \eta(t_j)\} \cup \delta(t_j))$

where $\delta(t_j)$ deterministically generates the axioms for the tree structure of the term t_j according to Def. 3 and $\eta(t_j)$ returns the individual of the head of t_j.

The properties match, var and term connect each event with its parameters. For example, the match v : layer0 of the first event in Ex. 4, generates

$$\texttt{match(e1, match0\_1), var(match0\_1, ``v"), term(match0\_1, layer0)}$$

where e1 is the representation of the event and match0_1 is the representation of the match in the KB. The complete direct mapping is given in the following example.

Example 10. The direct mapping of Ex. 4 is as follows. We apply the ϵ_{direct} function to all three events, where each event has one parameter.

$$\big\{\texttt{Event(e1), Event(e2), Event(e3), Next(e1, e2), Next(e2, e3), appliesRule(e1, ``depositStego"),}$$
$$\texttt{appliesRule(e2, ``erode"), appliesRule(e3, ``depositTRex"), match(e1, m1), var(m1, ``v"),}$$
$$\texttt{term(m1, layer0), match(e2, m2), var(m2, ``v"), term(m2, layer0), match(e3, m3),}$$
$$\texttt{var(m3, ``v"), term(m3, layer1)}\big\}$$

7 Discussion

Querying and Stability. The mapping can be used by the domain users to interact with the system. For one, it can be used to retrieve the result of the computation using the vocabulary of a domain. For example, the following SPARQL [44] query retrieves all depositions generated during the Jurassic:

```
SELECT ?l WHERE {?l a Layer. ?l during Jurassic}
```

Indeed, one of the main advantages of knowledge bases is that they enable ontology-based data access [46]: uniform data access in terms of a given domain. Another possibility is to use *justifications* [5]. Justifications are minimal sets of axioms responsible for entailments over a knowledge base, e.g., to find out why it is inconsistent. They are able to explain, during an interaction, why certain steps are not possible.

The programmers do not need to design a complete knowledge base – for many domains knowledge bases are available, for example in form of industrial standards [26,23]. For more specific knowledge bases, clear design principles based on experiences in ontology engineering are available [17]. Note that these KBs are stable and do rarely change. Our system requires a static domain knowledge, as changes in the DKDP can invalidate traces during execution without executing a rule, which is, thus, not a limitation if one uses stable ontologies.

The direct mapping uses a fixed vocabulary, but one can formulate the connection to the domain knowledge by using additional axioms. In Ex. 10, one can declare every event to be a layer. The axiom for depositStego is as follows.

appliesRule value "depositStego" SubClassOf contains value Stegosaurus

The exact mapping strategy is application-specific – for example, to remove information erode must be handled through additional axioms as well, for example by adding a special concept RemovedLayer that is defined as all layers that

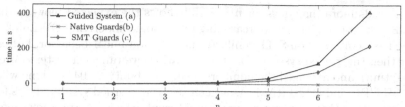

Fig. 3. Runtime comparison.

are matched on by some `erode` event. We next discuss some of the considerations when choosing the style of mapping, and the limitations of each.

There are, thus, two styles to connect trace and domain knowledge: One can add axioms connecting the vocabulary of traces with the vocabulary of the DKDP (direct mapping), or one can translate the trace into the vocabulary of the DKDP (first-order matching mapping, transducing mappings).

The two styles require different skills from the programmer to interact with the domain knowledge: The first style requires to express a trace as part of the domain as a set of ABox axioms, while the second one requires to connect *general* traces to the domain using TBox axioms. Thus, the second style operates on a higher level of abstraction and we conjuncture that such mappings may require more interaction with the domain expert and a deeper knowledge about knowledge graphs. However, the same insights needed to define the TBox axioms, are also needed to define the guards of a first-order matching mapping.

Naming Schemes. The transducing mappings and the first-order matching mapping have different naming schemes. A transducing mapping, and thus, a direct mapping, generate a new name *per event*, while the first-order matching mapping generates a fixed number of new names *per rule*: A transducing mapping can extract quite extensive knowledge from a trace, with the direct mapping giving a complete representation of it in a KB. As discussed, this requires the user to define general axioms. A first-order matching mapping must work with less names, and extract less knowledge from a trace. Its design requires to choose the right amount of abstraction to detect inconsistencies.

Evaluation. To evaluate whether the proposed system indeed gives a performance increase, we have implemented the running example[6] as follows: The system generates all traces up to length n, using three different transition systems: (a) The guided system (Def. 8) using the transducing mapping of Ex. 9. For reasoning, we use the Apache Jena framework [2]. (b) The guarded system (Def. 11) that uses a native implementation of the well-formedness predicate, and (c) the guarded system that uses the Z3 SMT solver [18] to check the first-order logic guards. The results are shown in Fig. 3. As we can see, the native implementation of the guarded systems is near instant for $n \leq 7$, while the guided

---

[6] https://github.com/Edkamb/KnowEnforce We slightly modified the example and replaced the asymmetry axioms by an equivalent formalization to fit the example into the fragment supported by the Jena OWL reasoner.

system needs more than 409s for $n = 7$ and shows the expected blow-up due to the N2ExpTime-completeness of reasoning in the logic underlying OWL [30]. The guarded system based on SMT similarly shows a non-linear behavior, but scales better then the guided system. For the evaluation, we ran each system for every n three times and averaged the numbers, using a Ubuntu 21.04 machine with an i7-8565U CPU and 32GB RAM. As we can see, the guarded system allows for an implementation that does not rely on an external, general-purpose reasoners to evaluate the guards and increases the scalability of the system, while the guided system does not scale even for small system and KBs.

8 Related Work

Runtime enforcement is a vast research field, for a recent overview we refer to the work of Falcone and Pinisetty [22], and give the related work for combinations of ontologies/knowledge bases and transitions systems in the following.

Concerning the combination of ontologies/knowledge bases and business process modeling, Corea et al. [16] point out that current approaches lack the foundation to annotate and develop ontologies together with business process rules. Our approach focuses explicitly on automating the mapping, or support developers in its development in a specific context, thus satisfying requirement 1 and 7 in their gap analysis for ontology-based business process modelling. Note that most work in this domain uses ontologies for the process model itself, similar to the ontology we give in Def. 13 and Def. 13 (e.g., Rietzke et al. [36]) or the current state (e.g., Corea and Delfmann [15]), not the trace. We refer to the survey of Corea et al. for a detailed overview.

Compared with existing simulators of hydrocarbon exploration [20,47], which formalized the domain knowledge of geological processes directly in the transition rules, we propose a *general* framework to formalize the domain knowledge in a knowledge base which is independent from the term rewriting system. This clear separation of concerns makes it easier for domain users to use the knowledge base for simulation without having the ability to program.

Tight interactions between programming languages, or transition systems, beyond logical programming and knowledge bases have recently received increasing research attention. The focus of the work of Leinberger [29,32] is the type safety of loading RDF data from knowledge bases into programming languages. Kamburjan et al. [28] semantically lift *states* for operations on the KB representation of the state, but are not able to access the trace. In logic programming, a concurrent extension of Golog [33] is extended to verify CTL properties with description logic assertions by Zarrieß and Claßen [48].

Cauli at al. [12] use knowledge bases to reason about the security properties of deployment configuration in the cloud, a high level representation of the overall system. As for traces, Pattipati et al. [34] introduce a debugger for C programs that operates on logs, i.e., special Traces. Their system operates post-execution and cannot guide the system. Al Haider et al. [1] use a similar technique to investigate logged traces of a program.

In runtime verification, knowledge bases has been investigated by Baader and Lippmann [6] in $\mathcal{ALC}$-LTL, which uses the description logic $\mathcal{ALC}$ instead of propositional variables inside of LTL. An overview over further temporalizations of description logics can be found in the work of Baader et al. [4]. Runtime enforcement has been using to temporal properties over traces since its beginnings [37], but, as a recent survey by Falcone and Pinisetty [22] points out, mainly for security/safety or usage control of libraries. In contrast, our work requires the enforcement to do any meaningful computation and uses a different way to express constraints than prior work: consistency with knowledge bases.

DatalogMTL extends Datalog with MTL operators [9,45] to enable ontology-based data access about sequences using inference rules. The ontology is expressed in these rules, i.e., it is not declarative but an additional programming layer, which we deem unpractical for domain users from non-computing domains. DatalogMTL has been used for queries [10] but not for runtime enforcement.

Traces have been explored from a logical perspective mainly in the style of CTL*, TLA and similar temporal logics. More recently, interest in more expressive temporal properties over traces of programming languages for verification using more complex approaches has risen and led to symbolic traces [11,19], integration of LTL and dynamic logics for Java-like languages [8] and trace languages based on type systems [27]. These approaches have in common that they aim for more expressive power and are geared towards better usability for programmers and simple verification calculi. They are only used for verification, not at runtime, and do not connect to formalized domain knowledge.

The guided system can be seen as a meta-computation, as put forward by Clavel et al. [14] for rewrite logics, which do not discuss the use of *consistency* as a meta-computation and instead program such meta computations explicitly.

9 Conclusion

We present a framework to use domain knowledge about dynamic processes to guide the execution of generic transition systems through runtime enforcement. We give a transformation to use of rule specific guards instead of using the domain knowledge directly as a consistency invariant over knowledge bases. The transformation is transparent and the domain user can interact with the system without being aware of the transformation or implementation details. To reduce the working load on the programmer, we discuss semi-automatic design of mappings using transducing approaches and a pre-defined direct mapping. We also discuss further alternatives, such as additional axioms on the events, and the use of local well-formedness predicates for certain classes of mappings.

Future Work. We plan to investigate how our system can interact with knowledge base evolution [24], a more declarative approach for changes in knowledge bases, as well as other approaches to modeling sequences in knowledge bases [40].

Acknowledgements This work was supported by University of Bergen and Research Council of Norway via SIRIUS (237898) and PeTWIN (294600).

References

1. N. Al Haider, B. Gaudin, and J. Murphy. Execution trace exploration and analysis using ontologies. In *RV*, volume 7186 of *LNCS*, pages 412–426. Springer, 2011.
2. Apache Foundation. Apache jena. https://jena.apache.org/.
3. F. Baader, D. Calvanese, D. L. McGuinness, D. Nardi, and P. F. Patel-Schneider, editors. *The Description Logic Handbook: Theory, Implementation, and Applications*. Cambridge University Press, 2003.
4. F. Baader, S. Ghilardi, and C. Lutz. LTL over description logic axioms. *ACM Trans. Comput. Log.*, 13(3):21:1–21:32, 2012.
5. F. Baader and B. Hollunder. Embedding defaults into terminological knowledge representation formalisms. *J. Autom. Reason.*, 14(1):149–180, 1995.
6. F. Baader and M. Lippmann. Runtime verification using the temporal description logic ALC-LTL revisited. *J. Appl. Log.*, 12(4):584–613, 2014.
7. S. Baset and K. Stoffel. Object-oriented modeling with ontologies around: A survey of existing approaches. *Int. J. Softw. Eng. Knowl. Eng.*, 28(11-12):1775–1794, 2018.
8. B. Beckert and D. Bruns. Dynamic logic with trace semantics. In *CADE*, volume 7898 of *LNCS*, pages 315–329. Springer, 2013.
9. S. Brandt, E. G. Kalayci, R. Kontchakov, V. Ryzhikov, G. Xiao, and M. Zakharyaschev. Ontology-based data access with a horn fragment of metric temporal logic. In *AAAI*, pages 1070–1076. AAAI Press, 2017.
10. S. Brandt, E. G. Kalayci, V. Ryzhikov, G. Xiao, and M. Zakharyaschev. Querying log data with metric temporal logic. *J. Artif. Intell. Res.*, 62:829–877, 2018.
11. R. Bubel, C. C. Din, R. Hähnle, and K. Nakata. A dynamic logic with traces and coinduction. In *TABLEAUX*, volume 9323 of *LNCS*, pages 307–322. Springer, 2015.
12. C. Cauli, M. Li, N. Piterman, and O. Tkachuk. Pre-deployment security assessment for cloud services through semantic reasoning. In *CAV (1)*, volume 12759 of *LNCS*, pages 767–780. Springer, 2021.
13. K. L. Clark and F. G. McCabe. Ontology oriented programming in go! *Appl. Intell.*, 24(3):189–204, 2006.
14. M. Clavel, F. Durán, S. Eker, P. Lincoln, N. Martí-Oliet, J. Meseguer, and C. L. Talcott. Reflection, metalevel computation, and strategies. In *All About Maude*, volume 4350 of *LNCS*, pages 419–458. Springer, 2007.
15. C. Corea and P. Delfmann. Detecting compliance with business rules in ontology-based process modeling. In J. M. Leimeister and W. Brenner, editors, *Towards Thought Leadership in Digital Transformation: 13. Internationale Tagung Wirtschaftsinformatik, WI 2017, St.Gallen, Switzerland, February 12-15, 2017*, 2017.
16. C. Corea, M. Fellmann, and P. Delfmann. Ontology-based process modelling - will we live to see it? In A. K. Ghose, J. Horkoff, V. E. S. Souza, J. Parsons, and J. Evermann, editors, *Conceptual Modeling - 40th International Conference, ER 2021, Virtual Event, October 18-21, 2021, Proceedings*, volume 13011 of *Lecture Notes in Computer Science*, pages 36–46. Springer, 2021.
17. J. Davies, R. Studer, and P. Warren. *Semantic Web technologies: trends and research in ontology-based systems*. John Wiley & Sons, 2006.
18. L. M. de Moura and N. S. Bjørner. Z3: an efficient SMT solver. In *TACAS*, volume 4963 of *Lecture Notes in Computer Science*, pages 337–340. Springer, 2008.
19. C. C. Din, R. Hähnle, E. B. Johnsen, K. I. Pun, and S. L. T. Tarifa. Locally abstract, globally concrete semantics of concurrent programming languages. In *TABLEAUX*, volume 10501 of *LNCS*, pages 22–43. Springer, 2017.

20. C. C. Din, L. H. Karlsen, I. Pene, O. Stahl, I. C. Yu, and T. Østerlie. Geological multi-scenario reasoning. In *NIK*. Bibsys Open Journal Systems, Norway, 2019.
21. C. C. Din and O. Owe. Compositional reasoning about active objects with shared futures. *Formal Aspects Comput.*, 27(3):551–572, 2015.
22. Y. Falcone and S. Pinisetty. On the runtime enforcement of timed properties. In *RV*, volume 11757 of *LNCS*, pages 48–69. Springer, 2019.
23. S. R. Fiorini, J. Bermejo-Alonso, P. J. S. Gonçalves, E. P. de Freitas, A. O. Alarcos, J. I. Olszewska, E. Prestes, C. Schlenoff, S. V. Ragavan, S. A. Redfield, B. Spencer, and H. Li. A suite of ontologies for robotics and automation [industrial activities]. *IEEE Robotics Autom. Mag.*, 24(1):8–11, 2017.
24. G. Flouris, D. Manakanatas, H. Kondylakis, D. Plexousakis, and G. Antoniou. Ontology change: classification and survey. *Knowl. Eng. Rev.*, 23(2):117–152, 2008.
25. M. Horridge, N. Drummond, J. Goodwin, A. L. Rector, R. Stevens, and H. Wang. The manchester OWL syntax. In *OWLED*, volume 216 of *CEUR Workshop Proceedings*. CEUR-WS.org, 2006.
26. IEEE ORA WG. IEEE standard ontologies for robotics and automation. *IEEE Std 1872-2015*, pages 1–60, 2015.
27. E. Kamburjan. Behavioral program logic. In *TABLEAUX*, volume 11714 of *LNCS*, pages 391–408. Springer, 2019.
28. E. Kamburjan, V. N. Klungre, R. Schlatte, E. B. Johnsen, and M. Giese. Programming and debugging with semantically lifted states. In *ESWC*, volume 12731 of *LNCS*, pages 126–142. Springer, 2021.
29. E. Kamburjan and D. V. Kostylev. Type checking semantically lifted programs via query containment under entailment regimes. In *Description Logics*, volume 2954 of *CEUR Workshop Proceedings*. CEUR-WS.org, 2021.
30. Y. Kazakov. SRIQ and SROIQ are harder than SHOIQ. In *Description Logics*, volume 353 of *CEUR Workshop Proceedings*. CEUR-WS.org, 2008.
31. E. Kharlamov, F. Martín-Recuerda, B. Perry, D. Cameron, R. Fjellheim, and A. Waaler. Towards semantically enhanced digital twins. In *IEEE BigData*, pages 4189–4193. IEEE, 2018.
32. M. Leinberger. *Type-safe Programming for the Semantic Web*. PhD thesis, University of Koblenz and Landau, Germany, 2021.
33. H. J. Levesque, R. Reiter, Y. Lespérance, F. Lin, and R. B. Scherl. GOLOG: A logic programming language for dynamic domains. *J. Log. Program.*, 31(1-3):59–83, 1997.
34. D. K. Pattipati, R. Nasre, and S. K. Puligundla. BOLD: an ontology-based log debugger for C programs. *Autom. Softw. Eng.*, 29(1):2, 2022.
35. A. Pnueli. The temporal logic of programs. In *FOCS*, pages 46–57. IEEE Computer Society, 1977.
36. E. Rietzke, R. Bergmann, and N. Kuhn. ODD-BP - an ontology- and data-driven business process model. In R. Jäschke and M. Weidlich, editors, *Proceedings of the Conference on "Lernen, Wissen, Daten, Analysen", Berlin, Germany, September 30 - October 2, 2019*, volume 2454 of *CEUR Workshop Proceedings*, pages 310–321. CEUR-WS.org, 2019.
37. F. B. Schneider. Enforceable security policies. *ACM Trans. Inf. Syst. Secur.*, 3(1):30–50, 2000.
38. SNOMED International. Snomed ct. https://www.snomed.org/.
39. A. Soylu, E. Kharlamov, D. Zheleznyakov, E. Jiménez-Ruiz, M. Giese, M. G. Skjæveland, D. Hovland, R. Schlatte, S. Brandt, H. Lie, and I. Horrocks. Optiquevqs: A visual query system over ontologies for industry. *Semantic Web*, 9(5):627–660, 2018.

40. E. D. Valle, S. Ceri, F. van Harmelen, and D. Fensel. It's a streaming world! reasoning upon rapidly changing information. *IEEE Intell. Syst.*, 24(6), 2009.
41. W. M. P. van der Aalst. Business process management: A comprehensive survey. *ISRN Software Engineering*, 2013:507984, Feb 2013.
42. W3C, OWL Working Group. Web ontology language. https://www.w3.org/OWL.
43. W3C, RDF Working Group. Resource description framework. https://www.w3. org/RDF.
44. W3C, SPARQL Working Group. Sparql 1.1 query language. https://www.w3. org/TR/sparql11-query/.
45. P. A. Walega, B. C. Grau, M. Kaminski, and E. V. Kostylev. Datalogmtl: Computational complexity and expressive power. In *IJCAI*, pages 1886–1892. ijcai.org, 2019.
46. G. Xiao, D. Calvanese, R. Kontchakov, D. Lembo, A. Poggi, R. Rosati, and M. Zakharyaschev. Ontology-based data access: A survey. In J. Lang, editor, *IJCAI 2018*, pages 5511–5519. ijcai.org, 2018.
47. I. C. Yu, I. Pene, C. C. Din, L. H. Karlsen, C. M. Nguyen, O. Stahl, and A. Latif. *Subsurface Evaluation Through Multi-scenario Reasoning*, pages 325–355. Springer International Publishing, Cham, 2021.
48. B. Zarrieß and J. Claßen. Verification of knowledge-based programs over description logic actions. In *IJCAI*, pages 3278–3284. AAAI Press, 2015.

Specification and Validation of Normative Rules for Autonomous Agents

Sinem Getir Yaman(✉), Charlie Burholt, Maddie Jones, Radu Calinescu,
and Ana Cavalcanti

Department of Computer Science, University of York, York, UK
`sinem.getir.yaman@york.ac.uk`

Abstract. A growing range of applications use autonomous agents such
as AI and robotic systems to perform tasks deemed dangerous, tedious
or costly for humans. To truly succeed with these tasks, the autonomous
agents must perform them without violating the social, legal, ethical,
empathetic, and cultural (SLEEC) norms of their users and operators.
We introduce SLEECVAL, a tool for specification and validation of rules
that reflect these SLEEC norms. Our tool supports the specification
of SLEEC rules in a DSL [1] we co-defined with the help of ethicists,
lawyers and stakeholders from health and social care, and uses the CSP
refinement checker FDR4 to identify redundant and conflicting rules in
a SLEEC specification. We illustrate the use of SLEECVAL for two case
studies: an assistive dressing robot, and a firefighting drone.

1 Introduction

AI and autonomous robots are being adopted in applications from health and
social care, transportation, infrastructure maintenance. In these applications,
the autonomous agents are often required to perform *normative tasks* that raise
social, legal, ethical, empathetic, and cultural (SLEEC) concerns [2]. There is
widespread agreement that these concerns must be considered throughout the development of the agents [3,4], and numerous guidelines propose high-level principles that reflect them [5,6,7,8]. However, to follow these guidelines, the engineers
developing the control software of autonomous agents need methods and tools
that support formalisation, validation and verification of SLEEC requirements.

The SLEECVAL tool introduced in our paper addresses this need by enabling
the specification and validation of *SLEEC rules*, i.e., nonfunctional requirements
focusing on SLEEC principles. To best of our knowledge, our tool is novel in its
support for the formalisation and validation of normative rules for autonomous
agents, and represents a key step towards an automated framework for specifying, validating and verifying autonomous agent compliance with such rules.

SLEECVAL is implemented as an Eclipse extension, and supports the definition of SLEEC rules in a domain-specific language (DSL). Given a set of such
rules, the tool extracts their semantics in tock-CSP [9]—a discrete-time variant
of the CSP process algebra [10], and uses the CSP refinement checker FDR4 [11]
to detect conflicting and redundant rules, providing counterexamples when such

© The Author(s) 2023
L. Lambers and S. Uchitel (Eds.): FASE 2023, LNCS 13991, pp. 241–248, 2023.
https://doi.org/10.1007/978-3-031-30826-0_13

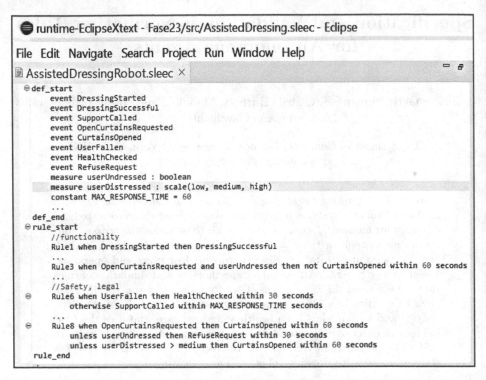

Fig. 1: Fragment of the SLEEC specification for an assistive dressing robot.

problems are identified. Our SLEECVAL tool and case studies, together with a description of its DSL syntax (BNF Grammar) and tock-CSP semantics are publicly available on our project webpage [12] and GitHub repository [13].

2   SLEECVAL: Notation, Components, and Architecture

SLEEC Rule Specification. As illustrated in Fig. 1, SLEEC DSL provides constructs for organising a SLEEC specification into a definition and a rule block. The definition block includes the declarations of events such as UserFallen, which corresponds to the detection of a user having fallen, and measures such as userDistressed, which becomes true when the user is distressed. Events and measures reflect the *capabilities* of the agent in perceiving and affecting its environment.

A SLEEC rule has the basic form 'when **trigger** then **response**'. The **trigger** defines an event whose occurrence indicates the need to satisfy the constraints defined in the **response**. For example, Rule1 applies when the event DressingStarted occurs. In addition, the **trigger** may include a Boolean expression over measures from the definition block. For instance, Rule3 applies when the event OpenCurtainsRequested occurs and, additionally, the Boolean measure userUndressed is true. The **response** defines requirements for that need to be satisfied when the triggers hold, and may include deadlines and timeouts.

```
//Conflicting Rules

RuleA when OpenCurtainsRequested then CurtainsOpened within 3 seconds

RuleB when OpenCurtainsRequested and userUndressed then not CurtainsOpened

//Redundant Rules

RuleC when DressingStarted then DressingFinished

RuleD when DressingStarted then DressingFinished within 2 minutes
```

(a) Example of conflicting and redundant rules written in SLEECVAL.

```
1      // CONFLICT CHECKING
2      SLEECRuleARuleB = timed_priority(intersectionRuleARuleB)
3      assert SLEECRuleARuleB:[deadlock-free]
4      // REDUNDANCY CHECKING
5      SLEECRuleCRuleD = timed_priority(intersectionRuleCRuleD)
6      assert not MSN::C3(SLEECRuleCRuleD) [T= MSN::C3(SLEECRuleD)
```

(b) Conflict and redundancy handling in CSP using FDR4.

Fig. 2: SLEECVAL conflict and redundancy checking.

The within construct specifies a deadline for the occurrence of a response. To accommodate situations where a response may not happen within its required time, the **otherwise** construct can be used to specify an alternative response. In Rule6, the response requires the occurrence of the event HealthChecked in 30 seconds, but provides an alternative to have SupportCalled if there is a timeout.

Importantly, a rule can be followed by one or more *defeaters* [14], introduced by the **unless** construct, and specifying circumstances that preempt the original response and provide an alternative. In Rule8, the first **unless** preempts the response if userUnderdressed is true, and a second defeater preempts both the response and the first defeater if the value of the measure userDistressed is 'high'.

SLEEC Rule Validation. SLEECVAL supports rule validation via conflict and redundancy checks. To illustrate the process, we consider the conflicting RuleA and RuleB from Fig. 2a, for the dressing robot presented above. Each rule is mapped to a tock-CSP process automatically generated by SLEECVAL. To define the checks, SLEECVAL computes the *alphabet* of each rule, i.e., the set of events and measures that the rule references, and examines each pair of rules.

For rule pairs with disjoint alphabets, there is no need to check consistency or redundancy. Otherwise (i.e., for rule pairs with overlapping alphabets), refinement assertions are generated as illustrated in Fig. 2b. Line 1 defines a tock-CSP process SLEECRuleARuleB that captures the intersection of the behaviours of the rules (in the example, RuleA and RuleB). The assertion in Line 3 is a deadlock check to reveal conflicts. If the assertion fails, there is a conflict between the two rules, and FDR4 provides a counterexample. For instance, the trace below is a counterexample that illustrates a conflict between RuleA and RuleB.

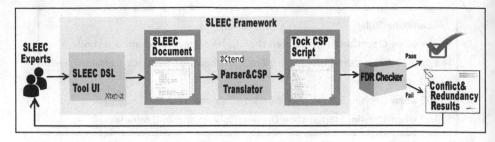

Fig. 3: SLEECVAL workflow.

$$OpenCurtainsRequested \rightarrow userUndressed.true \rightarrow tock \rightarrow tock \rightarrow tock$$

This trace shows a deadlock in a scenario in which *OpenCurtainsRequested* occurs, and the user is undressed, as indicated by the CSP event *userUndressed.true*. In these circumstances, RuleA imposes a deadline of 3 s for *CurtainsOpened* to occur, but RuleB forbids it. With a *tock* event representing 1 s, after three *tock* events, no further events can occur: *tock* cannot occur because the maximum 3 s allowed by RuleA have passed, and *CurtainsOpened* is disallowed by RuleB.

To illustrate our check of redundancy, we consider RuleC and RuleD in Fig. 2a. Line 5 in Fig. 2b defines the CSP process that captures the conjunction of these rules. Line 6 shows the assertion for checking whether RuleC is redundant under RuleD. It checks whether the behaviours allowed by RuleD are those allowed (according to trace-refinement '$[T =$') by the conjunction of RuleC and RuleD. If they are, it means that RuleC imposes no extra restrictions, and so is redundant. The assertion states that RuleC is *not* redundant. FDR4 shows that the assertion fails, as expected, since RuleD is more restrictive in its deadline. No counterexample is provided because the refinement holds.

The complexity of this process of validation is quadratic in the number of rules since the rules are considered pairwise. We refer the reader to [9] for background on refinement checking in tock-CSP using FDR4.

Specification and Validation Workflow. The SLEECVAL workflow relies on the three components shown in Fig. 3. We implemented the parser for the SLEEC DSL in Eclipse Xtext [15] using EBNF. The SLEEC concrete syntax provided by SLEECVAL supports highlighting of the keyword elements, and there is extra support in the form of pop-up warnings and errors. SLEECVAL also enforces a simple style for naming rules, events, and measures. Conflicts are treated as errors whereas redundant rules are indicated as warnings.

The tock-CSP processes that define the semantics of the rules are computed through a visitor pattern applied to each element of the SLEEC grammar's syntax tree, with each SLEEC rule converted to a tock-CSP *process*. The computation is based on translation rules. Each event and measure is modelled in tock-CSP as a *channel*, with measure types directly converted into existing CSP datatypes, or introduced as a new scalar datatype in CSP.

Table 1: Summary of evaluation results.

Case study	Related SLEEC principles	#rules	#conflicts	#redundancies
assistive dressing robot	social, ethical, empathetic, legal, cultural	9	4	2
firefighter drone	legal, social, ethical	7	1	7

3 Evaluation

Case studies. We used SLEECVAL to specify and validate SLEEC rules sets for agents in two case studies presented next and summarised in Table 1.

Case study 1. The autonomous agent from the first case study is an assistive dressing robot from the social care domain [16]. The robot needs to dress a user with physical impairments with a garment by performing an interactive process that involves finding the garment, picking it, and placing it over the user's arms and torso. The SLEEC specification for this agent comprises nine rules, a subset of which is shown in Fig. 1. SLEECVAL identified four pairs of conflicting rules and two pairs of redundant rules in the initial version of this SLEEC specification including the conflicting rules RuleA and RuleB, and the redundant rules RuleC and RuleD from Fig. 2a.

Case study 2. The autonomous agent from the second case study is a firefighter drone whose detailed description is available at [17]. Its model identifies 21 robotic-platform services (i.e., capabilities) corresponding to sensors, actuators, and an embedded software library of the platform. We consider scenarios in which the firefighter drone interacts with several stakeholders: human firefighters, humans affected by a fire, and teleoperators.

In these scenarios, the drone surveys a building where a fire was reported to identify the fire location, and it either tries to extinguish a clearly identified fire using its small on-board water reservoir, or sends footage of the surveyed building to teleoperators. If, however, there are humans in the video stream, there are privacy (ethical and/or legal) concerns. Additionally, the drone sounds an alarm when its battery is running out. There are social requirements about sounding a loud alarm too close to a human. The SLEEC specification for this agent consists of seven rules, within which SLEECVAL identified one conflict (between the rules shown in Fig. 4) and seven redundancies. The conflict is due to the fact that Rule3 requires that the alarm is triggered (event SoundAlarm) when the battery level is critical (signalled by the event BatteryCritical) and either the temperature is great than 35°C or a person is detected, while the defeater from Rule7 prohibits the triggering of the alarm when a person is detected.

Overheads. The overheads of the SLEECVAL validation depend on the complexity and size of the SLEEC specifications, which preliminary discussions with stakeholders suggested might include between several tens and a few hundred rules. In our evaluation, the checks of the 27 assertions from the assistive robot

```
Rule3 when BatteryCritical and temperature > 35 or personDetected then SoundAlarm
Rule7 when BatteryCritical then SoundAlarm unless personDetected then goGome unless temperature > 35
```

Fig. 4: Conflicting rules for the firefighter drone case study.

case study and of the 63 assertions from the firefighter drone case study were performed in under 30s and 70s, respectively, on a standard MacBook laptop. As the number of checks is quadratic in the size of the SLEEC rule set, the time required to validate a fully fledged rule set of, say, 100–200 rules should not exceed tens of minutes on a similar machine.

Usability. We have conducted a preliminary study in which we have asked eight tool users (including lawyers, philosophers, computer scientists, roboticists and human factors experts) to assess the SLEECVAL usability and expressiveness, and to provide feedback to us. In this trial, the users were asked to define SLEEC requirements for autonomous agents used in their projects, e.g. autonomous cars and healthcare systems. The feedback received from these users can be summarized as follows: (1) SLEECVAL is easy to use and the language is intuitive; (2) The highlighting of keywords, errors messages and warnings is particularly helpful in supporting the definition of a comprehensive and valid SLEEC specification; (3) Using the FDR4 output (e.g., counterexamples) directly is useful as a preliminary solution, but more meaningful messages are required to make rule conflicts and redundancies easier to comprehend and fix.

4   Conclusion

We have introduced SLEECVAL, a tool for definition and validation of normative rules for autonomous agents. SLEECVAL uses a DSL for encoding of timed SLEEC requirements, and provides them with a tock-CSP semantics that is automatically calculated by SLEECVAL, as are checks for conflicts and redundancy between rules. We also presented the results from the SLEECVAL use for an assistive dressing robot and a firefighter drone.

In the future, we will consider uncertainty in the agents and their environments by extending the SLEEC DSL with probability constructs. Additionally, we will develop a mechanism to annotate rules with labels that can be used to provide more insightful feedback to SLEEC experts. Finally, a systematic and comprehensive user study is also planned as future work. Our vision is to automate the whole process in Fig. 3 with a suggestive feedback loop allowing users to address validation issues within their rule sets.

Acknowledgements

This work was funded by the Assuring Autonomy International Programme, and the UKRI project EP/V026747/1 'Trustworthy Autonomous Systems Node in Resilience'.

References

1. Nordmann, A., Hochgeschwender, N., Wigand, D., Wrede, S.: A survey on domain-specific modeling and languages in robotics. Journal of Software Engineering for Robotics **7**(1), 75–99 (2016)
2. Townsend, B., Paterson, C., Arvind, T., Nemirovsky, G., Calinescu, R., Cavalcanti, A., Habli, I., Thomas, A.: From pluralistic normative principles to autonomous-agent rules. Minds and Machines (2022), `https://cutt.ly/SLEEC-rule-elicitation`, Minds & Machines **32**, 683–715
3. Dennis, L.A., Fisher, M., Winfield, A.: Towards verifiably ethical robot behaviour. In: Workshops at the Twenty-Ninth AAAI Conference on Artificial Intelligence (2015)
4. Floridi, L., Cowls, J., Beltrametti, M., Chatila, R., Chazerand, P., Dignum, V., Luetge, C., Madelin, R., Pagallo, U., Rossi, F., et al.: An ethical framework for a good AI society: Opportunities, risks, principles, and recommendations. In: Ethics, Governance, and Policies in Artificial Intelligence, pp. 19–39. Springer (2021)
5. Future of Life Institute: ASILOMAR AI Principles. `https://futureoflife.org/2017/08/11/ai-principles/` (2017), accessed 31 March 2022
6. IEEE Global Initiative on Ethics of Autonomous and Intelligent Systems: Ethically Aligned Design – Version II (2017), `https://standards.ieee.org/news/2017/ead_v2/`
7. BS8611, B.: Robots and robotic devices, guide to the ethical design and application of robots and robotic systems. British Standards Institute (2016)
8. UNESCO: Recommendation on the Ethics of Artificial Intelligence. `https://unesdoc.unesco.org/ark:/48223/pf0000380455` (2021), Accessed: 2022-03-18, Document code: SHS/BIO/REC-AIETHICS/2021
9. Baxter, J., Ribeiro, P., Cavalcanti, A.: Sound reasoning in tock-csp. Acta Informatica **59**(1), 125–162 (2022). https://doi.org/10.1007/s00236-020-00394-3, `https://doi.org/10.1007/s00236-020-00394-3`
10. Roscoe, A.W.: The Theory and Practice of Concurrency. Prentice Hall (1997)
11. Gibson-Robinson, T., Armstrong, P., Boulgakov, A., Roscoe, A.: FDR3 — A Modern Refinement Checker for CSP. In: Ábrahám, E., Havelund, K. (eds.) Tools and Algorithms for the Construction and Analysis of Systems. Lecture Notes in Computer Science, vol. 8413, pp. 187–201 (2014)
12. SLEECVAL project webpage (2022), `sleec.github.io`
13. SLEECVAL GitHub repository (2022), `anonymous.4open.science/r/SLEEC-tool`
14. Brunero, J.: Reasons and Defeasible Reasoning. The Philosophical Quarterly **72**(1), 41–64 (04 2021). https://doi.org/10.1093/pq/pqab013, `https://doi.org/10.1093/pq/pqab013`
15. Domain-specific language development. `https://www.eclipse.org/Xtext` (2022), [Online accessed: 13 October 2022]
16. Camilleri, A., Dogramadzi, S., Caleb-Solly, P.: A study on the effects of cognitive overloading and distractions on human movement during robot-assisted dressing. Frontiers in Robotics and AI **9** (May 2022), `https://eprints.whiterose.ac.uk/187214/`
17. MBZIRC-OC, "THE CHALLENGE 2020. `https://www.mbzirc.com/grand-challenge` (2020), [Online accessed: 13 October 2022]

Towards Log Slicing

Joshua Heneage Dawes[1](✉)(iD), Donghwan Shin[1,2](✉)(iD),
and Domenico Bianculli[1](✉)(iD)

[1] University of Luxembourg, Luxembourg, Luxembourg
{joshua.dawes,domenico.bianculli}@uni.lu
[2] University of Sheffield, Sheffield, UK
d.shin@sheffield.ac.uk

Abstract. This short paper takes initial steps towards developing a novel approach, called *log slicing*, that aims to answer a practical question in the field of log analysis: *Can we automatically identify log messages related to a specific message (e.g., an error message)?* The basic idea behind log slicing is that we can consider how different log messages are "computationally related" to each other by looking at the corresponding logging statements in the source code. These logging statements are identified by 1) computing a backwards program slice, using as criterion the logging statement that generated a *problematic* log message; and 2) extending that slice to include *relevant* logging statements.
The paper presents a problem definition of log slicing, describes an initial approach for log slicing, and discusses a key open issue that can lead towards new research directions.

Keywords: Log · Program Analysis · Static Slicing.

1 Introduction

When debugging failures in software systems of various scales, the logs generated by executions of those systems are invaluable [5]. For example, given an error message recorded in a log, an engineer can diagnose the system by reviewing log messages recorded before the error occurred. However, the sheer volume of the logs (e.g., 50 GB/h [9]) makes it infeasible to review all of the log messages. Considering that not all log messages are necessarily related to each other, in this paper we lay the foundations for answering the following question: *can we automatically identify log messages related to a specific message (e.g., an error message)?*

A similar question for programs is already addressed by *program slicing* [2,14]. Using this approach, given a program composed of multiple program statements and variables, we can identify a set of program statements (i.e., a program slice) that affect the computation of specific program variables (at specific positions in the source code).

Inspired by program slicing, in this paper we take initial steps towards developing a novel approach, called *log slicing*. We also highlight a key issue to

© The Author(s) 2023
L. Lambers and S. Uchitel (Eds.): FASE 2023, LNCS 13991, pp. 249–259, 2023.
https://doi.org/10.1007/978-3-031-30826-0_14

```
(1)  logger.info("check memory status: %s" % mem.status)
(2)  db = DB.init(mode="default")
(3)  logger.info("DB connected with mode: %s" % db.mode)
(4)  item = getItem(db)
(5)  logger.info("current item: %s" % item)
(6)  if check(item) is "error":
(7)      logger.error("error in item: %s" % item)
```

Fig. 1. An example program P_{ex}

```
(1)  check memory status: okay
(2)  DB connected with mode: default
(3)  current item: pencil
(4)  error in item: pencil
```

Fig. 2. An example execution log L_{ex} of P_{ex}

be addressed by further research. Once this issue has been addressed, we expect *log slicing* to be able to identify the log messages related to a given *problematic* log message by using static analysis of the code that generated the log. Further, since we will be using static analysis of source code, we highlight that our approach is likely to be restricted to identifying problems that can be localised at the source code level.

The rest of the paper is structured as follows: Section 2 illustrates a motivating example. Section 3 sketches an initial approach for *log slicing*, while Section 4 shows its application to the example, and discusses limitations and open issues. Section 5 discusses related work. Section 6 concludes the paper.

2   Motivating Example

Let us consider a simplified example program P_{ex} (Figure 1) connecting to a database and getting an item from it. For simplicity, we denote P_{ex} as a sequence of program statements $\langle s_1, s_2, \ldots, s_7 \rangle$ where s_k is the k-th statement. We can see that P_{ex} contains logging statements (i.e., $s_1, s_3, s_5,$ and s_7) that will generate log messages when executed[3]. Figure 2 shows a simplified execution log L_{ex} of P_{ex}. Similar to P_{ex}, we denote L_{ex} as a sequence of log messages $\langle m_1, m_2, m_3, m_4 \rangle$ where m_k is the k-th log message. Note that we do not consider additional information that is often found in logs, such as timestamp and log level (e.g., *info* and *debug*)[4], so these are omitted.

---

[3] If a program statement generates a log message when executed, it is considered a logging statement; otherwise, it is a non-logging statement.

[4] We ignore log levels since the user may choose a log message of any level to start log slicing.

The last log message "`error in item: pencil`" in L_{ex} indicates an error. Calling this log message m_{err}, let us suppose that a developer is tasked with addressing the error by reviewing the log messages leading up to m_{err}. Though we have only four messages in L_{ex}, it is infeasible in practice to review a huge amount of log messages generated by complex software systems. Furthermore, it is not necessary to review all log messages generated before m_{err} since only a subset of them is related to m_{err}; for example, if we look at L_{ex} and P_{ex} together, we can see that the first log message "`check memory status: okay`" does not contain information that is relevant to the error message, m_{err}. In particular, we can see this by realising that the variable `mem` logged in the first log message does not affect the computation of the variable `item` logged in the error message.

Ultimately, if we can automatically filter out such unrelated messages, with the goal of providing a log to the developer that only contains useful log messages, then the developer will better investigate and address issues in less time. We thus arrive at the central problem of this short paper: *How does one determine which log messages are related to a certain message of interest?*

An initial, naive solution would be to use keywords to identify related messages. In our example log L_{ex}, one could use the keyword "`pencil`" appearing in the error message to identify the messages related to the error, resulting in only the third log message. However, if we look at the source code in P_{ex}, we can notice that the second log message "`DB connected with mode: default`" could be relevant to the error because this message was constructed using the `db` variable, which is used to compute the value of variable `item`. This example highlights that keyword-based search cannot identify all relevant log messages, meaning that a more sophisticated approach to identifying relevant log messages is needed.

3   Log Slicing

A key assumption in this work is that it is possible to associate each log message with a unique logging statement in source code. We highlight that, while we do not describe a solution here, this is a reasonable assumption because there is already work on identifying the mapping between logging statements and log messages [4,11]. Therefore, we simply assume that the mapping is known.

Under this assumption, we observe that the relationship among *messages in the log* can be identified based on the relationship among their corresponding *logging statements in the source code*. Hence, we consider two distinct layers: the *program layer*, where program statements and variables exist, and the *log layer*, where log messages generated by the logging statements of the program exist.

To present our log slicing approach, as done in Section 2, let us denote a program P as a sequence of program statements and a log L as a sequence of log messages. Also, we say a program (slice) P' is a subsequence of P, denoted by $P' \sqsubseteq P$, if all statements of P' are in P in the same order. Further, we extend containment to sequences and write $s \in P$ when, with $P = \langle s_1, \ldots, s_u \rangle$, there is some k such that $s_k = s$. The situation is similar for a log message m contained in a log L, where we write $m \in L$. Now, for a program $P = \langle s_1, \ldots, s_u \rangle$ and its execution log $L = \langle m_1, \ldots, m_v \rangle$, let us consider a log message of interest $m_j \in L$ that indicates a problem. An example could be the log message "`error in item: pencil`" from the example log L_{ex} in Figure 2. Based on the assumption made at the beginning of this section, that we can identify the logging statement $s_i \in P$ (in the program layer) that generated $m_j \in L$ (in the log layer), our log slicing approach is composed of three abstract steps as follows:

Step 1: Compute a program slice $S_r \sqsubseteq P$ using the combination of the statement s_i and the program variables in s_i as a slicing criterion. Notice that, apart from the logging statement s_i that is a part of the slicing criterion, S_r is composed solely of non-logging statements because logging statements do not affect the computation of any program variable[5].

Step 2: Identify another program slice $S_l \sqsubseteq P$ composed of logging statements that are "*relevant*" to S_r. Here, a logging statement $s_l \in S_l$ is *relevant* to a non-logging statement $s_r \in S_r$ if the message that s_l writes to the log contains information that is relevant to the computation being performed by s_r. Formally, we write $\langle s_l, s_r \rangle \in$ relevance$_P$, that is, relevance$_P$ is a binary relation over statements in the program P.

Step 3: Remove any log message $m \in L$ that was not generated by some $s_l \in S_l$.

The result of this procedure would be a *log slice* that contains log messages that are *relevant* to m_j.

We highlight that defining the relation relevance$_P$ for a program P (intuitively, deciding whether the information written to a log by a logging statement is *relevant* to the computation being performed by some non-logging statement) is a central problem in this work, and will be discussed in more depth in the next section.

4   An Illustration of Log Slicing

We now illustrate the application of our log slicing procedure to our example program and log (Figures 1 and 2). Since, as we highlighted in Section 3, the definition of the relevance$_P$ relation is a central problem of this work, we will begin by fixing a provisional definition. A demonstration of our log slicing approach being applied using this definition of relevance$_P$ will then show why this definition is only provisional.

4.1   A Provisional Definition of Relevance

Our provisional definition makes use of some attributes of statements that can be computed via simple static analyses. In particular, for a statement s, we denote by vars(s) the set of variables that appear in s (where a variable x *appears in* a statement s if it is found in the abstract syntax tree of s). If s is a logging

---

[5] Assuming a logging statement does not call an impure function.

```
(2)  db = DB.init(mode="default")
(4)  item = getItem(db)
(6)  if check(item) is "error":
(7)      logger.error("error in item: %s" % item)
```

Fig. 3. Program slice S_r of the program P_{ex} when s_7 and its variable `item` are used as the slicing criterion

statement that writes a message m to the log, then, assuming that the only way in which a logging statement can use a variable is to add information to the message that it writes to the log, the set vars(s) corresponds to the set of variables used to construct the message m. If s is a non-logging statement, then vars(s) represents the set of variables used by s.

Now, let us consider a logging statement s_l, that writes a message m_l to the log, and a non-logging statement s_r. We define relevance$_P$[6] over the statements in a program P by $\langle s_l, s_r \rangle \in$ relevance$_P$ if and only if vars(s_l) $\cap$ vars(s_r) $\neq \emptyset$. In other words, a logging statement is *relevant* to a non-logging statement whenever the two statements share at least one variable.

4.2 Applying Log Slicing

Taking the program P_{ex} from Figure 1 and the log L_{ex} from Figure 2, we now apply the steps described in Section 3, while considering the log message $m_4 \in L_{ex}$ (i.e., "error in item: pencil") to be the message of interest m_i.

Step 1. Under our assumption that log messages can be mapped to their generating logging statements, we can immediately map m_4 to $s_7 \in P_{ex}$. Once we have identified the logging statement s_7 that generated m_4, we slice P_{ex} backwards, using s_7 and its variable `item` as the slicing criterion. This would yield the program slice $S_r = \langle s_2, s_4, s_6, s_7 \rangle$ as shown in Figure 3.

Step 2. The program slice $S_r = \langle s_2, s_4, s_6, s_7 \rangle$ yielded by Step 1 contains only non-logging statements (apart from the logging statement s_7 used as the slicing criterion). Hence, we must now determine which logging statements (found in P_{ex}) write messages that are *relevant* to the statements in S_r. More formally, we must find a sequence of logging statements $S_l \sqsubset P_{ex}$ such that $\langle s_l, s_r \rangle \in$ relevance$_P$ for any logging statement $s_l \in S_l$ and a non-logging statement $s_r \in S_r \setminus \{s_7\}$. For this, we use the provisional definition of relevance that we introduced in Section 4.1, that is, we identify the logging statements that share variables with the statements in our program slice S_r. For example, let us consider the non-logging statement $s_r = s_2 \in S_r$ (i.e., "db = `DB.init(mode="default")`"). Our definition tells us that the logging statement $s_l = s_3$ (i.e., "`logger.info("DB`

---

[6] We remark that this simple provisional definition of relevance misses relating statements that only share syntactically different aliased variables

```
(3)  logger.info("DB connected with mode: %s" % db.mode)
(5)  logger.info("current item: %s" % item)
(7)      logger.error("error in item: %s" % item)
```

Fig. 4. Logging statements S_l relevant to S_r

```
(2)  DB connected with mode: default
(3)  current item: pencil
(4)  error in item: pencil
```

Fig. 5. Log slicing result from L_{ex} when m_4 is the message of interest

connected with mode: %s" % db.mode)") should be included in S_l, since vars$(s_3) \cap$ vars$(s_2) = \{$db$\}$. Similarly, the logging statement s_5 should be included in S_l since vars$(s_3) \cap$ vars$(s_2) = \{$item$\}$, and the logging statement s_7 should be included in S_l since vars$(s_7) \cap$ vars$(s_6) = \{$item$\}$. Note that the logging statement s_2 (i.e., "logger.info("check memory status: %s" % mem.status)") would be omitted by our definition because no statements in S_r use the variable mem. As a result, with respect to our definition of relevance, $S_l = \langle s_3, s_5, s_7 \rangle$ as shown in Figure 4.

Step 3. Using $S_l = \langle s_3, s_5, s_7 \rangle$, we now remove log messages from L_{ex} that were generated by logging statements *not included* in S_l. The result is the sliced log in Figure 5.

4.3   Limitations and Open Issues

We now discuss the limitations of the definition of relevance presented so far, along with a possible alternative approach. We also highlight a key open issue.

Limitations. Using a combination of program slicing and our provisional definition of relevance seems, at least initially, to be an improvement on the keyword-based approach described in Section 2. However, the major limitation of this definition, that looks at program variables shared by logging and non-logging statements, is that a logging statement must use variables in the first place. Hence, this definition can no longer be used if we are dealing with log messages that are statically defined (i.e., do not use variables to construct part of the message written to the log). In this case, we must look to the semantic content of the log messages.

An Alternative. Our initial suggestion in this case is to introduce a heuristic based on the intuition that particular phrases in log messages will often accompany particular computation being performed in program source code. Such a heuristic would operate as follows:

1. For each non-logging statement s, inspect each variable v appearing in s.
2. For each such variable v, further inspect the *tokens* found in the string literals of logging statements that are reachable from s. The word *tokens* here is deliberately left vague; it could mean individual words found in string literals, or vectors of words.
3. For each variable/token pair that we find, we compute a score that takes into account 1) the frequency of that pair in the program source code; and 2) how close they are (in terms of the distance between the source code lines in which the variable/token appear), on average.
4. We say that, for a logging statement s_l and a non-logging statement s_r, $\langle s_l, s_r \rangle \in$ relevance$_P$ if and only if s_l contains tokens that score highly with respect to the variables found in s_r. Hence, we use the token-based heuristic to define the relation relevance$_P$ with respect to a single program P.

We highlight that this *token-based* approach is to be used in combination with the backwards program slicing described in Section 3.

Further Limitations. While this heuristic takes a step towards inspecting the semantic content of log messages, rather than relying on shared variables, initial implementation efforts have demonstrated the following limitations:

- It is difficult to choose an appropriate definition of a *token*. For example, should we use individual words found in string literals used by logging statements, or should we use sequences of words?
- Depending on the code base, there can be varying numbers of *coincidental* associations between tokens and variables. For example, a developer may always use the phrase "end transaction" near a use of the variable commit, but also near a use of the variable query. The developer may understand "end transaction" as being a phrase related to the variable commit and not to the variable query, despite the accidental co-occurrence of the two variables.
- Suppose that a phrase like "end transaction" appears only once, and is close to the variable commit. The developer may intend for the two to be related. However, if we use a heuristic that combines the frequency of a pair with the distance between the variable and token in the pair, a single occurrence will not score highly. Hence, there are some instances of relevance that this heuristic cannot identify.

More Issues. In Section 3, we assumed that the mapping between log messages and the corresponding logging statements that generated the log messages is known. However, determining the log message that a given logging statement might generate can be challenging, especially when the logging statement has a non-trivial structure. For example, while some logging statements might consist of a simple concatenation of a string and a variable value, others might involve nested calls of functions from a logging framework. This calls for more studies on finding the correspondence between logging statements and log messages.

Another key problem is the inconsistency of program slicing tools across programming languages (especially weakly-typed ones such as Python). If the underlying program slicing machinery made too many overapproximations, this would affect the applicability of our proposed approach. Furthermore, the capability of the tools for handling complex cases, such as nested function calls across different components, can hinder the success of log slicing.

5   Related Work

Log Analysis. The relationship between log messages has also been studied in various log analysis approaches (e.g., performance monitoring, anomaly detection, and failure diagnosis), especially for building a "reference model" [12] that represents the normal behavior (in terms of logged event flows) of the system under analysis. However, these approaches focus on the problem of identifying whether log messages *co-occur* (that is, one is always seen in the neighbourhood of the other) without accessing the source code [6,10,13,17,18]. On the other hand, we consider the *computational* relationship between log messages to filter out the log messages that do not affect the computation of the variable values recorded in a given log message of interest.

Log partitioning. Log partitioning, similarly to log slicing, involves separating a log into multiple parts, based on some criteria. In the context of process mining [1], log partitioning is used to allow parallelisation of model construction. In the context of checking an event log for satisfaction of formal specifications [3], *slices* of event logs are sent to separate instances of a checking procedure, allowing more efficient checking for whether some event log satisfies a formal specification written in a temporal logic. Hence, again, log partitioning, or slicing, is used to parallelise a task. Finally, we highlight that our log slicing approach could be used to generate multiple log slices to be investigated in parallel by some procedure.

Program Analysis including Logging Statements. Traditionally, program analysis [14,2] ignores logging statements since they usually do not affect the computation of program variables. Nevertheless, program analysis including logging statements has been studied as part of *log enhancement* to measure which program variables should be added to the existing logging statements [7,15] and where new logging statements should be added [16] to facilitate distinguishing program execution paths. Log slicing differs in that it actively tries to reduce the contents of a log. Finally, Messaoudi et al. [8] have proposed a log-based test case slicing technique, which aims to decompose complex test cases into simpler ones using, in addition to program analysis, data available in logs.

6   Conclusion

In this short paper, we have taken the first steps in developing *log slicing*, an approach to helping software engineers in their log-based debugging activities.

Log slicing starts from a log message that has been selected as indicative of a failure, and uses static analysis of source code (whose execution generated the log in question) to throw away log entries that are not relevant to the failure.

In giving an initial definition of the log slicing problem, we highlighted the central problem of this work: defining a good relevance relation. The provisional definition of relevance that we gave in Section 4.1 proved to be limited in that it required logging statements to use variables when constructing their log message. To remedy the situation, we introduced a frequency and proximity-based heuristic in Section 4.3. While this approach could improve on the initial definition of relevance, it possessed various limitations that we summarised.

Ultimately, as part of future work, we intend to investigate better definitions of relevance between logging statements and non-logging statements. If we were to carry on with the same idea for the heuristic (using frequency and proximity), future work would involve 1) finding a suitable way to define *tokens*; 2) reducing identification of coincidental associations between tokens and variables (i.e., reducing false positives); and 3) attempting to identify associations between tokens and variables with a lower frequency.

Acknowledgments. The research described has been carried out as part of the COSMOS Project, which has received funding from the European Union's Horizon 2020 Research and Innovation Programme under grant agreement No. 957254.

References

1. van der Aalst, W.M.P.: Distributed process discovery and conformance checking. In: de Lara, J., Zisman, A. (eds.) Fundamental Approaches to Software Engineering. pp. 1–25. Springer Berlin Heidelberg, Berlin, Heidelberg (2012)
2. Agrawal, H., Horgan, J.R.: Dynamic program slicing. SIGPLAN Not. **25**(6), 246–256 (jun 1990). https://doi.org/10.1145/93548.93576, https://doi.org/10.1145/93548.93576
3. Basin, D., Caronni, G., Ereth, S., Harvan, M., Klaedtke, F., Mantel, H.: Scalable offline monitoring. In: Bonakdarpour, B., Smolka, S.A. (eds.) Runtime Verification. pp 31–47. Springer International Publishing, Cham (2014)
4. Bushong, V., Sanders, R., Curtis, J., Du, M., Cerny, T., Frajtak, K., Bures, M., Tisnovsky, P., Shin, D.: On matching log analysis to source code: A systematic mapping study. In: Proceedings of the International Conference on Research in Adaptive and Convergent Systems. p. 181–187. RACS '20, Association for Computing Machinery, New York, NY, USA (2020). https://doi.org/10.1145/3400286.3418262, https://doi.org/10.1145/3400286.3418262
5. He, S., He, P., Chen, Z., Yang, T., Su, Y., Lyu, M.R.: A survey on automated log analysis for reliability engineering. ACM Comput. Surv. **54**(6) (Jul 2021). https://doi.org/10.1145/3460345
6. Jia, T., Yang, L., Chen, P., Li, Y., Meng, F., Xu, J.: Logsed: Anomaly diagnosis through mining time-weighted control flow graph in logs. In: 2017 IEEE 10th International Conference on Cloud Computing (CLOUD). pp. 447–455. IEEE, IEEE, Honolulu, CA, USA (2017). https://doi.org/10.1109/CLOUD.2017.64

7. Liu, Z., Xia, X., Lo, D., Xing, Z., Hassan, A.E., Li, S.: Which variables should I log? IEEE Transactions on Software Engineering **47**(9), 2012–2031 (2021). https://doi.org/10.1109/TSE.2019.2941943
8. Messaoudi, S., Shin, D., Panichella, A., Bianculli, D., Briand, L.C.: Log-based slicing for system-level test cases. In: Proceedings of the 30th ACM SIGSOFT International Symposium on Software Testing and Analysis. p. 517–528. ISSTA 2021, Association for Computing Machinery, New York, NY, USA (2021). https://doi.org/10.1145/3460319.3464824, https://doi.org/10.1145/3460319.3464824
9. Mi, H., Wang, H., Zhou, Y., Lyu, M.R.T., Cai, H.: Toward fine-grained, unsupervised, scalable performance diagnosis for production cloud computing systems. IEEE Transactions on Parallel and Distributed Systems **24**(6), 1245–1255 (2013). https://doi.org/10.1109/TPDS.2013.21
10. Nandi, A., Mandal, A., Atreja, S., Dasgupta, G.B., Bhattacharya, S.: Anomaly detection using program control flow graph mining from execution logs. In: 2016 26nd ACM International Conference on Knowledge Discovery and Data Mining (SIGKDD). pp. 215–224. KDD '16, Association for Computing Machinery, New York, NY, USA (2016). https://doi.org/10.1145/2939672.2939712
11. Schipper, D., Aniche, M., van Deursen, A.: Tracing back log data to its log statement: From research to practice. In: 2019 IEEE/ACM 16th International Conference on Mining Software Repositories (MSR). pp. 545–549 (2019). https://doi.org/10.1109/MSR.2019.00081
12. Shin, D., Bianculli, D., Briand, L.: PRINS: scalable model inference for component-based system logs. Empirical Software Engineering **27**(4),   87 (2022). https://doi.org/10.1007/s10664-021-10111-4, https://doi.org/10.1007/s10664-021-10111-4
13. Tak, B.C., Tao, S., Yang, L., Zhu, C., Ruan, Y.: Logan: Problem diagnosis in the cloud using log-based reference models. In: 2016 IEEE International Conference on Cloud Engineering (IC2E). pp. 62–67 (2016). https://doi.org/10.1109/IC2E.2016.12
14. Weiser, M.: Program slicing. IEEE Trans. Softw. Eng. **10**(4), 352–357 (Jul 1984). https://doi.org/10.1109/TSE.1984.5010248, https://doi.org/10.1109/TSE.1984.5010248
15. Yuan, D., Zheng, J., Park, S., Zhou, Y., Savage, S.: Improving software diagnosability via log enhancement. ACM Trans. Comput. Syst. **30**(1) (Feb 2012). https://doi.org/10.1145/2110356.2110360
16. Zhao, X., Rodrigues, K., Luo, Y., Stumm, M., Yuan, D., Zhou, Y.: Log20: Fully automated optimal placement of log printing statements under specified overhead threshold. In: 2017 26th Symposium on Operating Systems Principles (SOSP). p. 565–581. SOSP '17, Association for Computing Machinery, New York, NY, USA (2017). https://doi.org/10.1145/3132747.3132778
17. Zhao, X., Rodrigues, K., Luo, Y., Yuan, D., Stumm, M.: Non-Intrusive performance profiling for entire software stacks based on the flow reconstruction principle. In: 12th USENIX Symposium on Operating Systems Design and Implementation (OSDI 16). pp. 603–618. USENIX Association, Savannah, GA (Nov 2016), https://www.usenix.org/conference/osdi16/technical-sessions/presentation/zhao
18. Zhou, P., Wang, Y., Li, Z., Tyson, G., Guan, H., Xie, G.: Logchain: Cloud workflow reconstruction & troubleshooting with unstructured logs. Computer Networks **175**, 107279 (2020). https://doi.org/https://doi.org/10.1016/j.comnet.2020.107279, https://www.sciencedirect.com/science/article/pii/S1389128619316731

VAMOS:
Middleware for Best-Effort Third-Party Monitoring

Marek Chalupa[ID]([✉]), Fabian Muehlboeck[ID],
Stefanie Muroya Lei[ID], and Thomas A. Henzinger[ID]

Institute of Science and Technology Austria (ISTA), Klosterneuburg, Austria
marek.chalupa@ista.ac.at

Abstract. As the complexity and criticality of software increase every year, so does the importance of run-time monitoring. Third-party monitoring, with limited knowledge of the monitored software, and best-effort monitoring, which keeps pace with the monitored software, are especially valuable, yet underexplored areas of run-time monitoring. Most existing monitoring frameworks do not support their combination because they either require access to the monitored code for instrumentation purposes or the processing of all observed events, or both.

We present a middleware framework, VAMOS, for the run-time monitoring of software which is explicitly designed to support third-party and best-effort scenarios. The design goals of VAMOS are (i) efficiency (keeping pace at low overhead), (ii) flexibility (the ability to monitor black-box code through a variety of different event channels, and the connectability to monitors written in different specification languages), and (iii) ease-of-use. To achieve its goals, VAMOS combines aspects of event broker and event recognition systems with aspects of stream processing systems.

We implemented a prototype toolchain for VAMOS and conducted experiments including a case study of monitoring for data races. The results indicate that VAMOS enables writing useful yet efficient monitors, is compatible with a variety of event sources and monitor specifications, and simplifies key aspects of setting up a monitoring system from scratch.

1 Introduction

Monitoring—the run-time checking of a formal specification—is a lightweight verification technique for deployed software. Writing monitors is especially challenging if it is *third-party* and *real-time*. In third-party monitoring, the monitored software and the monitoring software are written independently, in order to increase trust in the monitor. In the extreme case, the monitor has very limited knowledge of and access to the monitored software, as in black-box monitoring. In real-time monitoring, the monitor must not slow down the monitored software while also following its execution close in time. In the extreme case, the monitor may not be able to process all observed events and can check the specification only approximately, as in best-effort monitoring.

We present middleware—called VAMOS ("Vigilant Algorithmic Monitoring of Software")—which facilitates the addition of best-effort third-party monitors to deployed software. The primary goals of our middleware are (i) performance

© The Author(s) 2023
L. Lambers and S. Uchitel (Eds.): FASE 2023, LNCS 13991, pp. 260–281, 2023.
https://doi.org/10.1007/978-3-031-30826-0_15

(keeping pace at low overhead), (ii) flexibility (compatibility with a wide range of heterogeneous event sources that connect the monitor with the monitored software, and with a wide range of formal specification languages that can be compiled into VAMOS), and (iii) ease-of-use (the middleware relieves the designer of the monitor from system and code instrumentation concerns).

All of these goals are fairly standard, but VAMOS' particular design tradeoffs center around making it as easy as possible to create a best-effort third-party monitor of actual software without investing much time into low-level details of instrumentation or load management. In practice, instrumentation—enriching the monitored system with code that is gathering observations on whose basis the monitor generates verdicts—is a key part of writing a monitoring system and affects key performance characteristics of the monitoring setup [11]. These considerations become even more important in third-party monitoring, where the limited knowledge of and access to the monitored software may force the monitor to spend more computational effort to re-derive information that it could not observe, or combine it from smaller pieces obtained from more (and different) sources. By contrast, current implementations of monitor specification languages mostly offer either very targeted instrumentation support for particular systems or some general-purpose API to receive events, or both, but little to organize multiple heterogeneous event streams, or to help with the kinds of best-effort performance considerations that we are concerned with. Thus, VAMOS fills a gap left open by existing tools.

Our vision for VAMOS is that users writing a best-effort third-party monitor start by selecting configurable instrumentation tools from a rich collection. This collection includes tools that periodically query webservices, generate events for relevant system calls, observe the interactions of web servers with clients, and of course standard code instrumentation tools. The configuration effort for each such *event source* largely consists of specifying patterns to look for and what events to generate for them. VAMOS then offers a simple specification language for filtering and altering events coming from the event sources, and simple yet expressive event recognition rules that produce a single, global event stream by combining events from a (possibly dynamically changing) number of event sources. Lastly, monitoring code as it is more generally understood—which could be written directly or generated from existing tools for run-time verification like LTL formulae [47], or stream verification specifications [8] such as TeSSLa [41]— processes these events to generate verdicts about the monitored system.

VAMOS thus represents middleware between event sources that emit events and higher-level monitoring code, abstracting away many low-level details about the interaction between the two. Users can employ both semi-synchronous and completely asynchronous [11] interactions with any or all event sources. Between these two extremes, to decouple the higher-level monitoring code's performance from the overhead incurred by the instrumentation, while putting a bound on how far the monitoring code can lag behind the monitored system, we provide a simple load-shedding mechanism that we call *autodrop buffers*, which are buffers that drop events when the monitoring code cannot keep up with the rate of incoming events, while maintaining summarization data about the dropped events. This summarization data can later be used by our event recognition system when it is notified that events were dropped; some standard monitoring specification systems can handle such *holes* in their event streams automatically [32,42,54]. The rule-based event recognition system allows grouping and ordering buffers dynamically to prioritize or rotate within variable sets of similar event sources, and specifying patterns over multiple events and buffers, to extract and combine the necessary information for a single global event stream.

Data from event sources is transferred to the monitor using efficient lock-free buffers in shared memory inspired by Cache-Friendly Asymmetric Buffers [29]. These buffers can transfer over one million events per second per event source on a standard desktop computer. Together with autodrop buffers, this satisfies our performance goal while keeping the specification effort low. As such, VA-MOS resembles a single-consumer version of an event broker [18,58,48,55,26,1] specialized to run-time monitoring.

The core features we built VAMOS around are not novel on their own, but to the best of our knowledge, their combination and application to simplify best-effort third-party monitoring setups is. Thus, we make the following contributions:

- We built middleware to connect higher-level monitors with event sources, addressing particular challenges of best-effort third-party monitoring (Section 2), using a mixture of efficient inter-process communication and easy-to-use facilities for load management (Section 3) on one hand, and *buffer groups* and other event recognition abstractions (Section 4) on the other hand.
- We implemented a compiler for VAMOS specifications, a number of event sources, and a connector to TeSSLa [41] monitors (Section 5).
- We conducted some stress-test experiments using our framework, as well as a case study in which we implemented a monitor looking for data races, providing evidence of the feasibility of low-overhead third-party monitoring with simple specifications (Section 6).

2   Architectural Overview

Writing a run-time monitor can be a complex task, but many tools to express logical reasoning over streams of run-time observations [19,34,16,49,24,27,41] exist. However, trying to actually obtain a concrete stream of observations from a real system introduces a very different set of concerns, which in turn have a huge effect on the performance properties of run-time monitoring [11].

The goal of VAMOS is to simplify this critical part of setting up a monitoring system, using the model shown in Figure 1. On the left side, we assume an arbitrary number of distinct event sources directly connected to the monitor. This is particularly important in third-party monitoring, as information may need to be collected from multiple different sources instead of just a single program, but can be also useful in other monitoring scenarios, e.g. for multithreaded programs.

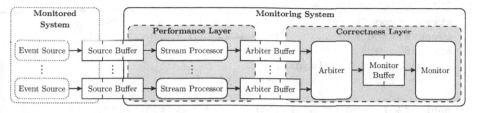

Fig. 1. The components of a VAMOS setup.

The right-most component is called the *monitor*, representing the part of the monitoring system that is typically generated by a monitoring specification tool, usually based on a single global event stream. As middleware, VAMOS connects the two, providing abstractions for common issues that monitor writers would otherwise have to address with boilerplate, but still complicated code.

Given that there are multiple event sources providing their own event streams, but only one global event stream consumed by the monitor, a key aspect is merging the incoming streams into one, which happens in the *arbiter*. Third-party monitoring often cannot rely on the source-code-based instrumentation that is otherwise common [21,4,14,16,25]; for example, TeSSLa[1] [41] comes with a basic way of instrumenting C programs by adding annotations into the specification that identify events with function calls or their arguments. Instead, it has to rely on things that can be reliably observed and whose meaning is clear, for example system calls, calls to certain standard library functions, or any other information one can gather from parts of the environment one controls, such as sensors or file system. These do not necessarily correspond in a straightforward way to the events one would like to feed into the higher-level monitor and thus need to be combined or split up in various ways. For example, when a program writes a line to the standard output, the data itself might be split into multiple system calls or just be part of a bigger one that contains multiple lines, and there are also multiple system calls that could be used. Therefore, the arbiter provides a way to specify a rule-based event recognition system to generate higher-level events from combinations of events on the different event sources.

Another common assumption in monitoring systems is some global notion of time that can be used to order events. This is not necessarily true for multiple, heterogeneous event sources, and even just observing the events of a multi-threaded program can cause events to arrive in an order that does not represent causality. VAMOS arbiter specifications are flexible enough to support many user-defined ways of expressing ways of merging events into a single global stream.

Doing this kind of sorting and merging and then potentially arbitrarily complex other computations in both the arbiter and the monitor may take longer than it takes the monitored system to generate events. Especially in third-party monitoring, a monitor may have to reconstruct information that is technically

---

[1] We keep referring to TeSSLa in the rest of the paper and also chose to use it in our implementation because it is one of the most easily available existing tools we could find. In general, the state of the field is that, while many papers describing similar tools exist, few are actually available [48].

```
1  stream type Observation { Op(arg : int, ret : int); }
2  event source Program : Observation to autodrop(16,4)
3  arbiter : Observation {
4      on Program: hole(n) | ;
5      on Program: Op(arg, ret) | yield;
6  }
7  monitor(2) { on Op(arg, reg) $$ CheckOp(arg, ret);  $$ }
```

Listing 1.1. A basic asynchronous best-effort monitor.

present in the monitored system but cannot be observed, or, worse, the monitor may have to consider multiple different possibilities if information cannot be reliably recomputed. However, as part of our performance goal, we want the monitor to not lag too far behind the monitored system. Therefore, our design splits the monitoring system into the *performance* and *correctness* layers. In between the two, events may be dropped as a simple load-shedding strategy.

The performance layer, on the other hand, sees all events and processes each event stream in parallel. *Stream processors* enable filtering and altering the events that come in, reducing pressure and computational load on the correctness layer. This reflects that in third-party monitoring, observing coarse-grained event types like system calls may yield many uninteresting events. For example, all calls to read may be instrumented, but only certain arguments make them interesting.

A Simple Example Listing 1.1 shows a full VAMOS specification (aside from the definition of custom monitoring code in a C function called CheckOp). *Stream types* describe the kinds of events and the memory layout of their data that can appear in a particular buffer; in this example, streams of type Observation contain only one possible event named Op with two fields of type **int**. For source buffers—created using event source descriptions as in line 2—these need to be based on the specification of the particular event source. Each event source is associated with a *stream processor*; if none is given (as in this example), a default one simply forwards all events to the corresponding arbiter buffer, here specified as an *autodrop* buffer that can hold up to 16 events and when full keeps dropping them until there is again space for at least four new events. Using an autodrop buffer means that in addition to the events of the stream type, the arbiter may see a special *hole* event notifying it that events were dropped. In this example, the arbiter simply ignores those events and forwards all others to the monitor, which runs in parallel to the arbiter with a blocking event queue of size two, and whose behavior we implemented directly in C code between $$ escape characters.

3 Efficient Instrumentation

Our goals for the performance of the monitor are to not incur too much overhead on the monitored system, and for the monitor to be reasonably up-to-date in terms of the lag between when an event is generated and when it is processed. The key features VAMOS offers to ensure these properties while keeping specifications simple are related to the performance layer, which we discuss here.

3.1 Source Buffers and Stream Processors

Even when instrumenting things like system calls, in order to extract information from them in a consistent state, the monitored system will have to be briefly interrupted while the instrumentation copies the relevant data. A common solution is to write this data to a log file that the monitor is incrementally processing. This approach has several downsides. First, in the presence of multiple threads, accesses to a single file require synchronization. Second, the common use of string encodings requires extra serialization and parsing steps. Third, file-based buffers are typically at least very large or unbounded in size, so slower monitors eventually exhaust system resources. Finally, writing to the log uses relatively costly system calls. Instead, VAMOS event sources transmit raw binary data via channels implemented as limited-size lock-free ring buffer in shared memory, limiting instrumentation overhead and optimizing throughput [29]. To avoid expensive synchronization of different threads in the instrumented program (or just to logically separate events), VAMOS also allows dynamically allocating new event sources, such that each thread can write to its own buffer(s). The total number of event sources may therefore vary across the run of the monitor.

For each event source, VAMOS allocates a new thread in the performance layer to process events from this source[2]. In this layer, event processors can filter and alter events before they are forwarded to the correctness layer, all in a highly parallel fashion. A default event processor simply forwards all events. The computations done here should be done at the speed at which events are generated on that particular source, otherwise the source buffer will fill up and eventually force the instrumentation to wait for space in the buffer.

3.2 Autodrop Buffers

As we already stated, not all computations of a monitor may be able to keep up with the monitored system. Our design separates these kinds of computations into the correctness layer, which is connected with the performance layer via *arbiter buffers*. The separation is achieved by using *autodrop buffers*. These buffers provide the most straightforward form of load management via load shedding [59]: if there is not enough space in the buffer, it gathers summarization information (like the count of events since the buffer became full) and otherwise drops the events forwarded to it. Once free space becomes available in the buffer, it automatically inserts a special *hole* event containing the summarization information. The summarization ensures that not all information about dropped

---

[2] When event sources can be dynamically added, the user may specify a limit to how many of them can exist concurrently to avoid accumulating buffers the monitor cannot process fast enough. When that limit is hit, new event sources are rejected and the instrumentation drops events that would be forwarded to them.

events is lost, which can help to reduce the impact of load shedding. At minimum, the existence of the *hole* event alone makes a difference in monitorability compared to not knowing whether any events have been lost [35], and is used as such in some monitoring systems [32,42,54].

In addition to autodrop buffers, arbiter buffers can also be finite-size buffers that block when space is not available, or ininite-size buffers. The former may slow down the stream processor and ultimately the event source, while the latter may accumulate data and exhaust available resources. For some event sources, this may not be a big risk, and it eliminates the need to deal with *hole* events.

4   Event Recognition, Ordering, and Prioritization

VAMOS' arbiter specifications are a flexible, yet simple way to organize the information gathered from a—potentially variable—number of heterogeneous event sources. In this section, we discuss the key relevant parts of such specifications—a more complete specification can be found in the Technical Report [13].

4.1   Arbiter Rules

We already saw simple arbiter rules in Listing 1.1, but arbiter rules can be much more complex, specifying arbitrary sequences of events at the front of arbitrarily many buffers, as well as buffer properties such as a minimum number of available events and emptiness. Firing a rule can also be conditioned by an arbitrary boolean expression. For example, one rule in the *Bank* example we use in our evaluation in Section 6 looks as follows:

```
1  on Out : transfer(t2, src, tgt) transferSuccess(t4) |,
2     In  : numIn(t0, act) numIn(t1, acc) numIn(t3, amnt) |
3     where $$ t2 == t0 + 4 $$
4  $$ $yield SawTransfer(src, tgt, amnt); ... $$
```

This rule matches multiple events on two different buffers (In and Out), describing a series of user input and program output events that together form a single higher-level event SawTransfer, which is forwarded to the *monitor* component of the correctness layer. Rules do not necessarily consume the events they have looked at; some events may also just serve as a kind of lookahead. The "|" character in the events sequence pattern separates the consumed events (left) from the lookahead (right). Code between $$ symbols can be arbitrary C code with some special constructs, such as the $yield statement (to forward events) above.

The rule above demonstrates the basic event-recognition capabilities of arbiters. By ordering the rules in a certain way, we can also prioritize processing events from some buffers over others. Rules can also be grouped into *rule sets* that a monitor can explicitly switch between in the style of an automaton.

4.2   Buffer Groups

The rules shown so far only refer to arbiter buffers associated with specific, named event sources. As we mentioned before, Vamos also supports creating event sources dynamically during the run of the monitoring system. To be able to refer to these in arbiter rules, we use an abstraction we call *buffer groups*.

As the name suggests, buffer groups are collections of arbiter buffers whose membership can change at run time. They are the only way in which the arbiter can access dynamically created event sources, so to allow a user to distinguish between them and manage associated data, we extend stream types with *stream fields* that can be read and updated by arbiter code. Buffer groups are declared for a specific stream type, and their members have to have that stream type[3]. Therefore, each member offers the same stream fields, which we can use to compare buffers and order them for the purposes of iterating through the buffer group. Now the arbiter rules can also be choice blocks with more rules nested within them, as follows (Both is a buffer group and pos is a stream field):

```
1  choose F,S from Both {
2    on F : Prime(n,p) | where $$ $F.pos < $S.pos $$
3    $$ ... $$
4    on F : hole(n) |
5    $$ $F.pos = $F.pos + n; $$
6  }
```

This rule is a slightly simplified version of one in the *Primes* example in Section 6. This example does not use dynamically created buffers, but only has two event sources, and uses the ordering capabilities of buffer groups to prioritize between the buffers based on which one is currently "behind" (expressed in the stream field pos, which the buffer group Both is ordered by). The choose rule tries to instantiate its variables with distinct members from the buffer group, trying out permutations in the lexicographic extension of the order specified for the buffer group. If no nested rule matches for a particular instantiation, the next one in order is tried, and the choose rule itself fails if no instantiation finds a match.

To handle dynamically created event sources, corresponding stream processor rules specify a buffer group to which to add new event sources, upon which the arbiter can access them through choose rules. In most cases, we expect that choose blocks are used to instantiate a single buffer, in which case we only need to scan the buffer group in its specified order. Here, a round-robin order allows for fairness, while field-based orderings allow more detailed control over buffers prioritization, as it may be useful to focus on a few buffers at the expense of others, as in our above example.

Another potential option for ordering schemes for buffer groups could be based on events waiting in them, or even the values of those events' associated data. Vamos currently does not support this because it makes sorting much more

---

[3] Note that stream processors may change the stream type between the source buffer and arbiter buffer, so event sources may use different types, but their arbiter buffers may be grouped together if processed accordingly.

expensive—essentially, all buffers may have to be checked in order to determine the order in which to try matching them against further rules. Some of our experiments could have made use of such a feature, but in different ways—future work may add mechanisms that capture some of these ways.

5   Implementation

In this section, we briefly review the key components of our implementation.

5.1   Source Buffers and Event Sources

The source buffer library allows low-overhead interprocess communication between a monitored system and the monitor. It implements lock-free asynchronous ring buffers in shared memory, inspired by Cache-Friendly Asymmetric Buffering [29], but extended to handle entries larger than 64 bits[4]. The library allows setting up an arbitrary number of source buffers with a unique name, which a monitor can connect to explicitly, and informing such connected monitors about dynamically created buffers. A user can also provide stream type information so connecting monitors can check for binary compatibility.

We have used the above library to implement an initial library of event sources: one that is used for detecting data races, and several which use either *DynamoRIO* [9] (a dynamic instrumentation framework) or the *eBPF* subsystem of the Linux Kernel [10,28,50] to intercept the read and write (or any other) system calls of an arbitrary program, or to read and parse data from file descriptors. The read/write related tools allow specifying an arbitrary number of regular expressions that are matched against the traced data, and associated event constructors that refer to parts of the regular expressions from which to extract the relevant data. Example uses of these tools are included in our artifact [12].

5.2   The VAMOS Compiler and the TeSSLa Connector

The compiler takes a VAMOS specification described in the previous sections and turns it into a C program. It does some minimal checking, for example whether events used in parts of the program correspond to the expected stream types, but otherwise defers type-checking to the C compiler. The generated program expects a command-line argument for each specified event source, providing the name of the source buffer created by whatever actual event source is used. Event sources signal when they are finished, and the monitor stops once all event sources are finished and all events have been processed.

The default way of using TeSSLa for online monitoring is to run an offline monitor incrementally on a log file of serialized event data from a single global

---

[4] Entries have the size of the largest event consisting of its fixed-size fields and identifiers for variable-sized data (strings) transported in separately managed memory.

event source. A recent version of TeSSLa [33] allows generating Rust code for the stream processing system with an interface to provide events and drive the stream processing directly. Our compiler can generate the necessary bridging code and replace the *monitor* component in VAMOS with a TeSSLa Rust monitor. We used TeSSLa as a representative of higher-level monitoring specification tools; in principle, one could similarly use other standard monitor specification languages, thus making it easier to connect them to arbitrary event sources.

6 Evaluation

Our stated design goals for VAMOS were (i) performance, (ii) flexibility, and (iii) ease-of-use. Of these, only the first is truly quantitative, and the majority of this section is devoted to various aspects of it. We present a number of benchmark programs, each of which used VAMOS to retrieve events from different event sources and organize them for a higher-level monitor in a different way, which provides some qualitative evidence for its flexibility. Finally, we present a case study to build a best-effort data-race monitor (Section 6.4), whose relative simplicity provides qualitative evidence for VAMOS' ease of use.

In evaluating performance, we focus on two critical metrics:

1. How much overhead does monitoring impose on the monitored system? We measure this as the difference of wall-clock running times.
2. How well can a best-effort third-party monitor cover the behavior of the monitored program? We measure this as the portion of errors a monitor can (not) find.

Our core claim is that VAMOS allows building useful best-effort third-party monitors for programs that generate hundreds of thousands of events per second without a significant slow down of the programs beyond the unavoidable cost of generating events themselves. We provide evidence that corroborates this claim based on three artificial benchmarks that vary various parameters and one case study implementation of a data race monitor that we test on 391 benchmarks taken from SV-COMP 2022 [7].

Experimental setup All experiments were run on a common personal computer with 16 *GB* of RAM and an *Intel(R) Core(TM) i7-8700* CPU with 6 physical cores running on 3.20 *GHz* frequency. Hyper-Threading was enabled and dynamic frequency scaling disabled. The operating system was Ubuntu 20.04. All provided numbers are based on at least 10 runs of the relevant experiments.

6.1 Scalability Tests

Our first experiment is meant to establish the basic capabilities of our arbiter implementation. An event source sends 10 million events carrying a single 64-bit number (plus 128 bits of metadata), waiting for some number of cycles between

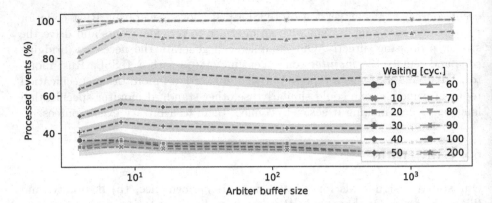

Fig. 2. The percentage of events that reached the final stage of the monitor in a stress test where the source sends events rapidly. Parameters are different arbiter buffer sizes (x-axis) and the delay (*Waiting*) of how many empty cycles the source waits between sending individual events. The shading around lines shows the 95 % confidence interval around the mean of the measured value. The source buffer was 8 pages large, which corresponds to a bit over 1 300 events.

each event. The performance layer simply forwards the events to autodrop buffers of a certain size, the arbiter retrieves the events, including holes, and forwards them to the monitor, which keeps track of how many events it saw and how many were dropped. We varied the number of cycles and the arbiter buffer sizes to see how many events get dropped because the arbiter cannot process them fast enough—the results can be seen in Figure 2.

At about 70 cycles of waiting time, almost all events could be processed even with very small arbiter buffer sizes (4 and up). In our test environment, this corresponds to a delay of roughly $700\,ns$ between events, which means that VAMOS is able to transmit approximately 1.4 million of events per second.

6.2   Primes

As a stress-test where the monitor actually has some work to do, this benchmark compares two parallel runs of a program that generates streams of primes and prints them to the standard output, simulating a form of differential monitoring [45]. The task of the monitor is to compare their output and alert the user whenever the two programs generate different data. Each output line is of the form #n : p, indicating that p is the nth prime. This is easy to parse using regular expressions, and our DynamoRIO-based instrumentation tool simply yields events with two 32-bit integer data fields (n and p).

While being started at roughly the same time, the programs as event sources run independently of each other, and scheduling differences can cause them to run out of sync quickly. To account for this, a VAMOS specification needs to allocate large enough buffers to either keep enough events to make up for possible scheduling differences, or at least enough events to make it likely that there is

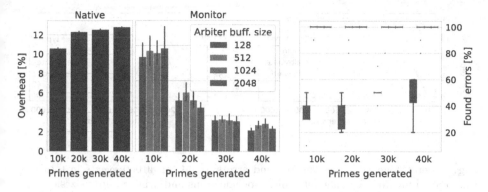

Fig. 3. Overheads (left) and percentage of found errors (right) in the primes benchmark for various numbers of primes and arbiter buffer sizes relative to DynamoRIO-optimized but not instrumented runs. DynamoRIO was able to optimize the program so much that the native binary runs slower than the instrumented one.

some overlap between the parts of the two event streams that are not automatically dropped. The arbiter uses the event field for the index variable n to line up events from both streams, exploiting the buffer group ordering functionality described in Section 4.2 to preferentially look at the buffer that is "behind", but also allowing the factor buffer to cache a limited number of events while waiting for events to show up on the other one. Once it has both results for the same index, the arbiter forwards a single pair event to the monitor to compare them.

Figure 3 shows results of running this benchmark in 16 versions, generating between 10 000 and 40 000 primes with arbiter buffer sizes ranging between 128 and 2024 events. The overheads of running the monitor are small, do not differ between different arbiter buffer sizes, and longer runs amortize the initial cost of dynamic instrumentation. We created a setting where one of the programs generates a faulty prime about once every 10 events and measured how many of these discrepancies the monitor can find (which depends on how many events are dropped). Unsurprisingly, larger buffer sizes are better at balancing out the scheduling differences that let the programs get out of sync. As long as the programs run at the same speed, there should be a finite arbiter buffer size that counters the desynchronization. In these experiments, this size is 512 elements.

Primes with TeSSLa We experimented with a variation of the benchmark that uses a very simple TeSSLa [17,41] specification receiving two streams for each prime generator (i.e., four streams in total): one stream of indexed primes as in the original experiment, and the other with hole events. The specification expects the streams to be perfectly lined up and checks that, whenever the last-seen pairs on both streams have the same index, they also contain the same prime (and ignores non-aligned pairs of primes). We wrote three variants of an arbiter to go in front of that TeSSLa monitor:

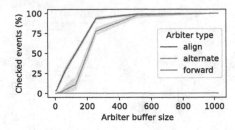 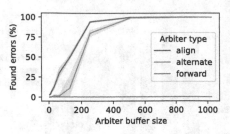

Fig. 4. Percentage of primes checked and errors found (of 40000 events in total) by the TeSSLa monitor for different arbiter specifications and arbiter buffer sizes.

1. the *forward* arbiter just forwards events as they come; it is equivalent to writing a script that parses output of generators and (atomically) feeds events into a pipe from which TeSSLa reads events.
2. the *alternate* arbiter always forwards the event from the stream where we have seen fewer events so far; if streams happen to be aligned (that is, contain no or only equally-sized *hole* events), the events will perfectly alternate.
3. the *align* arbiter is the one we used in our original implementation to intelligently align both streams

Figure 4 shows the impact of these different arbiter designs on how well the monitor is able to do its task, and that indeed more active arbiters yield better results—without them, the streams are perfectly aligned less than 1% of the time. While one could write similar functionality to align different, unsynchronized streams in TeSSLa directly, the language does not easily support this. As such, a combination of TeSSLa and VAMOS allows simpler specifications in a higher-level monitoring language, dealing with the correct ordering and preprocessing of events on the middleware level.

6.3   Bank

In this classic verification scenario, we wrote an interactive console application simulating a banking interface. Users can check bank account balances, and deposit, withdraw, or transfer money to and from various accounts. The condition we want to check is that no operations should be permitted that would allow an account balance to end up below 0.

We use an event source that employs DynamoRIO [9] to dynamically instrument the program to capture its inputs and outputs, which it parses to forward the relevant information to the monitor. The monitor in turn starts out with no knowledge about any of the account balances (and resets any gathered knowledge when hole events indicate that some information was lost), but discovers them through some of the observations it makes: the result of a check balance operation gives precise knowledge about an account's balance, while the success or failure of the deposit/withdraw/transfer operations provides lower and upper bounds on the potential balances. For example, if a withdrawal of some amount

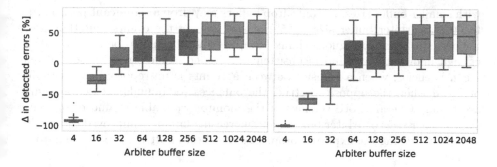

Fig. 5. Results of monitoring a simple banking simulator with VAMOS monitor (left) and TeSSLa monitor (right). Boxplots show the difference in the number of reported errors versus the number of errors the application made, in percent.

fails, this amount provides an upper bound on an account's balance, and any higher successive withdrawal attempt must surely fail too.

In the spirit of third-party monitoring, however, the stateful interface does not necessarily make it easy to derive these higher level events. For example, there is no individual confirmation that says that the withdrawal of some amount from some account was successful or not. Instead, the user selects an account, then the withdraw action, is then prompted which amount they would like to withdraw from said account, and after entering said amount, the system only displays a message that the withdrawal failed or was successful. The event source parses each individual step and provides them on two separate streams, one for the inputs and one for the outputs. This is where VAMOS' higher-level event recognition capabilities (see also the example in Section 4.1) allow the arbiter to recognize the higher-level events to forward to the monitor, which itself is therefore again much easier to specify.

To conduct measurements, we randomly generated 10 000 (well-formed) inputs and fed them to the banking application as fast as possible. We also let the application generate erroneous outputs (wrong balances, swapping success and failure messages) at random and measured how many those our best-effort third-party monitor was able to detect. The size of the source buffer was one page (128 events) and we varied the size of arbiter buffers from 4 to 2048.

The heavyweight instrumentation we used in this scenario caused the banking application to run through its script about 40% slower than without instrumentation for all sizes of the arbiter buffer, which is more than in our other benchmarks, but seems still plausible for interactive programs, and could be much more optimized. Our second metric is how many errors the monitor actually detects. Figure 5 shows this for both the monitor we described above and a TeSSLa variant that only considers exact knowledge about account balances (no upper or lower bounds) and thus finds fewer errors, demonstrating both an alternate monitor design and the use of our TeSSLa connector. The results vary quite a bit with arbiter buffer sizes and between runs, and the monitor may report more errors than were inserted into the run. This is because, first, especially with smaller buffer sizes, the autodrop buffers may drop a significant portion (up to 60% at arbiter buffer size 4, 5% at size 256) of the events, but the monitor needs to see a contiguous chunk of inputs and outputs to be able to gather enough information to find inconsistencies. Second, some errors cause multiple inconsistencies: when a transfer between accounts is misreported as successful or failed when the opposite is true, the balances (or bounds) of two accounts are wrong. Overall, both versions of the monitor were able to find errors with even smaller sizes of arbiter buffers, and increasing numbers improved the results steadily, matching the expected properties of a best-effort third-party monitor.

6.4   Case Study: Data Race Detection

While our other benchmarks were written artificially, we also used VAMOS to develop a best-effort data race monitor. Most tools for dynamic data race detection use some variation of the Eraser algorithm [51]: obtain a single global sequence of synchronization operations and memory accesses, and use the former to establish happens-before relationships whenever two threads access the same memory location in a potentially conflicting way. This entails keeping track of the last accessing threads for each location, as well as of the ways in which any two threads might have synchronized since those last accesses. Implemented naïvely, every memory access causes the monitor to pause the thread and atomically update the global synchronization state. Over a decade of engineering efforts directed at tools like ThreadSanitizer [52] and Helgrind [57] have reduced the resulting overhead, but it can still be substantial.

VAMOS enabled us to develop a similar monitor at significantly reduced engineering effort in a key area: efficiently communicating events to a monitor running in parallel in its own process, and building the global sequence of events. To build our monitor, we used ThreadSanitizer's source-code-based approach[5] to instrument relevant code locations, and for each such location, we reduce the need for global synchronization to fetching a timestamp from an atomically increased counter. Based on our facilities for dynamically creating event sources, each thread forms its own event source to which it sends events. In the correctness layer, the arbiter builds the single global stream of events used by our implementation of a version of the Goldilocks [22] algorithm (a variant of Eraser [51]), using the timestamps to make sure events are processed in the right order. Autodrop buffers may drop some events to avoid overloading the monitor; when this happens to a thread, we only report data races that the algorithm finds if all involved events were generated after the last time that events were dropped. This means that our tool may not find some races, often those that can only be detected looking at longer traces. However, it still found many races in our experiments, and other approaches to detecting data races in best-effort ways have similar restrictions [56].

Our implementation (contained in our artifact [12]) consists of:

---

[5] This decision was entirely to reduce our development effort; a dynamic instrumentation source could be swapped in without other changes.

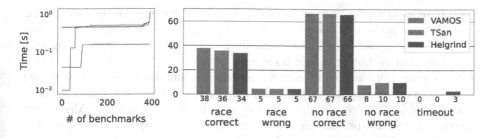

Fig. 6. Comparing running times of the three tools on all 391 benchmarks (left) and the correctness of their verdicts on the subset of 118 benchmarks for which it was possible to determine the ground truth (right). *Race* vs. *no race* indicates whether the tool found at least one data race, *correct* vs. *wrong* indicates whether that verdict matches the ground truth. For benchmarks with unknown ground truth, the three tools agreed on the existence of data races more than 99% of the time.

– a straightforward translation of the pseudocode in [22], using the C++ standard library set and map data structures, with extensions to handle holes;
– a small VAMOS specification to retrieve events from the variable number of event streams in order of their timestamps to forward to the monitor; the biggest complication here is deciding when to abandon looking for the next event in the sequence if it may have been dropped;
– an LLVM [40] instrumentation pass post-processing ThreadSanitizer's instrumentation to produce an event source compatible with VAMOS.

As such, we were able to use VAMOS to build a reasonable best-effort data-race monitor with relatively little effort, providing evidence that our ease-of-use design goal was achieved. To evaluate its performance, we tested it on 391 SV-COMP [7] concurrency test cases supported by our implementation, and compared it to two state-of-the-art dynamic data race detection tools, ThreadSanitizer [52] and Helgrind [57]. Figure 6 shows that the resulting monitor in most cases caused less overhead than both ThreadSanitizer and Helgrind in terms of time while producing largely the same (correct) verdicts.

7   Related Work

As mentioned before, VAMOS' design features a combination of ideas from works in run-time monitoring and related fields, which we review in this section.

Event Brokers/Event Recognition A large number of event broker systems with facilities for event recognition [18,58,55,26,1] already exist. These typically allow arbitrary event sources to connect and submit events, and arbitrarily many observers to subscribe to various event feeds. Mansouri-Samani and Sloman [44] outlined the features of such systems, including filtering and combining events, merging multiple monitoring traces into a global one, and using a database to store (parts of) traces and additional information for the longer term. Modern industrial implementations of this concept, like Apache Flink [1], are built for massively parallel stream processing in distributed systems, supporting arbitrary applications but providing no special abstractions for monitoring, in contrast to more run-time-monitoring-focused implementations like ReMinds [58]. Complex event recognition systems also sometimes provide capabilities for load-shedding [59], of which autodrop buffers are the simplest version. Most event recognition systems provide more features than VAMOS, but are also harder to set up for monitoring; in contrast, VAMOS offers a simple specification language that is efficient and still flexible enough for many monitoring scenarios.

Stream Run-Time Verification LoLa [19,24], TeSSLa [41], and Striver [27] are stream run-time verification [8] systems that allow expressing a monitor as a series of mutually recursive data streams that compute their current values based on each other's values. This requires some global notion of time, as the streams are updated with new values at time ticks and refer to values in other streams relative to the current tick, which is not necessarily available in a heterogeneous setting. Stream run-time verification systems also do not commonly support handling variable numbers of event sources. Some systems allow for dynamically instantiating sub-monitors for parts of the event stream [3,6,49,24] in a technique called *parametric trace slicing* [15]. This is used for logically splitting the events on a given stream into separate streams, making them easier to reason about, and can sometimes be exploited for parallelizing the monitor's work. These additional streams are internal to the monitoring logic, in contrast, VAMOS' ability to dynamically add new event sources affects the monitoring system's outside connections, while, internally, the arbiter still unifies the events coming in on all such connections into one global stream.

Instrumentation The two key questions in instrumentation revolve around the technical side of how a monitor accesses a monitored system as well as the behavioral side of what effects these accesses can have. On the technical side, static instrumentation can be either applied to source code [39,30,36,37,40,34] or compiled binaries [23,20], while dynamic instrumentation, like DyanmoRIO, is applied to running programs [43,46,9]. Alternatively, monitored systems or the platforms they run on may have specific interfaces for monitors already, such as PTrace and DTrace [10,28,50] in the Linux kernel. Any of these can be used to create an instrumentation tool for VAMOS.

On the behavioral side, Cassar et al. surveyed various forms of instrumentation between completely synchronous and offline [11]. Many of the systems surveyed [21,4,14,16] use a form of static instrumentation that can either do the necessary monitoring work while interrupting the program's current thread whenever an event is generated, or offer the alternative of using the interruption to export the necessary data to a log to be processed asynchronously or offline. A mixed form called *Asynchronous Monitoring with Checkpoints* allows stopping the monitored system at certain points to let the monitor catch up [25]. Our autodrop buffers instead trade precision for avoiding this kind of overhead. Aside from the survey, some systems (like TeSSLa [41]) incrementalize their default offline behavior to provide a monitor that may eventually significantly lag behind the monitored system.

Executing monitoring code or even just writing event data to a file or sending it over the network is costly in terms of overhead, even more so if multiple threads need to synchronize on the relevant code. Ha et al. proposed Cache-Friendly Asymmetric Buffering [29] to run low-overhead run-time analyses on multicore platforms. They only transfer 64-bit values, which suffices for some analyses, but not for general-purpose event data. Our adapted implementation thus has to do some extra work, but shares the idea of using a lock-free single-producer-single-consumer ring buffer for low overhead and high throughput.

While we try to minimize it, we accept some overhead for instrumentation as given. Especially in real-time systems, some run-time monitoring solutions adjust the activation status of parts of the instrumentation according to some metrics of overhead, inserting hole events for phases when instrumentation is deactivated [5,31,2]. In contrast, the focus of load-shedding through autodrop buffers is on ensuring that the higher-level part of the monitor is working with reasonably up-to-date events while not forcing the monitored system to wait. For monitors that do not rely on extensive summarization of dropped events, the two approaches could easily be combined.

Monitorability and Missing Events Monitorability [38,47] studies the ability of a runtime monitor to produce reliable verdicts about the monitored system. The possiblity of missing arbitrary events on an event stream without knowing about it significantly reduces the number of monitorable properties [35]. The *autodrop* buffers of VAMOS instead insert *hole* information, which some LTL [32], TeSSLa [42], and Mealy machine [54] specifications can be patched to handle automatically. Run-time verification with state estimation [53] uses a Hidden Markov Model to estimate the data lost in missing events.

8   Conclusion

We have presented VAMOS, which we designed as middleware for best-effort third-party run-time monitoring. Its goal is to significantly simplify the instrumentation part of monitoring, broadly construed as the gathering of high-level observations that serve as the basis for traditional monitoring specifications, particularly for best-effort third-party run-time monitoring, which may often need some significant preprocessing of the gathered information, potentially collected from multiple heterogeneous sources. We have presented preliminary evidence that the way we built VAMOS can handle large numbers of events and lets us specify a variety of monitors with relative ease. In future work, we plan to apply VAMOS' to more diverse application scenarios, such as multithreaded webservers processing many requests in parallel, or embedded software, and to integrate our tools with other higher-level languages. If a system's behavior conforms to the expectation of a third party, this is generally recognized as inspiring a higher level of trust than if that monitor was written by the system's developers. We hope that our design can help making best-effort third-party run-time monitoring more common.

Acknowledgements This work was supported in part by the ERC-2020-AdG 101020093. The authors would like to thank the anonymous FASE reviewers for their valuable feedback and suggestions.

References

1. Apache Software Foundation: Apache Flink (2023), https://flink.apache.org/
2. Arafa, P., Kashif, H., Fischmeister, S.: Dime: Time-aware dynamic binary instrumentation using rate-based resource allocation. In: EMSOFT 2013. pp. 1–10 (2013). https://doi.org/10.1109/EMSOFT.2013.6658603
3. Barringer, H., Falcone, Y., Havelund, K., Reger, G., Rydeheard, D.E.: Quantified event automata: Towards expressive and efficient runtime monitors. In: FM 2012. pp. 68–84 (2012). https://doi.org/10.1007/978-3-642-32759-9_9
4. Barringer, H., Goldberg, A., Havelund, K., Sen, K.: Rule-based runtime verification. In: VMCAI 2004. pp. 44–57 (2004). https://doi.org/10.1007/978-3-540-24622-0_5
5. Bartocci, E., Grosu, R., Karmarkar, A., Smolka, S.A., Stoller, S.D., Zadok, E., Seyster, J.: Adaptive runtime verification. In: RV 2012. pp. 168–182 (2012). https://doi.org/10.1007/978-3-642-35632-2_18
6. Basin, D., Klaedtke, F., Müller, S., Zălinescu, E.: Monitoring metric first-order temporal properties. Journal of the ACM **62**(2) (May 2015). https://doi.org/10.1145/2699444
7. Beyer, D.: Progress on software verification: SV-COMP 2022. In: TACAS 2022. pp. 375–402 (2022). https://doi.org/10.1007/978-3-030-99527-0_20
8. Bozzelli, L., Sánchez, C.: Foundations of boolean stream runtime verification. Theoretial Computer Science **631**, 118–138 (June 2016). https://doi.org/10.1016/j.tcs.2016.04.019
9. Bruening, D., Zhao, Q., Amarasinghe, S.: Transparent dynamic instrumentation. In: VEE 2012. p. 133–144 (2012). https://doi.org/10.1145/2151024.2151043
10. Cantrill, B., Shapiro, M.W., Leventhal, A.H.: Dynamic instrumentation of production systems. In: USENIX 2004. pp. 15–28 (2004), http://www.usenix.org/publications/library/proceedings/usenix04/tech/general/cantrill.html
11. Cassar, I., Francalanza, A., Aceto, L., Ingólfsdóttir, A.: A survey of runtime monitoring instrumentation techniques. In: PrePost@iFM 2017. EPTCS, vol. 254, pp. 15–28 (2017). https://doi.org/10.4204/EPTCS.254.2
12. Chalupa, M., Muehlboeck, F., Muroya Lei, S., Henzinger, T.A.: VAMOS: Middleware for best-effort third-party monitoring, artifact (2023). https://doi.org/10.5281/zenodo.7574688
13. Chalupa, M., Muehlboeck, F., Muroya Lei, S., Henzinger, T.A.: VAMOS: Middleware for best-effort third-party monitoring, technical report. Tech. Rep. 12407, Institute of Science and Technology Austria (2023), https://research-explorer.ista.ac.at/record/12407

14. Chen, F., Roşu, G.: Java-MOP: A monitoring oriented programming environment for java. In: TACAS 2005. pp. 546–550 (2005). https://doi.org/10.1007/978-3-540-31980-1_36

15. Chen, F., Rosu, G.: Parametric trace slicing and monitoring. In: TACAS 2009. pp. 246–261 (2009). https://doi.org/10.1007/978-3-642-00768-2_23

16. Colombo, C., Pace, G.J., Schneider, G.: LARVA — safer monitoring of real-time java programs (tool paper). In: SEFM 2009. pp. 33–37 (2009). https://doi.org/10.1109/SEFM.2009.13

17. Convent, L., Hungerecker, S., Leucker, M., Scheffel, T., Schmitz, M., Thoma, D.: TeSSLa: Temporal stream-based specification language. In: SBMF 2018. pp. 144–162 (2018). https://doi.org/10.1007/978-3-030-03044-5_10

18. Cugola, G., Margara, A.: Processing flows of information: From data stream to complex event processing. ACM Computing Surveys 44(3), 15:1–15:62 (2012). https://doi.org/10.1145/2187671.2187677

19. D'Angelo, B., Sankaranarayanan, S., Sánchez, C., Robinson, W., Finkbeiner, B., Sipma, H.B., Mehrotra, S., Manna, Z.: LOLA: runtime monitoring of synchronous systems. In: TIME 2005. pp. 166–174 (2005). https://doi.org/10.1109/TIME.2005.26

20. De Bus, B., Chanet, D., De Sutter, B., Van Put, L., De Bosschere, K.: The design and implementation of FIT: A flexible instrumentation toolkit. In: PASTE 2004. p. 29–34 (2004). https://doi.org/10.1145/996821.996833

21. Drusinsky, D.: Monitoring temporal rules combined with time series. In: CAV 2003. pp. 114–117 (2003). https://doi.org/10.1007/978-3-540-45069-6_11

22. Elmas, T., Qadeer, S., Tasiran, S.: Goldilocks: A race and transaction-aware java runtime. In: PLDI 2007. p. 245–255 (2007). https://doi.org/10.1145/1250734.1250762

23. Eustace, A., Srivastava, A.: ATOM: A flexible interface for building high performance program analysis tools. In: USENIX 1995. pp. 303–314 (1995), https://www.usenix.org/conference/usenix-1995-technical-conference/atom-flexible-interface-building-high-performance

24. Faymonville, P., Finkbeiner, B., Schirmer, S., Torfah, H.: A stream-based specification language for network monitoring. In: RV 2016. pp. 152–168 (2016). https://doi.org/10.1007/978-3-319-46982-9_10

25. Francalanza, A., Seychell, A.: Synthesising correct concurrent runtime monitors. Formal Methods in System Design 46(3), 226–261 (2015). https://doi.org/10.1007/s10703-014-0217-0

26. Giatrakos, N., Alevizos, E., Artikis, A., Deligiannakis, A., Garofalakis, M.: Complex event recognition in the big data era: A survey. The VLDB Journal 29(1), 313–352 (July 2019). https://doi.org/10.1007/s00778-019-00557-w

27. Gorostiaga, F., Sánchez, C.: Striver: Stream runtime verification for real-time event-streams. In: RV 2018. pp. 282–298 (2018). https://doi.org/10.1007/978-3-030-03769-7_16

28. Gregg, B.: DTrace: Dynamic Tracing in Oracle Solaris, Mac OS X, and FreeBSD. Prentice Hall (2011)

29. Ha, J., Arnold, M., Blackburn, S.M., McKinley, K.S.: A concurrent dynamic analysis framework for multicore hardware. In: OOPSLA 2009. pp. 155–174 (2009). https://doi.org/10.1145/1640089.1640101

30. Havelund, K., Rosu, G.: Monitoring Java programs with Java pathexplorer. In: RV 2001. pp. 200–217 (2001). https://doi.org/10.1016/S1571-0661(04)00253-1

31. Huang, X., Seyster, J., Callanan, S., Dixit, K., Grosu, R., Smolka, S.A., Stoller, S.D., Zadok, E.: Software monitoring with controllable overhead. International Journal on Software Tools for Technology Transfer **14**(3), 327–347 (2012). https://doi.org/10.1007/s10009-010-0184-4

32. Joshi, Y., Tchamgoue, G.M., Fischmeister, S.: Runtime verification of LTL on lossy traces. In: SAC 2017. p. 1379–1386 (2017). https://doi.org/10.1145/3019612.3019827

33. Kallwies, H., Leucker, M., Schmitz, M., Schulz, A., Thoma, D., Weiss, A.: TeSSLa - an ecosystem for runtime verification. In: RV 2022. pp. 314–324 (2022). https://doi.org/10.1007/978-3-031-17196-3_20

34. Karaorman, M., Freeman, J.: jMonitor: Java runtime event specification and monitoring library. In: RV 2004. pp. 181–200 (2005). https://doi.org/10.1016/j.entcs.2004.01.027

35. Kauffman, S., Havelund, K., Fischmeister, S.: What can we monitor over unreliable channels? International Journal on Software Tools for Technology Transfer **23**(4), 579–600 (2021). https://doi.org/10.1007/s10009-021-00625-z

36. Kiczales, G., Hilsdale, E., Hugunin, J., Kersten, M., Palm, J., Griswold, W.G.: An overview of AspectJ. In: ECOOP 2001. pp. 327–353 (2001). https://doi.org/10.1007/3-540-45337-7_{1}{8}

37. Kim, M., Kannan, S., Lee, I., Sokolsky, O., Viswanathan, M.: Java-MaC: A runtime assurance tool for Java programs. In: RV 2001. pp. 218–235 (2001). https://doi.org/10.1016/s1571-0661(04)00254-3

38. Kim, M., Kannan, S., Lee, I., Sokolsky, O., Viswanathan, M.: Computational analysis of run-time monitoring - fundamentals of java-mac. In: RV 2002. pp. 80–94 (2002). https://doi.org/10.1016/S1571-0661(04)80578-4

39. Kim, M., Viswanathan, M., Ben-Abdallah, H., Kannan, S., Lee, I., Sokolsky, O.: Formally specified monitoring of temporal properties. In: ECRTS 1999. pp. 114–122 (1999). https://doi.org/10.1109/EMRTS.1999.777457

40. Lattner, C., Adve, V.S.: LLVM: A compilation framework for lifelong program analysis & transformation. In: CGO 2004. pp. 75–88 (2004). https://doi.org/10.1109/CGO.2004.1281665

41. Leucker, M., Sánchez, C., Scheffel, T., Schmitz, M., Schramm, A.: TeSSLa: runtime verification of non-synchronized real-time streams. In: SAC 2018. pp. 1925–1933 (2018). https://doi.org/10.1145/3167132.3167338

42. Leucker, M., Sánchez, C., Scheffel, T., Schmitz, M., Thoma, D.: Runtime verification for timed event streams with partial information. In: RV 2019. pp. 273–291 (2019). https://doi.org/10.1007/978-3-030-32079-9_16

43. Luk, C., Cohn, R.S., Muth, R., Patil, H., Klauser, A., Lowney, P.G., Wallace, S., Reddi, V.J., Hazelwood, K.M.: Pin: building customized program analysis tools with dynamic instrumentation. In: PLDI 2005. pp. 190–200 (2005). https://doi.org/10.1145/1065010.1065034

44. Mansouri-Samani, M., Sloman, M.: Monitoring distributed systems. IEEE Network **7**(6), 20–30 (1993). https://doi.org/10.1109/65.244791

45. Muehlboeck, F., Henzinger, T.A.: Differential monitoring. In: RV 2021. pp. 231–243 (2021). https://doi.org/10.1007/978-3-030-88494-9_12

46. Nethercote, N., Seward, J.: Valgrind: a framework for heavyweight dynamic binary instrumentation. In: PLDI 2007. pp. 89–100 (2007). https://doi.org/10.1145/1250734.1250746

47. Pnueli, A., Zaks, A.: PSL model checking and run-time verification via testers. In: FM 2006. pp. 573–586 (2006). https://doi.org/10.1007/11813040_38

48. Rabiser, R., Guinea, S., Vierhauser, M., Baresi, L., Grünbacher, P.: A comparison framework for runtime monitoring approaches. Journal of Systems and Software **125**, 309–321 (2017). https://doi.org/10.1016/j.jss.2016.12.034

49. Reger, G., Cruz, H.C., Rydeheard, D.: MarQ: Monitoring at runtime with QEA. In: TACAS 2015. pp. 596–610 (2015). https://doi.org/10.1007/978-3-662-46681-0_55

50. Rosenberg, C.M., Steffen, M., Stolz, V.: Leveraging DTrace for runtime verification. In: RV 2016. pp. 318–332 (2016). https://doi.org/10.1007/978-3-319-46982-9_20

51. Savage, S., Burrows, M., Nelson, G., Sobalvarro, P., Anderson, T.: Eraser: A dynamic data race detector for multithreaded programs. ACM Transactions on Computer Systems **15**(4), 391–411 (November 1997). https://doi.org/10.1145/265924.265927

52. Serebryany, K., Iskhodzhanov, T.: ThreadSanitizer: Data race detection in practice. In: WBIA 2009. p. 62–71 (2009). https://doi.org/10.1145/1791194.1791203

53. Stoller, S.D., Bartocci, E., Seyster, J., Grosu, R., Havelund, K., Smolka, S.A., Zadok, E.: Runtime verification with state estimation. In: RV 2011. pp. 193–207 (2012). https://doi.org/10.1007/978-3-642-29860-8_15

54. Taleb, R., Khoury, R., Hallé, S.: Runtime verification under access restrictions. In: FormaliSE@ICSE 2021. pp. 31–41 (2021). https://doi.org/10.1109/FormaliSE52586.2021.00010

55. Tawsif, K., Hossen, J., Raja, J.E., Jesmeen, M.Z.H., Arif, E.M.H.: A review on complex event processing systems for big data. In: CAMP 2018. pp. 1–6 (2018). https://doi.org/10.1109/INFRKM.2018.8464787

56. Thokair, M.A., Zhang, M., Mathur, U., Viswanathan, M.: Dynamic race detection with O(1) samples. PACMPL **7**(POPL) (January 2023). https://doi.org/10.1145/3571238, https://doi.org/10.1145/3571238

57. Valgrind: Helgrind (2023), https://valgrind.org/docs/manual/hg-manual.html

58. Vierhauser, M., Rabiser, R., Grünbacher, P., Seyerlehner, K., Wallner, S., Zeisel, H.: ReMinds: A flexible runtime monitoring framework for systems of systems. Journal of Systems and Software **112**, 123–136 (2016). https://doi.org/10.1016/j.jss.2015.07.008

59. Zhao, B., Viet Hung, N.Q., Weidlich, M.: Load shedding for complex event processing: Input-based and state-based techniques. In: ICDE 2020. pp. 1093–1104 (2020). https://doi.org/10.1109/ICDE48307.2020.00099

Yet Another Model! A Study on Model's Similarities for Defect and Code Smells

Geanderson Santos[1]($\boxtimes$) (iD), Amanda Santana[1] (iD), Gustavo Vale[2] (iD),
and Eduardo Figueiredo[1] (iD)

[1] Federal University of Minas Gerais, Belo Horizonte, Brazil
{geanderson,amandads,figueiredo}@dcc.ufmg.br
[2] Saarland University, Saarbrücken, Germany
vale@cs.uni-saarland.de

Abstract. Software defect and code smell prediction help developers
identify problems in the code and fix them before they degrade the quality or the user experience. The prediction of software defects and code
smells is challenging, since it involves many factors inherent to the development process. Many studies propose machine learning models for
defects and code smells. However, we have not found studies that explore
and compare these machine learning models, nor that focus on the explainability of the models. This analysis allows us to verify which features
and quality attributes influence software defects and code smells. Hence,
developers can use this information to predict if a class may be faulty or
smelly through the evaluation of a few features and quality attributes.
In this study, we fill this gap by comparing machine learning models
for predicting defects and seven code smells. We trained in a dataset
composed of 19,024 classes and 70 software features that range from different quality attributes extracted from 14 Java open-source projects. We
then ensemble five machine learning models and employed explainability concepts to explore the redundancies in the models using the top-10
software features and quality attributes that are known to contribute to
the defects and code smell predictions. Furthermore, we conclude that
although the quality attributes vary among the models, the complexity,
documentation, and size are the most relevant. More specifically, Nesting
Level Else-If is the only software feature relevant to all models.

Keywords: Defect Prediction · Code Smells Detection · Explainable
Machine Learning · Quality Attributes

1 Introduction

Software defects appear in different stages of the life-cycle of software systems
degrading the software quality and hurting the user experience [25]. Sometimes,
the damage caused by software defects is in-reversible [44]. As consequence, the
software cost increases as developers need time to fix defects [43]. As a result,
it is better to avoid them as much as possible. Several studies showed that the

© The Author(s) 2023
L. Lambers and S. Uchitel (Eds.): FASE 2023, LNCS 13991, pp. 282–305, 2023.
https://doi.org/10.1007/978-3-031-30826-0_16

presence of code smells and anti-patterns are normally related to defecting code [24,34,49,51]. Code smells are symptoms of decisions on the implementation that may degrade the code quality [22]. Anti-patterns are the misuse of solutions to recurring problems [9]. For instance, Khomh et al. (2012) found that classes classified as God Classes are more defect-prone than classes that are not smelly. In this paper, we refer to code smells and anti-patterns as code smells.

One technique to mitigate the impact of defects and code smells is the application of strategies that anticipate problematic code [47], usually with the use of machine learning models that predict a defect or code smell [12,13,14,26,35,45,47,52,73]. Training and evaluating machine learning models is a hard task, since (i) it needs a large dataset, to avoid overfitting; (ii) the process of obtaining the labels and features to serve as input is costly, and it requires the use of different tools to support it; (iii) setting up the environment for training and evaluating models is time-consuming and computationally expensive, even though some tools help to automatize the process, and; (iv) understanding the importance of the features and how they affect the model is complex [39].

With these difficulties in mind, our goal is to identify a set of features that can be used by developers to simplify the process of defect and code smell prediction. To simplify, we aim at reducing the number of features that need to be collected to predict or identify possible candidates to present defects and code smells, through an analysis of model redundancies. To the best of our knowledge, no other studies have investigated similarities between the defect and code smell models. Instead, most studies focus on proposing and assessing the performance of models that predict defects or code smells [27,35,41,44]. In this work, we fill this gap through an analysis of which features are redundant or different in models built for defects and for seven code smells. Even more, we highlight which quality attributes are relevant to their prediction. This analysis is possible by the use of the SHAP technique, which determines the contribution of each feature to the prediction. As a result, using SHAP allows the verification of the features that contributed the most to the prediction and whether the features had high or low values.

To achieve our goal, we use a subset of 14 open-source Java systems that had its features and defects annotated [15,16]. We then employ the Organic tool [48] to detect nine code smells. We merged three of these smells due to similar definitions. After merging the data, we train and evaluate an ensemble machine learning model composed of five algorithms for each of our targets, i.e., defects and code smells. After evaluating the performance of our ensemble, we apply the SHAP technique to identify which features are relevant for each model. Finally, we analyze the results in terms of: (i) which features are relevant for each model; (ii) which features contribute the most for two or more models to identify redundancies in the models; (iii) which quality attributes are important to the defect and code smell prediction.

Our main findings are: (i) from the seven code smells evaluated, we identified that the most similar models to the Defect are the God Class, Refused Bequest, and Spaghetti Code; (ii) Nesting Level Else-If (NLE) and Comment Density

(CD) are the most important features; (iii) most features have high values, except on Refused Bequest; (iv) we identified sets of features that are common in trios of problems, such as API Documentation (AD), which is important for Defects, God Class, and Refused Bequest; (v) documentation, complexity, and size are the quality attributes that contribute the most for the prediction of defects and code smells; (vi) the intersection of features between the defects and code smells ranges from 40% for Refused Bequest to 60% of the God Class. We also contributed to the community by providing an extension of the previous dataset of defects [15,16] through the addition of nine smells, available in our online appendix [64]. As a consequence of these analyses, we obtained a smaller set of features that contributes to the prediction of defects and code smells. Developers and researches may train machine learning models with less effort using these findings, or they may use these features to identify possible candidates for introducing defects and code smells.

We organize the remainder of this work as follows. Section 2 describes the background of our work. Section 3 shows how we structured the methodology. Then, Section 4 presents the results of our evaluation comparing the defect model with the code smells. Section 5 discusses the main threats to validity of our investigation. Section 6 presents the related work our investigation is based on. Finally, Section 7 concludes this paper with remarks for further explorations about the subject.

2 Background

2.1 Defects

A software defect represents an error, failure, or bug [1] in a software project, that harm the appearance, operation, functionality, or performance of the target software project [25]. Defects may appear on different development stages [71] and may interrupt the development progress and increase the planned budget of software projects [43]. Furthermore, a software team may discover software defects after code release, generating a significant effort to tackle defects in production [37]. To mitigate these defects in software development, defect prediction may find the defective classes [42,43,73] before system testing and release. For instance, if a software team has limited resources for software inspection, a defect predictor may indicate which modules are most likely to be defective.

2.2 Code Smells

Brown et al. [9] proposed a catalog of anti-patterns, that are solutions to recurring problems based on design patterns, but instead of providing reusable code, it impacts negatively on the source code. Later, Fowler [22] introduced the code smells as symptoms of sub-optimal decisions in the software implementation that leads to code quality degradation. Since our defect dataset is class-level, we only consider the problems related to classes. In our work, we considered the following smells: Refused Bequest (RB), Brain Class (BC), Class Data Should be Private (CP), Complex Class (CC), Data Class (DC), God Class (GC), Lazy Class (LC), Spaghetti Code (SC), and Speculative Generality (SG). The definitions of the problems presented in this paper are: God Class is a large class that has too many responsibilities and centralizes the module functionality [61]. Refused Bequest is a class that does not use its parent behavior [22]. Spaghetti Code is a class that has methods with large and unique multistage process flow [9]. Due to space constraints, the definitions of all evaluated problems can be found in our replication package [64].

3   Study Design

3.1   Research Questions

In this paper, we investigate the similarities and redundancies between the software features used to predict defects and code smells. We can use this information to simplify the prediction model or identify possible candidates for introducing defects or smells. We employed data preparation to find the software features for the defect and code smell prediction models. Therefore, our main objective is to examine the software features applied for both predictions. Our paper investigates the following research questions.

RQ1. Are the defect and class-level code smell models explainable?

RQ2. Which software features are present in both defect and code smell models?

RQ3. Which software quality attributes are more relevant for the prediction of both defects and code smells?

3.2   Data

Predicting a defect or a code smell is a supervised learning problem that requires a dataset with the values of the independent and dependent variables for each sample. Many datasets were proposed in the literature [13,31,44]; however, in this work, the selected dataset portrays a joined version of several resources publicly available in the literature [15,16,17,74]. In total, five data sources compose this dataset: PROMISE [65], Eclipse Bug Prediction [84], Bug Prediction Dataset [13], Bugcatchers Bug Dataset [24], and GitHub Bug Dataset [74][3]. The dataset has classes from 34 open-source Java projects [77]. Furthermore, the data comprises 70 software features related to different aspects of the code. We can divide the features into seven quality attributes: documentation, coupling, cohesion, clone, size, complexity, and inheritance. We also highlight that the dataset is imbalanced. Only around 20% of the classes have a defect, and for the code smells, the range of classes they affect is between 4 to 16.2%. For these reasons, the dataset has a wide range of software features that may promote interesting

---

[3] https://zenodo.org/record/3693686

analysis of the defects and code smells. Finally, the open-source data facilitates the collection of code smells.

Data Collection. The first step of our study is to collect the data about the code smells to merge with the defect data [15]. We applied the Organic tool [48] to detect the code smells. As all projects are available on GitHub, we manually cloned the source code matching the project version included in the dataset. Since most of the systems in the original dataset have less than 1000 classes (20 systems), we collected data from the ones with more than 1000 classes (14 projects). We decided to focus on these projects because they represent 75% of the entire defect data and are readily available on GitHub. Additionally, we matched the name of the detected instances of code smells to the class name present in our defect dataset. Hence, independently of whether a class had a smell or not, we only consider it if the match was found in both datasets (i.e., the one with the defects and the one with the code smells). In the case that we could not find a match, we do not consider the class for further investigation. We use this approach to avoid bias as it would be unfair to determine that a class that Organic could not find in the defect dataset is non-smelly. Furthermore, this approach decreased the number of classes for most of the projects.

Table 1. Summary of the data for each project.

Project	Version	Classes	CP	DC	GC	LC	RB	SC	SG	defects
Ant	1.7	1592	12	161	403	211	57	102	36	330
Broadleaf	3.0	1303	3	231	168	97	66	36	36	277
Camel	1.6	2456	7	115	198	519	53	7	87	550
Elasticsearch	0.9	2605	52	42	380	374	187	88	88	362
Hazelcast	3.3	1443	19	71	74	123	115	26	46	232
JDT	3.4	960	308	44	358	1	54	150	31	197
Jedit	4.3	1108	101	56	331	133	9	144	58	264
Lucene	2.4	500	51	13	96	67	66	36	15	208
Neo4J	1.9	1654	64	20	101	187	67	22	92	18
OrientDB	1.6	880	54	30	181	141	40	58	53	171
PDE	3.4	1130	5	34	206	0	22	56	84	167
POI	3.0	822	6	103	58	130	219	18	17	434
Titan	0.5	765	28	11	75	96	18	29	54	66
Xalan	2.7	1794	102	113	456	298	211	159	60	947
Total		**19012**	**812**	**1044**	**3085**	**2377**	**1184**	**931**	**757**	**4223**
Percentage		**100%**	**4.3%**	**5.5%**	**16.2%**	**12.5%**	**6.2%**	**4.9%**	**4%**	**22.2%**

CP: *Class Data Should be Private; **DC***: *Data Class; **GC***: *God Class; **LC***: *Lazy Class;* ***RB***: *Refused Bequest; **SC***: *Spaghetti Code; **SG***: *Speculative Generality.*

Organic collects a wide range of code smells, including method and class ones. However, as the defect dataset is class-level, we only use the code smells found in classes. For this reason, we obtained the ground truth of nine smells, as described in Section 2.2. After collecting the data, we merged three code smells: Brain Class (BC), God Class (GC), and Complex Class (CC) into one code smell. Beyond the similar definitions, we merged the BC and CC to GC due to their low occurrence on the dataset. Hence, we named the code smell as God Class (GC), since it is more used in the literature [66]. Consequently, we evaluate seven smells in total.

Table 1 shows a summary of the data for each project. The first column presents the project's name. The second column presents the project version included in the dataset. The third column shows the number of classes for each system. Columns 4 through 10 show the number of smells found. The last column presents the number of defects in the system. The Total row presents the absolute number of classes and smelly/defective classes. The Percentage row presents the percentage of classes affected by smell/defect. We can observe from Table 1 that the projects vary in size, Lucene has the least classes (500), while Elasticsearch has the most (2605). We also observe that the number of smells and defects varies greatly for each system. For instance, the Xalan system has 456 instances of God Class and 947 defects. Meanwhile, even though the Neo4J is a large system, it had only 18 defects, i.e., 1% of its classes are defective.

Code Smells Validation. To validate the code smells collected with Organic, we conducted a manual validation with developers. First, we selected three of the most frequent code smells (GC, RB, and SC), since manual validation is costly and developers have to first understand the code. Then, we elaborate questions about each code smell based on the current literature: God Class (GC) [66], Refused Bequest (RB) [36] and Spaghetti Code (SC) [9]. We then produced a pilot study with four developers to improve the questions using classes that Organic classified as either one of the code smells. This allowed us to verify if the questions are suitable for our goals and whether the surveyed developers understood them. For each instance in our sample, we asked nine questions (3 for each smell). The developer was blind to which code smells they were evaluating and had four possible responses: "Yes", "No", "Don't Know", and "NA" (Not Applicable). The questions and developers' answers can be found in our replication package [64].

To make our validation robust, we calculated the sample size based on the number of instances for each of the three smells in our dataset. We then set a confidence level of 90% and a margin error of 10%. As a result, the sample size should have at least eighteen classes of each target code smell. Furthermore, to avoid biasing the analysis, we determine that two developers should evaluate each instance in our sample. In this case, developers had to validate 108 software classes (54 unique). To validate the 108 software classes, we invited fifteen developers from different backgrounds, including two co-authors. One of the authors was the moderator of the analysis and did not participate in the validation. As there were three questions for each smell, in order to consider the instance as truly containing the smell, developers needed to reach an agreement with the expected answer that supports the presence of the code smell on two out of three questions. In addition, if the two developers that evaluated the same instance disagreed on the presence of the smell, a third and more experienced developer checked the instance to make the final decision. This tiebreaker evaluation was

done by two software specialists that did not participate in the previous validation.

In the end, the developers agree that all GC classified by the tool was correct
(i.e., 18 out of 18 responses). For RB, the developers agree in 14 out of the
18 software classes (meaning that approximately 77% of developers agree with
the tool). Finally, SC is slightly worse, where the developers classified 13 out of
the 18 classes as SC. Thus, SC classes achieved an agreement of 72% between
the developers and the tool. The results demonstrate that Organic can identify
code smells with an appropriate level of accuracy (around 84% of agreement
between them). For this reason, we conclude that the Organic data is adequate
to represent code smells.

3.3   Quality Attributes

Although the literature proposes many quality attributes to group software features [4,8,68], we focus on the quality attributes previously discussed in the
selected dataset [15,16]. These quality attributes cluster the entire collection of
software features. Therefore, we separate the aforementioned software features
into seven quality attributes: (i) *Complexity*, (ii) *Coupling*, (iii) *Size*, (iv) *Documentation*, (v) *Clone*, (vi) *Inheritance*, and (vii) *Cohesion*. Table 2 presents
the quality attributes with their definition and reference. The complete list of
software features (66 in total) and the quality attributes are available under the
replication package of this study [64].

Table 2. Quality Attributes.

Class	Definition	Reference
Clone	Measure the code cloning. They may be a copy and paste of an existing piece of source code, and may present smaller modifications considering the original code.	[15,74]
Cohesion	Measure to what extent the source code elements are coherent in the system.	[16,74]
Complexity	Measure the complexity of source code elements (typically algorithms).	[8,16,68]
Coupling	Measure the amount of dependencies of source code elements.	[3,16,68]
Documentation	Measure the amount of comments and documentation of source code elements in the system.	[4,16,22]
Inheritance	Measure the different aspects of the inheritance hierarchy of the system.	[4,16,22]
Size	Measure the basic properties of the analyzed system in terms of different aspects (e.g., number of code lines, number of classes, or methods).	[16,22,78]

3.4 Machine Learning

The predictive accuracy of machine learning classification models depends on the association between the structural software properties and a binary outcome. In this case, the properties are the software features widely evaluated in the literature [15,16], and the binary outcome is the prediction if the class is defective or non-defective or if the class presents each of the evaluated code smells. To compare the defect and code smell prediction models, we rely on the same set of software features, i.e., the models are trained with the same 66 measures, except on the target representing the presence/absence of defect/code smell. We train each machine learning model for each target (i.e., defect and code smell). To build these models, we employ a tool known as PyCaret [6] to assist in the different parts of the process, described later. Finally, to test the capacity of the models, we apply five evaluation metrics: accuracy, recall, precision, F1, and AUC [11].

Data Preparation. To build our models, we follow these fundamental steps described in Figure 1. The three rounded rectangles indicate the steps and the actions we performed to build the models. First, we clean the data (i). Then, we explore the data identifying how better to represent them for our models (ii). After, we prepare the features to avoid overfitting (iii).

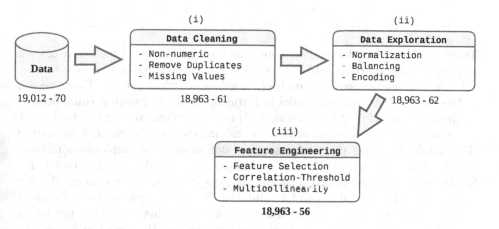

Fig. 1. Data Preparation Process Overview.

Data Cleaning. We first applied data cleaning to eliminate duplicated classes, non-numeric data, and missing values [56]. Hence, it was possible to vertically reduce the data as we removed a small chunk of repeated entries (61 classes). Further, we also reduced the horizontal dimension of the data from 70 to 65 features eliminating the non-numeric features. We also removed four over-represented software features. These software features gathered information about the exact line and column of the source code a class started and ended.

In the end, we executed data imputation to track the missing values, but the dataset had none.

Data Exploration. In the second step of the machine learning processing, we executed the data exploration. Therefore, we used one-hot encoding [38] to the *type* feature, which stores information about the class type. For instance, we created two new features for class and interface types. Subsequently, we applied data normalization using Standard Scaler [59]. Finally, we employed Synthetic Minority Oversampling Technique (SMOTE) [70] to deal with the imbalanced nature of the dataset. Table 1 summarizes the imbalanced nature of the targets compared to the data collection. For instance, from 19K classes, only 757 present Spaghetti Code (almost 4% of classes).

Feature Engineering. In the final step, we applied feature engineering to select the relevant software features. As a result, we executed feature selection, correlation analysis, and multicollinearity thresholds. First, the feature selection technique chooses a subset of software features from the combination of various permutation importance techniques, including Random Forest, Adaboost, and Linear correlation. Second, we checked the correlation between the subset of software features (99% of threshold). In doing so, we removed five software features (LLDC, TNLPA, TNA, TNPA, and TCLOC) because they were highly correlated with other software features (LDC, CLOC, NA, NLPA, and NPA). Additionally, we set the multicollinearity threshold to 85%, meaning that we remove software features with a correlation higher than the threshold. In the end, we ended up with 56 software features.

Training the Models. To build our classifier, we employ a technique known as the ensemble machine learning model [6]. This technique learns how to best combine the predictions from multiple machine learning models. Thus, we use a stronger machine learning model in terms of prediction, since it combines the prediction power of multiple models. To train the models, we divided the dataset into two sets: 70% of the data is used for training the models, and 30% for testing the models. To assess the performance of our models, we employed a method called k-fold cross-validation. This technique splits the data into K partitions. In our work, we used K=10 [11], and at each iteration, we use nine folds for training and the remaining fold for validation. We then permute these partitions on each iteration. As a result, we use each fold as training and as the validation set at least once. This method allows us to compare distinct models, helping us to avoid overfitting, as the training set varies on each iteration.

To identify which models are suitable to our goal, we evaluated 15 machine learning algorithms: CatBoost Classifier [6], Random Forest [23], Decision Tree [16], Extra Trees [6], Logistic Regression [29], K-Neighbors Classifier (KNN) [80], Gradient Boosting Machine [83], Extreme Gradient Boosting [63], Linear Discriminant Analysis [6], Ada Boost Classifier [55], Light Gradient Boosting Machine (LightGBM) [32], Naive Bayes [75], Dummy Classifier [55], Quadratic Discriminant Analysis [6], and Support Vector Machines (SVM) [23]. Furthermore, to tune the hyper-parameters of each model, we apply a technique called Optuna [5]. Optuna uses Bayesian optimization to find the best hyper-parameters for each model. After experimenting with all the targets, we observed that five models are able of achieving good performance independently of the target (i.e., defects or code smells): Random Forest [23], LightGBM [32], Extra Trees [10], Gradient Boosting Machine [72], and KNN [80]. For this reason, these models are carried out for the ensemble model. The data on the performance of the evaluated models can be found in our replication package [64]. To evaluate our models, we focus on the F1 and AUC metrics. F1 represents the harmonic mean of precision and recall. Additionally, AUC is relevant because we are dealing with binary classification and this metric shows the performance of a model at all thresholds. For these reasons, both metrics are suitable for the imbalanced nature of data [11].

Explaining the Models. The current literature offers many possibilities to explain machine learning models in multiple problems. One of the most prominent techniques spread in the literature is the application of SHAP (SHapley Addictive exPlanation) values [39]. These values compute the importance of each feature in the prediction model. Therefore, we can reason why a machine learning model made such decisions about the specific domain. For this reason, SHAP is appropriate as machine learning models are hard to explain [69] and features interact in complex patterns to create models that provide more accurate predictions. Consequently, knowing the logic behind a software class is a determinant factor that can help to tackle the reasons behind a defect or code smell in the target class.

4   Results

4.1   Predictive Capacity

Before explaining the models, we evaluate if they can effectively predict the code smells and defects. Even though we originally built models for the entire set of code smells, we observed that only three code smells (God Class, Refused Bequest, and Spaghetti Code) have comparable models to the defects. For this reason, we only present the results of these three code smells. We believe some code smells are not similar to the defect model because they indicate simple code with less chance of having a defect, for instance, Lazy Class and Data Class. As a result, these code smells seem to not have similarities with the defects. The remaining code smells results are available in the replication package [64].

Table 3. Performance of the Machine Learning Models.

Target	Accuracy	AUC	Recall	Precision	F1
God Class	0.944	0.973	0.801	0.844	0.823
Refused Bequest	0.976	0.951	0.645	0.939	0.765
Spaghetti Code	0.971	0.977	0.715	0.692	0.705
Defect	0.843	0.865	0.701	0.609	0.652

Table 3 shows the performance of each ensemble machine learning model with our four targets (i.e., defects and the three code smells). The values in the columns represent the mean of the 10-fold cross-validation. We present in each column the performance for the five evaluation metrics. We can observe from Table 3 that the performance of the ensemble model for the four targets is fairly acceptable, with models presenting an F1 score ranging from approximately 65% (defect model) to 82% (God Class model). These numbers are similar to other studies with similar purposes [15,16]. We conclude that the models can predict the targets with acceptable accuracy, as shown by the high AUC values in Table 3. For this reason, we may exploit these machine learning models to explain their prediction using the SHAP technique. In doing so, we can reason about the similarities of the software features associated with defects and code smell.

> *RQ1. The results show that the predictive accuracy of the defect and code smell models can be used to compare the models in terms of their features, with good F1 measures and high AUC. We also found that the class-level code smell models are slightly superior to the defect model in all five evaluation metrics.*

4.2   Explaining the Models

This section discusses the explanation of each target model. We rely on SHAP to support the model explanation [39]. To simplify our analysis, we consider the top-10 most influential software features on the target in each prediction model. We then compare each code smell model with the defective one. Our goal is to find similarities and redundancies between the software features that help the machine learning model to predict the target code smells and defects. We extract these ten software features from each of the four target models (i.e., the defect model and the three code smell models presented in this paper).

To illustrate our results, we employ a Venn diagram to check the intersection of features between the four models (Figures 2, 3, and 4). The Venn diagram displays two dashed circles, one for the code smell model and another for the defect model. Inside each dashed circle, we present the top-10 software features that contributed the most to the prediction of the target within inner circles. The color of these inner circles represents the feature's quality attribute. Likewise, the size of the inner circle represents the influence of the feature on the model, meaning that the bigger the size, the more it contributes to the target prediction. On each side of the inner circles, we have an arrow that indicates the direction of the feature value. For instance, a software feature with an arrow pointing up means that the software feature contributes to the prediction when its value is high. On the other hand, a software feature with an arrow pointing down means that the feature contributes to the prediction when its value is low. The software features on the intersection have two inner circles because they have a different impact on each target (i.e., defects and the three code smells). For a better understanding of the acronyms, we show on the right side of each diagram, a table with the acronym and the feature full name of all features that appears on the diagram.

God Class. Figure 2 shows the top-10 features that contribute to the Defect and God Class models, and their feature intersection. We can observe from Figure 2 that the defect model has an intersection with God Class of 6 out of 10 features. This means that 60% of the top-10 features that contribute the most to predictions are the same for both models. These features are: CD, CLOC, AD, NL, NLE, and CLLC; and most of them are related to documentation (3 out of 6) and complexity (2 out of 6). The only difference is for the CD, which needs to have low values to help in the God Class prediction. All remaining software features require a high value to predict a defect or a God Class (see arrows up). Moreover, in terms of importance, for both models, the largest inner circles are for NLE, NL, and AD. For the AD, its importance is smaller for the GC model compared to the defect model. Meanwhile, for the NLE, the importance of God Class is a bit larger than for the defect model. For the NL feature, their importance was equivalent.

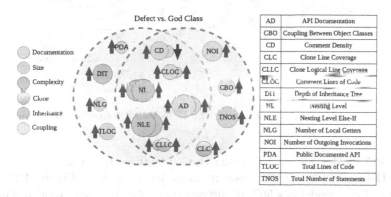

Fig. 2. Top-10 Software Features for the Defect and God Class Models.

Refused Bequest. Figure 3 shows the top-10 features that contribute the most to the Defect and Refused Bequest models. We can observe from the Venn diagram in Figure 3 that the defect model has an intersection of 40% (4 out of 10 features) with the Refused Bequest model when considering their top-10 software features. The features that intersect are CD, AD, NLE, and DIT. It is interesting to notice that for 3 out of the 4 software features in the intersection, the values that help to detect the Refused Bequest have to be low (see arrows pointing down), while for the defect model, all of them require to have high values. Furthermore, most of the Refused Bequest features have to be low (6 or 60%). In terms of importance, the DIT and NLE features were similar for both models. However, for both CD and AD, their contribution to the Refused Bequest model was smaller. Additionally, two features that highly contributed to the Refused Bequest are not in the intersection (NOP and NOA), while one (NL) is outside the intersection for the defect model. We also note that three features are related to the inheritance quality attribute, but only one intersects for both models, the

DIT one. We also observe that the size is relevant for both models. However, we do not have any size feature on the intersection of the models. The cohesion aspect was important only for the Refused Bequest model. The documentation attribute, which is relevant for the defect model (4 out of 10), has two of them with small importance (CLOC and PDA). The complexity attribute, indicated by NLE, is also very relevant for both models. CBO is the only coupling metric in the Refused Bequest model.

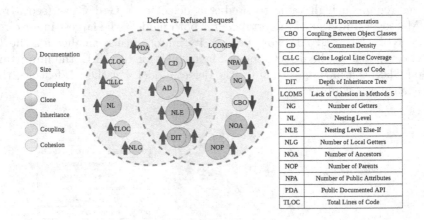

AD	API Documentation
CBO	Coupling Between Object Classes
CD	Comment Density
CLLC	Clone Logical Line Coverage
CLOC	Comment Lines of Code
DIT	Depth of Inheritance Tree
LCOM5	Lack of Cohesion in Methods 5
NG	Number of Getters
NL	Nesting Level
NLE	Nesting Level Else-If
NLG	Number of Local Getters
NOA	Number of Ancestors
NOP	Number of Parents
NPA	Number of Public Attributes
PDA	Public Documented API
TLOC	Total Lines of Code

Fig. 3. Top-10 Software Features for the Defect and Refused Bequest Models.

Spaghetti Code. Figure 4 presents the 10 features that are most important to the Defect and Spaghetti Code models. We observe in Figure 4 that the Spaghetti Code model has 50% of intersection with the defect model. They intersect with the CD, CLOC, CLLC, NL, and NLE features. For both models, most features need high values, except one for Spaghetti Code, the CD. The features NL, NLE, and CLOC had similar importance. On the other hand, the CD feature contributes less to the Spaghetti Code. Meanwhile, the CLLC feature contributes less to the defect model than to the Spaghetti Code model. It is interesting to notice that most features that highly contribute to the Spaghetti Code prediction are outside the intersection (NOI, TNOS, and CBO). Furthermore, the complexity quality attribute intersects both models (i.e., 2 out of 5). In addition, two of the documentation features on the defect model are important for the Spaghetti Code model. In terms of clone duplication, it also intersects half of the features of the Spaghetti Code model (CLLC). The size is relevant for both models, but none of the features intersects (2 out of 10 for both models). The features TLOC and NLG appear on the defect model, while the TNOS and TNLA on the Spaghetti Code model. The coupling is exclusive to the Spaghetti Code model, while the inheritance is exclusive to the defect model.

After observing the three figures (Figures 2, 3, and 4), we notice some intersections between the four models. For instance, CLOC is important for Defect, God Class, and Spaghetti Code models, even though the importance for God

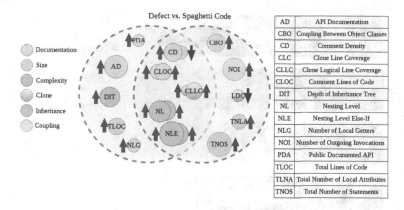

Fig. 4. Top-10 Software Features for the Defect and Spaghetti Code Models.

Class was smaller (see inner circle sizes). For this trio, we also have that NL and CLLC are important for the three models, but the CLLC has a small contribution in comparison to other features. For the Defect, God Class, and Refused Bequest, we highlight that the AD feature has high importance for all three models. Meanwhile, we also have some intersections between smells models. For the God Class and Spaghetti Code pair, we note that both NOI and TNOS are highly relevant to the models. Finally, CBO is important for the God Class, Refused Bequest, and Spaghetti Code, but with moderate importance.

RQ2. There is a group of software features that intersect between the defect models and the three code smells. More importantly, Nesting Level Else-If (NLE) and Comment density (CD) appear in the four models, although the CD influence is considerably low for the evaluated code smells. Furthermore, CBO is important for all the code smells, but not the defect model.

Figure 5 presents the number of features that correspond to the evaluated quality attributes according to the top-10 features discovered by SHAP. We stack each quality attribute horizontally to facilitate the comparison between them. Hence, our results indicate that practitioners do not need to concentrate on all software features to predict defects and the investigated code smells. A subset of features is enough to predict the targets. For instance, software features related to the documentation are the most relevant for the Defect and God Class models, with 4 and 3 features on the top-10, respectively. The Refused Bequest model needs software features related to the inheritance (3 features), but size and documentation are also relevant with two features each. Meanwhile, the Spaghetti Code model is the most comprehensive, requiring features linked to documentation, size, complexity, coupling, and clone duplication, with all of them having two features.

Based on the results discussed, we conclude that the four ensemble machine learning models require at least one software feature related to documentation (CD) and complexity (NLE) to predict the target. Hence, future studies about

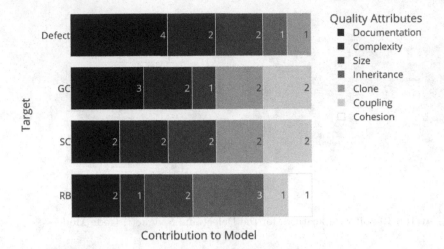

Fig. 5. Comparison between the Top-10 Features of each Target.

defect and code smell prediction, independently of the dataset and domain, could focus on these two feature collections. Furthermore, as we can observe in Figure 5, considering all the machine learning models evaluated, the documentation, complexity, and size are the most important quality attributes that contribute to the detection of defects and the code smell.

> *RQ3. The most relevant quality attributes to predict defects and code smells vary greatly between each model. For instance, documentation is more important for the Defect and God Class models, while Spaghetti Code has all of its five quality attributes with the same importance, and Refused Bequest prioritizes the inheritance. In general, documentation, complexity, and size contribute more to the prediction of defects and the investigated code smells.*

5   Threats to Validity

– **Internal Validity**: In our investigation, the chosen dataset is a potential threat to internal validity [79], as we employed the data documented in the current literature [15,16]. For this reason, we cannot reason on data quality, as any storing process could insert erroneous data into the dataset, which is common in a complex context such as software development. Furthermore, the use of Organic is also a threat; however, we validated the outcome by asking developers for a statistical sample of the results. Finally, the limited number of projects evaluated may interfere with the model's generalization to other contexts, although we covered 75% of the defect data with the chosen projects.

– **External Validity**: In this study, the external threat to validity [79] connects to the limited number of programming languages we examined to compare the defects and code smell. In this case, we limit the scope to the Java programming language to make our analysis feasible. However, we selected relevant systems that vary in domains, maturity, and development practices. For this reason, we cannot guarantee that our results generalize to other programming languages.

– **Construct Validity**: The use of SHAP is a possible threat to construct validity [79]. There are other tools to explain a machine learning model in the literature, such as Lime [60]. However, we tested only SHAP for our experimentation. Further interactions of this data could compare to other tools that focus on model explainability.
– **Conclusion Validity**: Our study could only match a chunk of the data collected with Organic with the defect dataset. Even though we pulled the same version from GitHub, we could not find some matching classes within the dataset. One of the main reasons for unmatched software classes is probably the refactoring of the class name and dependencies. For this reason, we cannot guarantee how different the results would be if we could match more classes. Furthermore, our study focuses on a diverse set of domains, which is a potential issue for generalization.

6   Related Work

Defect Prediction. Several studies [42,75] share the ability of applying code metrics for defect prediction. They vary in terms of accuracy, complexity, target programming language, input prediction density, and machine learning models. Menzies et al. [42] presented defect classifiers using code attributes defined by McCabe and Halstead metrics. They concluded that the choice of the learning method is more important than which subset of the available data we use for learning the software defects. In a similar approach, Turhan et al. [75] used cross-company data for building localized defect predictors. They used principles of analogy-based learning to cross-company data to fine-tune these models for localization and used static code features extracted from the source code, such as complex software features and Halstead metrics. They concluded that cross company data are useful in extreme cases and when within-company data is not available [75].

In the same direction, the study of Turhan et al. [76] evaluate the effect of mixing data from different projects stages. In this case, the authors use within and cross-project data to improve the prediction performance. They show that mixing project data based on the same project stage does not significantly improve the model performance. Hence, they concluded that optimal data for defect prediction is still an open challenge for researchers [76]. Similarly, He at al. [27] investigate defect prediction based on data selection. The authors propose a brute force approach to select the most relevant data for learning the software defects. To do so, they experiment with three large-scale experiments on 34 datasets obtained from ten open-source projects. They conclude that training data from the same project does not always help to improve the prediction performance [27]. On the other hand, we base our investigation on ensemble learning to improve the prediction performance and a wide set of software features.

Code Smells Prediction. Several automated detection strategies for code smells, and anti-patterns were proposed in the literature [18]. They also use diverse strategies in their identification. For instance, some methods are based on combination of metrics [48,57]; refactoring opportunities [19]; textual information [54]; historical data [52]; and machine learning techniques [7,12,14,20,21,35,40,41]. Khomh et al. [35] used Bayesian Belief Networks to detect three anti-patterns. They trained the models using two Java open-source systems. Maiga et al. [41] investigated the performance of the Support Vector Machine trained in three systems to predict four anti-patterns. Later, the authors introduced a feedback system to their model [40]. Amorim et al. [7] investigated the performance of Decision Trees to detect four code smells in one version of the Gantt project. Differently from these works, our dataset is composed of 14 systems, and we evaluate 9 code smells at the class level.

Cruz et al. [12] evaluated seven models to detect four code smells in 20 systems. The authors found that algorithms based on trees had a better F1 score than other models. Fontana et al. [20] evaluated six models to predict four smells. However, they have used the severity of the smells as the target. They reported high-performance numbers of the evaluated models. Later, Di Nucci et al. [14] replicated it [20] to address several limitations that potentially generated bias on the models' performance. Thus, the authors found out that the models' performance, when compared to the reference study, was 90% lower, indicating the need to further explore how to improve code smell prediction. Differently from previous work on code smell prediction, we are interested in exploring the similarities and differences between models for predicting code smells, in contrast with the models for defect prediction.

Defects and Code Smells. Several works tried to understand how code smells can affect software, evaluating different aspects of quality, such as maintainability [21,67,82], modularity [62], program comprehension [2], change-proneness [33,34], and how developers perceive code smells [53,81]. Other studies aim to evaluate how code smells impact the defect proneness [24,28,34,49,50,51]. Olbrich et al. [49] evaluated the fault-proneness evolution of the God Class and Brain Class of three open-source systems. They discovered that classes with these two smells can be more faulty, however, this did not hold for all analyzed systems. Similarly, Khomh et al. [34] evaluated the impact on fault-proneness of 13 different smells in several versions of three large open-source systems. They report the existence of a relationship between some code smells with defects, but it is not consistent for all system versions. Openja et al. [50] evaluated how code smells can make the class more fault-prone in quantum projects. Differently from these studies, we aim to understand whether models build for defects and code smells are similar or not.

Hall et al. [24] investigated if files with smells present more defects than files that do not have them. They found that for most of these smells, there is no statistical difference between smelly and non-smelly classes. Palomba et al. [51] evaluated how 13 code smells affect the presence of defects using a dataset of

30 open-source java systems. They reported that classes with smells have more bug fixes than classes that do not have any smells. Jebnoun et al. [28] evaluated how Code Clones are related to defects in three different programming languages. They concluded that smelly classes are more defect prone, but it varies according to the programming language. Differently from these three studies, we aim to understand how the prediction of defects differs from the models used to detect code smells, not on establishing a correlation between defect and code smell.

Explainable Machine Learning for Software Features. Software defect explainability is a relatively recent topic in the literature [30,46,58]. Mori and Uchihira [46] analyzed the trade-off between accuracy and interpretability of various models. The experimentation displays a comparison between the balanced output that satisfies both accuracy and interpretability criteria. Likewise, Jiarpakdee et al. [30] empirically evaluated two model-agnostic procedures, Local Interpretability Model-agnostic Explanations (LIME) [60] and BreakDown techniques. They improved the results obtained with LIME using hyperparameter optimization, which they called LIME-HPO. This work concludes that model-agnostic methods are necessary to explain individual predictions of defect models. Finally, Pornprasit et al. [58] proposed a tool that predicts defects for systems developed in Python. The input data consists of software commits, and the authors compare its performance with the LIME-HPO [30]. They conclude that the results are comparable to the state-of-the-art technology to explain models.

7 Conclusion

In this work, we investigated the relationship between defects and code smell machine learning models. To do so, we identified and validated the code smells collected with Organic. Then, we applied an extensive data processing step to clean the data and select the most relevant features for the prediction model. Subsequently, we trained and evaluated the models using an ensemble of models. In the end, as the models performed well, we employed an explainability tech nique to understand the models' decisions known as SHAP. We concluded that among the seven code smells initially collected, only three of them were similar to the defect model (Refused Bequest, God Class, and Spaghetti Code). In addition, we found that the features Nesting Level Else-If and Comment Density were relevant for the four models. Furthermore, most features require high values to predict defects and code smells, except for the Refused Bequest. Finally, we reported that the documentation, complexity, and size quality attributes are the most relevant for these models. In the future steps of this investigation, we can compare the SHAP results with other techniques (e.g., Lime) and employ white-box models to simplify the explainability. Another potential application of our study is the comparison between the reported code smells with other tools. We encourage the community to further investigate and replicate our results. For this reason, we made all data available under the replication package [64].

References

1. Ieee standard glossary of software engineering terminology. In: IEEE Std 610.12-1990 (1990)
2. Abbes, M., Khomh, F., Guéhéneuc, Y., Antoniol, G.: An empirical study of the impact of two antipatterns, blob and spaghetti code, on program comprehension. In: European Conference on Software Maintenance and Reengineering (CSMR) (2011)
3. Abdullah AlOmar, E., Wiem Mkaouer, M., Ouni, A., Kessentini, M.: Do Design Metrics Capture Developers Perception of Quality? An Empirical Study on Self-Affirmed Refactoring Activities. In: International Symposium on Empirical Software Engineering and Measurement (ESEM) (2019)
4. Aghajani, E., Nagy, C., Linares-Vásquez, M., Moreno, L., Bavota, G., Lanza, M., Shepherd, D.C.: Software documentation: The practitioners' perspective. In: Proceedings of the ACM/IEEE 42nd International Conference on Software Engineering (ICSE) (2020)
5. Akiba, T., Sano, S., Yanase, T., Ohta, T., Koyama, M.: Optuna: A next-generation hyperparameter optimization framework. In: International Conference on Knowledge Discovery & Data Mining (SIGKDD) (2019)
6. Ali, M.: PyCaret: An open source, low-code machine learning library in Python, https://www.pycaret.org
7. Amorim, L., Costa, E., Antunes, N., Fonseca, B., Ribeiro, M.: Experience report: Evaluating the effectiveness of decision trees for detecting code smells. In: International Symposium on Software Reliability Engineering (ISSRE) (2015)
8. Basili, V.R., Briand, L.C., Melo, W.L.: A validation of object-oriented design metrics as quality indicators. IEEE Transactions on Software Engineering (TSE) (1996)
9. Brown, W.H., Malveau, R.C., McCormick, H.W.S., Mowbray, T.J.: AntiPatterns: refactoring software, architectures, and projects in crisis. John Wiley & Sons, Inc. (1998)
10. Bui, X.N., Nguyen, H., Soukhanouvong, P.: Extra trees ensemble: A machine learning model for predicting blast-induced ground vibration based on the bagging and sibling of random forest algorithm. In: Proceedings of Geotechnical Challenges in Mining, Tunneling and Underground Infrastructures (ICGMTU) (2022)
11. Cawley, G.C., Talbot, N.L.: On over-fitting in model selection and subsequent selection bias in performance evaluation. Journal of Machine Learning Research (JMLR) (2010)
12. Cruz, D., Santana, A., Figueiredo, E.: Detecting bad smells with machine learning algorithms: an empirical study. In: International Conference on Technical Debt (TechDebt) (2020)
13. D'Ambros, M., Lanza, M., Robbes, R.: An extensive comparison of bug prediction approaches. In: 7th IEEE Working Conference on Mining Software Repositories (MSR) (2010)
14. Di Nucci, D., Palomba, F., Tamburri, D.A., Serebrenik, A., De Lucia, A.: Detecting code smells using machine learning techniques: Are we there yet? In: 2018 IEEE 25th International Conference on Software Analysis, Evolution and Reengineering (SANER) (2018)
15. Ferenc, R., Tóth, Z., Ladányi, G., Siket, I., Gyimóthy, T.: A public unified bug dataset for java. In: Proceedings of the 14th International Conference on Predictive Models and Data Analytics in Software Engineering (PROMISE) (2018)

16. Ferenc, R., Tóth, Z., Ladányi, G., Siket, I., Gyimóthy, T.: A public unified bug dataset for java and its assessment regarding metrics and bug prediction. In: Software Quality Journal (SQJ) (2020)
17. Ferenc, R., Tóth, Z., Ladányi, G., Siket, I., Gyimóthy, T.: Unified bug dataset, https://doi.org/10.5281/zenodo.3693686
18. Fernandes, E., Oliveira, J., Vale, G., Paiva, T., Figueiredo, E.: A review-based comparative study of bad smell detection tools. In: Proceedings of the 20th International Conference on Evaluation and Assessment in Software Engineering (EASE) (2016)
19. Fokaefs, M., Tsantalis, N., Stroulia, E., Chatzigeorgiou, A.: Jdeodorant: identification and application of extract class refactorings. In: 2011 33rd International Conference on Software Engineering (ICSE) (2011)
20. Fontana, F.A., Mäntylä, M.V., Zanoni, M., Marino, A.: Comparing and experimenting machine learning techniques for code smell detection. In: Empirical Software Engineering (EMSE) (2016)
21. Fontana, F.A., Zanoni, M., Marino, A., Mäntylä, M.V.: Code smell detection: Towards a machine learning-based approach (icsm). In: Int'l Conf. on Software Maintenance (2013)
22. Fowler, M.: Refactoring: Improving the Design of Existing Code. Addison-Wesley (1999)
23. Fukushima, T., Kamei, Y., McIntosh, S., Yamashita, K., Ubayashi, N.: An empirical study of just-in-time defect prediction using cross-project models. In: Working Conference on Mining Software Repositories (MSR) (2014)
24. Hall, T., Zhang, M., Bowes, D., Sun, Y.: Some code smells have a significant but small effect on faults. In: Transactions on Software Engineering and Methodology (TOSEM) (2014)
25. Haskins, B., Stecklein, J., Dick, B., Moroney, G., Lovell, R., Dabney, J.: Error cost escalation through the project life cycle. In: INCOSE International Symposium (2004)
26. Hassan, A.E.: Predicting faults using the complexity of code changes. In: International Conference of Software Engineering (ICSE) (2009)
27. He, Z., Shu, F., Yang, Y., Li, M., Wang, Q.: An investigation on the feasibility of cross-project defect prediction. In: Automated Software Engineering (ASE) (2012)
28. Jebnoun, H., Rahman, M.S., Khomh, F., Muse, B.: Clones in deep learning code: What, where, and why? In: Empirical Software Engineering (EMSE) (2022)
29. Jiang, T., Tan, L., Kim, S.: Personalized defect prediction. In: 28th IEEE/ACM International Conference on Automated Software Engineering (ASE) (2013)
30. Jiarpakdee, J., Tantithamthavorn, C., Dam, H.K., Grundy, J.: An empirical study of model-agnostic techniques for defect prediction models. In: Transactions on Software Engineering (TSE) (2020)
31. Jureczko, M., D., S.D.: Using object-oriented design metrics to predict software defects. In: Models and Methods of System Dependability (MMSD) (2010)
32. Ke, G., Meng, Q., Finley, T., Wang, T., Chen, W., Ma, W., Ye, Q., Liu, T.Y.: Lightgbm: A highly efficient gradient boosting decision tree. In: 31st Conference on Neural Information Processing System (NIPS) (2017)
33. Khomh, F., Di Penta, M., Gueheneuc, Y.: An exploratory study of the impact of code smells on software change-proneness. In: Proceedings of the 16th Working Conference on Reverse Engineering (WCRE) (2009)
34. Khomh, F., Di Penta, M., Guéhéneuc, Y., Antoniol, G.: An exploratory study of the impact of antipatterns on class change- and fault-proneness. In: Empirical Software Engineering (EMSE) (2012)

35. Khomh, F., Vaucher, S., Guéhéneuc, Y., Sahraoui, H.: Bdtex: A gqm-based bayesian approach for the detection of antipatterns. In: Journal of Systems and Software (JSS) (2011)
36. Lanza, M., Marinescu, R., Ducasse, S.: Object-Oriented Metrics in Practice. Springer-Verlag (2005)
37. Levin, S., Yehudai, A.: Boosting automatic commit classification into maintenance activities by utilizing source code changes. In: Proceedings of the 13rd International Conference on Predictor Models in Software Engineering (PROMISE) (2017)
38. Lin, Z., Ding, G., Hu, M., Wang, J.: Multi-label classification via feature-aware implicit label space encoding. In: International Conference on International Conference on Machine Learning (ICML) (2014)
39. Lundberg, S.M., Lee, S.: A unified approach to interpreting model predictions. In: Conference on Neural Information Processing Systems (NIPS) (2017)
40. Maiga, A., Ali, N., Bhattacharya, N., Sabané, A., Guéhéneuc, Y., Aimeur, E.: Smurf: A svm-based incremental anti-pattern detection approach. In: Working Conference on Reverse Engineering (WCRE) (2012)
41. Maiga, A., Ali, N., Bhattacharya, N., Sabané, A., Guéhéneuc, Y., Antoniol, G., Aïmeur, E.: Support vector machines for anti-pattern detection. In: Proceedings of International Conference on Automated Software Engineering (ASE) (2012)
42. Menzies, T., Greenwald, J., Frank, A.: Data mining static code attributes to learn defect predictors. In: Transactions on Software Engineering (TSE) (2007)
43. Menzies, T., Milton, Z., Turhan, B., Cukic, B., Jiang, Y., Bener, A.: Defect prediction from static code features: current results, limitations, new approaches. In: Automated Software Engineering (ASE) (2010)
44. Menzies, T., Zimmermann, T.: Software analytics: So what? In: IEEE Software (2013)
45. Menzies, T., Distefano, J., Orrego, A., Chapman, R.: Assessing predictors of software defects. In: In Proceedings, Workshop on Predictive Software Models (PROMISE) (2004)
46. Mori, T., Uchihira, N.: Balancing the trade-off between accuracy and interpretability in software defect prediction. In: Empirical Software Engineering (EMSE) (2018)
47. Nagappan, N., Ball, T., Zeller, A.: Mining metrics to predict component failures. In: International Conference on Software Engineering (ICSE) (2006)
48. Oizumi, W., Sousa, L., Oliveira, A., Garcia, A., Agbachi, A.B., Oliveira, R., Lucena, C.: On the identification of design problems in stinky code: experiences and tool support. In: Journal of the Brazilian Computer Society (JBCS) (2018)
49. Olbrich, S.M., Cruzes, D.S., Sjøberg, D.I.K.: Are all code smells harmful? a study of god classes and brain classes in the evolution of three open source systems. In: IEEE International Conference on Software Maintenance (ICSM) (2010)
50. Openja, M., Morovati, M.M., An, L., Khomh, F., Abidi, M.: Technical debts and faults in open-source quantum software systems: An empirical study. Journal of Systems and Software (JSS) (2022)
51. Palomba, F., Bavota, G., Di Penta, M., Fasano, F., Oliveto, R., De Lucia, A.: On the diffuseness and the impact on maintainability of code smells: A large scale empirical investigation. In: IEEE/ACM 40th International Conference on Software Engineering (ICSE) (2018)
52. Palomba, F., Bavota, G., Di Penta, M., Oliveto, R., De Lucia, A., Poshyvanyk, D.: Detecting bad smells in source code using change history information. In: 28th IEEE/ACM International Conference on Automated Software Engineering (ASE) (2013)

53. Palomba, F., Bavota, G., Penta, M.D., Oliveto, R., Lucia, A.D.: Do they really smell bad? a study on developers' perception of bad code smells. In: IEEE International Conference on Software Maintenance and Evolution (ICSME) (2014)

54. Palomba, F., Panichella, A., De Lucia, A., Oliveto, R., Zaidman, A.: A textual-based technique for smell detection. In: 2016 IEEE 24th international conference on program comprehension (ICPC) (2016)

55. Pedregosa, F., Varoquaux, G., Gramfort, A., Michel, V., Thirion, B., Grisel, O., Blondel, M., Prettenhofer, P., Weiss, R., Dubourg, V., Vanderplas, J., Passos, A., Cournapeau, D., Brucher, M., Perrot, M., Duchesnay, E.: Scikit-learn: Machine learning in Python. Journal of Machine Learning Research (JMLR) (2011)

56. Petrić, J., Bowes, D., Hall, T., Christianson, B., Baddoo, N.: The jinx on the nasa software defect data sets. In: International Conference on Evaluation and Assessment in Software Engineering (EASE) (2016)

57. PMD: Pmd source code analyser, https://pmd.github.io/

58. Pornprasit, C., Tantithamthavorn, C., Jiarpakdee, J., Fu, M., Thongtanunam, P.: Pyexplainer: Explaining the predictions of just-in-time defect models. In: International Conference on Automated Software Engineering (ASE) (2021)

59. Raju, V.N.G., Lakshmi, K.P., Jain, V.M., Kalidindi, A., Padma, V.: Study the influence of normalization/transformation process on the accuracy of supervised classification. In: 2020 Third International Conference on Smart Systems and Inventive Technology (ICSSIT) (2020)

60. Ribeiro, M.T., Singh, S., Guestrin, C.: "why should i trust you?": Explaining the predictions of any classifier. In: International Conference on Knowledge Discovery and Data Mining (KDD) (2016)

61. Riel, A.: Object Oriented Design Heuristics. Addison-Wesley Professional (1996)

62. Santana, A., Cruz, D., Figueiredo, E.: An exploratory study on the identification and evaluation of bad smell agglomerations. In: Proceedings of the 36th Annual ACM Symposium on Applied Computing (SAC) (2021)

63. Santos, G., Figueiredo, E., Veloso, A., Viggiato, M., Ziviani, N.: Understanding machine learning software defect predictions. In: Automated Software Engineering Journal (ASEJ) (2020)

64. Santos, G.: gesteves91/artifact-fase-santos-23: FASE Artifact Evaluation 2023 (Jan 2023), https://doi.org/10.5281/zenodo.7502546

65. Sayyad S., J., Menzies, T.: The PROMISE Repository of Software Engineering Databases. (2005), http://promise.site.uottawa.ca/SERepository

66. Schumacher, J., Zazworka, N., Shull, F., Seaman, C.B., Shaw, M.A.: Building empirical support for automated code smell detection. In: International Symposium on Empirical Software Engineering and Measurement (ESEM) (2010)

67. Sjøberg, D.I.K., Yamashita, A., Anda, B.C.D., Mockus, A., Dybå, T.: Quantifying the effect of code smells on maintenance effort. In: IEEE Transactions on Software Engineering (TSE) (2013)

68. Stroulia, E., Kapoor, R.: Metrics of refactoring-based development: An experience report. 7th International Conference on Object Oriented Information Systems (OOIS) (2001)

69. Tantithamthavorn, C., Hassan, A.E.: An experience report on defect modelling in practice: Pitfalls and challenges. In: International Conference on Software Engineering: Software Engineering in Practice (ICSE-SEIP) (2018)

70. Tantithamthavorn, C., Hassan, A.E., Matsumoto, K.: The impact of class rebalancing techniques on the performance and interpretation of defect prediction models. In: Transactions on Software Engineering (TSE) (2019)

71. Tantithamthavorn, C., McIntosh, S., Hassan, A.E., Ihara, A., Matsumoto, K.: The impact of mislabelling on the performance and interpretation of defect prediction models. In: International Conference on Software Engineering (ICSE) (2015)
72. Tantithamthavorn, C., McIntosh, S., Hassan, A.E., Matsumoto, K.: An empirical comparison of model validation techniques for defect prediction models. In: IEEE Transactions on Software Engineering (TSE) (2017)
73. Tantithamthavorn, C., McIntosh, S., Hassan, A.E., Matsumoto, K.: The impact of automated parameter optimization on defect prediction models. In: Transactions on Software Engineering (TSE) (2019)
74. Tóth, Z., Gyimesi, P., Ferenc, R.: A public bug database of github projects and its application in bug prediction. In: Computational Science and Its Applications (ICCSA) (2016)
75. Turhan, B., Menzies, T., Bener, A.B., Di Stefano, J.: On the relative value of cross-company and within-company data for defect prediction. Empirical Software Engineering (EMSE) (2009)
76. Turhan, B., Tosun, A., Bener, A.: Empirical evaluation of mixed-project defect prediction models. In: Proceedings of the 37th Conference on Software Engineering and Advanced Applications (SEAA) (2011)
77. Vale, G., Hunsen, C., Figueiredo, E., Apel, S.: Challenges of resolving merge conflicts: A mining and survey study. In: Transactions on Software Engineering (TSE) (2021)
78. Wang, S., Liu, T., Tan, L.: Automatically learning semantic features for defect prediction. In: International Conference of Software Engineering (ICSE) (2016)
79. Wohlin, C., Runeson, P., Hst, M., Ohlsson, M.C., Regnell, B., Wessln, A.: Experimentation in Software Engineering. Springer (2012)
80. Xuan, X., Lo, D., Xia, X., Tian, Y.: Evaluating defect prediction approaches using a massive set of metrics: An empirical study. In: Proceedings of the 30th Annual ACM Symposium on Applied Computing (SAC) (2015)
81. Yamashita, A., Moonen, L.: Do developers care about code smells? an exploratory survey. In: 20th Working Conference on Reverse Engineering (WCRE) (2013)
82. Yamashita, A., Counsell, S.: Code smells as system-level indicators of maintainability: An empirical study. In: Journal of Systems and Software (JSS) (2013)
83. Yatish, S., Jiarpakdee, J., Thongtanunam, P., Tantithamthavorn, C.: Mining software defects: Should we consider affected releases? In: International Conference on Software Engineering (ICSE) (2019)
84. Zimmermann, T., Premraj, R., Zeller, A.: Predicting defects for eclipse. In: International Workshop on Predictor Models in Software Engineering (PROMISE) (2007)

Competition Contributions

Software Testing: 5th Comparative Evaluation: Test-Comp 2023

Dirk Beyer(✉)

LMU Munich, Munich, Germany

Abstract. The 5th edition of the Competition on Software Testing (Test-Comp 2023) provides again an overview and comparative evaluation of automatic test-suite generators for C programs. The experiment was performed on a benchmark set of 4 106 test-generation tasks for C programs. Each test-generation task consisted of a program and a test specification (error coverage, branch coverage). There were 13 participating test-suite generators from 6 countries in Test-Comp 2023.

Keywords: Software Testing · Test-Case Generation · Competition · Program Analysis · Software Validation · Software Bugs · Test Validation · Test-Comp · Benchmarking · Test Coverage · Bug Finding · Test Suites · SV-Benchmarks · BenchExec · TestCov · CoVeriTeam

1 Introduction

In its 5th edition, the International Competition on Software Testing (Test-Comp, https://test-comp.sosy-lab.org, [7,8,9,10,11]) again compares automatic test-suite generators for C programs, in order to showcase the state of the art in the area of automatic software testing. This competition report is an update of the previous reports, referring to the rules and definitions, presents the competition results, and give some interesting data about the execution of the competition experiments. We use BenchExec [24] to execute the benchmarks and the results are presented in tables and graphs on the competition web site (https://test-comp.sosy-lab.org/2023/results) and are available in the accompanying archives (see Table 3).

Competition Goals. In summary, the goals of Test-Comp are the following [8]:

- Establish *standards* for software test generation. This means, most prominently, to develop a standard for marking input values in programs, define an exchange format for test suites, agree on a specification language for test-coverage criteria, and define how to validate the resulting test suites.

This report extends previous reports on Test-Comp [7,8,9,10,11].
Reproduction packages are available on Zenodo (see Table 3).

(✉) dirk.beyer@sosy-lab.org

L. Lambers and S. Uchitel (Eds.): FASE 2023, LNCS 13991, pp. 309–323, 2023.
https://doi.org/10.1007/978-3-031-30826-0_17

- Establish a set of *benchmarks* for software testing in the community. This means to create and maintain a set of programs together with coverage criteria, and to make those publicly available for researchers to be used in performance comparisons when evaluating a new technique.
- Provide an overview of *available tools* for test-case generation and a snapshot of the state-of-the-art in software testing to the community. This means to compare, independently from particular paper projects and specific techniques, different test generators in terms of effectiveness and performance.
- Increase the visibility and credits that *tool developers* receive. This means to provide a forum for presentation of tools and discussion of the latest technologies, and to give the participants the opportunity to publish about the development work that they have done.
- Educate PhD students and other participants on how to set up performance experiments, package tools in a way that supports reproduction, and how to perform *robust and accurate research experiments*.
- Provide *resources* to development teams that do not have sufficient computing resources and give them the opportunity to obtain results from experiments on large benchmark sets.

Related Competitions. In the field of formal methods, competitions are respected as an important evaluation method and there are many competitions [5]. We refer to the report from Test-Comp 2020 [8] for a more detailed discussion and give here only the references to the most related competitions [5,13,46,48].

2   Definitions, Formats, and Rules

Organizational aspects such as the classification (automatic, off-site, reproducible, jury, training) and the competition schedule is given in the initial competition definition [7]. In the following, we repeat some important definitions that are necessary to understand the results.

Test-Generation Task. A *test-generation task* is a pair of an input program (program under test) and a test specification. A *test-generation run* is a non-interactive execution of a test generator on a single test-generation task, in order to generate a test suite according to the test specification. A *test suite* is a sequence of test cases, given as a directory of files according to the format for exchangeable test-suites.[1]

Execution of a Test Generator. Figure 1 illustrates the process of executing one test-suite generator on the benchmark suite. One test run for a test-suite generator gets as input (i) a program from the benchmark suite and (ii) a test specification (cover bug, or cover branches), and returns as output a test suite (i.e., a set of test cases). The test generator is contributed by a competition participant as a software archive in ZIP format. The test runs are executed centrally by the competition organizer. The test-suite validator takes as input the test suite from

---

[1] https://gitlab.com/sosy-lab/software/test-format

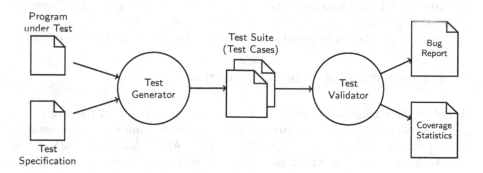

Fig. 1: Flow of the Test-Comp execution for one test generator (taken from [8])

Table 1: Coverage specifications used in Test-Comp 2023 (similar to 2019–2022)

Formula	Interpretation
COVER EDGES(@CALL(reach_error))	The test suite contains at least one test that executes function reach_error.
COVER EDGES(@DECISIONEDGE)	The test suite contains tests such that all branches of the program are executed.

the test generator and validates it by executing the program on all test cases: for bug finding it checks if the bug is exposed and for coverage it reports the coverage. We use the tool TESTCOV [23] [2] as test-suite validator.

Test Specification. The specification for testing a program is given to the test generator as input file (either properties/coverage-error-call.prp or properties/coverage-branches.prp for Test-Comp 2023).

The definition init(main()) is used to define the initial states of the program under test by a call of function main (with no parameters). The definition FQL(f) specifies that coverage definition f should be achieved. The FQL (FSHELL query language [36]) coverage definition COVER EDGES(@DECISIONEDGE) means that all branches should be covered (typically used to obtain a standard test suite for quality assurance) and COVER EDGES(@CALL(foo)) means that a call (at least one) to function foo should be covered (typically used for bug finding). A complete specification looks like: COVER(init(main()), FQL(COVER EDGES(@DECISIONEDGE))).

Table 1 lists the two FQL formulas that are used in test specifications of Test-Comp 2023; there was no change from 2020 (except that special function __VERIFIER_error does not exist anymore).

Task-Definition Format 2.0. Test-Comp 2023 used again the task-definition format in version 2.0.

---

[2] https://gitlab.com/sosy-lab/software/test-suite-validator

License and Qualification. The license of each participating test generator must allow its free use for reproduction of the competition results. Details on qualification criteria can be found in the competition report of Test-Comp 2019 [9].

3   Categories and Scoring Schema

Benchmark Programs. The input programs were taken from the largest and most diverse open-source repository of software-verification and test-generation tasks[3], which is also used by SV-COMP [13]. As in 2020 and 2021, we selected all programs for which the following properties were satisfied (see issue on GitLab[4] and report [9]):

1. compiles with `gcc`, if a harness for the special methods[5] is provided,
2. should contain at least one call to a nondeterministic function,
3. does not rely on nondeterministic pointers,
4. does not have expected result 'false' for property 'termination', and
5. has expected result 'false' for property 'unreach-call' (only for category *Error Coverage*).

This selection yielded a total of 4 106 test-generation tasks, namely 1 173 tasks for category *Error Coverage* and 2 933 tasks for category *Code Coverage*. The test-generation tasks are partitioned into categories, which are listed in Tables 6 and 7 and described in detail on the competition web site.[6] Figure 2 illustrates the category composition.

Category Error-Coverage. The first category is to show the abilities to discover bugs. The benchmark set consists of programs that contain a bug. We produce for every tool and every test-generation task one of the following scores: 1 point, if the validator succeeds in executing the program under test on a generated test case that explores the bug (i.e., the specified function was called), and 0 points, otherwise.

Category Branch-Coverage. The second category is to cover as many branches of the program as possible. The coverage criterion was chosen because many test generators support this standard criterion by default. Other coverage criteria can be reduced to branch coverage by transformation [35]. We produce for every tool and every test-generation task the coverage of branches of the program (as reported by TESTCOV [23]; a value between 0 and 1) that are executed for the generated test cases. The score is the returned coverage.

Ranking. The ranking was decided based on the sum of points (normalized for meta categories). In case of a tie, the ranking was decided based on the run time, which is the total CPU time over all test-generation tasks. Opt-out from categories was possible and scores for categories were normalized based on the number of tasks per category (see competition report of SV-COMP 2013 [6], page 597).

---

[3] https://gitlab.com/sosy-lab/benchmarking/sv-benchmarks
[4] https://gitlab.com/sosy-lab/benchmarking/sv-benchmarks/-/merge_requests/774
[5] https://test-comp.sosy-lab.org/2023/rules.php
[6] https://test-comp.sosy-lab.org/2023/benchmarks.php

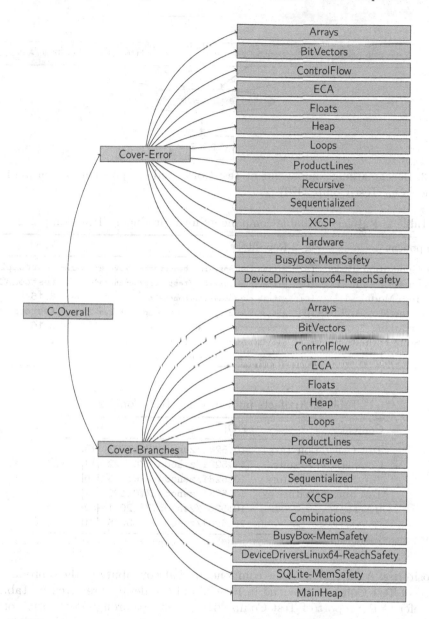

Fig. 2: Category structure for Test-Comp 2023; compared to Test-Comp 2022, sub-category *Hardware* was added to main category *Cover-Error*

4   Reproducibility

We followed the same competition workflow that was described in detail in the previous competition report (see Sect. 4, [10]). All major components that were used for the competition were made available in public version-control

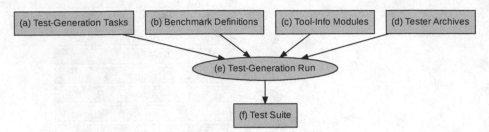

Fig. 3: Benchmarking components of Test-Comp and competition's execution flow (same as for Test-Comp 2020)

Table 2: Publicly available components for reproducing Test-Comp 2023

Component	Fig. 3	Repository	Version
Test-Generation Tasks	(a)	gitlab.com/sosy-lab/benchmarking/sv-benchmarks	testcomp23
Benchmark Definitions	(b)	gitlab.com/sosy-lab/test-comp/bench-defs	testcomp23
Tool-Info Modules	(c)	github.com/sosy-lab/benchexec	3.16
Test-Generator Archives	(d)	gitlab.com/sosy-lab/test-comp/archives-2023	testcomp23
Benchmarking	(e)	github.com/sosy-lab/benchexec	3.16
Test-Suite Format	(f)	gitlab.com/sosy-lab/software/test-format	testcomp23
Continuous Integration	(f)	gitlab.com/sosy-lab/software/coveriteam	1.0

Table 3: Artifacts published for Test-Comp 2023

Content	DOI	Reference
Test-Generation Tasks	10.5281/zenodo.7627783	[15]
Competition Results	10.5281/zenodo.7701122	[14]
Test-Suite Generators	10.5281/zenodo.7701118	[16]
Test Suites (Witnesses)	10.5281/zenodo.7701126	[17]
BenchExec	10.5281/zenodo.7612021	[52]
CoVeriTeam	10.5281/zenodo.7635975	[21]

repositories. An overview of the components that contribute to the reproducible setup of Test-Comp is provided in Fig. 3, and the details are given in Table 2. We refer to the report of Test-Comp 2019 [9] for a thorough description of all components of the Test-Comp organization and how we ensure that all parts are publicly available for maximal reproducibility.

In order to guarantee long-term availability and immutability of the test-generation tasks, the produced competition results, and the produced test suites, we also packaged the material and published it at Zenodo (see Table 3).

The competition used CoVeriTeam [20] [7] again to provide participants access to execution machines that are similar to actual competition machines. The

---

[7] https://gitlab.com/sosy-lab/software/coveriteam

Table 4: Competition candidates with tool references and representing jury members; [new] indicates first-time participants, [∅] indicates hors-concours participation

Tester	Ref.	Jury member	Affiliation
CoVeriTest	[19,39]	Marie-Christine Jakobs	TU Darmstadt, Germany
ESBMC-kind [new]	[33,32]	Rafael Sá Menezes	U. of Manchester, UK
FuSeBMC	[3,4]	Kaled Alshmrany	U. of Manchester, UK
FuSeBMC_IA [new]	[1,2]	Mohannad Aldughaim	U. of Manchester, UK
HybridTiger	[26,47]	(hors concours)	−
KLEE	[27,28]	(hors concours)	−
Legion	[42,43]	(hors concours)	−
Legion/SymCC	[43]	Gidon Ernst	LMU Munich, Germany
PRTest	[22,41]	Thomas Lemberger	QAware GmbH, Germany
Symbiotic	[29,30]	Marek Trtík	Masaryk U., Brno, Czechia
TracerX	[37,38]	Joxan Jaffar	National U. of Singapore, Singapore
VeriFuzz	[45]	Raveendra Kumar M.	Tata Consultancy Services, India
WASP-C [new]	[44]	Filipe Marques	INESC-ID, Lisbon, Portugal

competition report of SV-COMP 2022 provides a description on reproducing individual results and on trouble-shooting (see Sect. 3, [12]).

5   Results and Discussion

This section represents the results of the competition experiments. The report shall help to understanding the state of the art and the advances in fully automatic test generation for whole C programs, in terms of effectiveness (test coverage, as accumulated in the score) and efficiency (resource consumption in terms of CPU time). All results mentioned in this article were inspected and approved by the participants.

Participating Test-Suite Generators. Table 4 provides an overview of the participating test generators and references to publications, as well as the team representatives of the jury of Test-Comp 2023. (The competition jury consists of the chair and one member of each participating team.) An online table with information about all participating systems is provided on the competition web site.[8] Table 5 lists the features and technologies that are used in the test generators.

There are test generators that did not actively participate (e.g., tester archives taken from last year) and that are not included in rankings. Those are called *hors-concours* participations and the tool names are labeled with a symbol ([∅]).

Computing Resources. The computing environment and the resource limits were the same as for Test-Comp 2020 [8], except for the upgraded operating system: Each test run was limited to 8 processing units (cores), 15 GB of memory, and 15 min of CPU time. The test-suite validation was limited to 2 processing units,

---

[8] https://test-comp.sosy-lab.org/2023/systems.php

Table 5: Technologies and features that the test generators used

Tester	Bounded Model Checking	CEGAR	Evolutionary Algorithms	Explicit-Value Analysis	Floating-Point Arithmetics	Guidance by Coverage Measures	Predicate Abstraction	Random Execution	Symbolic Execution	Targeted Input Generation	Algorithm Selection	Portfolio
CoVeriTest		✓		✓	✓		✓					✓
ESBMC-kind [new]	✓			✓	✓							
FuSeBMC	✓				✓	✓				✓		✓
FuSeBMC_IA [new]	✓				✓	✓				✓		✓
HybridTiger		✓		✓	✓		✓					
KLEE					✓				✓	✓		
Legion			✓	✓	✓			✓	✓	✓		
Legion/SymCC			✓	✓	✓			✓	✓	✓		
PRTest					✓			✓				
Symbiotic					✓	✓			✓	✓		✓
TracerX	✓				✓				✓	✓		
VeriFuzz	✓		✓	✓	✓	✓		✓				
WASP-C [new]					✓				✓	✓		

7 GB of memory, and 5 min of CPU time. The machines for running the experiments are part of a compute cluster that consists of 168 machines; each test-generation run was executed on an otherwise completely unloaded, dedicated machine, in order to achieve precise measurements. Each machine had one Intel Xeon E3-1230 v5 CPU, with 8 processing units each, a frequency of 3.4 GHz, 33 GB of RAM, and a GNU/Linux operating system (x86_64-linux, Ubuntu 22.04 with Linux kernel 5.15). We used BenchExec [24] to measure and control computing resources (CPU time, memory, CPU energy) and VerifierCloud[9] to distribute, install, run, and clean-up test-case generation runs, and to collect the results. The values for time and energy are accumulated over all cores of the CPU. To measure the CPU energy, we use CPU Energy Meter [25] (integrated in BenchExec [24]). Further technical parameters of the competition machines are available in the repository which also contains the benchmark definitions.[10]

---

[9] https://vcloud.sosy-lab.org
[10] https://gitlab.com/sosy-lab/test-comp/bench-defs/tree/testcomp22

Table 6: Quantitative overview over all results; empty cells mark opt-outs; [new] indicates first-time participants, [ø] indicates hors-concours participation

Tester	Cover-Error 1173 tasks	Cover-Branches 2933 tasks	Overall 4106 tasks
CoVeriTest	581	1509	2073
ESBMC-kind [new]	289		
FuSeBMC	**936**	**1678**	**2813**
FuSeBMC_IA [new]	**908**	**1538**	**2666**
HybridTiger	463	1170	1629
KLEE	721	999	1961
Legion		838	
Legion/SymCC	349	1027	1329
PRTest	222	770	927
Symbiotic	644	1430	2128
TracerX		1400	
VeriFuzz	**909**	**1546**	**2673**
WASP-C [new]	570	1103	1770

One complete test-generation execution of the competition consisted of 50 445 single test-generation runs in 25 run sets (tester × property). The total CPU time was 315 days and the consumed energy 89.9 kWh for one complete competition run for test generation (without validation). Test-suite validation consisted of 53 378 single test-suite validation runs in 26 run sets (validator × property). The total consumed CPU time was 19 days. Each tool was executed several times, in order to make sure no installation issues occur during the execution. Including preruns, the infrastructure managed a total of 254 445 test-generation runs (consuming 3.0 years of CPU time). The prerun test-suite validation consisted of 338 710 single test-suite validation runs in 152 run sets (validator × property) (consuming 63 days of CPU time). The CPU energy was not measured during preruns.

New Test-Suite Generators. To acknowledge the test-suite generators that participated for the first time in Test-Comp, we list the test generators that participated for the first time. ESBMC-kind [new], FuSeBMC_IA [new], and WASP-C [new] participated for the first time in Test-Comp 2023, and Legion/SymCC participated first in Test-Comp 2022. Table 8 reports also the number of sub-categories in which the tools participated.

Table 7: Overview of the top-three test generators for each category (measurement values for CPU time and energy rounded to two significant digits)

Rank	Tester	Score	CPU Time (in h)	CPU Energy (in kWh)
Cover-Error				
1	FuSeBMC	**936**	72	0.96
2	VeriFuzz	909	4.5	0.049
3	FuSeBMC_IA [new]	908	37	0.48
Cover-Branches				
1	FuSeBMC	**1678**	720	9.2
2	VeriFuzz	1546	730	9.1
3	FuSeBMC_IA [new]	1538	470	6.0
Overall				
1	FuSeBMC	**2813**	790	10
2	VeriFuzz	2673	730	9.2
3	FuSeBMC_IA [new]	2666	500	6.5

Table 8: New test-suite generators in Test-Comp 2022 and Test-Comp 2023; column 'Sub-categories' gives the number of executed categories

Tester	Language	First Year	Sub-categories
ESBMC-kind [new]	C	2023	14
FuSeBMC_IA [new]	C	2023	30
WASP-C [new]	C	2023	30
Legion/SymCC	C	2022	16

Quantitative Results. The quantitative results are presented in the same way as last year: Table 6 presents the quantitative overview of all tools and all categories. The head row mentions the category and the number of test-generation tasks in that category. The tools are listed in alphabetical order; every table row lists the scores of one test generator. We indicate the top three candidates by formatting their scores in bold face and in larger font size. An empty table cell means that the test generator opted-out from the respective main category (perhaps participating in subcategories only, restricting the evaluation to a specific topic). More information (including interactive tables, quantile plots for every category, and also the raw data in XML format) is available on the competition web site [11] and in the results artifact (see Table 3). Table 7 reports the top three test generators for each category. The consumed run time (column 'CPU Time') is given in hours and the consumed energy (column 'Energy') is given in kWh.

---

[11] https://test-comp.sosy-lab.org/2023/results

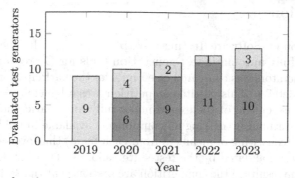

Fig. 4: Number of evaluated test generators for each year (top: number of first-time participants; bottom: previous year's participants)

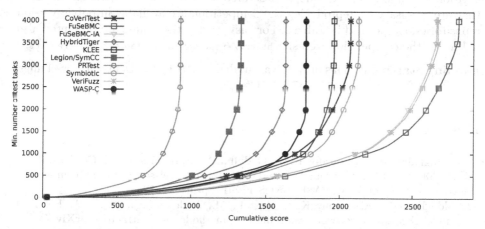

Fig. 5: Quantile functions for category *Overall*. Each quantile function illustrates the quantile (x-coordinate) of the scores obtained by test-generation runs below a certain number of test-generation tasks (y-coordinate). More details were given previously [9]. The graphs are decorated with symbols to make them better distinguishable without color.

Score-Based Quantile Functions for Quality Assessment. We use score-based quantile functions [24] because these visualizations make it easier to understand the results of the comparative evaluation. The web site [11] and the results artifact (Table 3) include such a plot for each category; as example, we show the plot for category *Overall* (all test-generation tasks) in Fig. 5. We had 11 test generators participating in category *Overall*, for which the quantile plot shows the overall performance over all categories (scores for meta categories are normalized [6]). A more detailed discussion of score-based quantile plots for testing is provided in the Test-Comp 2019 competition report [9].

6   Conclusion

The Competition on Software Testing took place for the 5th time and provides an overview of fully-automatic test-generation tools for C programs. A total of 13 test-suite generators was compared (see Fig. 4 for the participation numbers and Table 4 for the details). This off-site competition uses a benchmark infrastructure that makes the execution of the experiments fully-automatic and reproducible. Transparency is ensured by making all components available in public repositories and have a jury (consisting of members from each team) that oversees the process. All test suites were validated by the test-suite validator TESTCOV [23] to measure the coverage. The results of the competition are presented at the 26th International Conference on Fundamental Approaches to Software Engineering at ETAPS 2023.

Data-Availability Statement. The test-generation tasks and results of the competition are published at Zenodo, as described in Table 3. All components and data that are necessary for reproducing the competition are available in public version repositories, as specified in Table 2. For easy access, the results are presented also online on the competition web site `https://test-comp.sosy-lab.org/2023/results`.

Funding Statement. This project was funded in part by the Deutsche Forschungs-gemeinschaft (DFG) — 418257054 (Coop).

References

1. Aldughaim, M., Alshmrany, K.M., Gadelha, M.R., de Freitas, R., Cordeiro, L.C.: FuSeBMC_IA: Interval analysis and methods for test-case generation (competition contribution). In: Proc. FASE. LNCS 13991, Springer (2023)
2. Aldughaim, M., Alshmrany, K.M., Mustafa, M., Cordeiro, L.C., Stancu, A.: Bounded model checking of software using interval methods via contractors. arXiv/CoRR **2012**(11245) (December 2020). `https://doi.org/10.48550/arXiv.2012.11245`
3. Alshmrany, K., Aldughaim, M., Cordeiro, L., Bhayat, A.: FuSeBMC v.4: Smart seed generation for hybrid fuzzing (competition contribution). In: Proc. FASE. pp. 336–340. LNCS 13241, Springer (2022). `https://doi.org/10.1007/978-3-030-99429-7_19`
4. Alshmrany, K.M., Aldughaim, M., Bhayat, A., Cordeiro, L.C.: FuSeBMC: An energy-efficient test generator for finding security vulnerabili-ties in C programs. In: Proc. TAP. pp. 85–105. Springer (2021). `https://doi.org/10.1007/978-3-030-79379-1_6`
5. Bartocci, E., Beyer, D., Black, P.E., Fedyukovich, G., Garavel, H., Hartmanns, A., Huisman, M., Kordon, F., Nagele, J., Sighireanu, M., Steffen, B., Suda, M., Sutcliffe, G., Weber, T., Yamada, A.: TOOLympics 2019: An overview of competitions in formal methods. In: Proc. TACAS (3). pp. 3–24. LNCS 11429, Springer (2019). `https://doi.org/10.1007/978-3-030-17502-3_1`
6. Beyer, D.: Second competition on software verification (Summary of SV-COMP 2013). In: Proc. TACAS. pp. 594–609. LNCS 7795, Springer (2013). `https://doi.org/10.1007/978-3-642-36742-7_43`
7. Beyer, D.: Competition on software testing (Test-Comp). In: Proc. TACAS (3). pp. 167–175. LNCS 11429, Springer (2019). `https://doi.org/10.1007/978-3-030-17502-3_11`

8. Beyer, D.: Second competition on software testing: Test-Comp 2020. In: Proc. FASE. pp. 505–519. LNCS 12076, Springer (2020). https://doi.org/10.1007/978-3-030-45234-6_25
9. Beyer, D.: First international competition on software testing (Test-Comp 2019). Int. J. Softw. Tools Technol. Transf. **23**(6), 833–846 (December 2021). https://doi.org/10.1007/s10009-021-00613-3
10. Beyer, D.: Status report on software testing: Test-Comp 2021. In: Proc. FASE. pp. 341–357. LNCS 12649, Springer (2021). https://doi.org/10.1007/978-3-030-71500-7_17
11. Beyer, D.: Advances in automatic software testing: Test-Comp 2022. In: Proc. FASE. pp. 321–335. LNCS 13241, Springer (2022). https://doi.org/10.1007/978-3-030-99429-7_18
12. Beyer, D.: Progress on software verification: SV-COMP 2022. In: Proc. TACAS (2). pp. 375–402. LNCS 13244, Springer (2022). https://doi.org/10.1007/978-3-030-99527-0_20
13. Beyer, D.: Competition on software verification and witness validation: SV-COMP 2023. In: Proc. TACAS (2). LNCS , Springer (2023)
14. Beyer, D.: Results of the 5th Intl. Competition on Software Testing (Test-Comp 2023). Zenodo (2023). https://doi.org/10.5281/zenodo.7701122
15. Beyer, D.: SV-Benchmarks: Benchmark set for softwware verification and testing (SV-COMP 2023 and Test-Comp 2023). Zenodo (2023). https://doi.org/10.5281/zenodo.7697790
16. Beyer, D.: Test-suite generators and validator of the 5th Intl. Competition on Software Testing (Test-Comp 2023). Zenodo (2023). https://doi.org/10.5281/zenodo.7701118
17. Beyer, D.: Test suites from test-generation tools (Test-Comp 2023). Zenodo (2023). https://doi.org/10.5281/zenodo.7701126
18. Beyer, D., Chlipala, A.J., Henzinger, T.A., Jhala, R., Majumdar, R.: Generating tests from counterexamples. In: Proc. ICSE. pp. 326–335. IEEE (2004). https://doi.org/10.1109/ICSE.2004.1317455
19. Beyer, D., Jakobs, M.C.: CoVeriTest: Cooperative verifier-based testing. In: Proc. FASE. pp. 389–408. LNCS 11424, Springer (2019). https://doi.org/10.1007/978-3-030-16722-6_23
20. Beyer, D., Kanav, S.: CoVeriTeam: On-demand composition of cooperative verification systems. In: Proc. TACAS. pp. 561–579. LNCS 13243, Springer (2022). https://doi.org/10.1007/978-3-030-99524-9_31
21. Beyer, D., Kanav, S., Wachowitz, H.: Coveriteam Release 1.0. Zenodo (2023). https://doi.org/10.5281/zenodo.7635975
22. Beyer, D., Lemberger, T.: Software verification: Testing vs. model checking. In: Proc. HVC. pp. 99–114. LNCS 10629, Springer (2017). https://doi.org/10.1007/978-3-319-70389-3_7
23. Beyer, D., Lemberger, T.: TestCov: Robust test-suite execution and coverage measurement. In: Proc. ASE. pp. 1074–1077. IEEE (2019). https://doi.org/10.1109/ASE.2019.00105
24. Beyer, D., Löwe, S., Wendler, P.: Reliable benchmarking: Requirements and solutions. Int. J. Softw. Tools Technol. Transfer **21**(1), 1–29 (2019). https://doi.org/10.1007/s10009-017-0469-y
25. Beyer, D., Wendler, P.: CPU Energy Meter: A tool for energy-aware algorithms engineering. In: Proc. TACAS (2). pp. 126–133. LNCS 12079, Springer (2020). https://doi.org/10.1007/978-3-030-45237-7_8

26. Bürdek, J., Lochau, M., Bauregger, S., Holzer, A., von Rhein, A., Apel, S., Beyer, D.: Facilitating reuse in multi-goal test-suite generation for software product lines. In: Proc. FASE. pp. 84–99. LNCS 9033, Springer (2015). https://doi.org/10.1007/978-3-662-46675-9_6

27. Cadar, C., Dunbar, D., Engler, D.R.: KLEE: Unassisted and automatic generation of high-coverage tests for complex systems programs. In: Proc. OSDI. pp. 209–224. USENIX Association (2008)

28. Cadar, C., Nowack, M.: KLEE symbolic execution engine in 2019 (competition contribution). Int. J. Softw. Tools Technol. Transf. 23(6), 867 – 870 (December 2021). https://doi.org/10.1007/s10009-020-00570-3

29. Chalupa, M., Novák, J., Strejček, J.: SYMBIOTIC 8: Parallel and targeted test generation (competition contribution). In: Proc. FASE. pp. 368–372. LNCS 12649, Springer (2021). https://doi.org/10.1007/978-3-030-71500-7_20

30. Chalupa, M., Strejček, J., Vitovská, M.: Joint forces for memory safety checking. In: Proc. SPIN. pp. 115–132. Springer (2018). https://doi.org/10.1007/978-3-319-94111-0_7

31. Cok, D.R., Déharbe, D., Weber, T.: The 2014 SMT competition. JSAT 9, 207–242 (2016)

32. Gadelha, M.Y.R., Monteiro, F.R., Cordeiro, L.C., Nicole, D.A.: ESBMC v6.0: Verifying C programs using k-induction and invariant inference (competition contribution). In: Proc. TACAS (3). pp. 209–213. LNCS 11429, Springer (2019). https://doi.org/10.1007/978-3-030-17502-3_15

33. Gadelha, M.Y., Ismail, H.I., Cordeiro, L.C.: Handling loops in bounded model checking of C programs via k-induction. Int. J. Softw. Tools Technol. Transf. 19(1), 97–114 (February 2017). https://doi.org/10.1007/s10009-015-0407-9

34. Godefroid, P., Sen, K.: Combining model checking and testing. In: Handbook of Model Checking, pp. 613–649. Springer (2018). https://doi.org/10.1007/978-3-319-10575-8_19

35. Harman, M., Hu, L., Hierons, R.M., Wegener, J., Sthamer, H., Baresel, A., Roper, M.: Testability transformation. IEEE Trans. Software Eng. 30(1), 3–16 (2004). https://doi.org/10.1109/TSE.2004.1265732

36. Holzer, A., Schallhart, C., Tautschnig, M., Veith, H.: How did you specify your test suite. In: Proc. ASE. pp. 407–416. ACM (2010). https://doi.org/10.1145/1858996.1859084

37. Jaffar, J., Maghareh, R., Godboley, S., Ha, X.L.: TRACERX: Dynamic symbolic execution with interpolation (competition contribution). In: Proc. FASE. pp. 530–534. LNCS 12076, Springer (2020). https://doi.org/10.1007/978-3-030-45234-6_28

38. Jaffar, J., Murali, V., Navas, J.A., Santosa, A.E.: TRACER: A symbolic execution tool for verification. In: Proc. CAV. pp. 758–766. LNCS 7358, Springer (2012). https://doi.org/10.1007/978-3-642-31424-7_61

39. Jakobs, M.C., Richter, C.: COVERITEST with adaptive time scheduling (competition contribution). In: Proc. FASE. pp. 358–362. LNCS 12649, Springer (2021). https://doi.org/10.1007/978-3-030-71500-7_18

40. King, J.C.: Symbolic execution and program testing. Commun. ACM 19(7), 385–394 (1976). https://doi.org/10.1145/360248.360252

41. Lemberger, T.: Plain random test generation with PRTEST (competition contribution). Int. J. Softw. Tools Technol. Transf. 23(6), 871–873 (December 2021). https://doi.org/10.1007/s10009-020-00568-x

42. Liu, D., Ernst, G., Murray, T., Rubinstein, B.: LEGION: Best-first concolic testing (competition contribution). In: Proc. FASE. pp. 545–549. LNCS 12076, Springer (2020). https://doi.org/10.1007/978-3-030-45234-6_31

43. Liu, D., Ernst, G., Murray, T., Rubinstein, B.I.P.: LEGION: Best-first concolic testing. In: Proc. ASE. pp. 54–65. IEEE (2020). https://doi.org/10.1145/3324884.3416629
44. Marques, F., Santos, J.F., Santos, N., Adão, P.: Concolic execution for webassembly (artifact). Dagstuhl Artifacts Series **8**(2), 20:1–20:3 (2022). https://doi.org/10.4230/DARTS.8.2.20
45. Metta, R., Medicherla, R.K., Karmarkar, H.: VERIFUZZ: Fuzz centric test generation tool (competition contribution). In: Proc. FASE. pp. 341–346. LNCS 13241, Springer (2022). https://doi.org/10.1007/978-3-030-99429-7_20
46. Panichella, S., Gambi, A., Zampetti, F., Riccio, V.: SBST tool competition 2021. In: Proc. SBST. pp. 20–27. IEEE (2021). https://doi.org/10.1109/SBST52555.2021.00011
47. Ruland, S., Lochau, M., Jakobs, M.C.: HYBRIDTIGER: Hybrid model checking and domination-based partitioning for efficient multi-goal test-suite generation (competition contribution). In: Proc. FASE. pp. 520–524. LNCS 12076, Springer (2020). https://doi.org/10.1007/978-3-030-45234-6_26
48. Song, J., Alves-Foss, J.: The DARPA cyber grand challenge: A competitor's perspective, part 2. IEEE Security and Privacy **14**(1), 76–81 (2016). https://doi.org/10.1109/MSP.2016.14
49. Stump, A., Sutcliffe, G., Tinelli, C.: STAREXEC: A cross-community infrastructure for logic solving. In: Proc. IJCAR, pp. 367–373. LNCS 8562, Springer (2014). https://doi.org/10.1007/978-3-319-08587-6_28
50. Sutcliffe, G.: The CADE ATP system competition: CASC. AI Magazine **37**(2), 99–101 (2016).
51. Visser, W., Păsăreanu, C.S., Khurshid, S.: Test-input generation with Java PATHFINDER. In: Proc. ISSTA. pp. 97–107. ACM (2004). https://doi.org/10.1145/1007512.1007526
52. Wendler, P., Beyer, D.: sosy-lab/benchexec: Release 3.16. Zenodo (2023). https://doi.org/10.5281/zenodo.7612021

FuSeBMC_IA: Interval Analysis and Methods for Test Case Generation

(Competition Contribution)

Mohannad Aldughaim[1,4]($\boxtimes$)(ID), Kaled M. Alshmrany[1,5](ID), Mikhail R. Gadelha[2], Rosiane de Freitas[3], and Lucas C. Cordeiro[1,3](ID)

[1] University of Manchester, Manchester, UK
[2] Igalia, A Coruña, Spain
[3] Federal University of Amazonas, Manaus, Brazil
[4] King Saud University, Riyadh, Saudi Arabia
[5] Institute of Public Administration, Jeddah, Saudi Arabia
mohannad.aldughaim@manchester.ac.uk

Abstract. The cooperative verification of Bounded Model Checking and Fuzzing has proved to be one of the most effective techniques when testing C programs. FuSeBMC is a test-generation tool that employs BMC and Fuzzing to produce test cases. In Test-Comp 2023, we present an interval approach to FuSeBMC_IA, improving the test generator to use interval methods and abstract interpretation (via Frama-C) to strengthen our instrumentation and fuzzing. Here, an abstract interpretation engine instruments the program as follows. It analyzes different program branches, combines the conditions of each branch, and produces a Constraint Satisfaction Problem (CSP), which is solved using Constraint Programming (CP) by interval manipulation techniques called *Contractor Programming*. This process has a set of invariants for each branch, which are introduced back into the program as constraints. Experimental results show improvements in reducing CPU time (37%) and memory (13%), while retaining a high score.

Keywords: Automated Test-Case Generation · Bounded Model Checking · Fuzzing · Abstract Interpretation · Constraint Programming · Contractors.

1 Introduction

In Test-comp 2022 [1], cooperative verification tools showed their strength by being the best tools in each category. *FuSeBMC* [9,10] is a test-generation tool that employs cooperative verification using fuzzing and BMC. *FuSeBMC* starts with the analysis to instrument the Program Under Test (PUT); then, based on the results from BMC/AFL, it generates the initial seeds for the fuzzer. Finally, *FuSeBMC* keeps track of the goals covered and updates the seeds, while producing test cases using BMC/Fuzzing/Selective fuzzer. This year, we introduce abstract interpretation to *FuSeBMC* to improve the test case generation. In particular, we use interval methods to help our instrumentation and fuzzing by providing intervals to help reach (instrumented) goals faster. The selective fuzzer is a crucial component of *FuSeBMC*, which generates test cases for uncovered goals based on information obtained from test cases produced by BMC/fuzzer [9]. This work is based on our previous study, where CSP/CP by contractor techniques are applied to prune the state-space search [12]. Our approach also uses Frama-C [4,8] to

© The Author(s) 2023
L. Lambers and S. Uchitel (Eds.): FASE 2023, LNCS 13991, pp. 324–329, 2023.
https://doi.org/10.1007/978-3-031-30826-0_18

obtain variable intervals, further pruning the state space exploration. Our original contributions are: (1) improve instrumentation to allow abstract interpretation to provide information about variable intervals; (2) apply interval methods to improve the fuzzing and produce higher impact test cases by pruning the search space exploration; (3) reduce the usage of resources (incl. memory and CPU time).

2   Interval Analysis and Methods for Test Case Generation

FuSeBMC_IA improves the original *FuSeBMC* using Interval Analysis and Methods [3]. Fig. 1 illustrates the *FuSeBMC_IA*'s architecture. Our approach starts from the analysis phase of *FuSeBMC* [9,10]. It parses statement conditions required to reach a goal, to construct a Constraint Satisfaction Problem/Constraint Programming (CSP/CP) [5] with three components: constraints (program conditions), variables (used in a condition), and domains (provided by the static analyzer Frama-C via eva plugin [7]). We instrument the PUT with Frama-C intrinsic functions to obtain the domains, which generate intervals of a given set of variables at a specific program location. Then, we apply the contractor to each goal's CSP and output the results to a file used by the selective fuzzer. Contractor Programming is a set of interval methods that estimate the solution

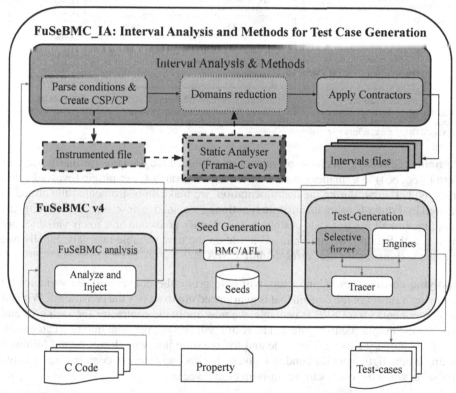

Fig. 1: *FuSeBMC_IA*'s architecture. The changes introduced in *FuSeBMC_IA* for Test-Comp 2023 are highlighted in green. The new Interval Analysis & Methods component generates intervals to be used by the selective fuzzer.

of a given CSP [5]. The used contractor technique is the Forward-Backward contractor, which is applied to a CSP/CP with a single constraint [3], which is implemented in the IBEX library [6]. IBEX is a C++ library for constraint processing over real numbers that implement contractors. More details regarding contractors can be found in our current work-in-progress [12].

Parsing Conditions and CSP/CP creation for each goal. While traversing the PUT clang AST [2], we consider each statement's conditions that lead to an injected goal: the conditions are parsed and converted from Clang expression [2] to IBEX expression [6]. The converted expressions are used as the constraints in CSP/CP to create a contractor. After parsing the goals, we have a CSP/CP for each goal. In case of a goal does not have a CSP/CP, the intervals for the variables are left unchanged. We also create a constraint for each condition in case of multiple conditions and take the intersection/union. At the end of this phase, we have a list of each goal and its contractor. Also, a list of variables for each contractor will be used to instrument the Frama-C file in the next phase.

```
1    int main() {
2    fuSeBMC_init:;
3        int x = __VERIFIER_nondet_int();
4        int y = 0;
5        if (x <= y) {
6        GOAL_1:;
7            x++;
8        }
9        if (x >= y) {
10           if (x <= 0) {
11           GOAL_2:;
12               x = y;
13           }
14       }
15       if (x > 1 && x < -1) {
16       GOAL_3:;
17           y++;
18       }
19       return 0;
20   }
```

```
1    int main() {
2        int x = __VERIFIER_nondet_int();
3        int y = 0;
4        if (x <= y) {
5            Frama_C_show_each_GOAL_1_2_(x, y);
6            x++;
7        }
8        if (x >= y)
9            if (x <= 0) {
10               Frama_C_show_each_GOAL_2_2_(x, y);
11               x = y;
12           }
13       if (x > 1 && x < -1) {
14           Frama_C_show_each_GOAL_3_1_(x);
15           y++;
16       }
17       return 0;
18   }
```

```
1    Goal 1:
2    x
3    -2147483648.000000
4    0.000000
5    y
6    0.000000
7    0.000000
8    Goal 2:
9    x
10   0.000000
11   0.000000
12   y
13   0.000000
14   0.000000
15   Goal 3:
16   Unreachable
```

Instrumented file   Instrumented file for Frama-C   Intervals file

Fig. 2: The figure illustrates an example of files produced. We are starting from the instrumented file that shows the goals injected. Then, we instrument the file with the Frama-C intrinsic function. Finally, we produce a file with each goal and the intervals to satisfy the conditions for each goal.

Domains reduction. In this step, we attempt to reduce the domains (primarily starting from $(-\infty, \infty)$) to a smaller range. This is done via Frama-C eva plugin (evolved value analysis) [7]. First, during the instrumentation, we make an instrumented file aimed to be used by Frama-C using its intrinsic functions `Frama_c_show_each()` (cf. Fig. 2). This function allows us to add custom text to identify goals and how many variables are in each call. Second, we run Frama-C to obtain the new variable intervals. Finally, we update the domains for the corresponding CSP/CP.

Applying contractors. Contractors will help prune the domains of the variables by removing a subset of the domain that is guaranteed not to satisfy the constraints. With all the components for a CSP/CP available, we now apply the contractor for each goal and produce the output file in Figure 2. The result will be split per goal into two categories. The first category lists each variable and the possible intervals (lower bound followed by upper bound) to enter the condition given. The second category contains unreachable goals, i.e. when the contractor result is an empty vector.

Selective Fuzzer. The Selective Fuzzer parses the file produced by the analyzer, extracts all the intervals, applies these intervals to each goal, and starts fuzzing within the given interval. Thus, pruning the search space from random intervals to informed intervals. The selective fuzzer will also prioritize the goals with smaller intervals and set a low priority to goals with unreachable results.

3 Strengths and Weaknesses

Using abstract interpretation in *FuSeBMC_IA* improved the test-case generation regarding resources. The new contractors generated by the Interval Analysis and Methods component are used by our selective fuzzer: (1) the information provided helps the selective fuzzer to start from a given range of values rather than a random range (as was our strategy in the previous version); (2) the selective fuzzer uses the information about unreachable goals to set their priority low for reachability; (3) when compared to *FuSeBMC* v4, this improvement helped saving CPU time by 37% and memory by 13%, which leads to saving 40% of energy; (4) although our approach produces fewer test cases for a given category, the impact of these test cases is higher in terms of reaching instrumented goals; (5) there is potential for future work to use the information provided by Frama-C, especially regarding overflow warnings. Finally, the intervals provided may not affect the *FuSeBMC_IA*'s outcome in the worst case. i.e., the selective fuzzer performs no better than not having interval information for seed generation. The time it takes to generate the intervals is only a tiny fraction of the time it takes to produce the test cases; its impact when the information is not useful is negligible.

Our approach suffers from a significant technical limitation: *FuSeBMC_IA* cannot create complementary contractors; we can only create intervals that satisfy the constraints of a branch (i.e., outer contractors). In practice, we can only create intervals to `if`-statements and ignore its `else`-statements (the inner contractor). We also skip any `if`-statement inside `else` statements, as this may lead to unsound intervals. This is a technical limitation rather than a theoretical one: we use run-time type information (RTTI) to identify ibex expressions. However, we link our tool with Clang, which requires compilation with no RTTI information. We are investigating approaches to address this limitation, e.g., to encapsulate all ibex expressions and manually store expression information, but currently, no proper fix has been implemented. Additionally, a bug has been found that caused *FuSeBMC_IA* to crash on some benchmarks that made *FuSeBMC_IA* scores much less than *FuSeBMC* in the coverage category.

4 Tool Setup and Configuration

When running *FuSeBMC_IA*, the user is required to set the architecture with $-a$, the property file path with $-p$, and the benchmark path, as:

```
fusebmc.py [-a {32, 64}] [-p PROPERTY_FILE]
    [-s {kinduction,falsi,incr,fixed}][BENCHMARK_PATH]
```

For Test-Comp 2023, *FuSeBMC_IA* uses `incr` for incremental BMC, which relies on the ESBMC's symbolic execution engine [11]. The `fusebmc.py` and `FuSeBMC.xml` files are the Benchexec tool info module and the benchmark definition file respectively.

5 Software Project

FuSeBMC_IA is publicly available on GitHub[1] under the terms of MIT License. In the repository, *FuSeBMC_IA* is implemented using a combination of Python and C++. Build instructions and dependencies are all available in `README.md` file. *FuSeBMC_IA* is a fork of the main project *FuSeBMC* available on GitHub[2].

---

[1] https://github.com/Mohannad-Aldughaim/FuSeBMC_IA
[2] https://github.com/kaled-alshmrany/FuSeBMC

6   Data-Availability Statement

All files necessary to run the tool are available on Zenodo [13].

Acknowledgment

King Saud University, Saudi Arabia[3] supports the *FuSeBMC_IA* development. The work in this paper is also partially funded by the UKRI/IAA project entitled "Using Artificial Intelligence/Machine Learning to assess source code in Escrow".

References

1. Beyer, D. Advances in Automatic Software Testing: Test-Comp 2022. *FASE*. pp. 321-335 (2022) DOI:https://doi.org/10.1007/978-3-030-99429-7_18
2. The Clang Team, Clang documentation. (2022), https://clang.llvm.org/docs/UsersManual.html, accessed: 19-12-2022
3. Jaulin, L., Kieffer, M., Didrit, O. & Walter, E. Applied Interval Analysis. *Springer London*. pp. 11-100 (2001) DOI:https://doi.org/10.1007/978-1-4471-0249-6_2
4. Cuoq, P., Kirchner, F., Kosmatov, N., Prevosto, V., Signoles, J. & Yakobowski, B. Frama-C. *International Conference On Software Engineering And Formal Methods*. pp. 233-247 (2012) DOI:https://doi.org/10.1007/978-3-642-33826-7_16
5. Mustafa, M., Stancu, A., Delanoue, N. & Codres, E. Guaranteed SLAM—An interval approach. *Robotics And Autonomous Systems*. **100** pp. 160-170 (2018) DOI:https://doi.org/10.1016/j.robot.2017.11.009
6. Chabert, G. ibex-lib.org. , http://www.ibex-lib.org/, accessed: 19-12-2022
7. Bühler, D. EVA, an evolved value analysis for Frama-C: structuring an abstract interpreter through value and state abstractions. (Rennes 1,2017) DOI:https://doi.org/10.1007/978-3-319-52234-0_7
8. Baudin, P., Bobot, F., Bühler, D., Correnson, L., Kirchner, F., Kosmatov, N., Maroneze, A., Perrelle, V., Prevosto, V., Signoles, J. & Others The dogged pursuit of bug-free C programs: the Frama-C software analysis platform. *Communications Of The ACM*. **64**, 56-68 (2021) DOI:https://doi-org.manchester.idm.oclc.org/10.1145/3470569
9. Alshmrany, K., Aldughaim, M., Bhayat, A. & Cordeiro, L. FuSeBMC: An energy-efficient test generator for finding security vulnerabilities in C programs. *International Conference On Tests And Proofs*. pp. 85-105 (2021) DOI: https://doi.org/10.1007/978-3-030-79379-1_6
10. Alshmrany, K., Aldughaim, M., Bhayat, A. & Cordeiro, L. FuSeBMC v4: Smart Seed Generation for Hybrid Fuzzing. *International Conference On Fundamental Approaches To Software Engineering*. pp. 336-340 (2022) DOI: https://doi.org/10.1007/978-3-030-99429-7_19
11. Gadelha, M., Monteiro, F., Morse, J., Cordeiro, L., Fischer, B. & Nicole, D. ESBMC 5.0: An Industrial-Strength C Model Checker. *ASE*. pp. 888-891 (2018) DOI: https://doi-org.manchester.idm.oclc.org/10.1145/3238147.3240481
12. Aldughaim, M., Alshmrany, K., Menezes, R., Stancu, A. & Cordeiro, L. Incremental Symbolic Bounded Model Checking of Software Using Interval Methods via Contractors.
13. Aldughaim, M., Alshmrany, K., Gadelha, M., Freitas, R. & Cordeiro, L. FuSeBMC v.5: Interval Analysis and Methods for Test Case Generation. DOI:https://doi.org/10.5281/zenodo.7473124(Zenodo,2022,12)

---

[3] https://ksu.edu.sa/en/

Correction to: Feature-Guided Analysis of Neural Networks

Divya Gopinath, Luca Lungeanu, Ravi Mangal, Corina Păsăreanu, Siqi Xie, and Huafeng Yu

Correction to:
Chapter "Feature-Guided Analysis of Neural Networks" in: L. Lambers and S. Uchitel (Eds.): *Fundamental Approaches to Software Engineering*, LNCS 13991, https://doi.org/10.1007/978-3-031-30826-0_7

In the originally published version of chapter 7, there was an error in the affiliations of some of the authors. In addition, the name of the author Huafeng Yu had been spelled incorrectly. This has been corrected.

The updated original version of this chapter can be found at
https://doi.org/10.1007/978-3-031-30826-0_7

L. Lambers and S. Uchitel (Eds.): FASE 2023, LNCS 13991, p. C1, 2023.
https://doi.org/10.1007/978-3-031-30826-0_19

Author Index

A

Aguirre, Nazareno   3, 111
Aldughaim, Mohannad   324
Alshmrany, Kaled M.   324
Ansari, Saba Gholizadeh   151

B

Baunach, Marcel   26
Bengolea, Valeria   111
Beyer, Dirk   309
Bianculli, Domenico   249
Bliudze, Simon   143
Brizzio, Matías   3
Burholt, Charlie   241

C

Calinescu, Radu   241
Carvalho, Luiz   3
Cavalcanti, Ana   241
Chalupa, Marek   260
Cordeiro, Lucas C.   324
Cordy, Maxime   3

D

d'Aloisio, Giordano   88
Dastani, Mehdi   151
Dawes, Joshua Heneage   249
de Freitas, Rosiane   324
Degiovanni, Renzo   3
Di Marco, Antinisca   88
Dignum, Frank   151
Din, Crystal Chang   220

E

El-Hokayem, Antoine   173

F

Falcone, Yliès   173
Figueiredo, Eduardo   282
Frias, Marcelo F.   111

G

Gadelha, Mikhail R.   324
Gopinath, Divya   133

H

Haltermann, Jan   195
Henzinger, Thomas A.   260
Huisman, Marieke   143

J

Jakobs, Marie-Christine   195
Jones, Maddie   241

K

Kamburjan, Eduard   220
Keller, Gabriele   151
Kifetew, Fitsum Meshesha   151

L

Larsen, Kim Guldstrand   26
Lei, Stefanie Muroya   260
Li, Zhe   67
Lorber, Florian   26
Lungeanu, Luca   133

M

Mangal, Ravi   133
Molina, Facundo   111
Muehlboeck, Fabian   260

N

Neele, Thomas   47
Nyman, Ulrik   26

© The Editor(s) (if applicable) and The Author(s) 2023
L. Lambers and S. Uchitel (Eds.): FASE 2023, LNCS 13991, pp. 331–332, 2023.
https://doi.org/10.1007/978-3-031-30826-0

P

Papadakis, Mike 3
Păsăreanu, Corina 133
Politano, Mariano 111
Ponzio, Pablo 111
Prandi, Davide 151
Prasetya, I. S. W. B. 151

R

Ribeiro, Leandro Batista 26
Richter, Cedric 195
Rubbens, Robert 143

S

Safina, Larisa 143
Sammartino, Matteo 47
Santana, Amanda 282
Santos, Geanderson 282
Shin, Donghwan 249

Soueidi, Chukri 173
Stilo, Giovanni 88

T

Traon, Yves Le 3

V

Vale, Gustavo 282
van den Bos, Petra 143

W

Wehrheim, Heike 195

X

Xie, Fei 67
Xie, Siqi 133

Y

Yaman, Sinem Getir 241
Yu, Huafeng 133

Printed in the United States
by Baker & Taylor Publisher Services